Schoolcraft's

INDIAN
Legends

Michigan State University Press Schoolcraft Series

Philip P. Mason, editor

Schoolcraft's
INDIAN Legends

from

Algic Researches, The Myth of Hiawatha, Oneóta, The Race in America, and *Historical and Statistical Information Respecting...the Indian Tribes of the United States*

Edited by
Mentor L. Williams

Michigan State University Press
East Lansing
1991

CONTENTS

FOREWORD

THE LAST TWO decades have witnessed a renewed interest in the career of Henry Rowe Schoolcraft, the famous nineteenth-century Indian agent, explorer, naturalist, writer, and student of the life and customs of the Indians of North America. For twenty years, from 1822 to 1841, he served as Indian agent of the Chippewa and Ottawa tribes of northern Michigan and Wisconsin.

During his twenty-year residency, Schoolcraft took an active role in the cultural life of Michigan. He was one of the founders and benefactors of the Historical Society of Michigan, the Michigan State Library, and the Algic Research Society. Schoolcraft was also interested in exploring the vast wilderness areas of the upper Great Lakes. In 1820 he accompanied Lewis Cass, Governor of Michigan Territory, as a mineralogist on an expedition to explore the Lake Superior region. In 1832 he led another expedition to discover the source of the Mississippi River in the northern wilds of Minnesota. On all of his numerous expeditions, Schoolcraft was careful to collect and record information about the mineral resources of the regions explored.

His main interest, however, was in the study of the Indians of North America, and especially those Algonquin-speaking tribes of the upper Great Lakes. This pursuit was greatly facilitated by Schoolcraft's marriage in 1825 to Jane Johnston, the charming, well-educated daughter of John Johnston, a prominent Lake Superior fur trader, and Ozhow-Guscodoy-Wayquay (Woman-of-the-Green-Prairie) daughter of Chippewa chieftain Waub-Ojeeg. With her assistance and with the help of her family, Schoolcraft was able to gather extensive information on the Indians of Lake Superior country. In what is probably the first "oral history" project conducted in the United States, he kept a detailed record of interviews with hundreds of the Indians who visited agency headquarters each summer at Sault Ste. Marie and later Mackinac Island and whom he visited in their tribal villages. He was particularly interested in Native American life, customs, religious beliefs, ceremonies, music, folk tales, and history.

Schoolcraft was not alone in his pursuit of this cultural data; other Indian agents, explorers, fur traders, and public officials recognized the importance of gathering and preserving information about Native Americans. Yet, Schoolcraft differed from his colleagues in one major respect. Not only did he systematically collect first-hand accounts, but he shared his findings in a series of publications—more than twenty books and scores of articles and monographs relating to the Indians of North America. Even after he resigned as Superintendent of Indian Affairs in 1841, he continued his research and published several major studies.

Despite Schoolcraft's once widespread popularity in the United States and Europe, few of his major works are available today except for those found in the rare book collections of research libraries or in the hands of private collectors.

In 1953, Michigan State University Press began an ambitious project to make Schoolcraft's major works generally available to the public. Mentor L. Williams, professor at the Illinois Institute of Technology, edited the first two publications: *Schoolcraft's Narrative Journal of Travels . . . to the Sources of the Mississippi River in the Year 1820* (1953), and *Schoolcraft's Indian Legends from Algic Researches, The Myth of Hiawatha, Oneóta, The Red Race of America and Historical and Statistical Information Respecting . . . the Indian Tribes of the United States* (1956). After Professor Williams's untimely death in 1956, I edited Schoolcraft's *Expedition to Lake Itasca: The Discovery of the Source of the Mississippi* (1958), which contained not only a reprint of Schoolcraft's original 1834 volume, but all of the extant diaries, journals, reports, and correspondence relating to this historic expedition.

Then, in 1962, the Press published *The Literary Voyageur or Muzzeniegun.* It was based upon a weekly manuscript magazine proposed by Schoolcraft at Sault Ste. Marie, Michigan Territory, in the winter of 1826–1827, and named *Muzzeniegun,* a Chippewa word meaning "a printed document or book." It contained articles, poems, and announcements on all aspects of Indian life and customs, especially ceremonies, superstitions, burials, war chants and songs, and the folktales of the Chippewa of the upper Great Lakes.

Since the early 1980s, interest in Native American culture has increased sharply, enhancing the research value of Schoolcraft's original work. In order to meet this demand, Michigan State University Press is now reissuing the most important of Schoolcraft's published and unpublished works. As a first step, it is publishing new editions of its four original Schoolcraft books. Also planned is the re-publication of *Personal Memories of a Residence of Thirty Years with the Indian Tribes on the American Frontier* (1851). Finally, the Press is planning a multi-volume edition of the "Papers of Henry R. Schoolcraft, an Indian Agent, 1822–1841," the outgrowth of a National Historical Publications and Records Commission Project.

PHILIP P. MASON
Wayne State University

PREFACE

THE PRIMARY TOOL of the editorial trade is a text with which to work. When the editor of this volume began his search for a copy of Schoolcraft's *Algic Researches,* his inquiries of Americana dealers were answered negatively. As weeks wore on with no copy turning up, he became more convinced than ever of the need for an accessible edition of this once popular collection to which scholars had been referring for a generation, though probably not reading. In fact, the entire output of Henry Rowe Schoolcraft, representing over thirty years of literary activity, has ceased to be public property. It is in the hands of collectors or stored in rare book repositories. The present edition is modestly offered to the students of American literature and culture, to the devotees of folklore, and to the general reading public in an effort to gain for Schoolcraft some of the honor he richly deserves as the first American to recognize the value and worth of the Indian heritage.

In presenting the tales the editor has followed the arrangement made by Schoolcraft in the 1839 edition of *Algic Researches.* Those legends that Schoolcraft collected later for inclusion in *Oneóta* and *The Myth of Hiawatha* may be found in Appendix A. In this way the totality of *Algic Researches* has been preserved, and, at the same time, the whole body of Schoolcraft's Indian legends has been made available for the first time in a single volume. The selection of the stories was governed by one principle: is this a legend? All biographical and historical Indian narratives were rigidly excluded. A large number of myths and legends which were mentioned in Schoolcraft's epitomes and compendiums of Indian lore were also omitted because they had been presented either by summary, by reference, or by expository fragment. To deserve collection here the legend must have been told as a narrative. Perhaps at some future date the other facets of Schoolcraft's exhaustive investigations of the Indians can be rescued from the chaotic state in which they now exist.

The original text of the legends has been preserved. All of the author's footnotes have been included and may be identified by his initials in brackets. Other footnote material, scrupulously kept to a minimum, has been supplied by the editor. Some changes in spelling have been made, changes which Schoolcraft himself observed in the later publication of the stories in *The Myth of Hiawatha.* Whenever Schoolcraft, or his printers, could not decide on the spelling of an Indian name, conformity was arbitrarily imposed. Where punctuation appeared to be following the common nineteenth century pepper-and-salt custom, modern innovations were adopted with no harm to the narratives. A statement of the publication record of every tale is given at the end of each, including publication in collections

ix

whose authors acknowledged Schoolcraft as their source. There has been no effort to appraise or analyze the tales anthropologically; this is a task for the professional.

In a second appendix, Appendix B, a body of related material has been brought together for the unusually curious scholar. Here may be found extracts from Schoolcraft's journal, letters, and other works illustrating his theories and concepts of collecting Indian materials, as well as his tribulations as a collector. The much argued relationship between *Hiawatha* and Schoolcraft is reviewed and documented. A background is provided for the furor about the "cult of Indian writing" that developed in America in the period between 1825-1855, and a select list of contemporary works dealing with Indian legends, life, and antiquities is included.

A bibliography is essential for a volume of this scope. Some of the earlier as well as the more recent studies of the North American Indians have been catalogued. Both secondary and primary source material has been listed, as have also the more prominent periodicals examined.

The editor acknowledges his very great indebtedness to Mr. and Mrs. Wright Howes, Northwest Americana collectors, for their help in ferreting out lost volumes, and to the staff of the Newberry Library for their patient and persevering labors in providing him with scores of volumes from their extensive Indian collections. He also wishes to thank the Houghton Mifflin Company for permission to reproduce materials from their editions of Longfellow's *Poetical Works* and Samuel Longfellow's *Henry Wadsworth Longfellow*. To Mr. Lyle Blair, Manager of the Michigan State University Press, he gives thanks for forgiveness of transgressions against editorial deadlines, as well as for the opportunity of getting this volume before the public on the centenary of the publication of *The Myth of Hiawatha*. Finally, to his family for enduring what they must have believed a state of perpetual curmudgeonishness, he offers his belated but heartfelt apologies.

July 9, 1955   MENTOR L. WILLIAMS.
Winnetka, Illinois

INTRODUCTION

I

IN A SOCIETY which has, within three hundred and fifty years, so completely absorbed one of its minority races that an annual beauty contest can be held to determine its most pulchritudinous female, a query might well be asked: Is it necessary to continue the study of the American Indian? Should we pursue the investigation of a past grandeur, a departed glory, and an empty mythology? Those who would answer in the negative forget that there are nearly 375,000 Indians living in the continental United States of whom sixty percent are full-blooded members of their race and live in basically Indian communities. Those who would give an affirmative answer ought not be so naïve as to base their reply on the tourist and museum value of the Red Man. He is more than an exhibit in a museum, more than a vendor of trinkets, more than an extra in a Hollywood western. The American Indian has left an indelible mark upon the culture of America, upon its customs, its habits, its language, and even upon its mode of thought.

The curiosity of European civilizations about the forest denizens of the New World gave rise to the dubious eighteenth century concept of the Noble Savage, a concept that was rudely shattered on these shores in the conflict between the hunter and the pastoral economies. American colonists saw little in their Indian antagonists to justify the notion that primeval man was free from the taints of old world degeneracy. Instead, when the occasion required, which was most of the time, they loudly voiced their belief that the only good Indian was a dead one. Some, like Jefferson, could still detect the inherent goodness of man in the Indian leaders, like John Logan. Some, smarting from conscience pangs, were roused to deep resentment against colonial and early national treatment of the land's first and rightful owners. A few, caught in the meshes of intellectual curiosity, wanted even then to study the Indian—as a specimen, as a waning race about to disappear forever from the view of mankind. Perhaps the most highly developed rationalization of the American mind, where the Indians were concerned, was to consider them a "provisional race"—placed on this hemisphere by a well-meaning Deity (who abhorred a vacuum) to occupy the area until the "chosen" white men should arrive to take title and reap the harvest of natural resources.

A pretense was maintained of being fair and just, in accord with the principles of English jurisprudence: always assemble, arrange a treaty, make proper payment for lands acquired. But the bargaining always terminated with the equally meaningful Anglo-Saxon legality: no trespassing and no poaching—this means you! Moreover, the Indians were heathens, their immaculate conceptions and tribal saviours notwithstanding. Could

xi

they be converted, clothed, and pastoralized all would be well in New Zion. The bow would be replaced by the hoe, the tomahawk with the blacksmith's hammer, and consumption or smallpox would do the rest.

Enough has been said to demonstrate that there are more ways to study the Indian than to botanize on the grave of his dead past. History and literature have too long done no more than that. To discover his ever-living impact on the society that we call modern is the function of anthropologists, ethnologists, sociologists, and folklorists. Add to these the social psychologists and the instrumentalists and we get a half-dozen intellectual disciplines with which to study the totality of American culture, a culture in which the Indian has had and still has a very significant part. It is not an answer to a specific problem, it is not a panacea for multiple social sclerosis that is sought. In fact, the single-mindedness of the problem-solution approach to any culture pattern may be the handicap under which modern man labors. What is needed may be scope, breadth, depth rather than pinpointed analysis. The new sciences of man applied to the examination of man in the time-space stream should yield the understanding and vision of function and purpose that materialistic individualism and strait-jacketed humanism have almost obscured. If these human sciences had a steady flow of material to examine, their professors might inaugurate a second Enlightenment. The Indian tributary has been clogged too long with underbrush and log-jams to run freely into the main stream. It is time for Teharonhiawakhon to return and clear the stream. Folklorists and ethnologists know who he is.

II

When the first white men, English, French, and Dutch, set foot on the Atlantic coast, the Indians they encountered were of tribes belonging to the Algonquin linguistic family. Before the white man came, the area east of the Mississippi, north of a line drawn through Tennessee and Virginia, extending across the Great Lakes and the St. Lawrence to the Hudson Bay was held by this great congeries of Algonquin tribes: along the coast were the Powhatan, Delaware, Mohegan, Pequot, Wampanoag, and Narraganset tribes; along the St. Lawrence and inland were the Montagnai, Algonquin, Ottowa, and Chippewa tribes; in the Ohio-Mississippi valley were the Illinois, Potawatomi, Miami, Menomini, Sauk and Fox tribes. Sometime before the white man's arrival members of the Iroquois linguistic family had muscled into the territory of the Algonquins, occupying the triangle between the Appalachians and Lake Erie. The Susquehanna, Huron, Erie, the Five Nations of New York (Seneca, Cayuga, Onondaga, Oneida, Mohawk), the Tuscarora and the Cherokee of the south were the major tribes of the Iroquois speaking group.

English colonists in Virginia and New England fell afoul the local tribes immediately. Invited to go west, the coastal Indians were blocked by the great triangle of Iroquois. It was a fight to the finish as the English found in their wars with Sassacus and King Philip. The Delawares under Tamenend (Tammany) were equally hard pressed, and the Powhatans led by Opechancanough were worse than decimated. Nevertheless, Pocahontas, Massasoit, King Philip, Tamenend, and Uncas left a record the white men have never been able to ignore or forget.

When the French began their colonization of the St. Lawrence region, they found a state of total war in progress. The Iroquois, a violently militant family, to whom guns had been sold by the Dutch and English traders, were bent on exterminating the older residents. Their fury fell first upon the Ottawa who were driven northwestward into the upper Lake Huron and Lake Superior country where they mingled with their cousins, the Chippewa. All the coastal tribes were subject to Iroquois raids and lived in a state of perpetual alert. Not content with their power, frequently the case with nations trained chiefly in the arts of war, the Five Nations turned on their own relatives-in-language, and all but annihilated the Hurons, the Eries, and the Susquehannas. Remnants of these tribes fled westward where, under the name of Wyandot, they affiliated with the Ottowa and settled in Michigan and Indiana.

In the contest between the French and the English the alignment of Indians is interesting to observe. The French gave guns and moral support to the Algonquins, and encouraged their depredations against the English frontier; the Iroquois, on the other hand, became allies of the English. King William's War, Queen Anne's War, King George's War, and the French and Indian War were fought largely in terms of the Indian allies and commando raids.

With the fall of Quebec the Algonquin leaders found themselves in a curious dilemma. Large numbers of warriors from the Ohio and lake country had successfully demonstrated their prowess at Fort Duquesne and Ticonderoga and had profited greatly in scalps, captives, and plunder from their numerous forays against English frontier settlements. What was to happen now that their colleagues, the French, had shown the white feather? Pontiac, leader of the Ottawa, decided to carry on the campaign against the droves of English settlers pouring across the Appalachians. The Delaware, Miami, Ottowa, Chippewa, and Potawatomi captured fort after fort and eventually laid seige to Detroit and Pittsburgh. For a while it looked as if the Indians might prevent the English from occupying the country they had won. But the beleaguered garrisons were relieved and the Ohio Indians (Delaware and Shawnee) were forced to make peace with the English.

A frontier is always a frontier, no matter who battles for it. When the colonies broke with Britain, all the Indians, Iroquois and Algonquin, were urged by the nonrebellious English of Canada and the west to continue their struggle against the colonial rebels. Burgoyne's army was swollen with Indian contingents from as far west as Michigan, Illinois, and Wisconsin. After the war the old line-up continued. English traders hoped, through Detroit and Sault Ste. Marie, to hold the Indian trade for themselves. In 1790 one of Washington's generals (Harmar) was defeated by the combined Algonquin under Little Turtle; in 1791 St. Clair was similarly routed. Thoroughly aroused, the Americans, led by General Wayne, engaged the allied forces of Delaware, Shawnee, Ottowa, Miami, and the refugee Wyandot, under Blue Jacket, and defeated them at Fallen Timbers. By the Greenville treaty the Indians gave up the greater part of Ohio and Indiana.

This was not yet the end. At Fallen Timbers a new Indian leader emerged, Tecumseh. Filled with the dream of Pontiac, the dream that the white advance could be stopped by a firm federation of Indian tribes, Tecumseh canvassed tribe after tribe for support of his plan. Before he was quite ready, however, his fanatical brother, the Prophet, Tenskwatawa, engaged General Harrison in pitched battle at Tippecanoe and was defeated. Tecumseh retired to Canada where he was made a brigadier general in the War of 1812 and lost his life at the Battle of the Thames. The Americans, however, felt the fury of the Indians at Fort Dearborn and the River Raisin. Participating in the Detroit campaign in the War of 1812 was a young Sauk named Black Hawk and upon him descended the somewhat tattered mantle of Pontiac and Tecumseh. He, too, attempted a federation against the white invader, and, ignoring the advice of the conservative, Keokuk, led his tribesmen to battle in Wisconsin (1832), where Winfield Scott clinched his reputation as an Indian fighter. Black Hawk was captured and, as a captive, made a triumphal tour through the United States. Among those who saw him in Boston was Henry Wadsworth Longfellow.

Little wonder that the white settlers saw the Indian only as a fierce savage whose breast was filled with hatred and violence. What opportunity had the Indian, pawn of European power politics, defender of his tribal soil, to show his true character as a man of thought, humor, and feeling? What opportunity had the white settler, self-appointed tamer of the wilderness, defender of home and fireside, to know the Indian at home with his family, his rituals, and his tribal memories? Who really were these mighty men: Powhatan, Massasoit, King Philip, Tammany, Uncas, Pontiac, Tecumseh, Black Hawk, and Keokuk?

Gradually, from returned white captives, from traders, missionaries, and curious travelers, there began to emerge a different picture of the Indian. He was not, they found, devoid of feeling or solely devoted to the arts of rapine and torture. First, it was his customs and crafts that caught the white man's eye; later, it was the mystery of his origin that stimulated their imagination; finally, it was the discovery that he had an oral tradition that encouraged them to begin systematic study. The language, the religion, the ethic, the art, and the literature of the Indian were actually discovered in the first quarter of the nineteenth century.

It was with considerable surprise that the newer arrivals in the field of Indian investigations learned that the lake, forest, and plains Indians entertained themselves with lodge stories. With this discovery a curtain was lifted from before the red race and the Indian was revealed as a creator of tales, a teacher of wisdom, an instructor of youth, a singer of songs, a preserver of traditions. In short, he was transformed into an intellectual.

His legends were both gospel and story book, intended to instruct and amuse.

In the Algonquin mythology there was a hierarchy of supernatural beings ranging downward from the Great Spirit, Gitche Monedo, through Matche Monedo, the spirit of evil, to the minor deities or demigods, and the manitos or wizards and necromancers. The demigods were the chief subject of the lodge narratives. Each of the cardinal compass points was represented by a man-god, who controlled the winds. Kabeyun, by virtue of his age, controlled the West wind. His sons, Kabebonicca, Shawondasee, and Wabun ruled over the North, South and East winds. Kabeyun surprised an incautious maiden at play and begat a son, Manabozho, through whose birth the mother died. The son, reared by his grandmother, grew up in ignorance of his origin until he reached manhood. Then he pried the secret from his grandmother, and went off to avenge his mother's death. Kabeyun and Manabozho met in a mighty encounter, reminiscent of the Miltonic war in heaven or the battles of the Titans. Neither could destroy the other. Peace was declared and Kabeyun awarded the Northwest wind to Manabozho. When he had lived his allotted time on earth, Manabozho was transported to his seat in the Northwest, beside his brother Kabebonicca.

Manabozho next learned of the great serpent, the material manifestation of evil. This serpent lived in the north, under a great lake, and wreaked constant vengeance against mankind. Once he destroyed the earth with a flood and only Manabozho survived by climbing a tall tree on a mountain top. Being master of the animals, he sent the diving creatures into the depths to bring up the primordial earth (the beaver was the successful contestant) and from a speck of soil he caused a new world to grow.

A wicked manito, Pearl Feather, an agent of the serpent, had killed Manabozho's grandfather. The grandson had to destroy this evildoer also. With cunning and brawn, he eliminated the guardian fire-hissing reptiles, crossed the great pitch-lake, and destroyed the Shining Manito by shooting him in the scalplock with his last three arrows.

Manabozho was also a trickster and practical joker; sometimes he was just a born fool, a Till Eulenspiegel. *Tripe-de-roche* resulted from one of his foolish episodes. While cooking his game he grew sleepy and commanded his rump to watch his food during his nap. Upon waking, he found his meal stolen and punished his rump by squatting over the fire. After adequate scorching, Manabozho roared in pain and rushed for the lake, sliding down the rocks as he did so. The roasted flesh of his rump rubbed off on the rocks and, in a pinch, constitutes a survival diet, to this day.[1]

Other demigods were Iagoo, the teller of tall tales; Weeng, the sleep bringer; Pauguk, the spirit of death; and Kwasind, the strong man and Indian Paul Bunyan who helped Manabozho to clear the streams and move fallen forests.[2] In the water were fairies and mermen, on the land were the little people or Puk-Wudj-Ininees, and the cannibal giants, Windigoes. Magicians were numerous; perhaps the most noted was Mishosha, possessor of a wonderful canoe which, when a certain charm was spoken, could outstrip the wind in speed—and no paddles. Sometimes this canoe had ribs made of live rattlesnakes. No wonder the "lifted curtain" revealed to the white man a new world, fantastic and fearful, in which the Indian lived.

The Iroquois were equally facile at filling their world with supernatural beings. Their cosmogenic personages were the Ice King or god of winter, Tawiskaron (the flinty one), and Teharonhiawakhon, the friend of man and master of animals. These feuding brothers had a remarkable ancestry, similar to that of Manabozho. Their grandmother, Awenhai, fell from the sky and landed on the back of the Great Turtle where she conceived and bore, parthogenetically, a daughter. In due time the daughter matured and was impregnated by the Wind. Teharonhiawakhon was delivered normally, but Tawiskaron performed his own Caesarian section, through the navel, an easy operation because his flint head was shaped like an arrow point.

From the Turtle, Teharonhiawakhon received an ear of corn which he roasted. Tawiskaron smelled it and told his grandmother, who ordered him to get some for her. Teharonhiawakhon refused to grant the favor unless Tawiskaron would surrender the flint of his life. To this request the winter god agreed and stuck out his "flint thing" to be broken off. Teharonhiawakhon demanded that his brother break it off himself. Tawiskaron did so, thus surrendering his co-equality with the life deity.

Teharonhiawakhon created animals and birds; Tawiskaron made, in imitative but lesser degree, frogs, bats, worms, and owls. He also hid his brother's animals in a cave (hibernation). To cap his evil doings he built a bridge of white rocks (ice) over which he brought monsters to destroy Teharonhiawakhon's creatures, but Teharonhiawakhon outwitted him by sending a bluebird (spring), to sing before his flint brother. Tawiskaron fled in terror and the white stones melted. To escape capture he floated away on a cake of ice. In a final battle between the two, Tawiskaron was smashed to bits, his blood and bones becoming fruit-bearing vines that grew from crevices in the rocks.

Teharonhiawakhon, it was asserted, made the springs, lakes, and rivers to water an arid earth, and also kept the streams of obstacles and grisly monsters. In function and origin, then, there is relatively little difference between Teharonhiawakhon and Manabozho.[3] In other respects there is a wide divergence; the Iroquois deity is sober and dedicated to his task of helping man, whereas the Algonquin demigod has a mischievous and playful quality quite foreign to the other. The Iroquois legend provides many other names (from different informants) for Teharonhiawakhon: Teharonhiawagon, Taounyawatha, Tharonhiawakon, and Ioskeha.

At this point confusion confounded enters the story. Another Iroquois tale, this time a tradition, concerns the formation of the Iroquois League. About 1570 the Iroquois tribes, because of rivalry, were on the verge of internecine war. A tyrant of the Mohawks, Wathatotarho (Atotarho), refused to reach an agreement with kindred tribes. Another Mohawk, Hiawatha (Haiyonhwatha, Hayowentha), working in collaboration with Dekanawida, campaigned among the Oneidas and Cayugas for a federation. Conditional approval from these tribes eventually won over the Onondagas and Senecas. Only Wathatotarho refused. According to tradition, the Mohawk leader was a fit subject for analysis. His shape was inhuman: he had serpents for hair, turtle claws for hands, bear claws for feet, and his *membrum virile* was wrapped around his body many times. Hiawatha, it was said, suffered grievously from the arts of this tyrant; his pregnant daughter was trampled to death by a mob of people gazing up at a falling object to which Wathatotarho had directed their attention. Another version had her crushed by the plummeting object, a gigantic white-plumed bird. Hiawatha went into seclusion beside a lake whose waters he had lifted by a band of ducks. From the shells in the lake he made thirteen strings of wampum. Then he and Dekanawida sought out Wathatotarho's hiding place and cured him of his wretched condition by singing six· songs and arguing the thirteen points inherent in the strings of wampum. Hiawatha was credited with combing the snakes from the tyrant's hair.[4] Wathatotarho was made human again and agreed to join the league of the Hodenosaunee, or Longhouse. When the plan of a league was adopted, Hiawatha announced that his work was finished and he stepped into his canoe and rose out of sight above the heads of the assembled warriors.

Because the Iroquois came to believe in this tale they assumed he had magical power, and because they had lost their wampum belts, in which their history was recorded, they easily confused the political hero with their chief god, Teharonhiawakhon.[5]

III

Although a handful of the seventeenth and eighteenth century colonists took a scholarly interest in the Indian, primarily because he was a savage and a curiosity, and partly because he was a heathen in need of conversion, it remained for the men of rationalism to initiate investigations at a deeper level. Bearers of the Word had become experts in tribal tongues in order to communicate God's message, and had made some tentative conjectures about linguistic similarities between Hebrew and Algonquin, leading to the conclusion that at last the Lost Tribes were accounted for.

Franklin and Jefferson, with no qualifications beyond extraordinarily facile minds, encouraged the kind of scholarship that led to the great work of Albert Gallatin, their protégé, on the Indian tribes. All the resources of the federal government were thrown into the vast system of exploration that Jefferson, Madison, and Calhoun fathered. Every expedition was expected to report on the character and differences of the Indian tribes with whom it came in contact, to collect linguistic data, and to study the rituals and ceremonies. As reports of these expeditions were published, more and more persons became interested in the subject. The men of the Enlightenment sought to unravel the mystery of ante-Columbian civilizations through a variety of ingenious theories, including one that tied the Indian rituals to the Masonic order. Books on American antiquities—the mounds and tumuli, especially—made the terms Aztec, Mound-builder, Fort Ancient household words. Monographs on specific tribal dialects became available. The first serious efforts at scientific classification of the Indians on other than a geographic basis were made. Antiquarian, linguistic, and classificatory studies constituted a sort of primitive ethnology long before that science came into being.

Add to these the accounts of travelers, American and European, the histories of tribes, the biographies of celebrated Red Men, and the imaginative poems and dramas built around famous Indian leaders of the resistance and there results what can best be called a fad or a rage for things aboriginal, as the select list of early nineteenth century works on the Indian (Appendix B) indicates. Popular magazines were flooded with genuine and spurious Indian materials; no issue of the *American Monthly,* the *Knickerbocker,* the *Southern Literary Messenger,* or the *Columbian* failed to carry its monthly quota; by 1835 *Knickerbocker* was running a series of "Indian Sketches and Legends" and a series of letters burlesquing the accounts of travelers among the Indians—"Travels of an Indian Prince in the United States," by "Wawanosh." Burlesque is an infallible sign of the presence of a cult, sentimental and indiscriminate.

The man most responsible for popularizing the oral literature *(polite literature* in sentimental terms) of the aborigine was Henry Rowe Schoolcraft. The story of Schoolcraft is one of those incredible biographies that only the nineteenth century could produce, the story of a jack-of-all-trades who commanded respect from everyone. Not a charlatan, not a pseudo-, but a self-educated man in a dozen fields. There were many like him; for example, Elihu Burritt, the learned blacksmith, who mastered a dozen languages and founded the League for Universal Brotherhood, and Horace Greeley, dean of American journalism, who, in his own words, "converted obstacle into opportunity, and wrested achievement from difficulty."

Born in 1793, Schoolcraft spent his boyhood in Hamilton, New York on the Norman's Kill (Longfellow's "Vale of Tawasentha"). His father, Col. Lawrence Schoolcraft, had a distinguished military career. The family had long been engaged in glassmaking, and Henry was encouraged in the craft. After a few terms at Union College, where he taught himself Hebrew and German and where he first contracted the disease *cacoethes scribendi* from writing for local newspapers, he was sent to Vermont in 1812 to build a glass manufactory. While there he furthered his education by attending lectures at Middlebury and wrote sections of a work on vitreology. With the collapse of the American glass industry after the war of 1812, young Schoolcraft decided to see the West. In 1817 he set forth on a journey that took him down the Ohio to the mounds of Illinois, then to Missouri's Ozarks and the mineral district of Potosi. From there he went down river to New Orleans and by ship to New York. He published the results of his travels in 1819. When the volume was called to the attention of John C. Calhoun, then Secretary of War, he appointed Schoolcraft official geologist with the expedition being led by Governor Lewis Cass to Lake Superior and the headwaters of the Mississippi.[6]

Governor Cass was so satisfied with the geologist's performance that he invited Schoolcraft to accompany him in 1821 on a journey up the Maumee and down the Wabash, to St. Louis; then up the Illinois to Chicago where a treaty conference with the Lake Michigan tribes was held.[7] In 1822 Cass had Schoolcraft appointed Indian agent at Sault Ste. Marie where the federal government had just established a military outpost (Fort Brady) to counteract the economic power being exerted by the British in that region.

At the Sault the new agent entered into his duties with gusto. First on his agenda was the preparation of answers to a questionnaire the governor had circulated requesting information about the Indian tribes.[8] In pursuit of this information he cultivated the Johnstons, a trading family of great influence on the St. Mary's. John Johnston had married the daughter of Wabojeeg, a Chippewa chief, and had reared a family of four girls and four boys. Naturally, their connections with the Indians afforded an opportunity Schoolcraft could not neglect. Nor could he refrain from courting and marrying Jane Johnston, a well-educated half-breed, in 1823.[9]

Meanwhile, he was making trips along the Lake Superior coast, and to Mackinac, and Detroit superintending Indian affairs. At the agency a stream of Indians was in constant attendance. To assist him he employed an Irish-American interpreter. Wearily, he recorded in his journal that the interpreter was very indifferent to his attempts to elicit answers to questions on cosmogony, religion, and the supernatural. The Irishman's vocabulary was limited to supplies and the price of furs and whiskey, the trader's jargon. With the help of his numerous relatives he plunged into a study of the Chippewa language and had soon mastered it to the extent of writing learned articles about its grammar.

In 1828 Schoolcraft was elected to the territorial legislature of Michigan and introduced the legislation setting up the system of township and county names. At the same time he became a founding father of the Michigan Historical Society. He was requested by the national government to investigate conditions at the western end of Lake Superior in 1831, and the request was repeated in 1832. Both journeys were followed by published reports which were filled out with appendices on the Indian language. By this time he had collected a mass of legends about which he was so enthusiastic that he organized the Algic Society, whose purpose was to study and rehabilitate the Indians.[10]

The closing of Fort Brady in 1833 made it advisable to remove the agency from the Sault to Mackinac, where he began to play the squire to the rapidly swelling volume of English and American tourists. Two such tourists, Dr. G. R. Gilman and Mrs. Anna Jameson, an English lady, found the Schoolcrafts delightful hosts. His manuscript magazines, which were circulated among his friends, were raided freely by his visitors, who were searching for the unusual and the novel. In a journal entry for 1835 he announced that he had decided his collection would fare better if he published it than it would at the hands of literary weavers like Washington Irving.

From the reception accorded a few magazine articles he came to the decision to offer his volume, now labeled *Algic Researches,* to an eastern publisher. Harpers' brought it out in 1839. It was favorably noticed, but was not popular enough to warrant a second edition. The legends were too close to the Indian originals to arouse the widespread attention of an audience sated with the sentimental viands served by the whipped syllabub vendors of the period. Even though his own religious bias (he had been converted through the influence of his wife and a missionary brother-in-law while still at Sault Ste. Marie) was evident in the exclusion of the more off-color legends, the tales were not sentimental enough to suit the popular taste.

Schoolcraft was retired from the Indian Agency in 1841 and immediately moved to New York state. In 1842 he went to England, hoping to interest publishers there in *Algic Researches,* but without success. Mrs. Johnston, always frail, and frequently in ill health, died while he was abroad. On his return he made a trip through Western Virginia, Ohio, and Canada, seeking further material on the Algonquin. He helped to found the American Ethnological Society and became an active member of the New York Historical Society. His further researches were followed by the publication of *Oneóta,* in 1844-45, and *Notes on the Iroquois,* in 1847. For the latter task he was given a subvention by the state of New York.

The United States Congress, in 1847, authorized Schoolcraft to collect statistics on all the Indian tribes within the nation and prepare them for publication. His initial volume appeared in 1851 and others followed, six in all, in rapid succession. The series was completed in 1857 and was published by order of the Congress.[11] Meanwhile, Longfellow had brought out *Hiawatha* (1855), and the public reception was so overwhelming that Schoolcraft decided the profit from such popularity should not all go into the Cambridge poet's pocket. He prepared a new and slightly modified collection of the tales, adding many from *Oneóta* and omitting some from *Algic Researches,* identified the stories boldly with Hiawatha, and published the work under the title, *The Myth of Hiawatha* in 1856. Even with the fillip afforded by Longfellow's book, the public failed to respond and a second edition was not needed.

The later years of Schoolcraft's life were clouded by illness and shrouded in some family mystery never fully explained. He had remarried in 1847; his children appear to have been a source of disappointment, and there was much talk about miscegenation. He died in 1864. It is saddening to reflect on the sudden fall into obscurity of a man who should justly be called a father of American ethnology and folklore.

IV

Schoolcraft's Indian legends have been constantly exploited since the publication of the first four in *Travels in the Central Portion of the Mississippi Valley* (1825). John Ahearn Jones, an Englishman, who justly acquired a reputation as a fraud, pirated all four legends for his *Tales of an Indian Camp* (1829). An American doctor, G. R. Gilman published several of them in 1838, no doubt with Schoolcraft's permission since he copied them directly from their collector's manuscripts. In *Life on the Lakes* Gilman wrote: "He has been for many years a diligent collector of facts, not a spinner out of theories; and much, I think, may yet be expected from his vast and daily increasing store." (Vol. I, p. 158.) Mrs. Anna Jameson, on the other hand, having formed a close friendship with Mrs. Schoolcraft, claimed that she transcribed her "Indian fictions" from the lady of the house. Five of the legends were published in *Winter Studies and Summer Rambles* (1848).[12] Schoolcraft was fearful lest, in the hands of a professional craftsman, the lodge stories would lose the "roughness that gave them their characteristic originality." No doubt this and the persistent urging of friends like Bancroft and Gallatin led him to overcome his personal scruples and fears about offering them to a wider public.

After the appearance of *Algic Researches* in 1839 there were no borrowings of complete tales. They were imitated, however, in the popular journals, and excerpts from several were printed in so-called newspaper reviews. Probably many of them got into cheap editions of Indian *stuff* manufactured for the sensational trade to which Ingraham and his ilk were to pander later.

Longfellow noticed Schoolcraft's legends shortly after they were published. His interest in the Indians had been lifelong, and he had considered the possibility of doing something about them early in his poetic career. A college student, recently returned from the west in the forties, reawakened his interest enough for him to invite the Ojibway lecturer and writer, George Copway, to his home for tea and conversation. A little later he was re-reading Schoolcraft, and in 1854 he lugged the huge quartos of the first three volumes of *Historical and Statistical Information* home to examine their "ill digested" contents.

The much-debated question of Longfellow's indebtedness to Schoolcraft has been rather effectually stilled by the strident argument of the Osborns in their *Hiawatha-Schoolcraft-Longfellow* tome. There was never any real argument about it, because Longfellow acknowledged his debt handsomely. Professor Stith Thompson's charge is a horse of another color. Repeated many times by others since he first made it in 1922, it deserves full presentation here.

"Through the labor of Henry Rowe Schoolcraft, the legends of the Ojibwa and their neighbors were re-printed at some length. Unfortunately, the scientific value of his work is marred by the manner in which he reshaped the stories to suit his own literary taste. Several of his tales, indeed, are distorted almost beyond recognition. Nevertheless, he introduced to the civilized world a considerable body of Indian legend. Among these tales are the myths of Manabozho, though he caused great confusion by adapting to his myth the name of the Iroquois hero, Hiawatha. Through the poem of Longfellow, the details of the myth have become a part of American literature. Another mythical tale known anew through the work of Schoolcraft was 'The Sun Snarer,' already mentioned as reported by the Jesuits. He also tells a number of trickster incidents. His work serves as a landmark in the history of the recording of American Indian tales.

"A result of Schoolcraft's sentimentality has been the attitude of a large part of the general public toward Indian tradition. All sections of the country have acquired legends of 'lovers' leaps.' The courtship of Hiawatha and Minnehaha, the least Indian of any of the events in Hiawatha, has come for many readers to stand as the typical American Indian tale. If a collection of authentic tales, like the present, can help correct so erroneous an impression, it will have been well worth preparing." *Tales of the North American Indians* (1929), p. xv.

Behind this damning with faint praise lie two questionable statements and two others that are matters of judgment. First, was Schoolcraft's work as a collector partly invalidated by his adaptation of the legends "to suit his own literary taste"? It is quite irrefutable that Schoolcraft was a deeply religious man and was moved to "cut short off" some of his tales. He was not a prude, however. He could make a sly sexual innuendo whenever he chose, as in the incident illustrating the Indian's sense of humor. When one Indian laughed at another for crushing his testicles while climbing a tree, the sufferer drove a pothook through the laugher's head. "He died for a laugh." In comparing the Indians with the Greeks for lewdness, the Greeks came off second best in Schoolcraft's opinion. Whenever Schoolcraft wrote about his tales he expressed fear that their original roughness, meaning their closeness to natural physical function, would be worn off if put in the "literary loom." In one tale he even went so far as to mention the unmentionable menses of an Indian girl. Furthermore, it must be remembered that part of a complaint such as this must be borne by his informants. The Johnston girls were gentle, secluded, and very Christian; they suffered the same sentimental afflictions to which the females of the time were subject. They were devout and prayerful. Charlotte McMurray, Schoolcraft's sister-in-law and wife of a minister, supplied him with "The Enchanted Moccasins." There are three or four tales specifically ascribed to Mrs. H. R. Schoolcraft. It is more than probable that a large number of those stories that were "marred," were marred by the teller rather than the recorder. In this connection, the reader should examine the legends supplied by Chusco, the convert. The editor has noted at least two such cases in the text where the conversion shows through the story.

Second, are any of the tales "distorted beyond recognition"? The answer again must lie in the sources Schoolcraft used. Schoolcraft, by his own testimony, might cut off a tale, but he was too much the dedicated man to recast one to suit a moral prejudice. He might omit, as he did the *tripe-de-roche* yarn, but he would not change any tale beyond recognition.

Next, was it Schoolcraft's sentimentality that was responsible for the public attitude Professor Thompson describes? If "Schoolcraft" is a printer's error for Longfellow, the statement may stand. But, if Schoolcraft *is* meant, then the facts must be made clear. Except for the "Swing on Lake Superior" no woman hurtles from a cliff in Schoolcraft's tales, and in that story it is the wicked mother-in-law who cuts the ropes that plunge the wife involuntarily into space. In the 1821 *Narrative Journal* there is a reference to a lovers' leap at Lake Pepin (August 3rd entry), but this was the kind of tale that Schoolcraft, on principle, excluded from his collection of legends. No Schoolcraft story contains a Minnehaha, nor is there a tale in all Schoolcraft that deals with a love of this type and this outcome. In *Algic Researches* the "love affair" of Manabozho and the arrow-maker's daughter fills exactly one sentence.

Finally, did Schoolcraft cause great confusion by adapting the name of an Iroquois hero to the myth of Manabozho?[13] The answer is no. In *Algic Researches* (1839) there was no such identification. In *Oneóta* (1844) there was no such identification. In *Notes on the Iroquois* (1847), where he told the distorted version of Hiawatha, he did not link the two names; in fact, the word Manabozho did not occur in the recital. Schoolcraft did compare Hiawatha to Quetzalcoatl. In *Historical and Statistical Information* (1851-1854), the three volumes accessible to Longfellow, there was an account of the Iroquois Hiawatha, but it did not associate him with Manabozho. Not until *The Myth of Hiawatha* (1856), one year after *Hiawatha* was published, did Schoolcraft make a connection between the Algonquin myth-hero and the Iroquois political figure. In this case Schoolcraft copied Longfellow, probably to get on the bandwagon. Why did Longfellow make the shift? Perhaps because the Iroquois, themselves, were confused. As was pointed out earlier, there are two Hiawathas, the political figure of the League, and the myth which the Iroquois created about Hiawatha two hundred years after his death, a myth that had absorbed much of the Teharonhiawakhon legend.

After Longfellow, the use of Schoolcraft's legends has been of little consequence. The hack, Cornelius Matthews, reworked the tales, some from *Algic Researches* and some from *The Myth of Hiawatha,* under the title of *The Indian Fairy Book* (1869).[14] The book was designed to fit into a series of national fairy tales being prepared for children. As *The Enchanted Moccasins* it was reprinted in 1877. Florence Choate and Elizabeth Curtis published a volume, *The Indian Fairy Book* (1916), that follows Matthews more closely than Schoolcraft, although they acknowledged Schoolcraft as their source. This book was aimed at the juvenile audience. Both Matthews and the Choate-Curtis combination took liberties with the tales that cannot be accepted by anyone who has read the originals. Another children's volume was compiled in 1938 by Alden O. Deming. Its chief merits are that only Manabozho tales are used, and each is carefully written without reference to the Schoolcraft text although Schoolcraft is credited as originator of the stories.

Schoolcraft's Indian legends are significant if not artistic. He did not intend them to be tales of literary merit; they were, he said, the "scattered bones of aboriginal lore," and they awaited the "arranger" who could touch them "with the spear of truth and cause the skeleton of their ancient society to arise and live."

NOTES

1. The Manabozho cycle has yet to be told for modern readers by some uninhibited author who can bring order out of the folklorist's chaos.

2. It is a matter for speculation whether Paul Bunyan may be traced in origin to the lumberjacks of mixed breed who might have created Paul in the image of Kwasind.

3. J. N. B. Hewitt says, "Few, if any, of the characteristic acts and functions of the one may not safely and correctly be predicated of the other." *Handbook of American Indians*, "Manabozho."

4. According to Lewis Morgan, Hayowentha means "man who combs hair." *League of the Iroquois*, p. 64.

5. This is Hewitt's conclusion: "In this mystified form he became the central figure of a cycle of interrelated legends." As a result of this confusion, by the Iroquois, the tradition, as told to Joshua V. H. Clark, got into Schoolcraft's *Notes on the Iroquois*, a volume which Longfellow used. Several scholars writing about the use of Hiawatha's name for Manabozho, blame Schoolcraft for this. The matter is discussed later in this Introduction.

6. For the story of the expedition of 1820 see Mentor L. Williams (ed.), *Schoolcraft's Narrative Journal of an Expedition . . .* , Michigan State College Press (1953).

7. See Schoolcraft's *Travels in the Central Portion of the Mississippi Valley* (1825), in which he published for the first time some examples of Indian legends.

8. See Appendix B 1.

9. "My connection with the Johnston family has thrown open the whole arcana of the Indian's thoughts." *Personal Memoirs of a Residence of Thirty Years* (Philadelphia, 1851), p. 639.

10. Schoolcraft coined the word "Algic" by which he meant "an adjective term . . . to denote a genus or family of tribes who take their characteristic from the use of the Algonquin language. It is a derivative from the words *Algonquin* and *Akee*, earth, or land." Article on "Ethnology" in *Oneóta*.

11. In its several editions this work acquired many titles, but the best known is *Historical and Statistical Information Respecting the History, Condition, and Prospects of the Indian Tribes of the United States. . . .*

12. Of such visits Schoolcraft wrote: "It seems to me that Englishwomen and Englishmen, for I have had a good many of both sexes to visit me recently, look on America very much as one does when he peeps through a magnifying glass on pictures of foreign views. . . . It is all an optical deception. . . . Even Mrs. Jameson, who had the most accurate and artistic eye of all . . . appeared to regard our vast woods, and wilds, and lakes as a magnificent panorama, a painting in oil." *Pers. Mem.*, p. 566.

13. Albert Keiser, in *The Indian in American Literature*, p. 198, makes the same error.

14. For a discussion of the date of Matthews' volume, examine J. A. Hallowell's article in *Jour. Am. Folklore* (1946) 59:139.

ALGIC RESEARCHES,

COMPRISING

INQUIRIES RESPECTING THE MENTAL CHARACTERISTICS

OF THE

NORTH AMERICAN INDIANS

FIRST SERIES

INDIAN TALES AND LEGENDS

IN TWO VOLUMES

VOL. I

BY HENRY ROWE SCHOOLCRAFT

Author of a Narrative Journal of Travels to the Source of the Mississippi;
Travels in the Central Portions of the Mississippi Valley;
An Expedition to Itasca Lake, &c.

NEW-YORK:

HARPER & BROTHERS, 82 CLIFF-STREET

1839.

TO

LIEUT. COL. HENRY WHITING

OF THE UNITED STATES ARMY

SIR,

The position taken by you in favor of the literary susceptibilities of the Indian character, and your tasteful and meritorious attempts in imbodying their manners and customs, in the shape of poetic fiction, has directed my thoughts to you in submitting my collection of their oral fictions to the press. Few have given attention to the intellectual traits and distinctive opinions of these scattered branches of the human family, without finding the subject interesting and absorbing. But in an age of multifarious excitement, in which topic after topic, and invention after invention, have poured in upon us with an almost overwhelming rapidity, the interest felt on the subject, and the tribes themselves, and their strong claims to attention, have been thrown into the background and nearly lost sight of.

It is a pleasing coincidence, that, in addressing one whose feelings and sentiments, in relation to them, have preserved their equanimity, amid the din of the intellectual and moral novelties of the day, I can, at the same time, appeal to the ties of literary sympathy and of personal friendship.[1] Accept these expressions of my respect, and believe me,

Most truly yours,

HENRY R. SCHOOLCRAFT.

1. Henry Whiting, army careerist (1788-1851), was the respected author of long narrative poems as well as several short biographies for Jared Sparks' Library of American Biography. *Ontwa, the Son of the Forest* (New York, 1822) and *Sannillac* (Boston, 1831) were his most popular works. Schoolcraft contributed notes to the latter.

GENERAL CONSIDERATIONS

IT IS PROPOSED BY THE AUTHOR to publish the result of his observation on the mythology, distinctive opinions, and intellectual character of the aborigines. Materials exist for separate observations on their oral tales, fictitious and historical; their hieroglyphics, music, and poetry; and the grammatical structure of the languages, their principles of combination, and the actual state of their vocabulary. The former topic has been selected as the commencement of the series. At what time the remaining portions will appear, will depend upon the interest manifested by the public in the subject, and the leisure and health necessary to the examination of a mass of original papers, the accumulation of nearly twenty years.[1]

The character and peculiarities of the tribes have been studied under favorable circumstances and new aspects; offering, it is believed, an insight into their mental constitution, as yet but imperfectly understood. Hitherto our information has related rather to their external customs and manners, their physical traits and historical peculiarities, than to what may be termed the philosophy of the Indian mind. Such an examination required time and diligence. Much of the earlier part of it was necessarily devoted to clearing the ground of inquiry, by acquiring the principles of the languages, and obtaining data for generalization. This was to be done, too, at remote points of the Continent, away from all the facilities and encouragements of literary society, and with the aid of persons profoundly ignorant of the grammatical principles of the languages they spoke, and incapable of discriminating the fabulous from the true in the histories they related. The severe axioms of commerce had, from the first, caused the Indians to be regarded merely as the medium of a peculiar branch of trade, which was pursued at great hazards, excited deep animosity in the breasts of the respective commercial factors, and gave an absorbing interest to all that took place in the Indian country for two centuries. The interpretership of the languages became, of necessity, the business of a class of men who were generally uneducated, and who, imbued strongly with the feelings and prejudices of their employers, sought no higher excellence in their profession than to express the common ideas connected with the transactions of trade. The result was, then as now, that they comprehended the scope and genius of none of the languages they spoke. Whoever will submit to the labor of a critical examination into the subject, will soon become satisfied that the mediums of communication he is compelled to use are jargons, and not languages. It is impossible not to attribute to this imperfect state of oral translation, a considerable share of the errors and misunderstandings which have characterized our intercourse, political and commercial, with the tribes. Made sensible of this defect in the mode of com-

4

munication, at an early period after my entrance into the Indian territories, my collections in Indian lexicography have been withheld from my journals of travel for further opportunity to examine the principles of the languages themselves.[2] Nothwithstanding this impression, and the care adopted to ensure accuracy, much of my earlier information, derived through the ordinary channels of interpretation, proved either wholly fallacious, or required to be tested and amended by a diligent course of subsequent scrutiny.

Language constituted the initial point of inquiry, but it did not limit it. It was found necessary to examine the mythology of the tribes as a means of acquiring an insight into their mode of thinking and reasoning, the sources of their fears and hopes, and the probable origin of their opinions and institutions. This branch of inquiry connected itself, in a manner which could not have been anticipated, with their mode of conveying instruction, moral, mechanical, and religious, to the young, through the intervention of traditionary fictitious tales and legends; and naturally, as the next effort of a barbarous people, to hieroglyphic signs to convey ideas and sounds. Rude as these characters were, however, they furnish very striking illustrations of their intellectual efforts, and exhibit evidences of that desire, implanted in the minds of all men, to convey to their contemporaries and transmit to posterity the prominent facts of their history and attainments. Nothing in the whole inquiry has afforded so ample a clue to their opinions and thoughts, in all the great departments of life and nature, as their oral imaginative tales; and it has, therefore, been deemed proper to introduce copious specimens of these collections from a large number of the tribes, embracing three of the generic stocks of language.[3]

In adopting an original nominative for the series, the object has been to convey definite general impressions. The term ALGIC[4] is introduced, in a generic sense, for all that family of tribes who, about A.D. 1600, were found spread out, with local exceptions, along the Atlantic, between Pamlico Sound and the Gulf of St. Lawrence, extending northwest to the Mississippi of Hudson's Bay, and west to the Mississippi. The exceptions embrace the Yemassees and Catawbas on the coast, and the Tuscaroras, Iroquois, Wyandots, and Winnebagoes, and a part of the Sioux, in the interior, all of whom appear to have been intruders within the circle, and three of which, namely, the Tuscaroras, Iroquois, and Wyandots, speak dialects of a generic language, which we shall denominate the OSTIC.[5] The Winnebagoes are clearly of the Abanic[6] stock, and the Yemassees and Catawbas—extinct tribes, of whom but little has been preserved, of the restless and warlike Muskogee race. The latter, who, together with the Cherokees and Choctaws, fill up the southern portion of the Union, quite to the banks of the Mississippi, exist in juxtaposition to, and not as intruders within, the Algic circle. The Chickasaws are a scion of the Choctaws, as the Seminoles are of the Muskogees. The Choctaw and Muskogee are, radically, the same language. The Cherokees do not appear to have put forth any distant branches, and have come down to our times, as a distinct people. It thus appears that four mother stocks occupied the entire area of North America, east of the Mississippi, and lying between the Gulf of Mexico and Hudson's Bay, with the exception of a single tribe and a portion of another. The Winnebagoes, who are of the Abanic race, had, however, merely crossed from the west to the east banks of the Mississippi, but never proceeded beyond the shores of Green Bay. The Dacotahs had crossed this stream higher north, and proceeded to the west shores of Superior, whence they were beat back by the van of the Algics under the name of Odjibwas.

The object of inquiry is thus defined with general precision, although it is not intended to limit the inquiry itself to geographical boundaries. It will be perceived that the territory formerly occupied by the Algic nations comprehended by far the largest portion of the United States east of the Mississippi, together with a large area of the British possessions. They occupied the Atlantic coast as far south as the river Savannah in Georgia, if Shawnee tradition is entitled to respect, and as high north as the coast of Labrador, where the tribes of this stock are succeeded by the Esquimaux. It was into the limits of these people [Algics] that the Northmen, according to appearances, pushed their daring voyages previous to the discovery of Columbus;[7] and it was also among these far-spreading and independent hordes that the earliest European colonies were planted. Cabot, and Hudson, and Verrazani made their principal landings among the tribes of this type. The Pilgrims first set foot ashore in their midst, and they landed near the spot where, several centuries before, Thorwald Ericson had fallen a sacrifice to the spirit of Norwegian and Icelandic discovery. If the country had ever been occupied by Esquimaux, as indicated by Scandinavian history, there was not an Esquimaux there at that period. The entire coast of New-England was possessed by the Algics. They extended north of it to Cape Breton. Cartier found them in the Bay of Chaleur, the Pilgrims at Plymouth, Hudson at the island of Manhattan, Barlow and Amidas on the coasts of Virginia. They lined the seaboard; they appear to have migrated along its borders from southwest to northeast, and were privately attached to the open coast by the double facility which it afforded of a spontaneous subsistence, having the resources of the sea on one side and of the forest on the other. It is probable that these advantages led them to underrate the interior, which, being left unguarded, their enemies pushed in from the west, and seated themselves in Western New-York and Pennsylvania on the sources of the principal streams. It is evident that the Algics did not penetrate the interior to a great extent, their camps and towns forming, as it were, but a hem or cordon along the Atlantic. At the only points where this edging was penetrated, the discoverers found tribes of the Ostic stock, a fierce and indomitable race, of a sanguinary character, and speaking a harsh and guttural language. Such were the Iroquois, who were encountered on the Upper Hudson and the Mohawk, and the Wyandots found by Cartier at the islands of Orleans and Hochelaga. Regard these two leading races of the north in whatever light we may, it is impossible to overlook the strong points of character in which they differed. Both were dexterous and cunning woodsmen, excelling in all the forest arts necessary to their condition, and having much in their manners and appearance in common. But they spoke a radically different language, and they differed scarcely less in their distinctive character and policy. The one was mild and conciliating, the other fierce and domineering. They were alike in hospitality, in their misconception of virtue, and their high estimate of bravery. Independence was strikingly characteristic of both; but the one was satisfied with personal or tribal freedom, while the other sought to secure it by general combination. And if the two races be closely compared, there appears to be grounds for the opinion, that one is descended from a race of shepherds or pastoral nomads, and the other from a line of adventurers and warlike plunderers. It may, perhaps, be deemed among the auspicious circumstances which awaited the Europeans in this hemisphere, that they planted their earliest colonies among the former race.

In giving this enlarged signification to the terms Algic and Ostic, reference has been had to the requisitions of a general philological classification. But it is proper to remark of the Algic tribes, to whom our attention is to be particularly directed, that they were marked by peculiarities and shades of language and customs deemed to be quite striking among themselves. They were separated by large areas of territory, differing considerably in their climate and productions. They had forgotten the general points in their history, and each tribe and subtribe was prone. to regard itself as independent of all others, if not the leading or parent tribe. Their languages exhibited diversities of sound, where there was none whatever in its syntax. Changes of accent and interchanges of consonants had almost entirely altered the aspect of words, and obscured their etymology. Some of the derivatives were local, and not understood beyond a few hundred miles, and all the roots of the language were buried, as we find them at this day, beneath a load of superadded verbiage. The identity of the stock is, however, to be readily traced amid these discrepancies. They are assimilated by peculiar traits of a common physical resemblance; by general coincidence of manners, customs, and opinions; by the rude rites of a worship of spirits, everywhere the same; by a few points of general tradition; and by the peculiar and strongly-marked features of a transpositive language, identified by its grammar, alike in its primitive words, and absolutely fixed in the number and mode of modification of its radical sounds.

One or two additional remarks may be made in relation to the general traits of the Algic race. It was the chiefs of these nomadic bands who welcomed the Europeans to the shore. They occupied the Atlantic States. They everywhere received the strangers with open arms, established pacific relations with them, and evinced, both by their words and their policy, the abiding sense they had of the advantages of the intercourse. They existed so completely in the hunter state as to have no relish for any other kind of labor, looking with an inward and deep contempt on the arts of husbandry and mechanics. They had skill enough to construct their canoes; knew sufficient of the elementary art of weaving to make bags and nets of bark, and the simple tapestry or mats to cover their lodges; and, above all, they were expert in fabricating the proper missiles of war and hunting. They had no smiths, supplying their place by a very considerable skill in the cleavage of silicious stones. They knew enough of pottery to form a mixture which would stand the effects of repeated and sudden heating and cooling, and had probably retained the first simple and effectual arts of the human race in this branch. They had but little knowledge of numbers, and none of letters; but found a substitute for the latter in a system of hieroglyphics of a general character, but quite exact in their mode of application, and absolutely fixed in the elements. They were formal, and inclined to stateliness in their councils and public intercourse, and very acute and expert in the arrangement and discussion of minor matters, but failed in comprehensive views, deep-reaching foresight, and powers of generalization. Hence they were liable to be called cunning rather than wise. They were, emphatically, men of impulse, capable of extraordinary exertions on the instant, but could not endure the tension, mental and physical, of long-continued exertions. Action appeared to be always rather the consequence of nervous, than of intellectual excitement. Above all, they were characterized by habits of sloth, which led them utterly to despise the value of time; and this has appeared so constant a trait, under every vicissitude of their history, that it may be regarded as the probable effect of a luxurious effeminacy, produced upon the race under a climate more adverse to personal activity. It should be borne in mind, that the character first drawn of the Algic race is essentially that which has been attributed to the whole of the North American tribes, although it is not minutely applicable to some of the interior nations. The first impressions made upon the strangers from the Old World, sank deep; and there was, naturally, but little disposition to re-examine the justice of the conclusions thus formed. These people were, from the outset, regarded as of eastern origin; and, if nothing before adverted to had been suited to give coloring to the idea, it would have resulted, almost as a matter of course, from their having, in all their tribes and every band of them, a class of Magii, who affected to exert the arts of magic, offered sacrifices to idolatrous things, and were consulted as oracles both in peace and war. These pseudo priests were called *Powows* by the English, *Jongleurs* by the French, and by various other terms by themselves and by others; but their office and general character were identical. They upheld a spurious worship, and supported it by all sorts of trick and deception. There was no regular succession in this priesthood, so far as is known; but the office, like that of the war-captain, was generally assumed and exercised by men of more than ordinary acuteness and cunning. In other words, it was conferred by the election of opinion, but not of votes.

The Algics entered the present limits of the United States from the southwest. They appear to have crossed the Mississippi at the point where the heavy formations of boulder and gravel, southwest of the Alleghenies, are heaved up close along its banks. They were followed, at distinct eras, by the Ostic, the Muskogee; and the Tsallanic[8] hordes, by the first of whom they were driven, scattered, and harassed, and several of the tribes not only conquered, but exterminated. The Iroquois, who, in their sixfold dialects, constitute the type of the Ostics, appear to have migrated up the Valley of the Ohio, which they occupied and named; and, taking a most commanding and central position in Western New-York, interposed themselves between the New-England and the Algonquin sub-types, and thus cut off their communication with each other. This separation was complete. They pushed their conquests successfully down the Hudson, the Delaware, the Susquehanna, and the St. Lawrence, and westward up the Great Lakes. The Wyandots, an Ostic tribe, who, at the discovery of the St. Lawrence by the French, were posted as low down as the island of Orleans, formed an alliance with the French and with the Algonquins north of that stream. This exposed them to dissension with their warlike and jealous relatives the Iroquois, and led to their expulsion into the region of the upper lakes, even to the farther shores of Lake Superior. They were, however, supported by all the influence of the French, and by the whole of the confederate Algic tribes, and finally fixed themselves upon the Straits of Detroit, where they were privileged with a high political power, as keepers of the great council fire, and enjoyed much respect among the Western tribes through the whole of the eighteenth century. It was this tribe that it required most address to bring over, in the combined struggle which the lake tribes made for independence under the noted Algic leader, Pontiac, between 1759 and 1764.

History first takes notice of the Algics in Virginia, and some parts of the Carolinas and Georgia. The Powhattanic tribes were a clearly-marked scion of this stock. They occupied all the streams of Virginia and Maryland flowing into the Ocean or into Chesapeake Bay. They were ever prone to divide and assume new names, which were generally taken from some prominent or characteristic feature in the geography or natural productions of the country. The farther they wandered, the more striking were their diversities, and the more obscure became every link by which identity is traced. Under the name of Lenawpees and of Mohegans, they extended along the seashore through the present limits of Delaware, Pennsylvania, New-Jersey, and New-York, and various petty independent tribes of the same race swept round the whole coast of New-England, and the British provinces beyond it, to Cape Breton and the Gulf of St. Lawrence. The traditions of all these tribes pointed southwest as the place of their origin, and it was there that they located the residence of their God. The Odjibwas and Algonquins proper, and their numerous progeny of tribes in the west and northwest, date their origin in the east, and to this day call the north and northwest winds the *home wind,*[9] indicating, probably, that it blows back on the track of their migration. Whether this be considered in a local or general sense, it is equally interesting of a people, whose original terms are simple in meaning, and constitute, as it were, so many links in the investigation of their history. The whole of these tribes, interior and Atlantic, spoke branches of one radical language. Scattered as they were in geographical position, and marked by peculiarities of language and history, they are yet readily recognized as descendants from a common stock. Wherever the process of philological analysis is applied, the Algic roots are found. The tribes coincide also in their general characteristics, mental and physical. They employed the same hieroglyphic signs to express names and events; possessed the same simple, and, in some respects, childlike attainments in music and poetry, and brought with them to this Continent, and extensively propagated, a mythology, the strong belief in which furnishes the best clue to their hopes and fears, and lies at the foundation of the Indian character. Simple although their music is, there is something strikingly characteristic in it. Their Pib-e-gwun is but another name for the Arcadian pipe;[10] but they did not appropriate the same music to love and religion. The latter was of a totally different, and of a louder and harsher kind. Their hieroglyphics, bearing quite a resemblance to the Egyptian, express a series of whole images, without adjuncts, and stand as general memoranda to help the recollection, and to be interpreted according to the mythology, customs, and arts of the people. There is nothing whatever in this system analogous to the Runic character. Nor does there appear to be, in either language or religion, anything approximating either to the Scandinavian or to the Hindoo races. With a language of a strongly Semitic cast,[11] they appear to have retained leading principles of syntax where the lexicography itself has changed; and while they fell into a multiplicity of bands from the most common causes, they do not appear to have advanced an iota in their original stock of knowledge, warlike arts, or political tact, but rather fell back. The ancient bow and arrow, javelin, and earth kettle, remained precisely the same things in their hands. And whatever mechanical skill they had in architecture, weaving, or any other art, dwindled to a mere knowledge of erecting a wigwam, and weaving nets and garters. At least, if they possessed superior attainments in the Southern portions of this Continent, where they certainly dwelt, these were lost amid the more stern vicissitudes and frigid climate of the North. And this was perfectly natural. Of what use were these arts to a comparatively sparse population, who occupied vast regions, and lived, very well, by hunting the flesh and wearing the skins of animals? To such men a mere subsistence was happiness, and the killing of a few men in war glory. It may be doubted whether the very fact of the immensity of an unoccupied country, spread out before a civilized or half civilized people, with all its allurements of wild game and personal independence, would not be sufficient, in the lapse of a few centuries, to throw them back into a complete state of barbarism.[12]

But we will not anticipate the results of research, where the object is merely to direct attention to the interest of the inquiry itself. To discover and fix the comprehensive points of their national resemblance, and the concurring circumstances of their history and traditions; to point out the affinities of their languages, and to unveil the principles of their mythology, are conceived to be essential prerequisites to the formation of right notions of their probable origin and mental peculiarities. And it is obvious that the true period for this inquiry must be limited to the actual existence of the tribes themselves. Every year is diminishing their numbers and adding to the obscurity of their traditions. Many of the tribes and languages are already extinct, and we can allude to at least one of the still existing smaller tribes who have lost the use of their vernacular tongue and adopted the English.[13] Distinct from every benevolent consideration, weighty as these are, it is exceedingly desirable that the record of facts, from which they are to be judged, should be completed as early as possible. It is conceived that, in rescuing their oral tales and fictitious legends, an important link in the chain has been supplied. But it is believed that still higher testimony remains. History, philosophy, and poetry regard with deep interest these recorded and accumulating materials on the character and origin of races of men, who are associated with the geographical nomenclature of the country, and to whom at least, it may be assumed, posterity will render poetic justice. But revelation has a deeper stake in the question, and it is one calculated to infuse new energy in the cause of benevolence, and awaken fresh ardor in the heart of piety.

It is not the purpose of these remarks to excite the expectation that a long residence in the Indian country, and official intercourse with the tribes, have given the author such access to the Indian mind, or enabled him to push his inquiries so far into their former history and mental characteristics, as to clear up fully the obscurities referred to; but the hope is indulged that data have been obtained of a new and authentic character, which will prove important in any future researches on these topics.[14]

NOTES

1. Some of the plan for Schoolcraft's monumental work, *Historical and Statistical Information on the Indians of North America,* 6 vols. (Philadelphia, 1851-57), is foreshadowed in these "considerations."

2. Schoolcraft frequently commented on Indian linguistics, even in his first northwest travel journal (1821). That he should become more than an amateur linguist was inevitable.

3. No statement by Schoolcraft better summarizes his gropingly scientific approach to ethnology, anthropology, and linguistics than this paragraph.

4. Derived from the words Allegheny and Atlantic, in reference to the race of Indians anciently located in this geographical area, but who, as expressed in the text, had extended themselves, at the end of the 15th century, far toward the north and west. [H. R. S.]

5. From the Algic, Oshtegwon, a head, &c. [H. R. S.] Schoolcraft's cumbersome nomenclature is frequently close to the presently accepted data of North American Indian anthropology. His language groupings are fundamentally sound.

6. Denoting occidental. From Kabeyun the west—and embracing the tribes who, at the commencement of 1800, were located west of the Mississippi. The Sioux, Otoes, Omahaws, Osages, and Quapaws, constitute the leading members of this group. [H. R. S.]

7. For some remarks on this question, see *Am. Biblical Repository,* second series, No. 2, April, 1839. [H. R. S.] "Ante-Columbian History of America," Vol. I, pp. 430-449.

8. From *Tsallakee*—the name by which, according to David Brown, the Cherokees call themselves. [H. R. S.] David Brown and his sister Catharine

Brown were Christian Cherokees who labored valiantly for Christ among their fellows. Both received mission school education. The early death of the sister elevated her to tract fame. See Rufus Anderson, *Memoir of Catharine Brown,* Cincinnati, 1827 (3rd Ed.).

9. Keewaydin. [H. R. S.]

10. When Schoolcraft re-edited his Indian tales in 1856, *The Myth of Hia-watha,* he named the appended collection of Indian poems in translation "Wild Notes of the Pibbigwun." Many of the poems in *Algic Researches* were transferred from the story text to this appendix in 1856.

11. The notion that Indians were descended from the lost tribes of Israel was firmly rooted in the thinking of most early nineteenth century intellectuals.

12. J. F. Cooper held a similar view of cultural retrogression. See Chapter VI, *The Prairie.*

13. The Brothertons. [H. R. S.] This group of Mohegans, Pequots, Narragansets, and Montauks from New England and Long Island settled in 1788 on Oneida land in Oneida County, New York. They were removed to Wisconsin with the Stockbridges in 1833. Because of dialect differences English was adopted as the common tongue. See *Pers. Mem.,* pp. 658-659.

14. It should be observed that Schoolcraft's modest hope that he had contributed something of importance to future researches was the understatement of 1839.

INDIAN TALES AND LEGENDS

MYTHOLOGIC AND ALLEGORIC

RENDERED FROM

THE ORAL TRADITIONS OF THE NORTH AMERICAN INDIANS

BY COMPETENT INTERPRETERS

AND WRITTEN OUT

FROM THE ORIGINAL NOTES

PRELIMINARY OBSERVATIONS

ON THE TALES

THE FOLLOWING TALES are published as specimens of an oral imaginative lore existing among the North American aborigines. In the long period of time in which these tribes have been subjects of observation, we are not aware that powers of this kind have been attributed to them. And it may be asked, Why the discovery of this peculiar trait in their intellectual character has not been made until the first quarter of the nineteenth century? The force of the query is acknowledged; and, in asserting the claim for them, the writer of these pages proposes first to offer to the public some proofs of the correctness of his own conclusions on this point.[1]

The era of the discovery was the era of maritime adventure. The master spirits of those times were men of shrewd, keen sense and adventurous tempers, who wished to get ahead in the world, and relied for their success, rather upon the compass and sword, than upon their pens. It was the age of action and not of research. Least of all, had they the means or the inclination to inquire into the mental capacities of fierce and warlike races of hunters and warriors, who claimed to be lords of the soil, and actually exterminated the first settlement made in St. Domingo and in Virginia. They set out from Europe with a lamentable want of true information respecting them, and were disappointed in not finding them wild animals on two legs. Long after the discovery, it was debated whether any faith ought to be kept with them; and the chief point of inquiry was, not whether they had any right to the soil, but how they could be turned to the best account in the way of trade and merchandise. The Spaniards, who occupy the foreground in the career of discovery, began by selling the Indian and compelling him to feudal servitude, and would probably have driven as profitable a traffic as was subsequently carried on with the Africans, had it not soon appeared that the Indian was a lazy man, and not a productive laborer. He sank under the overwhelming idea of hopeless servitude, lingered a few years an unprofitable miner, and died. The project was therefore relinquished, not because of the awakened sensibilities of the conquerors, but because it was (in the mercantile acceptation of the term) a bad business. The history of the manners, customs, and languages of the ancient nations, and particularly of the oriental branches of the human family, from whom they were thought to have descended, was deeply in the dark. Comparative philology was unknown, and the spirit of critical and historical acumen, which has evinced itself in Germany in modern days, and is rapidly extending itself over the world, still slumbered under the intellectual darkness which spellbound the human mind after the overthrow of

15

Greece and Rome, and the dispersion of the Jews. To expect, therefore, that the hardy commanders of exploring voyages should have, at the opening of the sixteenth century, entered into any minute inquiries of the kind referred to, would be to expect that the human mind should reverse its ordinary mode of operation. These men do not appear to have troubled themselves with the inquiry whether the Indians *had* a history: certainly they took no pains to put on record facts in the department of inquiry to which our attention is now directed. This view results from an attentive examination of the earlier voyages and histories of adventure in this hemisphere, in which is exhibited the coldest air of mercantile calculation. The journals themselves are mere logbooks, rigid and dry in their details, destitute of any powers of reflection upon the events they narrate, and unrelieved by exact research, tact of observation, or high-souled sentiment.[2]

History is required to pass a less censorious judgment on the moral character of those of the colonists who settled north of the latitudes of the West Indies. The great Anglo-Saxon stock, which spread along the shores of the North Atlantic, carried with it notions of liberty and justice, which shielded the aboriginal tribes from the curse of slavery. They treated them as having a just right to the occupancy of the soil, and formed treaties with them. They acknowledged, by these acts, their existence as independent political communities, and maintained, in their fullest extent, the doctrine of political faith and responsibility. Some of the colonies went farther, and early directed their attention to their improvement and conversion to Christianity. The two powers were, however, placed in circumstances adverse to the prosperous and contemporaneous growth of both, while they occupied a territory over which there was a disputed sovereignty. It must needs have happened, that the party which increased the fastest in numbers, wanted most land, and had most knowledge (to say nothing of the influence of temperance and virtue), should triumph, and those who failed in these requisites, decline. It is believed that this is the true cause why the transplanted European race overspread the land, and the Indians were driven before them. And that result is by no means owing to a proper want of sympathy for the latter, or of exertions both to better their condition and avert their fate. The Indians could not, however, be made to understand this. They did not look to causes, but reasoned wholly from effects. They saw the white race occupying the prominent harbors, pushing up the navigable streams, spreading over the uplands, and multiplying in numbers "like sands on the seashore." And they attributed to hostile purpose, breach of faith, and cupidity, what was, to a very great extent, owing to their own idle habits, vices, and short-sightedness. The two races soon came to measure swords; and this contest extended, with short periods of intervening peace, from about A.D. 1600 to the close of 1814. The Indians staked stratagem and the geographical obstacles of a vast unknown wilderness, against knowledge, resources, and discipline. Their policy was to fly when pursued, and pursue when relieved from pursuit; to avoid field fights, and carry on a most harassing war of detail. By avoiding concentration in camps, and occupying a comparatively large area of country, they have compelled their assailants, at all times, to employ a force entirely disproportioned to that required to cope with the same number of civilized troops. The result of this long-continued, and often renewed contest for supremacy, it is only necessary to advert to. It has been anything but favorable to the production of right feelings and a reciprocal knowledge of real character on both sides. The Indians could never be made to appreciate the offers of education and Christianity by one portion of the community, while others were arrayed against them in arms. Their idea of government was, after all, the Eastern notion of a unity or despotism, in which everything emanates from the governing power, and is responsible to it. Nor has their flitting and feverish position on the frontiers been auspicious to the acquisition of a true knowledge of their character, particularly in those things which have relation to the Indian mind, their opinions on abstract subjects, their mythology, and other kindred topics. Owing to illiterate interpreters and dishonest men, the parties have never more than half understood each other. Distrust and misapprehension have existed by the century together. And it is, therefore, no cause for astonishment, that the whole period of our contemporaneous history should be filled up with so many negotiations and cessions, wars and treaties.

These remarks are offered to indicate, that the several periods of our colonial and confederate history, and wars, were unfavorable to the acquisition of that species of information respecting their mental capacities and social institutions, of which it is our purpose to speak. The whole tendency of our intercourse with them has been, to demonstrate rather the physical than moral capabilities of the Indian, his expertness in war, his skill, stratagem, powers of endurance, and contempt of suffering. Indian fortitude has been applauded at the stake, and Indian kindness and generosity acknowledged in the wigwam, and in the mazes of the wilderness. Admiration had been excited by his noble sentiments of independence and exaltation above personal fear. Above all, perhaps, had he been accredited for intellect in his acuteness in negotiation and simple force of his oratory. But the existence of an intellectual invention had never been traced, so far as it is known, to the amusements of his domestic fireside; nor could it well have been conjectured to occupy so wide a field for its display in legendary tales and fables.

My attention was first arrested by the fact of the existence of such tales among the Odjibwa nation inhabiting the region about Lake Superior in 1822. Two years previous, I had gone out in that quarter as one of the members of a corps of observation, on an exploratory expedition to the head waters of the Mississippi.[3] The large area of territory which it was found this tribe occupied, together with their number and warlike character, induced the department of war to extend a military post to the Falls or *Sault* of St. Mary's, near the outlet of Lake Superior, in the year above named. I accompanied this force, and assumed, at the sime time, an official relation to this tribe, as Agent of Indian affairs, which led me to inquire into their distinctive history, language, and characteristic traits. It was found that they possessed a story-telling faculty, and I wrote down from

their narration a number of these fictitious tales;[4] some of which were
amusing merely, other were manifestly intended to convey mythological
or allegorical information. The boundaries between truth and fiction are
but feebly defined among the aborigines of this Continent, and it was found
in this instance, that the individuals of the tribe who related the tales were
also the depositories of their historical traditions, such as they were; and
these narrators wove the few and scattered incidents and landmarks of their
history into the web and woof of their wildest tales. I immediately announced this interesting discovery in their moral character to a few friends
and correspondents, who were alike interested in the matter;[5] and a new
zest was thus given to the inquiry, and the field of observation greatly extended. The result was the finding of similar tales among all the north-
western tribes whose traditions were investigated. They were also found
among some of the tribes west of the Mississippi, and the present state of
the inquiry demonstrates that this species of oral lore is common to the
Algic, the Ostic, and some tribes of the Abanic stock. It is conjectured to
exist among the rather extended branches of the Muskogee, and also the
Cherokee, although no actual proof is possessed and it becomes a question
of interest to ascertain how far a similar trait can be traced among the
North American tribes, and where the exceptions and limitations are to be
found. To find a trait which must hereafter be deemed characteristic of the
mental habits of these tribes, so diffused, furnishes a strong motive for extending inquiries farther and wider. It may be asked whether the South
American aborigines possessed, or still possess, this point of intellectual
affinity with the tribes of the North. Did Manco Capac and Montezuma
employ this means to strengthen political power, inspire courage, or console themselves under misfortune? Do the icebound and impoverished
natives of the Arctic circle draw inspiration in their cruel vicissitudes from
a similar intellectual source? What sound deductions can be drawn from a
comparison of Eastern with Western fable, as thus developed? And, finally,
is this propensity connected, in other of the American stock tribes, with a
hieroglyphic system of notation, as we find it in the Algic, which will bear
any useful comparison with the phonetic system of Egypt, the Runic of
Iceland and Norway, or with any other mode of perpetuating the knowledge of events or things known to the human race?

A few remarks may be added respecting the character of the tales now
submitted to inspection. And the first is, that they appear to be of a homoge-
neous and vernacular origin. There are distinctive tribal traits, but the
general features coincide. The ideas and incidents do not appear to be
borrowed or unnatural. The situations and circumstances are such as are
common to the people. The language and phraseology are of the most
simple kind. Few adjectives are used, and few comparisons resorted to.
The style of narration, the cast of invention, the theory of thinking, are
eminently peculiar to a people who wander about in woods and plains,
who encounter wild beasts, believe in demons, and are subject to the
vicissitudes of the seasons. The tales refer themselves to a people who are
polytheists; not believers in one God or Great Spirit, but of thousands of

spirits; a people who live in fear, who wander in want, and who die in misery. The machinery of spirits and necromancy, one of the most ancient and prevalent errors of the human race, supplies the framework of these fictitious creations. Language to carry out the conceptions might seem to be wanting, but here the narrator finds a ready resource in the use of metaphor, the doctrine of metamorphosis, and the personification of inanimate objects; for the latter of which, the grammar of the language has a peculiar adaptation. Deficiencies of the vocabulary are thus supplied, life and action are imparted to the whole material creation, and every purpose of description is answered. The belief of the narrators and listeners in every wild and improbable thing told, helps wonderfully, in the original, in joining the sequence of parts together. Nothing is too capacious for Indian belief. Almost every declaration is a prophecy, and every tale a creed. He believes that the whole visible and invisible creation is animated with various orders of malignant or benign spirits, who preside over the daily affairs and over the final destinies of men. He believes that these spirits must be conciliated by sacrifices, and a series of fasts and feasts either follow or precede these rites, that by the one they may be rendered acceptable, and by the other, his gratitude may be shown. This constitutes the groundwork of the Algic religion: but superstition has ingrafted upon the original stock, till the growth is a upas of giant size, bearing the bitter fruits of demonology, witchcraft, and necromancy. To make the matter worse, these tribes believe that animals of the lowest, as well as highest class in the chain of creation, are alike endowed with reasoning powers and faculties. And as a natural conclusion, they endow birds, and bears, and all other animals with souls, which, they believe, will be encountered in other shapes in another state of existence. So far the advantages of actual belief come in aid of their fictitious creations, and this is the true cause why so much importance is attached to the flight and appearance of particular birds, who, being privileged to ascend in the air, are supposed by them to be conversant with the wishes, or to act in obedience to the mandates of the spirits: and the circumstance of this belief deserves to be borne in mind in the perusal of their tales, as it will be found that the words put into the mouths of the actors express the actual opinions of the natives on life, death, and immortality, topics which have heretofore been impenetrably veiled.[6]

The value of these traditionary stories appeared to depend, very much, upon their being left, as nearly as possible, in their original forms of thought and expression. In the original there is no attempt at ornament. Great attention is paid, in the narration, to repeating the conversations and speeches, and imitating the very tone and gesture of the actors. This is sometimes indulged at the risk of tautology. Moral point has been given to no tale which does not, in the original, justify it; and it is one of the unlooked-for features connected with the subject, that so considerable a proportion of them possess this trait. It is due to myself, and to those who have aided me in the collection and translation of the materials, to say, that the advantages enjoyed in this respect have been of the most favorable character.

The whole examination, extending, with intervals, through a period of seventeen years, has been conducted not only with the aid that a public station, as an executive officer for the tribes, has supplied, but with the super-added intelligence and skill in the languages existing within the range of my domestic and affiliated circle.[7]

Of the antiquity of the tales, the surest external evidence may probably be drawn from the lexicography. In a language in which the actor and the object are riveted, so to speak, by transitive inflections, it must needs happen that the history of its names for objects, whether preserved orally or by letters, is, in fact, the history of the introduction of the objects named, and this fixes eras in the enlargement of the vocabulary. Although it is true, that without letters these eras cannot be accurately fixed, yet valuable inferences may be drawn from an examination of this branch of the inquiry. Words are like coins, and may, like them, be examined to illustrate history. It has been found that those of the highest antiquity are simple and brief. Most of the primitive nouns are monosyllabic, and denote but a single object or idea. A less number are disyllabic; few exceed this; and it may be questioned, from the present state of the examination, whether there is a single primitive trisyllable. The primitives become polysyllabic by adding an inflection indicating the presence or absence of vitality (which is the *succedaneum* for gender), and a farther inflection to denote number. They also admit of adjective terminations. Pronouns are denoted by particles prefixed or suffixed. The genius of the language is accumulative, and tends rather to add syllables or letters, making farther distinctions in objects already before the mind, than to introduce new words. A simple word is thus oftentimes converted into a descriptive phrase, at once formidable to the eye and the ear. And it is only by dissecting such compounds that the radix can be attained.

Judged by this test, most of the tales are of the era of flint arrow-heads, earthen pots, and skin clothes. Their fishnets are represented as being made of the bark of trees. No mention is made of a blanket, gun, knife, or any metallic instrument; we do not hear of their cutting down trees, except in a single instance, yet there is nothing to indicate that their economical labors were not well performed. *Au* is an original, causative particle, and appears to be the root of a numerous class of words, sometimes with, and sometimes without a consonant added. *Aukee* is earth, and may be, but is rather too remote for a derivative from אֶרֶץ. By adding *k* to this root the term is made specific, and denotes an earthen pot or kettle. *Aubik* is the radix for metal, ore, rock. By prefixing the particle *Pe,* we have the name for iron, *Misk* for copper, and so forth; but as euphony requires, in forming compounds, that two vowels should not come together, the sound of *w* is interposed in these particular instances. *Gunzh* is the radix for plant; *Tig* for tree; *Asee* for animal, etc.; and either by suffixing or prefixing syllabical increments, the terminology of the three great departments of nature is formed. The terms of consanguinity are derived from *Ai,* a heart, hence *Si-ai,* elder brother, *Sheem-ai,* younger brother, or younger sister, etc. *Konaus,* a loose wrapper, is the most ancient and generic term for a garment which has been found. The principal female garment, leggon, etc., are derivatives from it. *Muttataus,* a beaver robe, is from the same root. *Wyaun,* a furred skin, and *Waigin,* a dressed skin, appear to form the bases of the nomenclature for the Indian wardrobe. Blanket is a modern term, meaning white furred skin. Woolen cloth took the name of dressed skin, and its various colors and qualities are indicated by adjective prefixes. Calicoes or printed cottons are named from a generic, meaning speckled or spotted. All these are modern terms, as modern as those for a horse, a sheep, or a hog, and, like the latter, are descriptive and polysyllabic. Tobacco and the zea mays, both indigenous productions, are mentioned. The latter is the subject of a simple allegoric tale.

These particulars may suffice to indicate the importance of etymological analysis in examining the antiquity of tales. Narrations of a later era are denoted by the introduction of the modern compounds, such as their names for the domestic animals of Europe, a gun, a rifle, a ship, a spyglass, compass, watch, hat, etc. The bow and arrow, club and lance, are the only species of arms actually described as in use, except in a single instance, and this tale is manifestly an interpolated version of an ancient story. The father of the winds makes battle with a huge flagroot, and the king of reptiles is shot with a dart.

Geographical terms and allusions to the climate supply another branch of comparison. Some of the grand features of the country are referred to by their modern Indian names, but this is nearly restricted to what may be termed the historical legends. There are frequent allusions to the Northern hemisphere. Snow, ice, and lakes are referred to. Warm latitudes are once or twice mentioned, and the allusions are coupled with admonitions against the danger of corrupt and effeminate manners and habits.

Astronomy and cosmogony constitute subjects of frequent notice; and this might naturally be expected from a people who are quick in their perceptions of external nature, and pass a large share of their time under the open sky. The phenomena of thunder, lightning, the aurora borealis, meteors, the rainbow, the galaxy of the milky way, the morning and evening stars, and the more prominent groups of the fixed and minor stars, are specifically named and noticed. The cardinal points are accurately distinguished. They entertain the semi-ancient theory that the earth is spheroidal, and the sun and moon perform their circuits round it. The visitors to these luminaries, described in the text, personify the former as a male and the latter as a female, under the idea of brother and sister. We are left to infer, from another passage, that they believe the sky revolves. Nothing, however, in the "open firmament," is a subject of more constant and minute observation, and a more complex terminology, than the clouds. Their color, shape, transparency or obscurity, movements, and relative position to the sun and to each other, constitute objects of minute notice and deep importance. A large proportion of the names of individuals in the Algic tribes is drawn from this fruitful source of Indian observation. The Great Spirit is invariably located in the sky, and the Evil Spirit, and the train of minor malignant Spirits, in the earth. Their notions of the position of seas and continents are altogether vague and confused. Nor has it been observed that they have any knowledge of volcanic action. The idea of a universal deluge appears to be equally entertained by the tribes of North and South America.[8] The Algics certainly have it incorporated in their traditionary tales, and I have found the belief in these traditions the most firmly seated among the bands the farthest removed from the advances of civilization and Christianity.

It is the mythology, however, of these tribes which affords the deepest insight into their character, and unfolds, perhaps, some of the clearest co-incidences with Oriental rites and opinions. Were the terms Baalim and Magii introduced into the descriptions of their worship, instead of Manito and Meeta, this coincidence would be very apparent. Medical magic spread the charms of its delusion over the semibarbaric tribes who, at a very early epoch, spread from the Persian and the Arabian Gulfs to the Mediterranean; and it would not be a light task to find branches of the human race who are more completely characterized by its doctrines and practices than the wide-spreading members of the Algic stock of this Continent. Their prophets, jugglers, and meetays occupy the same relative importance in the political scale. They advise the movement of armies, and foretell the decrees of fate to individuals. They interpret dreams, effect the performance of miraculous cures, and preside over the most sacred rites. Oracles alike to chiefs and kings, warriors and hunters, nothing can be accomplished without their aid, and it would be presumptuous and impious to attempt anything, in war or peace, which they had decreed to be wrong. But our more immediate object is the class of oral fictions among the Western tribes, and for the growth and development of which their peculiar belief in the doctrine of spirits and magicians has furnished so wide a field. Come from what quarter of the world they may, the propensity to amusing and serio-comic fiction appears to have been brought with them. What traits, if any, of the original threadwork of foreign story remain, it would be premature, in the present state of these collections, to decide. The character and incidents of the narrations are adapted to the condition they are now in, as well as the position they now occupy. There is, it is true, a spirit of reminiscence apparent which pleases itself in allusions to the past; they speak of a sort of golden age, when all things were better with them than they now are; when they had better laws and leaders; when crimes were more promptly punished; when their language was spoken with greater purity, and their manners were freer from barbarism. But all this seems to flit through the Indian mind as a dream, and furnishes him rather the source of a pleasing secret retrospection than any spring to present and future exertions. He pines away as one that is fallen, and despairs to rise. He does not seem to open his eyes on the prospect of civilization and mental exaltation held up before him, as one to whom the scene is new or attractive. These scenes have been pictured before him by teachers and philanthropists for more than two centuries; but there has been nothing in them to arouse and inspire him to press onward in the career of prospective civilization and refinement. He has rather turned away with the air of one to whom all things "new" were "old," and chosen emphatically to re-embrace his woods, his wigwam, and his canoe.

Perhaps the trait that was least to have been anticipated in the tales is the moral often conveyed by them. But, on reflection, this is in accordance with the Indian maxim, which literally requires "an eye for an eye, and a tooth for a tooth." And the more closely this feature of poetic justice is scrutinized, the more striking does it appear. Cruelty, murder, and sorcery are eventually punished, although the individual escapes for the time and his career may be long drawnout. Domestic infidelity meets the award of death in the only instance narrated. Religious vows are held inviolate. Respect for parents and for age, fraternal affection, hospitality, bravery, self-denial, endurance under fatigue or suffering, and disinterestedness, are uniformly inculcated. Presumption and pride are rebuked, and warnings given against the allurements of luxury and its concomitant vices. With a people who look back to some ancient and indefinite period in their history as an age of glory, an adherence to primitive manners and customs naturally occupies the place of virtue. The stories are generally so constructed as to hold up to admiration a bold and independent spirit of enterprise and adventure. Most of their heroes are drawn from retired or obscure places, and from abject circumstances. Success is seen to crown the efforts of precocious boys, orphans, or castaways. But whatever success is had, it is always through the instrumentality of the spirits or Manitoes—the true deities worshiped by all the Algic tribes.

The legend of Manabozho reveals, perhaps, the idea of an incarnation.[9] He is the great spirit-man of northern mythology. The conception of the character reveals rather a monstrosity than a deity, displaying in strong colors far more of the dark and incoherent acts of a spirit of carnality than the benevolent deeds of a god. His birth is shrouded in allegoric mystery. He is made to combine all that is brave, warlike, strong, wise, and great in Indian conception, both of mortal and immortal. He conquers the greatest magician, overcomes fiery serpents, and engages in combats and performs exploits the most extravagant. He has no small share in the Adamic-like labor of naming the animals. He destroys the king of the reptile creation, is drawn into the mouth of a gigantic fish with his canoe, survives a flood by climbing a tree, and recreates the earth from a morsel of ground brought up in the paws of a muskrat. In contrast with these high exploits, he goes about playing low tricks, marries a wife, travels the earth, makes use of low subterfuges, is often in want of food, and, after being tricked and laughed at, is at one time made to covet the ability of a woodpecker, and at another outdone by the simple skill of a child. The great points in which he is exultingly set forth in the storytelling circle, are his great personal strength, readiness of resource, and strong powers of necromancy. Whatever other parts he is made to play, it is the Indian Hercules, Samson, or Proteus that is prominently held up to admiration. It is perhaps natural that rude nations in every part of the world should invent some such mythological existence as the Indian Manabozho, to concentrate their prime exploits upon; for it is the maxim of such nations that "the race *is* always to the swift, and the battle to the strong."

In closing these remarks, it will not be irrelevant to notice the evidence of the vernacular character and antiquity of the tales, which is furnished by the Pontiac manuscript, preserved in the collections of the Historical Society of Michigan. By this document, which is of the date of 1763, it is shown that this shrewd and talented leader of the Algic tribes, after he had formed the plan of driving the Saxon race from the Continent, appealed to the mythologic belief of the tribes to bring them into his views. It was the Wyandots whom he found it the hardest to convert; and in the general council which he held with the Western chiefs, he narrated before them a tale of a Delaware magician, which is admirably adapted in its incidents to the object he had in view, and affords proof of his foresight and powers of invention. It is deemed of further interest in this connection, as carrying back the existence of the tales and fables to a period anterior to the final fall of the French powers in the Canadas, reaching to within a fraction more than sixty years of their establishment at Detroit.[10] While, however, the authenticity of this curious politico-mythologic tale is undisputed, the names and allusions would show it to be of the modern class of Indian fictions, were not the fact historically known. The importance of this testimony, in the absence of any notice of this trait in the earlier writers, has induced me to submit a literal translation of the tale, from the original French MS., executed by Professor Fasquelle.[11]

NOTES

1. For other statements of "preliminary observations" see "Preface" and "Introduction" to *The Myth of Hiawatha* in Appendix B.

2. Schoolcraft's censure of Spanish colonialism must be read against a background of militant American sympathy for Latin-American independence.

3. The *Narrative Journal* of the Cass expedition in 1820 contained but three legends: one an account of serpent guardians of the Isle of Yellow Sands which he extracted from Jonathan Carver, one a lovers' leap tale, and one a fanciful yarn told by his Indian guide about a lump of copper.

4. Some specimens of these tales were published in my "Travels in the Central Portions of the Mississippi Valley" in 1825, and a "Narrative of the Expedition to Itasca Lake" in 1834, and a few of them have been exhibited to literary friends, who have noticed the subject. *Vide* Dr. Gilman's "Life on the Lakes," and Mrs. Jameson's "Winter Studies and Summer Rambles," received at the moment these sheets are going through the press. [H. R. S.] Publication records will be found at the end of each story.

5. Shortly after completing the expedition to the Upper Lakes country in 1820, Schoolcraft and Governor Cass initiated a questionnaire that sought information on this and many other aspects of Indian life. See Appendix B.

6. Cf. "Introduction" to *The Myth of Hiawatha* in Appendix B.

7. See "Note" at the conclusion of this chapter.

8. Humboldt found it among the traditions of the Auricanians. [H. R. S.]

9. It is most important to the student of Indian legends to note that School-craft, *before* the publication of *Hiawatha,* associated his basic legend with Manabozho, the Algonquin equivalent of the Iroquois, Teharonhiawakhon. From the standpoint of anthropology the two are identical. In Schoolcraft's mind Hiawatha was not the later political figure of that name, but was the deity, Teharonhiawakhon. Much needless ink has been wasted because of this alleged confusion. See editor's Introduction.

10. Although Quebec was taken in 1759, the Indians did not acquiesce in the transference of power, in the upper lakes, till the *raising of the siege* of Detroit in 1763. This is the true period of the Pontiac war. [H. R. S.]

11. Louis John Fasquelle came to the United States from France in 1832. He was appointed Professor of Modern Languages at the University of Michigan in 1845.

NOTE

THE MATERIALS OF THESE TALES and legends have been derived from the aborigines, and interpreted from their languages by various individuals, among whom it is deemed important to name the following: Mrs. Henry R. Schoolcraft, Mr. William Johnston, of Mackinac; Mrs. James Lawrence Schoolcraft, Henry Connor, Esq., of Detroit; Mrs. [Rev.] William McMurray, of Dundas, George C. Martin, of Amherstburg, U. Canada; Mrs. La Chapelle, of Prairie du Chien; Mr. John Quinney, Stockbridge Reserve, Wisconsin; John H. Kinzie, Esq., of Chicago; Miss Eleanor Bailly, of Konamik, Illinois; Mr. George Johnston, Miss Mary Holiday, of Sault Ste. Marie, Michigan. These persons are well versed in the respective tongues from which they have given translations; and being residents of the places indicated, a reference to them for the authenticity of the materials is thus brought within the means of all who desire it.

It is also deemed proper to refer, in this connection, to Gen. Cass, American Minister at Paris, and to C. C. Trowbridge, Esq., of Detroit, and James D. Doty, Esq., Green Bay, whose inquiries have been, at my instance, respectively directed to this new feature in the oral traditions of the Indians.[1]

New-York, January 31, 1839.

---

1. Further identification of some of the persons here referred to gives evidence of the authenticity of the tales. Mrs. Henry R. Schoolcraft (1800-1842) was Obahbahn-wawa-geezhags-quay or Jane, daughter of Susan (Ozhaw-guscoday-wayquay) and John Johnston, a British trader of Sault Ste. Marie. Mrs. Johnston, Schoolcraft's mother-in-law, was the daughter of the Chippewa chief, Wabojeeg (c. 1747-1793). William Johnston (b. 1811), a son of Susan and John, was Schoolcraft's brother-in-law, as was also George Johnston (b. 1796). Both were assistants at the Indian Agency administered by Schoolcraft. Mrs. James Lawrence Schoolcraft, a daughter of Susan and John Johnston (b. 1814) married Schoolcraft's brother. Her name was Omiskabu-goquay or Ann Maria. Mrs. William McMurray was another sister-in-law (b. 1806) named Ogebu-noquay or Charlotte.

Cass, Doty, and Trowbridge were members of the 1820 expedition.

OJEEG ANNUNG[1]

OR

THE SUMMER-MAKER

AN ODJIBWA TALE[2]

THERE LIVED A CELEBRATED HUNTER on the southern shores of Lake Superior, who was considered a Manito by some, for there was nothing but what he could accomplish. He lived off the path, in a wild, lonesome place, with a wife whom he loved, and they were blessed with a son, who had attained his thirteenth year. The hunter's name was Ojeeg, or the Fisher, which is the name of an expert, sprightly little animal common to the region. He was so successful in the chase, that he seldom returned without bringing his wife and son a plentiful supply of venison, or other dainties of the woods. As hunting formed his constant occupation, his son began early to emulate his father in the same employment, and would take his bow and arrows, and exert his skill in trying to kill birds and squirrels. The greatest impediment he met with, was the coldness and severity of the climate. He often returned home, his little fingers benumbed with cold, and crying with vexation at his disappointment. Days, and months, and years passed away, but still the same perpetual depth of snow was seen, covering all the country as with a white cloak.

One day, after a fruitless trial of his forest skill, the little boy was returning homeward with a heavy heart, when he saw a small red squirrel gnawing the top of a pine bur. He had approached within a proper distance to shoot, when the squirrel sat up on its hind legs and thus addressed him:

"My grandchild, put up your arrows, and listen to what I have to tell you." The boy complied rather reluctantly, when the squirrel continued: "My son, I see you pass frequently, with your fingers benumbed with cold, and crying with vexation for not having killed any birds. Now, if you will follow my advice, we will see if you cannot accomplish your wishes. If you will strictly pursue my advice, we will have perpetual summer, and you will then have the pleasure of killing as many birds as you please; and I will also have something to eat, as I am now myself on the point of starvation.

"Listen to me. As soon as you get home you must commence crying. You must throw away your bow and arrows in discontent. If your mother asks you what is the matter, you must not answer her, but continue crying and sobbing. If she offers you anything to eat, you must push it away with apparent discontent, and continue crying. In the evening, when your father

27

returns from hunting, he will inquire of your mother what is the matter with you. She will answer that you came home crying, and would not so much as mention the cause to her. All this while you must not leave off sobbing. At last your father will say, 'My son, why is this unnecessary grief? Tell me the cause. You know I am a spirit, and that nothing is impossible for me to perform.' You must then answer him, and say that you are sorry to see the snow continually on the ground, and ask him if he could not cause it to melt, so that we might have perpetual summer. Say it in a supplicating way, and tell him this is the cause of your grief. Your father will reply, 'It is very hard to accomplish your request, but for your sake, and for my love for you, I will use my utmost endeavors.' He will tell you to be still, and cease crying. He will try to bring summer with all its loveliness. You must then be quiet, and eat that which is set before you."

The squirrel ceased. The boy promised obedience to his advice, and departed. When he reached home, he did as he had been instructed, and all was exactly fulfilled, as it had been predicted by the squirrel.

Ojeeg told him that it was a great undertaking. He must first make a feast, and invite some of his friends to accompany him on a journey. Next day he had a bear roasted whole. All who had been invited to the feast came punctually to the appointment. There were the Otter, Beaver, Lynx, Badger and Wolverine. After the feast, they arranged it among themselves to set out on the contemplated journey in three days. When the time arrived, the Fisher took leave of his wife and son, as he foresaw that it was for the last time. He and his companions traveled in company day after day, meeting with nothing but the ordinary incidents. On the twentieth day they arrived at the foot of a high mountain, where they saw the tracks of some person who had recently killed an animal, which they knew by the blood that marked the way. The Fisher told his friends that they ought to follow the track, and see if they could not procure something to eat. They followed it for some time; at last they arrived at a lodge, which had been hidden from their view by a hollow in the mountain. Ojeeg told his friends to be very sedate, and not to laugh on any account. The first object that they saw was a man standing at the door of the lodge, but of so deformed a shape that they could not possibly make out who or what sort of a man it could be. His head was enormously large; he had such a queer set of teeth, and no arms. They wondered how he could kill animals. But the secret was soon revealed. He was a great Manito. He invited them to pass the night, to which they consented.

He boiled his meat in a hollow vessel made of wood, and took it out of this singular kettle in some way unknown to his guests. He carefully gave each their portion to eat, but made so many odd movements that the Otter could not refrain from laughing, for he is the only one who is spoken of as a jester. The Manito looked at him with a terrible look, and then made a spring at him, and got on him to smother him, for that was his mode of killing animals. But the Otter, when he felt him on his neck, slipped his head back and made for the door, which he passed in safety; but went out with the curse of the Manito. The others passed the night, and they conversed on different subjects. The Manito told the Fisher that he would accomplish his object, but that it would probably cost him his life. He gave them his advice, directed them how to act, and described a certain road which they must follow, and they would thereby be led to the place of action.

They set off in the morning, and met their friend, the Otter, shivering with cold; but Ojeeg had taken care to bring along some of the meat that had been given him, which he presented to his friend. They pursued their way, and traveled twenty days more before they got to the place which the Manito had told them of. It was a most lofty mountain. They rested on its highest peak to fill their pipes and refresh themselves. Before smoking, they made the customary ceremony, pointing to the heavens, the four winds, the earth, and the zenith; in the meantime, speaking in a loud voice, addressed the Great Spirit, hoping that their object would be accomplished. Then they commenced smoking.

They gazed on the sky in silent admiration and astonishment, for they were on so elevated a point, that it appeared to be only a short distance above their heads. After they had finished smoking, they prepared themselves.Ojeeg told the Otter to make the first attempt to try and make a hole in the sky. He consented with a grin. He made a leap, but fell down the hill stunned by the force of his fall; and the snow being moist, and falling on his back, he slid with velocity down the side of the mountain. When he found himself at the bottom, he thought to himself, it is the last time I make such another jump, so I will make the best of my way home. Then it was the turn of the Beaver, who made the attempt, but fell down senseless; then of the Lynx and Badger, who had no better success.

"Now," says the Fisher to the Wolverine, "try your skill; your ancestors were celebrated for their activity, hardihood, and perseverance, and I depend on you for success. Now make the attempt." He did so, but also without success. He leaped the second time, but now they could see that the sky was giving way to their repeated attempts. Mustering strength, he made the third leap, and went in. The Fisher nimbly followed him.

They found themselves in a beautiful plain, extending as far as the eye could reach, covered with flowers of a thousand different hues and fragrance. Here and there were clusters of tall, shady trees, separated by innumerable streams of the purest water, which wound around their courses under the cooling shades, and filled the plain with countless beautiful lakes, whose banks and bosom were covered with water-fowl, basking and sporting in the sun. The trees were alive with birds of different plumage, warbling their sweet notes, and delighted with perpetual spring.

The Fisher and his friend beheld very long lodges, and the celestial inhabitants amusing themselves at a distance. Words cannot express the beauty and charms of the place. The lodges were empty of inhabitants, but they saw them lined with mocuks[3] of different sizes, filled with birds and fowls of different plumage. Ojeeg thought of his son, and immediately commenced cutting open the mocuks and letting out the birds, who descended in whole flocks through the opening which they had made. The warm air of those regions also rushed down through the opening, and spread its genial influence over the north.

When the celestial inhabitants saw the birds let loose, and the warm gales descending, they raised a shout like thunder, and ran for their lodges. But it was too late. Spring, summer, and autumn had gone; even perpetual summer had almost all gone; but they separated it with a blow, and only a part descended; but the ends were so mangled, that, wherever it prevails among the lower inhabitants, it is always sickly.[4]

When the Wolverine heard the noise, he made for the opening and safely descended. Not so the Fisher. Anxious to fulfill his son's wishes, he continued to break open the mocuks. He was, at last, obliged to run also, but the opening was now closed by the inhabitants. He ran with all his might over the plains of heaven, and, it would appear, took a northerly direction. He saw his pursuers so close that he had to climb the first large tree he came to. They commenced shooting at him with their arrows, but without effect, for all his body was invulnerable except the space of about an inch near the tip of his tail. At last one of the arrows hit the spot, for he had in this chase assumed the shape of the Fisher after whom he was named.

He looked down from the tree, and saw some among his assailants with the totems[5] of his ancestors. He claimed relationship, and told them to desist, which they only did at the approach of night. He then came down to try and find an opening in the celestial plain, by which he might descend to the earth. But he could find none. At last, becoming faint from the loss of blood from the wound on his tail, he laid himself down towards the north of the plain, and, stretching out his limbs, said, "I have fulfilled my promise to my son, though it has cost me my life; but I die satisfied in the idea that I have done so much good, not only for him, but for my fellow-beings. Hereafter I will be a sign to the inhabitants below for ages to come, who will venerate my name for having succeeded in procuring the varying seasons. They will now have from eight to ten moons without snow."

He was found dead next morning, but they left him as they found him, with the arrow sticking in his tail, as it can be plainly seen, at this time, in the heavens.[6]

NOTES

1. There is a group of stars in the Northern hemisphere which the Odjibwas call *Ojeeg Annung,* or the Fisher Stars. It is believed to be identical with the group of the Plough. They relate the following tale respecting it. [H. R. S.]

2. This term is used, in these tales, as synonymous with Chippewa. [H. R. S.]

3. Baskets, or cages. [H. R. S.]

4. The idea here indicated is among the peculiar notions of these tribes, and is grafted in the forms of their language, which will be pointed out in the progress of these researches. [H. R. S.]

5. Family arms, or armorial mark. [H. R. S.]

6. This story was printed without alteration in *The Myth of Hiawatha* (Philadelphia, 1856) hereafter referred to as *M. H.,* pp. 121-128.

THE CELESTIAL SISTERS

A SHAWNEE TALE

WAUPEE, OR THE WHITE HAWK, lived in a remote part of the forest, where animals and birds were abundant. Every day he returned from the chase with the reward of his toil, for he was one of the most skillful and celebrated hunters of his tribe. With a tall, manly form, and the fire of youth beaming from his eye, there was no forest too gloomy for him to penetrate, and no track made by the numerous kinds of birds and beasts which he could not follow.

One day he penetrated beyond any point which he had before visited. He traveled through an open forest, which enabled him to see a great distance. At length he beheld a light breaking through the foliage, which made him sure that he was on the borders of a prairie. It was a wide plain covered with grass and flowers. After walking some time without a path, he suddenly came to a ring worn through the sod, as if it had been made by footsteps following a circle. But what excited his surprise was, that there was no path leading to or from it. Not the least trace of footsteps could be found, even in a crushed leaf or broken twig. He thought he would hide himself, and lie in wait to see what this circle meant. Presently he heard the faint sounds of music in the air. He looked up in the direction they came from, and saw a small object descending from above. At first it looked like a mere speck, but rapidly increased, and, as it came down, the music became plainer and sweeter. It assumed the form of a basket, and was filled with twelve sisters of the most lovely forms and enchanting beauty. As soon as the basket touched the ground, they leaped out, and began to dance round the magic ring, striking, as they did so, a shining ball as we strike the drum. Waupee gazed upon their graceful forms and motions from his place of concealment. He admired them all, but was most pleased with the youngest. Unable longer to restrain his admiration, he rushed out and endeavored to seize her. But the sisters, with the quickness of birds, the moment they descried the form of a man, leaped back into the basket and were drawn up into the sky.

Regretting his ill luck and indiscretion, he gazed till he saw them disappear, and then said, "They are gone, and I shall see them no more." He returned to his solitary lodge, but found no relief to his mind. Next day he went back to the prairie, and took his station near the ring; but in order to deceive the sisters, he assumed the form of an opossum. He had not waited long, when he saw the wicker car descend, and heard the same sweet music. They commenced the same sportive dance, and seemed even more beautiful and graceful than before. He crept slowly towards the ring, but the instant

31

the sisters saw him they were startled, and sprang into their car. It rose but a short distance, when one of the elder sisters spoke. "Perhaps," said she, "it is come to show us how the game is played by mortals." "Oh no!" the youngest replied; "quick, let us ascend." And all joining in a chant, they rose out of sight.

The White Hawk returned to his own form again, and walked sorrowfully back to his lodge. But the night seemed a very long one, and he went back betimes the next day. He reflected upon the sort of plan to follow to secure success. He found an old stump near by, in which there were a number of mice. He thought their small form would not create alarm, and accordingly assumed it. He brought the stump and sat it up near the ring. The sisters came down and resumed their sport. "But see," cried the younger sister, "that stump was not there before." She ran affrighted towards the car. They only smiled, and gathering round the stump, struck it in jest, when out ran the mice, and Waupee among the rest. They killed them all but one, which was pursued by the youngest sister; but just as she had raised her stick to kill it, the form of White Hawk rose, and he clasped his prize in his arms. The other eleven sprang to their basket and were drawn up to the skies.

Waupee exerted all his skill to please his bride and win her affections. He wiped the tears from her eyes. He related his adventures in the chase. He dwelt upon the charms of life on the earth. He was incessant in his attentions, and picked out the way for her to walk as he led her gently toward his lodge. He felt his heart glow with joy as she entered it, and from that moment he was one of the happiest of men. Winter and summer passed rapidly away, and their happiness was increased by the addition of a beautiful boy to their lodge. Waupee's wife was a daughter of one of the stars, and as the scenes of earth began to pall upon her sight, she sighed to revisit her father. But she was obliged to hide these feelings from her husband. She remembered the charm that would carry her up, and took occasion, while the White Hawk was engaged in the chase, to construct a wicker basket, which she kept concealed. In the meantime she collected such rarities from the earth as she thought would please her father, as well as the most dainty kinds of food. When all was in readiness, she went out one day, while Waupee was absent, to the charmed ring, taking her little son with her. As soon as they got into the car, she commenced her song and the basket rose. As the song was wafted by the wind, it caught her husband's ear. It was a voice which he well knew, and he instantly ran to the prairie. But he could not reach the ring before he saw his wife and child ascend. He lifted up his voice in loud appeals, but they were unavailing. The basket still went up. He watched it till it became a small speck, and finally it vanished in the sky. He then bent his head down to the ground, and was miserable.

Waupee bewailed his loss through a long winter and a long summer. But he found no relief. He mourned his wife's loss sorely, but his son's still more. In the meantime his wife had reached her home in the stars, and almost forgot, in the blissful employments there, that she had left a husband on the earth. She was reminded of this by the presence of her son, who, as he grew up, became anxious to visit the scene of his birth. His grandfather said to his daughter one day, "Go, my child, and take your son down to his father, and ask him to come up and live with us. But tell him to bring along a specimen of each kind of bird and animal he kills in the chase." She accordingly took the boy and descended. The White Hawk, who was ever near the enchanted spot, heard her voice as she came down the sky. His heart beat with impatience as he saw her form and that of his son, and they were soon clasped in his arms.

He heard the message of the Star, and began to hunt with the greatest activity, that he might collect the present. He spent whole nights, as well as days, in searching for every curious and beautiful bird or animal. He only preserved a tail, foot, or wing of each, to identify the species; and, when all was ready, they went to the circle and were carried up.

Great joy was manifested on their arrival at the starry plains. The Star Chief invited all his people to a feast, and, when they had assembled, he proclaimed aloud, that each one might take of the earthly gifts such as he liked best. A very strange confusion immediately arose. Some chose a foot, some a wing, some a tail, and some a claw. Those who selected tails or claws were changed into animals, and ran off; the others assumed the form of birds, and flew away. Waupee chose a white hawk's feather. His wife and son followed his example, when each one became a white hawk. He spread his wings, and, followed by his wife and son, descended with the other birds to the earth, where his species are still to be found.[1]

NOTE

1. This sentence is altered in *M. H.* where it reads: "Pleased with his transformation, and new vitality, the chief spread out gracefully his white wings, and followed by his wife and son, descended to the earth, where the species are still to be found." Reprinted without other significant change as "The Star Family, or the Celestial Sisters," *M. H.*, pp. 116-120. Using the same title, Cornelius Matthews reprinted the tale in *The Indian Fairy Book* (New York, 1869) pp. 7-15. Florence Choate and Elizabeth Curtis reworked the tale in their *Indian Fairy Book* (New York, 1916) pp. 72-79. Hereafter Matthews will be referred to as *C. M.*, and Choate and Curtis as *C-C.* In Henry Whiting's *Sannilac* (Boston, 1831), there is a long verse addendum titled "Waupee, the White Hawk, and the Star Woman." Here C. C. Trowbridge is credited with collecting the legend. A poem, "The Star Family," in the poetic appendix to *M. H.*, Wild notes of the Pibbigwun, pp. 335-339, develops the same theme in *Hiawatha* metre.

TAU-WAU-CHEE-HEZKAW

OR

THE WHITE FEATHER

A SIOUX TALE[1]

THERE WAS AN OLD MAN living in the center of a forest, with his grandson, whom he had taken when quite an infant. The child had no parents, brothers, or sisters; they had all been destroyed by six large giants, and he had been informed that he had no other relative living besides his grandfather. The band to whom he belonged had put up their children on a wager in a race against those of the giants, and had thus lost them. There was an old tradition in the band, that it would produce a great man, who would wear a white feather, and who would astonish everyone with his skill and feats of bravery.

The grandfather, as soon as the child could play about, gave him a bow and arrows to amuse himself. He went into the edge of the woods one day, and saw a rabbit; but, not knowing what it was, he ran home and described it to his grandfather. He told him what it was, that its flesh was good to eat, and that, if he would shoot one of his arrows into its body, he would kill it. He did so, and brought the little animal home, which he asked his grandfather to boil, that they might feast on it. He humored the boy in this, and encouraged him to go on on acquiring the knowledge of hunting, until he could kill deer and larger animals; and he became, as he grew up, an expert hunter. As they lived alone, and away from other Indians, his curiosity was excited to know what was passing in the world. One day he came to the edge of a prairie, where he saw ashes like those at his grandfather's lodge, and lodge-poles left standing. He returned and inquired whether his grandfather had put up the poles and made the fire. He was answered no, nor did he believe that he had seen anything of the kind. It was all imagination.

Another day he went out to see what there was curious; and, on entering the woods, he heard a voice calling out to him, "Come here, you destined wearer of the White Feather. You do not yet wear it, but you are worthy of it. Return home and take a short nap. You will dream of hearing a voice, which will tell you to rise and smoke. You will see in your dream a pipe, smoking-sack, and a large white feather. When you awake you will find these articles. Put the feather on your head, and you will become a great hunter, a great warrior, and a great man, capable of doing anything. As a proof that you will become a great hunter, when you smoke the

34

smoke will turn into pigeons." The voice then informed him who he was, and disclosed the true character of his grandfather, who had imposed upon him. The voice-spirit then gave him a *vine,* and told him he was of an age to revenge the injuries of his relations. "When you meet your enemy," continued the spirit, "you will run a race with him. He will not see the vine, because it is enchanted. While you are running, you will throw it over his head and entangle him, so that you will win the race."

Long ere this speech was ended he had turned to the quarter from which the voice proceeded, and was astonished to behold a man, for as yet he had never seen any man besides his grandfather, whose object it was to keep him in ignorance. But the circumstance that gave him the most surprise was, that this man, who had the looks of great age, was composed of *wood* from his breast downward, and appeared to be fixed in the earth.

He returned home, slept, heard the voice, awoke, and found the promised articles. His grandfather was greatly surprised to find him with a white feather on his forehead, and to see flocks of pigeons flying out of his lodge. He then recollected what had been predicted, and began to weep at the prospect of losing his charge.

Invested with these honors, the young man departed the next morning to seek his enemies and gratify his revenge. The giants lived in a very high lodge in the middle of a wood. He traveled on till he came to this lodge, where he found that his coming had been made known by *the little spirits who carry the news.* The giants came out, and gave a cry of joy as they saw him coming. When he approached nearer, they began to make sport of him, saying, "Here comes the little man with the white feather, who is to achieve such wonders." They, however, spoke very fair to him when he came up, saying he was a brave man, and would do brave things. This they said to encourage, and the more surely to deceive him. He, however, understood the object.

He went fearlessly up to the lodge. They told him to commence the race with the smallest of their number. The point to which they were to run was a peeled tree towards the rising sun, and then back to the starting-place, which was marked by a CHAUNKAHPEE, or war-club, made of iron. This club was the stake, and whoever won it was to use it in beating the other's brains out. If he beat the first giant, he was to try the second, and so on until they had all measured speed with him. He won the first race by a dexterous use of the vine, and immediately despatched his competitor, and cut off his head. Next morning he ran with the second giant, whom he also outran, killed, and decapitated. He proceeded in this way for five successive mornings, always conquering by the use of his vine, and cutting off the heads of the vanquished. The survivors acknowledged his power, but prepared secretly to deceive him. They wished him to leave the heads he had cut off, as they believed they could again reunite them with the bodies, by means of one of their *medicines.* White Feather insisted, however, in carrying all the heads to his grandfather. One more contest was to be tried, which would decide the victory; but, before going to the giant's lodge on the sixth morning, he met his old counselor in the woods, who was stationary. He told him that he was about to be deceived. That he had never known any other sex but his own; but that, as he went on his way to the lodge, he would meet the most beautiful woman in the world. He must pay no attention to her, but, on meeting her, he must wish himself changed into a male elk. The transformation would take place immediately, when he must go to feeding and not regard her.

He proceeded towards the lodge, met the female, and became an elk. She reproached him for having turned himself into an elk on seeing her; said she had traveled a great distance for the purpose of seeing him, and becoming his wife. Now this woman was the sixth giant, who had assumed this disguise; but Tau-Wau-Chee-Hezkaw remained in ignorance of it. Her reproaches and her beauty affected him so much, that he wished himself a man again, and he at once resumed his natural shape. They sat down together, and he began to caress her, and make love to her. He finally ventured to lay his head on her lap and went to sleep. She pushed his head aside at first, for the purpose of trying if he was really asleep; and when she was satisfied he was, she took her axe and broke his back. She then assumed her natural shape, which was in the form of the sixth giant, and afterward changed him into a dog, in which degraded form he followed his enemy to the lodge. He took the white feather from his brow, and wore it as a trophy on his own head.

There was an Indian village at some distance, in which there lived two girls, who were rival sisters, the daughters of a chief. They were fasting to acquire power for the purpose of enticing the wearer of the white feather to visit their village. They each secretly hoped to engage his affections. Each one built herself a lodge at a short distance from the village. The giant, knowing this, and having now obtained the valued plume, went immediately to visit them. As he approached, the girls saw and recognized the feather. The eldest sister prepared her lodge with great care and parade, so as to attract the eye. The younger, supposing that he was a man of sense, and would not be enticed by mere parade, touched nothing in her lodge, but left it as it ordinarily was. The eldest went out to meet him, and invited him in. He accepted her invitation, and made her his wife. The younger invited the enchanted dog into her lodge, and made him a good bed, and treated him with as much attention as if he were her husband.

The giant, supposing that whoever possessed the white feather possessed also all its virtues, went out upon the prairie to hunt, but returned unsuccessful. The dog went out the same day a-hunting upon the banks of a river. He drew a stone out of the water, which immediately became a beaver. The next day the giant followed the dog, and, hiding behind a tree, saw the manner in which the dog went into the river and drew out a stone, which at once turned into a beaver. As soon as the dog left the place, the giant went to the river, and observing the same manner, drew out a stone, and had the satisfaction of seeing it transformed into a beaver. Tying it to his belt, he carried it home, and, as is customary, threw it down at the door of the lodge before he entered. After being seated a short time, he told his wife to bring in his belt or hunting girdle. She did so, and returned with it, with nothing tied to it but a *stone*.

The next day, the dog, finding his method of catching beavers had been discovered, went to a wood at some distance, and broke off a charred limb from a burned tree, which instantly became a bear. The giant, who had again watched him, did the same, and carried a bear home; but his wife, when she came to go out for it, found nothing but a black stick tied to his belt.

The giant's wife determined she would go to her father, and tell him what a valuable husband she had, who furnished her lodge with abundance. She set out while her husband went to hunt. As soon as they had departed, the dog made signs to his mistress to sweat him after the manner of the Indians. She accordingly made a lodge just large enough for him to creep in. She then put in heated stones, and poured on water. After this had been continued the usual time, he came out a very handsome young man, but had not the power of speech.

Meantime the elder daughter had reached her father's, and told him of the manner in which her sister supported a dog, treating him as her husband, and of the singular skill this animal had in hunting. The old man, suspecting there was some magic in it, sent a deputation of young men and women to ask her to come to him, and bring her dog along. When this deputation arrived, they were surprised to find, in the place of the dog, so fine a young man. They both accompanied the messengers to the father, who was no less astonished. He assembled all the old and wise men of the nation to see the exploits which, it was reported, the young man could perform. The giant was among the number. He took his pipe and filled it, and passed it to the Indians, to see if anything would happen when they smoked. It was passed around to the dog, who made a sign to hand it to the giant first, which was done, but nothing effected. He then took it himself. He made a sign to them to put the white feather upon his head. This was done, and immediately he regained his speech. He then commenced smoking, and behold! immense flocks of white and blue pigeons rushed from the smoke.

The chief demanded of him his history, which he faithfully recounted. When it was finished, the chief ordered that the giant should be transformed into a dog, and turned into the middle of the village, where the boys should pelt him to death with clubs. This sentence was executed.

The chief then ordered, on the request of the White Feather, that all the young men should employ themselves four days in making arrows. He also asked for a buffalo robe. This robe he cut into thin shreds, and sowed in the prairie. At the end of the four days he invited them to gather together all their arrows, and accompany him to a buffalo hunt. They found that these shreds of skin had grown into a very large herd of buffalo. They killed as many as they pleased, and enjoyed a grand festival, in honor of his triumph over the Giants.

Having accomplished their labor, the White Feather got his wife to ask her father's permission to go with him on a visit to his grandfather. He replied to this solicitation, that a woman must follow her husband into whatever quarter of the world he may choose to go.

The young man then placed the white feather in his frontlet, and, taking his war-club in his hand, led the way into the forest, followed by his faithful wife.[2]

NOTES

1. In *M. H.* the headnote reads "A Dacotah Legend."

2. Reprinted in *M. H.*, pp. 180-187; in *C. M.*, pp. 102-114 and *C-C*, pp. 147-158. In *Historical and Statistical Information*, I, pp. 329-332 (hereafter designated *H. S. I.*) the story is titled "The Little Orphan Who Carries the White Feather."

PEBOAN AND SEEGWUN

AN

ALLEGORY OF THE SEASONS[1]

FROM THE ODJIBWA

AN OLD MAN WAS SITTING alone in his lodge, by the side of a frozen stream. It was the close of winter, and his fire was almost out. He appeared very old and very desolate. His locks were white with age, and he trembled in every joint. Day after day passed in solitude, and he heard nothing but the sounds of the tempest, sweeping before it the new-fallen snow.

One day, as his fire was just dying, a handsome young man approached and entered his dwelling. His cheeks were red with the blood of youth, his eyes sparkled with animation, and a smile played upon his lips. He walked with a light and quick step. His forehead was bound with a wreath of sweet grass, in place of a warrior's frontlet, and he carried a bunch of flowers in his hand.

"Ah, my son," said the old man, "I am happy to see you. Come in. Come, tell me of your adventures, and what strange lands you have been to see. Let us pass the night together. I will tell you of my prowess and exploits, and what I can perform. You shall do the same, and we will amuse ourselves."

He then drew from his sack a curiously-wrought antique pipe, and having filled it with tobacco, rendered mild by an admixture of certain leaves, handed it to his guest. When this ceremony was concluded they began to speak.

"I blow my breath," said the old man, "and the streams stand still. The water becomes stiff and hard as clear stone."

"I breathe," said the young man, "and flowers spring up all over the plains."

"I shake my locks," retorted the old man, "and snow covers the land. The leaves fall from the trees at my command, and my breath blows them away. The birds get up from the water, and fly to a distant land. The animals hide themselves from my breath, and the very ground becomes as hard as flint."

"I shake my ringlets," rejoined the young man, "and warm showers of soft rain fall upon the earth. The plants lift up their heads out of the earth, like the eyes of children glistening with delight. My voice recalls the birds. The warmth of my breath unlocks the streams. Music fills the groves wherever I walk, and all nature rejoices."

39

At length the sun began to rise. A gentle warmth came over the place. The tongue of the old man became silent. The robin and bluebird began to sing on the top of the lodge. The stream began to murmur by the door, and the fragrance of growing herbs and flowers came softly on the vernal breeze.

Daylight fully revealed to the young man the character of his entertainer. When he looked upon him, he had the icy visage of Peboan.[2] Streams began to flow from his eyes. As the sun increased, he grew less and less in stature, and anon had melted completely away. Nothing remained on the place of his lodge fire but the miskodeed,[3] a small white flower, with a pink border, which is one of the earliest species of Northern plants.[4]

NOTES

1. In *M. H.* the subtitle reads "An Allegory of Winter and Spring."
2. Winter.
3. The Claytonia Virginica. [H. R. S.]
4. Printed in *M. H.* without change, pp. 96-98. It had been printed first in Mrs. Anna Jameson's *Winter Studies and Summer Rambles* (London, 1838) III, pp. 218-221. This was somewhat more sentimentalized than Schoolcraft's version. Under the title "The Winter Spirit and His Visitor," the story was reprinted in *C. M.*, pp. 261-263 and in *C-C The Indian Fairy Book* (New York, 1916), pp. 209-211.

THE RED LOVER

A CHIPPEWA TALE

MANY YEARS AGO there lived a warrior on the banks of Lake Superior, whose name was Wawanosh. He was the chief of an ancient family of his tribe, who had preserved the line of chieftainship unbroken from a remote time, and he consequently cherished a pride of ancestry. To the reputation of birth he added the advantages of a tall and commanding person, and the dazzling qualities of personal strength, courage, and activity. His bow was noted for its size, and the feats he had performed with it. His counsel was sought as much as his strength was feared, so that he came to be equally regarded as a hunter, a warrior, and a counselor. He had now passed the meridian of his days, and the term AKKEE-WAIZEE, i.e., one who has been long on the earth, was applied to him.

Such was Wawanosh, to whom the united voice of the nation awarded the first place in their esteem, and the highest authority in council. But distinction, it seems, is apt to engender haughtiness in the hunter state as well as civilized life. Pride was his ruling passion, and he clung with tenacity to the distinctions which he regarded as an inheritance.

Wawanosh had an only daughter, who had now lived to witness the budding of the leaves of the eighteenth spring. Her father was not more celebrated for his deeds of strength than she for her gentle virtues, her slender form, her full beaming hazel eyes, and her dark and flowing hair.

> "And through her cheek
> The blush would make its way, and all but speak.
> The sunborn blood suffused her neck, and threw
> O'er her clear brown skin a lucid hue,
> Like coral reddening through the darken'd wave,
> Which draws the diver to the crimson cave."

Her hand was sought by a young man of humble parentage, who had no other merits to recommend him but such as might arise from a tall and commanding person, a manly step, and an eye beaming with the tropical fires of youth and love. These were sufficient to attract the favorable notice of the daughter, but were by no means satisfactory to the father, who sought an alliance more suitable to the rank and the high pretensions of his family.

"Listen to me, young man," he replied to the trembling hunter, who had sought the interview, "and be attentive to my words. You ask me to bestow upon you my daughter, the chief solace of my age, and my choicest gift from the Master of Life. Others have asked of me this boon, who were as young, as active, and as ardent as yourself. Some of these persons have had better

41

claims to become my son-in-law. Have you reflected upon the deeds which have raised me in authority, and made my name known to the enemies of my nation? Where is there a chief who is not proud to be considered the friend of Wawanosh? Where, in all the land, is there a hunter who has excelled Wawanosh? Where is there a warrior who can boast the taking of an equal number of scalps? Besides, have you not heard that my fathers came from the East, bearing the marks of chieftaincy?

"And what, young man, have *you* to boast? Have *you* ever met your enemies in the field of battle? Have *you* ever brought home a trophy of victory? Have *you* ever proved your fortitude by suffering protracted pain, enduring continued hunger, or sustaining great fatigue? Is your *name* known beyond the humble limits of your native village? Go, then, young man, and earn a name for yourself. It is none but the brave that can ever hope to claim an alliance with the house of Wawanosh. Think not my warrior blood shall mingle with the humble mark of the Awasees[1]—fit totem for fishermen!"

The intimidated lover departed, but he resolved to do a deed that should render him worthy of the daughter of Wawanosh, or die in the attempt. He called together several of his young companions and equals in years, and imparted to them his design of conducting an expedition against the enemy, and requested their assistance. Several embraced the proposal immediately; others were soon brought to acquiesce; and, before ten suns set, he saw himself at the head of a formidable party of young warriors, all eager, like himself, to distinguish themselves in battle. Each warrior was armed, according to the custom of the period, with a bow and a quiver of arrows, tipped with flint or jasper. He carried a sack or wallet, provided with a small quantity of parched and pounded corn, mixed with pemmican or maple sugar. He was furnished with a PUGGAMAUGUN, or war-club of hard wood, fastened to a girdle of deer skin, and a stone or copper knife. In addition to this, some carried the ancient *shemagun,* or lance, a smooth pole about a fathom in length, with a javelin of flint, firmly tied on with deer's sinews. Thus equipped, and each warrior painted in a manner to suit his fancy, and ornamented with appropriate feathers, they repaired to the spot appointed for the war-dance.

A level, grassy plain extended for nearly a mile from the lodge of Wawanosh along the lake shore. Lodges of bark were promiscuously interspersed over this green, and here and there a cluster of trees, or a solitary tall pine. A belt of yellow sand skirted the lake shore in front, and a tall, thick forest formed the background. In the center of this plain stood a high shattered pine, with a clear space about, renowned as the scene of the war-dance time out of mind. Here the youths assembled, with their tall and graceful leader, distinguished by the feathers of the bald eagle, which he wore on his head. A bright fire of pine wood blazed upon the green. He led his men several times around this fire, with a measured and solemn chant. Then suddenly halting, the war-whoop was raised, and the dance immediately began. An old man, sitting at the head of the ring, beat time upon the drum, while several of the elder warriors shook their rattles, and "ever and anon" made the woods re-echo with their yells. Each warrior chanted alternately the verse of a song, all the rest joining in chorus.[2]

FIRST VOICE

The eagles scream on high,
    They whet their forked beaks:
Raise—raise the battle cry,
    'Tis fame our leader seeks.

SECOND VOICE

Tis fame my soul desires,
    By deeds of martial strife:
Give—give me warlike fires,
    Or take—ah take my life.

THIRD VOICE

The deer a while may go
    Unhunted o'er the heath,
For now I seek a nobler foe,
    And prize a nobler death.

FOURTH VOICE

Lance and quiver, club and bow,
    Now alone attract my sight;
I will go where warriors go,
    I will fight where warriors fight.

Thus they continued the dance,[3] with short intermissions, for two successive days and nights. Sometimes the village seer, who led the ceremony, would embrace the occasion of a pause to address them with words of encouragement.[4]

In the dreamy hours of night
I beheld the bloody fight.
As reclined upon my bed,
Holy visions crowned my head;
High our guardian spirit bright
Stood above the dreadful fight;
Beaming eye and dazzling brand
Gleamed upon my chosen band,
While a black and awful shade
O'er the faithless foeman spread.
Soon they wavered, sunk, and fled,
Leaving wounded, dying, dead,
While my gallant warriors high
Waved their trophies in the sky.

At every recurrence of this kind, new energy was infused into the dance, and the warriors renewed their gesticulations, and stamped upon the ground as if they were trampling their enemies under their feet.

FIFTH VOICE

Now my heart with valour burns,
I my lance in fury shake;
He who falters, he who turns,
Give him fagot, fire, and stake.

SIXTH VOICE

See my visage scarred and red—
See my brows with trophies bright—
Such the brows that warriors dread,
Such the trophies of the fight.[5]

At length the prophet uttered his final prediction of success; and the warriors dropping off, one by one, from the fire, each sought his way to the place appointed for the rendezvous, on the confines of the enemy's country. Their leader was not among the last to depart, but he did not leave the village without seeking an interview with the daughter of Wawanosh. He disclosed to her his firm determination never to return, unless he could establish his name as a warrior. He told her of the pangs he had felt at the bitter reproaches of her father, and declared that his soul spurned the imputation of effeminacy and cowardice implied by his language. He averred that he never could be happy, either with or without her, until he had proved to the whole tribe the strength of his heart, which is the Indian term for courage. He said that his dreams had not been propitious, but he should not cease to invoke the power of the Great Spirit. He repeated his protestations of inviolable attachment, which she returned, and, pledging vows of mutual fidelity, they parted.

All she ever heard from her lover after this interview was brought by one of his successful warriors, who said that he had distinguished himself by the most heroic bravery, but, at the close of the fight, he had received an arrow in his breast. The enemy fled, leaving many of their warriors dead on the field. On examining the wound, it was perceived to be beyond their power to cure. They carried him towards home a day's journey, but he languished and expired in the arms of his friends. From the moment the report was received, no smile was ever seen in the once happy lodge of Wawanosh. His daughter pined away by day and by night. Tears and sighs, sorrow and lamentation, were heard continually. Nothing could restore her lost serenity of mind. Persuasives and reproofs were alternately employed, but employed in vain. She would seek a sequestered spot, where she would sit under a shady tree, and sing her mournful laments for hours together.[6]

It was not long before a small bird of beautiful plumage flew upon the tree under which she usually sat, and with its sweet and artless notes seemed to respond to her voice. It was a bird of strange character, such as had not before been observed. It came every day and sang, remaining until dark.[7] Her fond imagination soon led her to suppose it was the spirit of her lover, and her visits were repeated with greater frequency. She passed her time in fasting, and singing her plaintive songs. Thus she pined away, until that death she so fervently desired came to her relief. After her decease the bird was never more seen, and it became a popular opinion that this mysterious bird had flown away with her spirit.

But bitter tears of regret fell in the lodge of Wawanosh. Too late he regretted his false pride and his harsh treatment of the noble youth.[8]

NOTES

1. Catfish. [H. R. S.]
2. In *M. H.* this sentence is changed to: "Each warrior chanted alternately the verse of a song, of which the words generally embraced some prominent idea, often repeated." This change permitted omission of the last three stanzas of the poem which follows.
3. The phrase "till each had introduced his verse" is inserted here in the version in *M. H.*
4. The *M. H.* sentence adds "in a prophetic voice and air, suited to raise their voices."
5. These stanzas omitted in *M. H.*
6. Another sentence is added here in *M. H.:* "Passages of these are yet repeated by tradition."
7. In *M. H.* Schoolcraft here identifies the bird as Chileeli and adds "and when it left its perch on the tree, it seemed, from the delicate play of the colors of its plumage, as if it had taken its hues from the rainbow." Several other minor changes occur later in the paragraph.
8. The first version of this story appeared as "Love and War" in Schoolcraft's *Travels in the Central Mississippi Valley* (New York, 1825) pp. 421-427. He specifically attributes this story to Jane Johnston, p. 426. Another version, "Love and War," is to be found in James A. Jones' *Traditions of the North American Indians* (London, 1829) I, pp. 213-223. Only in *M. H.* does the name of the bird appear and there the title is changed to "Chileeli, or the Red Lover," pp. 129-135. Schoolcraft was again moved to poetic expression by this theme. See "Chileeli," *M. H.* pp. 319-322.

IAMO

OR

THE UNDYING HEAD

AN OTTOWA TALE[1]

IN A REMOTE PART OF THE NORTH lived a man[2] and his only sister, who had never seen human being. Seldom, if ever, had the man any cause to go from home; for, as his wants demanded food, he had only to go a little distance from the lodge, and there, in some particular spot, place his arrows, with their barbs in the ground. Telling his sister where they had been placed, every morning she would go in search, and never fail of finding each struck through the heart of a deer. She had then only to drag them into the lodge and prepare their food. Thus she lived till she attained womanhood, when one day her brother, whose name was Iamo, said to her, "Sister, the time is near at hand when you will be ill. Listen to my advice. If you do not, it will probably be the cause of my death. Take the implements with which we kindle our fires. Go some distance from our lodge, and build a separate fire. When you are in want of food, I will tell you where to find it. You must cook for yourself, and I will for myself. When you are ill, do not attempt to come near the lodge, or bring any of the utensils you use. Be sure always to fasten to your belt the implements you need, for you do not know when the time will come. As for myself, I must do the best I can." His sister promised to obey him in all he had said.

Shortly after, her brother had cause to go from home. She was alone in her lodge, combing her hair. She had just untied the belt to which the implements were fastened, when suddenly the event, to which her brother had alluded, occurred.[3] She ran out of the lodge, but in her haste forgot the belt. Afraid to return, she stood for some time thinking. Finally she decided to enter the lodge and get it. For, thought she, my brother is not at home, and I will stay but a moment to catch hold of it. She went back. Running in suddenly, she caught hold of it, and was coming out when her brother came in sight. He knew what was the matter. "Oh," he said, "did I not tell you to take care? But now you have killed me." She was going on her way, but her brother said to her, "What can you do there now? the accident has happened. Go in, and stay where you have always stayed. And what will become of you? You have killed me."

He then laid aside his hunting dress and accouterments, and soon after both his feet began to inflame and turn black, so that he could not move. Still he directed his sister where to place the arrows, that she might always

46

have food. The inflammation continued to increase, and had now reached his first rib; and he said, "Sister, my end is near. You must do as I tell you. You see my medicine-sack, and my war-club tied to it. It contains all my medicines, and my war-plumes, and my paints of all colors. As soon as the inflammation reaches my breast, you will take my war-club. It has a sharp point, and you will cut off my head. When it is free from my body, take it, place its neck in the sack, which you must open at one end. Then hang it up in its former place. Do not forget my bow and arrows. One of the last you will take to procure food. The remainder tie to my sack, and then hang it up, so that I can look towards the door. Now and then I will speak to you, but not often." His sister again promised to obey.

In a little time his breast was affected. "Now," said he, "take the club and strike off my head." She was afraid, but he told her to muster courage. "*Strike,*" said he, and a smile was on his face. Mustering all her courage, she gave the blow and cut off the head. "Now," said the head, "place me where I told you." And fearfully she obeyed it in all its commands. Retaining its animation, it looked around the lodge as usual, and it would command its sister to go to such places as it thought would procure for her the flesh of different animals she needed. One day the head said, "The time is not distant when I shall be freed from this situation, but I shall have to undergo many sore evils. So the Superior Manito decrees, and I must bear all patiently." In this situation we must leave the head.

In a certain part of the country was a village inhabited by a numerous and warlike band of Indians. In this village was a family of ten young men —brothers. It was in the spring of the year that the youngest of these blackened his face and fasted. His dreams were propitious. Having ended his fast, he sent secretly for his brothers at night, so that none in the village could overhear or find out the direction they intended to go. Though their drum was heard, yet that was a common occurrence. Having ended the usual formalities, he told them how favorable his dreams were, and that he had called them together to know if they would accompany him in a war excursion. They all answered they would. The third brother from the eldest, noted for his oddities, coming up with his war-club when his brother had ceased speaking, jumped up, "Yes," said he, "*I* will go, and this will be the way I will treat those we are going to fight;" and he struck the post in the center of the lodge, and gave a yell. The others spoke to him, saying, "Slow, slow, Mudjikewis, when you are in other people's lodges." So he sat down. Then, in turn, they took the drum, and sang their songs, and closed with a feast. The youngest told them not to whisper their intention even to their wives, but secretly to prepare for their journey. They all promised obedience, and Mudjikewis was the first to say so.

The time for their departure drew near. Word was given to assemble on a certain night, when they would depart immediately. Mudjikewis was loud in his demands for his moccasins. Several times his wife asked him the reason. "Besides," said she, "you have a good pair on." "Quick, quick," he said, "since you must know, we are going on a war excursion. So be quick." He thus revealed the secret. That night they met and started. The snow was on the ground, and they traveled all night, lest others should follow them. When it was daylight, the leader took snow and made a ball of it; then tossing it into the air, he said, "It was in this way I saw snow fall in a dream, so that I could not be tracked." And he told them to keep close to each other for fear of losing themselves, as the snow began to fall in very large flakes. Near as they walked, it was with difficulty they could see each other. The snow continued falling all that day and the following night. So it was impossible to track them.

They had now walked for several days, and Mudjikewis was always in the rear. One day, running suddenly forward, he gave the *Saw-saw-quan*,[4] and struck a tree with his war-club, which broke into pieces as if struck with lightning. "Brothers," said he, "this will be the way I will serve those whom we are going to fight." The leader answered, "Slow, slow, Mudjikewis. The one I lead you to is not to be thought of so lightly." Again he fell back and thought to himself, "What, what: Who can this be he is leading us to?" He felt fearful, and was silent. Day after day they traveled on, till they came to an extensive plain, on the borders of which human bones were bleaching in the sun. The leader spoke. "They are the bones of those who have gone before us. None has ever yet returned to tell the sad tale of their fate." Again Mudjikewis became restless, and, running forward, gave the accustomed yell. Advancing to a large rock which stood above the ground, he struck it, and it fell to pieces. "See, brothers," said he, "thus will I treat those whom we are going to fight." "Still, still," once more said the leader; "he to whom I am leading you is not to be compared to that rock."

Mudjikewis fell back quite thoughtful, saying to himself, "I wonder who this can be that he is going to attack." And he was afraid. Still they continued to see the remains of former warriors, who had been to the place where *they* were now going, some of whom had retreated as far back as the place where they first saw the bones, beyond which no one had ever escaped. At last they came to a piece of rising ground, from which they plainly distinguished, sleeping on a distant mountain, a mammoth bear.

The distance between them was very great, but the size of the animal caused him plainly to be seen. "There," said the leader, "it is he to whom I am leading you; here our troubles only will commence, for he is a MISHE-MOKWA[5] and a Manito. It is he who has that we prize so dearly (i.e., *wampum*), to obtain which, the warriors whose bones we saw sacrificed their lives. You must not be fearful. Be manly. We shall find him asleep." They advanced boldly till they came near, when they stopped to view him more closely. He was asleep. Then the leader went forward and touched the belt around the animal's neck. "This," he said, "is what we must get. It contains the wampum." They then requested the eldest to try and slip the belt over the bear's head, who appeared to be fast asleep, as he was not in the least disturbed by the attempt to obtain the belt. All their efforts were in vain, till it came to the one next the youngest. He tried, and the belt moved nearly over the monster's head, but he could get it no farther. Then the youngest one and leader made his attempt, and succeeded. Placing it on the back of the oldest, he said, "Now we must run," and off they started. When one became fatigued with its weight, another would relieve him. Thus they ran till they had passed the bones of all former warriors, and were some distance beyond, when, looking back, they saw the monster slowly rising. He stood some time before he missed his wampum. Soon they heard his tremendous howl, like distant thunder, slowly filling all the sky; and then they heard him speak and say, "Who can it be that has dared to steal my wampum? Earth is not so large but that I can find them." And he descended from the hill in pursuit. As if convulsed, the earth shook with every jump he made. Very soon he approached the party. They however kept the belt, exchanging it from one to another, and encouraging each other. But he gained on them fast. "Brothers," said the leader, "has never any one of you, when fasting, dreamed of some friendly spirit who would aid you as a guardian?" A dead silence followed. "Well," said he, "fasting, I dreamed of being in danger of instant death, when I saw a small lodge, with smoke curling from its top. An old man lived in it, and I dreamed he helped me. And may it be verified soon," he said, running forward and giving the peculiar yell, and a howl as if the sounds came from the depths of his stomach, and which is called *Checaudum*. Getting upon a piece of rising ground, behold! a lodge, with smoke curling from its top, appeared. This gave them all new strength, and they ran forward and entered it. The leader spoke to the old man who sat in the lodge, saying, *"Nemesho,*[6] help us. We claim your protection, for the great bear will kill us." "Sit down and eat, my grandchildren," said the old man. "Who is a great Manito?" said he, "there is none but me; but let me look," and he opened the door of the lodge, when lo! at a little distance he saw the enraged animal coming on, with slow but powerful leaps. He closed the door. "Yes," said he, *"he* is indeed a great Manito. My grandchildren, you will be the cause of my losing my life. You asked my protection, and I granted it; so now, come what may, I will protect you. When the bear arrives at the door, you must run out of the other end of the lodge." Then putting his hand to the side of the lodge where he sat, he brought out a bag, which he opened. Taking out two small black dogs, he placed them before him. "These are the ones I use when I fight," said he; and he commenced patting, with both hands, the sides of one of them, and he began to swell out, so that he soon filled the lodge by his bulk. And he had great strong teeth. When he attained his full size he growled, and from that moment, as from instinct, he jumped out at the door and met the bear, who in another leap would have reached the lodge. A terrible combat ensued. The skies rang with the howls of the fierce monsters. The remaining dog soon took the field. The brothers, at the onset, took the advice of the old man, and escaped through the opposite side of the lodge. They had not proceeded far before they heard the dying cry of one of the dogs, and soon after of the other. "Well," said the leader, "the old man will share their fate; so run, run, he will soon be after us." They started with fresh vigor, for they had received food from the old man; but very soon the bear came in sight, and again was fast gaining upon them. Again the leader asked the brothers if they could do nothing for their safety.

All were silent. The leader, running forward, did as before. "I dreamed," he cried, "that, being in great trouble, an old man helped me who was a Manito. We shall soon see his lodge." Taking courage, they still went on. After going a short distance they saw the lodge of the old Manito. They entered immediately and claimed his protection, telling him a Manito was after them. The old man, setting meat before them, said, "Eat. Who is a Manito? there is no Manito but me. There is none whom I fear." And the earth trembled as the monster advanced. The old man opened the door and saw him coming. He shut it slowly, and said, "Yes, my grandchildren, you have brought trouble upon me." Procuring his medicine sack, he took out his small war-clubs of black stone, and told the young men to run through the other side of the lodge. As he handled the clubs they became very large, and the old man stepped out just as the bear reached the door. Then striking him with one of the clubs, it broke in pieces. The bear stumbled. Renewing the attempt with the other war-club, that also was broken, but the bear fell senseless. Each blow the old man gave him sounded like a clap of thunder, and the howls of the bear ran along till they filled the heavens.

The young men had now run some distance, when they looked back. They could see that the bear was recovering from the blows. First he moved his paws, and soon they saw him rise on his feet. The old man shared the fate of the first, for they now heard his cries as he was torn in pieces. Again the monster was in pursuit, and fast overtaking them. Not yet discouraged, the young men kept on their way; but the bear was now so close, that the leader once more applied to his brothers, but they could do nothing. "Well," said he, "my dreams will soon be exhausted. After this I have but one more." He advanced, invoking his guardian spirit to aid him. "Once," said he, "I dreamed that, being sorely pressed, I came to a large lake, on the shore of which was a canoe, partly out of water, having ten paddles all in readiness. Do not fear," he cried, "we shall soon get to it." And so it was, even as he had said. Coming to the lake, they saw the canoe with the ten paddles, and immediately they embarked. Scarcely had they reached the center of the lake, when they saw the bear arrive at its borders. Lifting himself on his hind legs, he looked all around. Then he waded into the water; then losing his footing, he turned back, and commenced making the circuit of the lake. Meanwhile, the party remained stationary in the center to watch his movements. He traveled around, till at last he came to the place from whence he started. Then he commenced drinking up the water, and they saw the current fast setting in towards his open mouth. The leader encouraged them to paddle hard for the opposite shore. When only a short distance from land, the current had increased so much, that they were drawn back by it, and all their efforts to reach it were vain.

Then the leader again spoke, telling them to meet their fates manfully. "Now is the time, Mudjikewis," said he, "to show your prowess. Take courage, and sit in the bow of the canoe; and when it approaches his mouth, try what effect your club will have on his head." He obeyed, and stood ready to give the blow; while the leader, who steered, directed the canoe for the open mouth of the monster.

Rapidly advancing, they were just about to enter his mouth, when Mudjikewis struck him a tremendous blow on the head, and gave the saw-saw-quan. The bear's limbs doubled under him, and he fell stunned by the blow. But before Mudjikewis could renew it, the monster disgorged all the water he had drank, with a force which sent the canoe with great velocity to the opposite shore. Instantly leaving the canoe, again they fled, and on they went till they were completely exhausted. The earth again shook, and soon they saw the monster hard after them. Their spirits drooped, and they felt discouraged. The leader exerted himself, by actions and words, to cheer them up; and once more he asked them if they thought of nothing, or could do nothing for their rescue; and, as before, all were silent. "Then," he said, "this is the last time I can apply to my guardian spirit. Now if we do not succeed, our fates are decided." He ran forward, invoking his spirit with great earnestness, and gave the yell. "We shall soon arrive," said he to his brothers, "to the place where my last guardian spirit dwells. In him I place great confidence. Do not, do not be afraid, or your limbs will be fear-bound. We shall soon reach his lodge. Run, run," he cried.

Returning now to Iamo, he had passed all the time in the same condition we left him, the head directing its sister, in order to procure food, where to place the magic arrows, and speaking at long intervals.[7] One day the sister saw the eyes of the head brighten, as if through pleasure. At last it spoke. "Oh, sister," it said, "in what a pitiful situation you have been the cause of placing me. Soon, very soon, a party of young men will arrive and apply to me for aid; but, alas! how can I give what I *would* have done with so much pleasure. Nevertheless, take two arrows, and place them where you have been in the habit of placing the others, and have meat prepared and cooked before they arrive. When you hear them coming and calling on my name, go out and say, 'Alas! it is long ago that an accident befell him. I was the cause of it.' If they still come near, ask them in and set meat before them. And now you must follow my directions strictly. When the bear is near, go out and meet him. You will take my medicine sack, bows and arrows, and my head. You must then untie the sack, and spread out before you my paints of all colors, my war eagle feathers, my tufts of dried hair, and whatever else it contains. As the bear approaches, you will take all these articles, one by one, and say to him, 'This is my deceased brother's paint,' and so on with all the other articles, throwing each of them as far from you as you can. The virtues contained in them will cause him to totter; and, to complete his destruction, you will take my head, and that too you will cast as far off as you can, crying aloud, 'See, this is my deceased brother's head.' He will then fall senseless. By this time the young men will have eaten, and you will call them to your assistance. You must then cut the carcass into pieces, yes, into *small* pieces, and scatter them to the four winds; for, unless you do this, he will again revive." She promised that all should be done as he said. She had only time to prepare the meat, when

the voice of the leader was heard calling upon Iamo for aid. The woman
went out and said as her brother had directed. But the war party, being
closely pursued, came up to the lodge. She invited them in, and placed the
meat before them. While they were eating they heard the bear approaching.
Untying the medicine sack and taking the head, she had all in readiness for
his approach. When he came up she did as she had been told;[8] and, before
she had expended the paints and feathers, the bear began to totter, but,
still advancing, came close to the woman. Saying as she was commanded,
she then took the head, and cast it as far from her as she could. As it rolled
along the ground, the blood, excited by the feelings of the head in this
terrible scene, gushed from the nose and mouth. The bear, tottering, soon
fell with a tremendous noise. Then she cried for help, and the young men
came rushing out, having partially regained their strength and spirits.

Mudjikewis, stepping up, gave a yell and struck him a blow upon the
head. This he repeated till it seemed like a mass of brains; while the others,
as quick as possible, cut him into very small pieces, which they then scattered in every direction. While thus employed, happening to look around
where they had thrown the meat, wonderful to behold! they saw starting
up and running off in every direction small black bears, such as are seen
at the present day. The country was soon overspread with these black
animals. And it was from this monster that the present race of bears[9] derived their origin.

Having thus overcome their pursuer, they returned to the lodge. In the
meantime, the woman, gathering the implements she had used and the
head, placed them again in the sack. But the head did not speak again,
probably from the effects of its great exertion to overcome the monster.[10]

Having spent so much time and traversed so vast a country in their flight,
the young men gave up the idea of ever returning to their own country,
and game being plenty, they determined to remain where they now were.[11]
One day they moved off some distance from the lodge for the purpose of
hunting, having left the wampum with the woman. They were very successful, and amused themselves, as all young men do when alone, by talking
and jesting with each other. One of them spoke and said, "We have all this
sport to ourselves; let us go and ask our sister if she will not let us bring
the head to this place, as it is still alive. It may be pleased to hear us talk
and be in our company. In the meantime, take food to our sister." They
went, and requested the head. She told them to take it, and they took it to
their hunting-grounds and tried to amuse it, but only at times did they see
its eyes beam with pleasure. One day, while busy in their encampment,
they were unexpectedly attacked by unknown Indians. The skirmish was
long contested and bloody. Many of their foes were slain, but still they
were thirty to one. The young men fought desperately till they were all
killed. The attacking party then retreated to a heighth of ground, to muster
their men, and to count the number of missing and slain. One of their young
men had strayed away, and, in endeavoring to overtake them, came to the
place where the head was hung up. Seeing that alone retain animation, he
eyed it for some time with fear and surprise. However, he took it down

and opened the sack, and was much pleased to see the beautiful feathers, one of which he placed on his head.

Starting off, it waved gracefully over him till he reached his party, when he threw down the head and sack, and told them how he had found it, and that the sack was full of paints and feathers. They all looked at the head and made sport of it. Numbers of the young men took the paint and painted themselves, and one of the party took the head by the hair and said, "Look, you ugly thing, and see your paints on the faces of warriors." But the feathers were so beautiful, that numbers of them also placed *them* on their heads. Then again they used all kinds of indignity to the head, for which they were in turn repaid by the death of those who had used the feathers. Then the chief commanded them to throw all away except the head. "We will see," said he, "when we get home, what we can do to it. We will try to make it shut its eyes."

When they reached their homes they took it to the council lodge, and hung it up before the fire, fastening it with raw hide soaked, which would shrink and become tightened by the action of the fire. "We will then see," they said, "if we cannot make it shut its eyes."

Meanwhile, for several days the sister had been waiting for the young men to bring back the head; till at last, getting impatient, she went in search of it. The young men she found lying within short distances of each other, dead, and covered with wounds. Various other bodies lay scattered in different directions around them. She searched for the head and sack, but they were nowhere to be found. She raised her voice and wept, and blackened her face. Then she walked in different directions, till she came to the place from whence the head had been taken. There she found the magic bow and arrows, where the young men, ignorant of their qualities had left them. She thought to herself that she would find her brother's head, and came to a piece of rising ground, and there saw some of his paints and feathers. These she carefully put up, and hung upon the branch of a tree till her return.

At dusk she arrived at the first lodge of a very extensive village. Here she used a charm, common among Indians when they wish to meet with a kind reception. On applying to the old man and woman of the lodge, she was kindly received. She made known her errand. The old man promised to aid her, and told her that the head was hung up before the council fire, and that the chiefs of the village, with their young men, kept watch over it continually. The former are considered as Manitoes. She said she only wished to see it, and would be satisfied if she could only get to the door of the lodge. She knew she had not sufficient power to take it by force. "Come with me," said the Indian, "I will take you there." They went, and they took their seats near the door. The council lodge was filled with warriors, amusing themselves with games, and constantly keeping up a fire to smoke the head, as they said, to make dry meat. They saw the head move, and not knowing what to make of it, one spoke and said, "Ha! ha! it is beginning to feel the effects of the smoke." The sister looked up from the door, and her eyes met those of her brother, and tears rolled down the cheeks of the head. "Well," said the chief, "I thought we would make you do something at last. Look! look at it—shedding tears," said he to those around him; and they all laughed and passed their jokes upon it. The chief, looking around and observing the woman, after some time said to the man who came with her, "Who have you got there? I have never seen that woman before in our village." "Yes," replied the man, "you have seen her; she is a relation of mine, and seldom goes out. She stays in my lodge, and asked me to allow her to come with me to this place." In the center of the lodge sat one of those young men who are always forward, and fond of boasting and displaying themselves before others. "Why," said he, "I have seen her often, and it is to his lodge I go almost every night to court her." All the others laughed and continued their games. The young man did not know he was telling a lie to the woman's advantage, who by that means escaped.[12]

She returned to the old man's lodge, and immediately set out for her own country. Coming to the spot where the bodies of her adopted brothers lay, she placed them together, their feet toward *the east*. Then taking an axe which she had, she cast it up into the air crying out, "Brothers, get up from under it, or it will fall on you." This she repeated three times, and the third time the brothers all arose and stood on their feet.

Mudjikewis commenced rubbing his eyes and stretching himself. "Why," said he, "I have overslept myself." "No, indeed," said one of the others, "do you not know we were all killed, and that it is our sister who has brought us to life?" The young men took the bodies of their enemies and *burned* them. Soon after, the woman went to procure wives for them, in a distant country, they knew not where; but she returned with ten young females, which she gave to the young men, beginning with the eldest. Mudjikewis stepped to and fro, uneasy lest he should not get the one he liked. But he was not disappointed, for she fell to his lot. And they were well matched, for she was a female magician. They then all moved into a very large lodge, and their sister[13] told them that the women must now take turns in going to her brother's head every night, trying to untie it. They all said they would do so with pleasure. The eldest made the first attempt, and with a rushing noise she fled through the air.

Towards daylight she returned. She had been unsuccessful, as she succeeded in untying only one of the knots. All took their turns regularly, and each one succeeded in untying only one knot each time. But when the youngest went, she commenced the work as soon as she reached the lodge; although it had always been occupied, still the Indians never could see any one.[14] For ten nights now, the smoke had not ascended, but filled the lodge and drove them out. This last night they were all driven out, and the young woman carried off the head.

The young people and the sister heard the young woman coming high through the air, and they heard her saying, "Prepare the body of our brother." And as soon as they heard it, they went to a small lodge where the black body of Iamo lay. His sister commenced cutting the neck part, from which the head had been severed. She cut so deep as to cause it to bleed; and the others who were present, by rubbing the body and applying medicines, expelled the blackness. In the meantime the one who brought it, by cutting the neck of the head, caused that also to bleed.

As soon as she arrived, they placed that close to the body, and by the aid of medicines and various other means, succeeded in restoring Iamo to all his former beauty and manliness. All rejoiced in the happy termination of their troubles, and they had spent some time joyfully together, when Iamo said, "Now I will divide the wampum;" and getting the belt which contained it, he commenced with the eldest, giving it in equal proportions. But the youngest got the most splendid and beautiful, as the bottom of the belt held the richest and rarest.

They were told that, since they had all once died, and were restored to life, they were no longer mortals, but *spirits,* and they were assigned different stations in the invisible world. Only Mudjikewis's place was, however, named. He was to direct the *west wind,* hence generally called Kabeyun,[15] there to remain forever. They were commanded, as they had it in their power, to do good to the inhabitants of the earth; and forgetting their sufferings in procuring the wampum, to give all things with a liberal hand. And they were also commanded that it should also be held by them *sacred;* those grains or shells of the pale hue to be emblematic of peace, while those of the darker hue would lead to evil and to war.

The spirits then, amid songs and shouts, took their flight to their respective abodes on high; while Iamo, with his sister Iamoqua, descended into the depths below.

---

[16] Some of the incidents of this tale furnish references to both Occidental as well as Oriental customs, which are appropriate subjects of comment. This is not the place to enter into their discussion. It may be sufficient to mention, that the burning of the dead is an Eastern, and not an Algic custom. Burying with the feet towards the east is common to the present and to many Eastern tribes; but there are tumuli or barrows in the Northwest, in which the bones lie north and south, indicating its occupancy by tribes of a prior race. The idea of the immortality of man is clearly indicated; but an idea more clearly shadowed forth here, than perhaps in any other of these fictions, is the necessity of a great boon or Savior to render men happy. This is placed symbolically in this tale in wampum, the most sacred of all objects known to these tribes, and its acquirement is the work of the Indian Mudjikewis or heir. It is not presumable that they possess, or ever possessed, the true idea of the Savior of mankind, as revealed by Holy Writ. The allusions are thought rather to show the original tendency of the human mind, unenlightened and uninstructed, to seek for some moral or physical panacea which is to introduce happiness to the race. Such an idea appears compatible with the condition of the erratic nations immediately at, and posterior to, the great biblical era of the introduction of new languages, and the consequent dispersion of men over the world. For it is rather to this era, than to the comparatively newer one of the fall of the Israelitish kingdom, that we are to look as the *first* point of historical and philological comparison. It is hence that the Hebrew, the initial language, becomes so

important in the investigation. We may, indeed, regard it as furnishing a key to the principles of grammatical utterance in the East.

It has been observed, that the custom of female separation, upon the violation of which the present tale is founded, is a Hebrew custom, identified with the written institutions of the Pentateuch. A lodge of separation is established at these periods by all the Algic tribes. Nothing is better attested, by those who have given attention to this subject, than that everything touched by the female during this period is polluted and rendered unclean. To cross her pathway even, is to fall under the bane of impurity; and a hunter or a warrior who should thus trespass, would feel his hopes blighted and his prospect of success destroyed.[17]

NOTES

1. In *M. H.* the title reads: "Mishemokwa; or the War of the Gigantic Bear Wearing the Precious Prize or the Necklace of Wampum, or the Origin of the Small Black Bear. An Ottowa Legend."

2. In *M. H.*: "a great magician called IAMO."

3. See last paragraph for explanation of her illness.

4. War-cry. [H. R. S.]

5. A she-bear—also a male having the ferocity of a she-bear. [H. R. S.]

6. My grandfather. [H. R. S.]

7. In *M. H.* the following lines replace this sentence: "They were now in sight of the lodge of Iamo, the magician of the undying head—of that great magician whose life had been the forfeit of the kind of necromantic leprosy caused by the careless steps of the fatal curse of uncleanliness in his sister. This lodge was the sacred spot of expected relief to which they had been fleeing, from the furious rage of the giant Bear, who had been robbed of her precious boon, the *magissauniqua*. For it had been the design of many previous war parties to obtain this boon.

"In the meantime, the undying head of Iamo had remained in the medicine sack, suspended on the sides of his wigwam, where his sister had placed it, with its mystic charms, and feathers and arrows. This head retained all life and vitality, keeping its eyes open, and directing its sister, in order to procure food, where to place the magic arrows, and speaking at long intervals."

8. A variation occurs in *M. H.* For the next clause and the following sentence read: " 'Behold, Mishemokwa,' she cried, 'this is the meda sack of Iamo. These are war eagle's feathers of Iamo (casting them aside). These are magic arrows of Iamo (casting them down). These are the sacred paints and magic charms of Iamo. These are dried tufts of the hair of furious beasts. And this (swinging it with all her might) is his undying head.' The monster began to totter, as she cast one thing after the other on the ground, but still, recovering strength, came close up to the woman till she flung the head."

9. The phrase, "the mukwahs" is inserted here in *M. H.*

10. The next paragraph begins with this sentence in *M. H.* "The war party were now triumphant, but they did not know what use to make of their triumph."

11. *M. H.* adds "and make this their home."

12. In *M. H.* the word "scrutiny" ends this sentence.

13. In *M. H.* the sister's name is here inserted, "Iamoqua."

14. *M. H.* adds "for they all possessed invisibility."

15. Additional identification supplied here in *M. H.:* "the father of Mana-bozho."

16. This passage on comparative mythology and Hebraic custom is omitted from *M. H.* Perhaps the open espousal of the theory of Hebrew origins was less tenable in 1856.

17. This tale was reprinted in *M. H.,* pp. 142-160.

MON-DAW-MIN

OR

THE ORIGIN OF INDIAN CORN

AN ODJIBWA TALE

IN TIMES PAST, a poor Indian was living with his wife and children in a beautiful part of the country. He was not only poor, but inexpert in procuring food for his family, and his children were all too young to give him assistance. Although poor, he was a man of a kind and contented disposition. He was always thankful to the Great Spirit for everything he received. The same disposition was inherited by his eldest son, who had now arrived at the proper age to undertake the ceremony of the Ke-ig-uish-im-o-win, or fast, to see what kind of a spirit would be his guide and guardian through life. Wunzh, for this was his name, had been an obedient boy from his infancy, and was of a pensive, thoughtful, and mild disposition, so that he was beloved by the whole family. As soon as the first indications of spring appeared, they built him the customary little lodge, at a retired spot some distance from their own, where he would not be disturbed during this solemn rite. In the meantime he prepared himself, and immediately went into it and commenced his fast. The first few days he amused himself in the mornings by walking in the woods and over the mountains, examining the early plants and flowers, and in this way prepared himself to enjoy his sleep, and, at the same time, stored his mind with pleasant ideas for his dreams. While he rambled through the woods, he felt a strong desire to know how the plants, herbs, and berries grew, without any aid from man, and why it was that some species were good to eat, and others possessed medicinal or poisonous juices. He recalled these thoughts to mind after he became too languid to walk about, and had confined himself strictly to the lodge; he wished he could dream of something that would prove a benefit to his father and family, and to all others. "True!" he thought, "the Great Spirit made all things, and it is to him that we owe our lives. But could he not make it easier for us to get our food, than by hunting animals and taking fish? I must try to find out this in my visions."

On the third day he became weak and faint, and kept his bed. He fancied, while thus lying, that he saw a handsome young man coming down from the sky and advancing towards him. He was richly and gaily dressed, having on a great many garments of green and yellow colors, but differing in their deeper or lighter shades. He had a plume of waving feathers on his head, and all his motions were graceful.

58

"I am sent to you, my friend," said the celestial visitor, "by that Great Spirit who made all things in the sky and on the earth. He has seen and knows your motives in fasting. He sees that it is from a kind and benevolent wish to do good to your people, and to procure a benefit for them, and that you do not seek for strength in war or the praise of warriors. I am sent to instruct you, and show you how you can do your kindred good." He then told the young man to arise, and prepare to wrestle with him, as it was only by this means that he could hope to succeed in his wishes. Wunzh knew he was weak from fasting, but he felt his courage rising in his heart, and immediately got up, determined to die rather than fail. He commenced the trial, and, after a protracted effort, was almost exhausted, when the beautiful stranger said, "My friend, it is enough for once; I will come again to try you;" and, smiling on him, he ascended in the air in the same direction from which he came. The next day the celestial visitor re-appeared at the same hour and renewed the trial. Wunzh felt that his strength was even less than the day before, but the courage of his mind seemed to increase in proportion as his body became weaker. Seeing this, the stranger again spoke to him in the same words he used before, adding, "Tomorrow will be your last trial. Be strong, my friend, for this is the only way you can overcome me, and obtain the boon you seek." On the third day he again appeared at the same time and renewed the struggle. The poor youth was very faint in body, but grew stronger in mind at every contest, and was determined to prevail or perish in the attempt. He exerted his utmost powers, and after the contest had been continued the usual time, the stranger ceased his efforts and declared himself conquered. For the first time he entered the lodge, and sitting down beside the youth, he began to deliver his instructions to him, telling him in what manner he should proceed to take advantage of his victory.

"You have won your desires of the Great Spirit," said the stranger. "You have wrestled manfully. Tomorrow will be the seventh day of your fasting. Your father will give you food to strengthen you, and as it is the last day of trial, you will prevail. I know this, and now tell you what you must do to benefit your family and your tribe. Tomorrow," he repeated, "I shall meet you and wrestle with you for the last time; and, as soon as you have prevailed against me, you will strip off my garments and throw me down, clean the earth of roots and weeds, make it soft, and bury me in the spot. When you have done this, leave my body in the earth, and do not disturb it, but come occasionally to visit the place, to see whether I have come to life, and be careful never to let the grass or weeds grow on my grave. Once a month cover me with fresh earth. If you follow my instructions, you will accomplish your object of doing good to your fellow-creatures by teaching them the knowledge I now teach you." He then shook him by the hand and disappeared.

In the morning the youth's father came with some slight refreshments, saying, "My son, you have fasted long enough. If the Great Spirit will favor you, he will do it now. It is seven days since you have tasted food, and you must not sacrifice your life. The Master of Life does not require that." "My father," replied the youth, "wait till the sun goes down. I have a particular reason for extending my fast to that hour." "Very well," said the old man, "I shall wait till the hour arrives, and you feel inclined to eat."

At the usual hour of the day the sky-visitor returned, and the trial of strength was renewed. Although the youth had not availed himself of his father's offer of food, he felt that new strength had been given to him, and that exertion had renewed his strength and fortified his courage. He grasped his angelic antagonist with supernatural strength, threw him down, took from him his beautiful garments and plume, and finding him dead, immediately buried him on the spot, taking all the precautions he had been told of, and being very confident, at the same time, that his friend would again come to life. He then returned to his father's lodge, and partook sparingly of the meal that had been prepared for him. But he never for a moment forgot the grave of his friend. He carefully visited it throughout the spring, and weeded out the grass, and kept the ground in a soft and pliant state. Very soon he saw the tops of the green plumes coming through the ground; and the more careful he was to obey his instructions in keeping the ground in order, the faster they grew. He was, however, careful to conceal the exploit from his father. Days and weeks had passed in this way. The summer was now drawing towards a close, when one day, after a long absence in hunting, Wunzh invited his father to follow him to the quiet and lonesome spot of his former fast. The lodge had been removed, and the weeds kept from growing on the circle where it stood, but in its place stood a tall and graceful plant, with bright-colored silken hair, surmounted with nodding plumes and stately leaves, and golden clusters on each side. "It is my friend," shouted the lad; "it is the friend of all mankind. It is *Mondawmin*.[1] We need no longer rely on hunting alone; for, as long as this gift is cherished and taken care of, the ground itself will give us a living." He then pulled an ear. "See, my father," said he, "this is what I fasted for. The Great Spirit has listened to my voice, and sent us something new,[2] and henceforth our people will not alone depend upon the chase or upon the waters."

He then communicated to his father the instructions given him by the stranger. He told him that the broad husks must be torn away, as he had pulled off the garments in his wrestling; and having done this, directed him how the ear must be held before the fire till the outer skin became brown, while all the milk was retained in the grain. The whole family then united in a feast on the newly-grown ears, expressing gratitude to the Merciful Spirit who gave it. So corn came into the world, and has ever since been preserved.[3]

NOTES

1. The Algic name for corn. The word is manifestly a trinary compound from *monedo,* spirit; *min,* a grain or berry; and *iaw,* the verb substantive. [H. R. S.]

2. The Zea mays, it will be recollected, is indigenous to America, and was unknown in Europe before 1495. [H. R. S.]

3. "Mon-Daw-Min" was reprinted in *Historical and Statistical Information* (1852) II, pp. 230-231 (hereafter referred to as *H. S. I.*), and in *M. H.*, pp. 99-104. As "Wunzh, Father of Indian Corn," it was collected in *C. M.*, pp. 330-338, and in *C-C*, pp. 295-303.

PEETA KWAY

OR

THE TEMPEST

AN ALGIC TALE

THERE ONCE LIVED A WOMAN called Monedo Kway[1] on the sand mountains called "the Sleeping Bear" of Lake Michigan, who had a daughter as beautiful as she was modest and discreet. Everybody spoke of the beauty of this daughter. She was so handsome that her mother feared she would be carried off, and to prevent it she put her in a box on the lake, which was tied by a long string to a stake on the shore. Every morning the mother pulled the box ashore, and combed her daughter's long, shining hair, gave her food, and then put her out again on the lake.

One day a handsome young man chanced to come to the spot at the moment she was receiving her morning's attentions from her mother. He was struck with her beauty, and immediately went home and told his feelings to his uncle, who was a great chief and a powerful magician. "My nephew," replied the old man, "go to the mother's lodge, and sit down in a modest manner, without saying a word. You need not ask her the question. But whatever *you think* she will understand, and what *she thinks* in answer you will also understand." The young man did so. He sat down, with his head dropped in a thoughtful manner, without uttering a word. He then thought, "I wish she would give me her daughter." Very soon he understood the mother's thoughts in reply. "Give you my daughter?" thought she; "*you!* No, indeed, my daughter shall never marry *you*." The young man went away and reported the result to his uncle. "Woman without good sense," said he, "who is she keeping her daughter for? Does she think she will marry the Mudjikewis?[2] Proud heart! we will try her magic skill, and see whether she can withstand our power." The pride and haughtiness of the mother was talked of by the spirits living on that part of the lake. They met together and determined to exert their power in humbling her. For this purpose they resolved to raise a great storm on the lake. The water began to toss and roar, and the tempest became so severe, that the string broke, and the box floated off through the straits down Lake Huron, and struck against the sandy shores at its outlet. The place where it struck was near the lodge of a superannuated old spirit called Ishkwon Daimeka, or the keeper of the gate of the lakes. He opened the box and let out the beautiful daughter, took her into his lodge, and married her.

When the mother found that her daughter had been blown off by the

62

storm, she raised very loud cries and lamented exceedingly. This she continued to do for a long time, and would not be comforted. At length, after two or three years the spirits had pity on her and determined to raise another storm and bring her back. It was even a greater storm than the first; and when it began to wash away the ground and encroach on the lodge of Ishkwon Daimeka she leaped into the box, and the waves carried her back to the very spot of her mother's lodge on the shore. Monedo Kway was overjoyed; but when she opened the box, she found that her daughter's beauty had almost all departed. However, she loved her still because she was her daughter, and now thought of the young man who had made her the offer of marriage. She sent a formal message to him, but he had altered his mind, for he knew that she had been the wife of another. "*I* marry your daughter?" said he; "*your* daughter! No, indeed! I shall never marry her."

The storm that brought her back was so strong and powerful, that it tore away a large part of the shore of the lake, and swept off Ishkwon Daimeka's lodge, the fragments of which, lodging in the straits, formed those beautiful islands which are scattered in the St. Clair and Detroit rivers. The old man himself was drowned, and his bones are buried under them. They heard him singing as he was driven off on a portion of his lodge; some fragments of his words are still repeated, which show what his thoughts were in the midst of his overthrow.[3]

ISHKWON DAIMEKA'S LAMENT

The waves, the waves, the angry waves,
    Have borne my bless'd away,
And cast me forth all reft and lone,
    With wrecks of wood and clay.

My power is gone, my guardian dead,
    My loved, my cherish'd lost,
And every dream of pleasure fled,
    And every bright hope cross'd.

I go—I go, a floating ball,
    A speck of earth at best;
But with my dying breath I call
    On Peeta Kway the bless'd.

Oh! was it kind in spirits high,
    Who rule these waters free,
To call the vengeance of the sky,
    And turn its wrath on me?

Yet shall I triumph; for the storm
    That sounds my funeral knell,

Shall lands, and coasts, and islands form,
  Where joy and peace shall dwell.

And every vestige of my lodge,
  And all my simple store,
Shall turn to pastures green and sweet,
  And many a winding shore.

There other tribes of men shall dwell,
  Who serve a purer power,
And oft of me the story tell,
  To while away the hour.

So shall I live, though now I'm toss'd,
  A poor, dishonour'd thing,
And where one Peeta Kway was lost,
  A thousand more shall spring.[4]

NOTES

1. Female spirit or prophetess. [H. R. S.]
2. A term indicative of the heir or successor to the first place in power. [H. R. S.]
3. The final sentence in *M. H.* reads: "They heard him singing his songs of lamentation as he was driven off on a portion of his lodge; as if he had been called to testify his bravery and sing his war song at the stake:

"I ride the waters like the winds
  No storms can blench my heart."

4. This story is reprinted in *M. H.*, pp. 213-215, with slight changes in wording, under the title "Peeta Kway, The Foam-Woman. An Ottowa Legend." The lament is not reprinted in *M. H.*

MANABOZHO

OR

THE GREAT INCARNATION OF THE NORTH

AN ALGIC LEGEND[1]

Introductory Note.—The accounts which the Indians hand down of a remarkable personage of miraculous birth, who waged a warfare with monsters, performed the most extravagant and heroic feats, underwent a catastrophe like Jonah's, and survived a general deluge, constitute a very prominent portion of their cabin lore. Interwoven with these leading traits are innumerable tales of personal achievement, sagacity, endurance, miracle, and trick, which place him in almost every scene of deep interest that could be imagined, from the competitor on the Indian playground, to a giant-killer, or a mysterious being of stern, all-knowing, superhuman power. [He is regarded as the messenger of the Great Spirit, sent down to them in the character of a wise man, and a prophet. But he comes clothed with all the attributes of humanity, as well as the power of performing miraculous deeds. He adapts himself perfectly to their manners, and customs, and ideas. He is brought up from a child among them. He is made to learn their mode of life. He takes a wife, builds a lodge, hunts and fishes like the rest of them, sings his war songs and medicine songs, goes to war, has his triumphs, has his friends and foes, suffers, wants, hungers, is in dread or joy—and, in fine, undergoes all the vicissitudes of his fellows. His miraculous gifts and powers are always adapted to his situation. When he is swallowed by a great fish, with his canoe, he escapes by the exertion of these powers, but always, as much as possible, in accordance with Indian maxims and means. He is provided with a magic canoe, which goes where it is bid; yet, in his fight with the great wampum prince, he is counseled by a woodpecker to know where the vulnerable point of his antagonist lies. He rids the earth of monsters and giants, and clears away windfalls, and obstructions to the navigation of streams. But he does not do these feats by miracles; he employs strong men to help him. When he means to destroy the great serpents, he changes himself into an old tree, and stands on the beach till they come out of the water to bask in the sun. Whatever man could do, in strength or wisdom, he could do. But he never does things above the comprehension or belief of his people; and whatever else he is, he is always true to the character of an Indian.] Whatever man could do, he could do. He affected all the powers of a necromancer. He wielded the arts of a demon, and had the ubiquity of a god. But in proportion as Mana-

65

bozho exercises powers and performs exploits wild or wonderful, the chain of narration which connects them is broken or vague. (He leaps over extensive regions of country like an *ignis fatuus*. He appears suddenly like an avatar, or saunters over weary wastes a poor and starving hunter. His voice is at one moment deep and sonorous as a thunder-clap, and at another clothed with the softness of feminine supplication. Scarcely any two persons agree in all the minor circumstances of the story, and scarcely any omit the leading traits. The several tribes who speak dialects of the mother language from which the narration is taken, differ, in like manner, from each other in the particulars of his exploits.) But he is not presented here as an historical personage, or in any other light than as the native narrators themselves depict him, when they have assembled a group of listeners in the lodge, and begin the story of Manabozho. [This myth is one of the most general in the Indian country. It is the prime legend of their mythology. He is talked of in every winter lodge—for the winter season is the only time devoted to such narrations. The moment the leaves come out, stories cease in the lodge. The revival of spring in the botanical world opens, as it were, so many eyes and ears to listen to the tales of men; and the Indian is far too shrewd a man, and too firm a believer in the system of invisible spirits by which he is surrounded, to commit himself by saying a word which they, with their acute senses on the opening of the spring, can be offended at.] (His birth and parentage are obscure. Story says his grandmother was the daughter of the moon. Having been married but a short time, her rival attracted her to a grapevine swing on the banks of a lake, and by one bold exertion pitched her into its center, from which she fell through to the earth. Having a daughter, the fruit of her lunar marriage, she was very careful in instructing her, from early infancy, to beware of the west wind, and never, in stooping, to expose herself to its influence. In some unguarded moment this precaution was neglected. In an instant, the gale, invading her robes, scattered them upon its wings, and accomplishing its Tarquinic purpose, at the same moment annihilated her.) At the scene of this catastrophe her mother found a fœtus-like mass, which she carefully and tenderly nursed till it assumed the beautiful and striking lineaments of the infant Manabozho.

(Very little is told of his early boyhood. We take him up in the following legend at a period of advanced youth, when we find him living with his grandmother. And at this time he possessed, although he had not yet *exercised,* all the anomalous and contradictory powers of body and mind, of manship and divinity, which he afterward evinced. The timidity and rawness of the boy quickly gave way in the courageous developments of the man. He soon evinced the sagacity, cunning, perseverance, and heroic courage which constitutes the admiration of the Indians. And he relied largely upon these in the gratification of an ambitious, vainglorious, and mischief-loving disposition. In wisdom and energy he was superior to any one who had ever lived before. Yet he was simple when circumstances required it, and was ever the object of tricks and ridicule in others. He could transform himself into any animal he pleased, being man or manito, as circumstances rendered necessary. He often conversed with animals, fowls, reptiles, and fishes. He deemed himself related to them, and invariably addressed them by the term "my brother;" and one of his greatest resources, when hard pressed, was to change himself into their shapes.

Manitoes constitute the great power and absorbing topic of Indian lore. Their agency is at once the groundwork of their mythology and demonology. They supply the machinery of their poetic inventions, and the belief in their multitudinous existence exerts a powerful influence upon the lives and character of individuals. As their Manitoes are of all imaginary kinds, grades, and powers, benign and malicious, it seems a grand conception among the Indians to create a personage strong enough in his necromantic and spiritual powers to baffle the most malicious, beat the stoutest, and overreach the most cunning. In carrying out this conception in the following tale, they have, however, rather exhibited an incarnation of the power of Evil than of the genius of Benevolence.)

MANABOZHO WAS LIVING with his grandmother near the edge of a wide prairie. On this prairie he first saw animals and birds of every kind. He there also saw exhibitions of divine power in the sweeping tempests, in the thunder and lightning, and the various shades of light and darkness, which form a never-ending scene of observation. Every new sight he beheld in the heavens was a subject of remark; every new animal or bird an object of deep interest; and every sound uttered by the animal creation a new lesson, which he was expected to learn. He often trembled at what he heard and saw. To this scene his grandmother sent him at an early age to watch. The first sound he heard was that of the owl, at which he was greatly terrified, and, quickly descending the tree he had climbed, he ran with alarm to the lodge. "Noko! Noko!"[2] he cried, "I have heard a monedo." She laughed at his fears, and asked him what kind of a noise it made. He answered, "It makes a noise like this: Ko-ko-ko-ho." She told him that he was young and foolish; that what he had heard was only a bird, deriving its name from the. noise it made.

He went back and continued his watch. While there, he thought to himself, "It is singular that I am so simple, and my grandmother so wise, and that I have neither father nor mother. I have never heard a word about them. I must ask and find out." He went home and sat down silent and dejected. At length his grandmother asked him, "Manabozho, what is the matter with you?" He answered, "I wish you would tell me whether I have any parents living, and who my relatives are." Knowing that he was of a wicked and revengeful disposition, she dreaded telling him the story of his parentage, but he insisted on her compliance. "Yes," she said, "you have a father and three brothers living. Your mother is dead. She was taken without the consent of her parents by your father the West. Your brothers are the North, East, and South, and, being older than yourself, your father has given them great power with the winds, according to their names. You are the youngest of his children. I have nourished you from your infancy, for your mother died in giving you birth, owing to the ill treatment of your father. I have no relations besides you this side of the planet in which I was born, and from which I was precipitated by female jealousy. Your mother was my only child, and you are my only hope."

He appeared to be rejoiced to hear that his father was living, for he had already thought in his heart to try and kill him. He told his grand-mother he should set out in the morning to visit him. She said it was a long distance to the place where Ningabiun[3] lived. But that had no effect to stop him, for he had now attained manhood, possessed a giant's height, and was endowed by nature with a giant's strength and power. He set out and soon reached the place, for every step he took covered a large sur-face of ground. The meeting took place on a high mountain in the West. His father was very happy to see him. He also appeared pleased. They spent some days in talking with each other. One evening Manabozho asked his father what he was most afraid of on earth. He replied, "Nothing." "But is there not something you dread here? tell me." At last his father said, yielding, "Yes, there is a black stone found in such a place. It is the only thing earthly I am afraid of; for if it should hit me or any part of my body, it would injure me very much." He said this as a secret, and in return asked his son the same question. Knowing each other's power, although the son's was limited; the father feared him on account of his great strength. Manabozho answered, "Nothing!" intending to avoid the question, or to refer to some harmless object as the one of which he was afraid. He was asked again and again, and answered "Nothing!" But the West said, "There must be something you are afraid of." "Well! I will tell you," says Man-abozho, "what it is." But, before he would pronounce the word, he af-fected great dread. "Ie-ee—Ie-ee—it is—it is," said he, "yeo! yeo![4] I cannot name it, I am seized with a dread." The West told him to banish his fears. He commenced again, in a strain of mock sensitiveness repeating the same words; at last he cried out, "It is the root of the apukwa."[5] He appeared to be exhausted by the effort of pronouncing the word, in all this skillfully acting a studied part.

Some time after he observed, "I will get some of the black rock." The West said, "Far be it from you; do not do so, my son." He still persisted. "Well," said the father, "I will also get the apukwa root." Manabozho im-mediately cried out, "Kago! kago!"[6] affecting, as before, to be in great dread of it, but really wishing, by this course, to urge on the West to procure it, that he might draw him into combat. He went out and got a large piece of the black rock, and brought it home. The West also took care to bring the dreaded root.

In the course of conversation he asked his father whether he had been the cause of his mother's death. The answer was "Yes!" He then took up the rock and struck him. Blow led to blow, and here commenced an ob-stinate and furious combat, which continued several days. Fragments of the rock, broken off under Manabozho's blows, can be seen in various places to this day.[7] The root did not prove as mortal a weapon as his well-acted fears had led his father to expect, although he suffered severely from the blows. This battle commenced on the mountains. The West was forced to give ground. Manabozho drove him across rivers, and over mountains and lakes, and at last he came to the brink of this world.

"Hold!" cried he, "my son, you know my power, and that it is impossible to kill me. Desist, and I will also portion you out with as much power as your brothers. The four quarters of the globe are already occupied; but you can go and do a great deal of good to the people of this earth, which is infested with large serpents, beasts, and monsters,[8] who make great havoc among the inhabitants. Go and do good. You have the power now to do so, and your fame with the beings of this earth will last forever. When you have finished your work, I will have a place provided for you. You will then go and sit with your brother Kabibboonocca in the north."

Manabozho was pacified. He returned to his lodge, where he was confined by the wounds he had received. But from his grandmother's skill in medicines he was soon recovered. She told him that his grandfather, who had come to the earth in search of her, had been killed by MEGISSOGWON,[9] who lived on the opposite side of the great lake. "When he was alive," she continued, "I was never without oil to put on my head, but now my hair is fast falling off for the want of it." "Well!" said he, "Noko, get cedar bark and make me a line, whilst I make a canoe." When all was ready, he went out to the middle of the lake to fish. He put his line down, saying, "Me-she-nah-ma-gwai (the name of the kingfish), take hold of my bait." He kept repeating this for some time. At last the king of the fishes said, "Manabozho troubles me. Here, Trout, take hold of his line." The trout did so. He then commenced drawing up his line, which was very heavy, so that his canoe stood nearly perpendicular; but he kept crying out, "Wha-ee-he! wha-ee-he!" till he could see the trout. As soon as he saw him, he spoke to him. "Why did you take hold of my hook? Esa! esa![10] you ugly fish." The trout, being thus rebuked, let go.

Manabozho put his line again in the water, saying, "King of fishes, take hold of my line." But the king of the fishes told a monstrous sunfish to take hold of it; for Manabozho was tiring him with his incessant calls. He again drew up his line with difficulty, saying as before, "Wha-ee-he! wha-ee-he!" while his canoe was turning in swift circles. When he saw the sunfish, he cried, "Esa! esa! you odious fish. why did you dirty my hook by taking it in your mouth? Let go, I say, let go." The sunfish did so, and told the king of fishes what Manabozho said. Just at that moment the bait came near the king, and hearing Manabozho continually crying out, "Me-she-nah-ma-gwai, take hold of my hook," at last he did so, and allowed himself to be drawn up to the surface, which he had no sooner reached than, at one mouthful, he took Manabozho and his canoe down. When he came to himself, he found that he was in the fish's belly, and also his canoe. He now turned his thoughts to the way of making his escape. Looking in his canoe, he saw his war-club, with which he immediately struck the heart of the fish. He then felt a sudden motion, as if he were moving with great velocity. The fish observed to the others, "I am sick at stomach for having swallowed this dirty fellow Manabozho." Just at this moment he received another more severe blow on the heart. Manabozho thought, "If I am thrown up in the middle of the lake, I shall be drowned; so I must prevent it." He drew his canoe and placed it across the fish's throat, and just as he had finished the fish commenced vomiting, but to no effect. In this he was aided by a squirrel, who had accompanied him unperceived until that moment. This animal had taken an active part in helping him to place his canoe across the fish's throat. For this act he named him, saying, "For the future, boys shall always call you Ajidaumo."[11]

He then renewed his attack upon the fish's heart, and succeeded, by repeated blows, in killing him, which he first knew by the loss of motion, and by the sound of the beating of the body against the shore. He waited a day longer to see what would happen. He heard birds scratching on the body, and all at once the rays of light broke in. He could see the heads of gulls, who were looking in by the opening they had made. "Oh!" cried Manabozho, "my younger brothers, make the opening larger, so that I can get out." They told each other that their brother Manabozho was inside of the fish. They immediately set about enlarging the orifice, and in a short time liberated him. After he got out he said to the gulls, "For the future you shall be called Kayoshk[12] for your kindness to me."

The spot where the fish happened to be driven ashore was near his lodge. He went up and told his grandmother to go and prepare as much oil as she wanted. All besides, he informed her, he should keep for himself.

Sometime after this, he commenced making preparations for a war excursion against the Pearl Feather, the Manito who lived on the opposite side of the great lake, who had killed his grandfather. The abode of this spirit was defended, first, by fiery serpents, who hissed fire so that no one could pass them; and, in the second place, by a large mass of gummy matter lying on the water, so soft and adhesive, that whoever attempted to pass, or whatever came in contact with it, was sure to stick there.

He continued making bows and arrows without number, but he had no heads for his arrows. At last Noko told him that an old man who lived at some distance could make them. He sent her to get some. She soon returned with her conaus or wrapper full.[13] Still he told her he had not enough, and sent her again. She returned with as much more. He thought to himself, "I must find out the way of making these heads." Cunning and curiosity prompted him to make the discovery. But he deemed it necessary to deceive his grandmother in so doing. "Noko," said he, "while I take my drum and rattle, and sing my war songs, go and try to get me some *larger* heads for my arrows, for those you brought me are all of the same size. Go and see whether the old man cannot make some a little larger." He followed her as she went, keeping at a distance, and saw the old artificer at work, and so discovered his process. He also beheld the old man's daughter, and perceived that she was very beautiful. He felt his breast beat with a new emotion, but said nothing. He took care to get home before his grandmother, and commenced singing as if he had never left his lodge. When the old woman came near, she heard his drum and rattle, without any suspicion that he had followed her. She delivered him the arrowheads.

One evening the old woman said, "My son, you ought to *fast* before you go to war, as your brothers frequently do, to find out whether you will be successful or not."[14] He said he had no objection, and immediately commenced a fast for several days. He would retire every day from the lodge so far as to be out of reach of his grandmother's voice. It seems she had indicated this spot, and was very anxious he should fast there, and not at another place. She had a secret motive, which she carefully hid from him. Deception always begets suspicion. After a while he thought to himself, "I must find out why my grandmother is so anxious for me to fast at this spot." Next evening he went but a short distance. She cried out, "A little farther off;" but he came nearer to the lodge, and cried out in a low, counterfeited voice, to make it appear that he was distant. She then replied, "That is far enough." He had got so near that he could see all that passed in the lodge. He had not been long in his place of concealment, when a paramour in the shape of a bear entered the lodge. He had very long hair. They commenced talking about him, and appeared to be improperly familiar. At that time people lived to a very great age, and he perceived, from the marked attentions of this visitor, that he did not think a grandmother too old to be pleased with such attentions. He listened to their conversation some time. At last he determined to play the visitor a trick. He took some fire, and when the bear had turned his back, touched his long hair. When the animal felt the flame, he jumped out, but the open air only made it burn the fiercer, and he was seen running off in a full blaze.

Manabozho ran to his customary place of fasting, and, assuming a tone of simplicity, began to cry out, "Noko! Noko! is it time for me to come home?" "Yes," she cried. When he came in she told him what had taken place, at which he appeared to be very much surprised.

After having finished his term of fasting and sung his war-song—from which the Indians of the present day derive the custom—he embarked in his canoe, fully prepared for war. In addition to the usual implements, he had a plentiful supply of oil. He traveled rapidly night and day, for he had only to will or speak, and the canoe went. At length he arrived in sight of the fiery serpents. He stopped to view them. He saw they were some distance apart, and that the flame only which issued from them reached across the pass. He commenced talking as a friend to them; but they answered, "We know you, Manabozho, you cannot pass." He then thought of some expedient to deceive them, and hit upon this. He pushed his canoe as near as possible. All at once he cried out, with a loud and terrified voice, "What is that behind you?" The serpents instantly turned their heads, when, at a single word, he passed them. "Well!" said he, placidly, after he had got by, "how do you like my exploit?" He then took up his bow and arrows, and with deliberate aim shot them, which was easily done, for the serpents were stationary, and could not move beyond a certain spot. They were of enormous length and of a bright color.

Having overcome the sentinel serpents, he went on in his canoe till he came to a soft gummy portion of the lake, called PIGIU-WAGUMEE, or Pitchwater. He took the oil and rubbed it on his canoe, and then pushed into

it. The oil softened the surface and enabled him to slip through it with
ease, although it required frequent rubbing, and a constant reapplication
of the oil. Just as his oil failed, he extricated himself from this impediment,
and was the first person who ever succeeded in overcoming it.

He now came in view of land, on which he debarked in safety, and could
see the lodge of the Shining Manito, situated on a hill. He commenced
preparing for the fight, putting his arrows and clubs in order, and just at the
dawn of day began his attack, yelling and shouting, and crying with triple
voices, "Surround him! surround him! run up! run up!" making it appear
that he had many followers. He advanced crying out, "It was you that killed
my grandfather," and with this shot his arrows. The combat continued
all day. Manabozho's arrows had no effect, for his antagonist was clothed
with pure wampum. He was now reduced to three arrows, and it was
only by extraordinary agility that he could escape the blows which the
Manito kept making at him. At that moment a large woodpecker (the
ma-ma) flew past, and lit on a tree. "Manabozho," he cried, "your adversary has a vulnerable point; shoot at the lock of hair on the crown of
his head." He shot his first arrow so as only to draw blood from that part.
The Manito made one or two unsteady steps, but recovered himself. He began to parley, but, in the act, received a second arrow, which brought him
to his knees. But he again recovered. In so doing, however, he exposed
his head, and gave his adversary a chance to fire his third arrow, which
penetrated deep, and brought him a lifeless corpse to the ground. Manabozho uttered his saw-saw-quan, and taking his scalp as a trophy, he
called the woodpecker to come and receive a reward for his information.
He took the blood of the Manito and rubbed it on the woodpecker's[15]
head, the feathers of which are red to this day.

After this victory he returned home, singing songs of triumph and
beating his drum. When his grandmother heard him, she came to the shore
and welcomed him with songs and dancing. Glory fired his mind. He
displayed the trophies he had brought in the most conspicuous manner,
and felt an unconquerable desire for other adventures. He felt himself
urged by the consciousness of his power to new trials of bravery, skill,
and necromantic prowess. He had destroyed the Manito of Wealth, and
killed his guardian serpents, and eluded all his charms. He did not long
remain inactive. His next adventure was upon the water, and proved him
the prince of fishermen. He captured a fish of such monstrous size, that
the fat and oil he obtained from it formed a small lake. He therefore invited all the animals and fowls to a banquet, and he made the order in
which they partook of this repast the measure of their fatness. As fast as
they arrived, he told them to plunge in. The bear came first, and was
followed by the deer, opossum, and such other animals as are noted for
their peculiar fatness at certain seasons. The moose and bison came
tardily. The partridge looked on till the reservoir was nearly exhausted.
The hare and marten came last, and these animals have, consequently, no
fat. When this ceremony was over, he told the assembled animals and birds
to dance, taking up his drum and crying, "New songs from the south, come,

brothers, dance." He directed them to pass in a circle around him, and to shut their eyes. They did so. When he saw a fat fowl pass by him, he adroitly wrung off its head, at the same time beating his drum and singing with greater vehemence, to drown the noise of the fluttering, and crying out, in a tone of admiration, "That's the way, my brothers, *that's* the way." At last a small duck (the diver), thinking there was something wrong, opened one eye and saw what he was doing. Giving a spring, and crying "Ha-ha-a! Manabozho is killing us," he made for the water. Manabozho followed him, and, just as the duck was getting into the water, gave him a kick, which is the cause of his back being flattened and his legs being straightened out backward, so that when he gets on land he cannot walk, and his tail feathers are few. Meantime the other birds flew off, and the animals ran into the woods.

After this Manabozho set out to travel. He wished to outdo all others, and to see new countries. But after walking over America and encountering many adventures, he became satisfied as well as fatigued. He had heard of great feats in hunting, and felt a desire to try his power in that way. One evening, as he was walking along the shores of a great lake, weary and hungry, he encountered a great magician in the form of an old wolf, with six young ones, coming towards him. The wolf, as soon as he saw him, told his whelps to keep out of the way of Manabozho, "for I know," continued he, "that it is he that we see yonder." The young wolves were in the act of running off, when Manabozho cried out, "My grandchildren, where are you going? Stop, and I will go with you." He appeared rejoiced to see the old wolf, and asked him whither he was journeying. Being told that they were looking out for a place where they could find most game, to pass the winter, he said he should like to go with them, and addressed the old wolf in the following words. "Brother, I have a passion for the chase; are you willing to change me into a wolf?" He was answered favorably, and his transformation immediately effected.

Manabozho was fond of novelty. He found himself a wolf corresponding in size with the others, but he was not quite satisfied with the change, crying out, "Oh, make me a little larger." They did so. "A little larger still," he exclaimed. They said, "Let us humor him," and granted his request. "Well," said he, "*that* will do." He looked at his tail. "Oh!" cried he, "do make my tail a little longer and more bushy." They did so. They then all started off in company, dashing up a ravine. After getting into the woods some distance, they fell in with the tracks of moose. The young ones went after them, Manabozho and the old wolf following at their leisure. "Well," said the wolf, "who do you think is the fastest of the boys? can you tell by the jumps they take?" "Why," he replied, "that one that takes such long jumps, he is the fastest, to be sure." "Ha! ha! you are mistaken," said the old wolf. "He makes a good start, but he will be the first to tire out; this one, who appears to be behind, will be the one to kill the game." Then they came to the place where the boys had started in chase. One had dropped his small bundle. "Take that, Manabozho," said the old wolf. "Esa," he replied, "what will I do with a dirty dogskin?" The wolf took it up; it was a beautiful robe. "Oh, I will carry it now," said Manabozho. "Oh, no," replied the wolf, who at the moment exerted his magic power; "it is a robe of pearls!" And from this moment he omitted no occasion to display his superiority, both in the hunter's and the magician's art; above his conceited companion. Coming to a place where the moose had lain down, they saw that the young wolves had made a fresh start after their prey. "Why," said the wolf, "this moose is poor. I know by the tracks, for I can always tell whether they are fat or not." They next came to a place where one of the wolves had bit at the moose, and had broken one of his teeth on a tree. "Manabozho," said the wolf, "one of your grandchildren has shot at the game. Take his arrow; there it is." "No," he replied; "what will I do with a dirty dog's tooth?" The old man took it up, and behold! it was a beautiful silver arrow. When they overtook the youngsters, they had killed a very fat moose. Manabozho was very hungry; but, alas! such is the power of enchantment, he saw nothing but the bones picked quite clean. He thought to himself, "Just as I expected, dirty, greedy fellows!" However, he sat down without saying a word. At length the old wolf spoke to one of the young ones, saying, "Give some meat to your grandfather." One of them obeyed, and, coming near to Manabozho, opened his mouth as if he was about to vomit. He jumped up, saying, "You filthy dog, you have eaten so much that your stomach refuses to hold it. Get you gone into some other place." The old wolf, hearing the abuse, went a little to one side to see, and behold, a heap of fresh ruddy meat, with the fat, lying all ready prepared. He was followed by Manabozho, who, having the enchantment instantly removed, put on a smiling face. "Amazement!" said he; "how fine the meat is." "Yes," replied the wolf; "it is always so with us; we know our work, and always get the best. It is not a long tail that makes a hunter." Manabozho bit his lip.

They then commenced fixing their winter quarters, while the youngsters went out in search of game, and soon brought in a large supply. One day, during the absence of the young wolves, the old one amused himself in cracking the large bones of a moose. "Manabozho," said he, "cover your head with the robe, and do not look at me while I am at these bones, for a piece may fly in your eye." He did as he was told; but, looking through a rent that was in the robe, he saw what the other was about. Just at that moment a piece flew off and hit him on the eye. He cried out, "Tyau, why do you strike me, you old dog?" The wolf said, "You must have been looking at me." But deception commonly leads to falsehood. "No, no," he said, "why should I want to look at you?" "Manabozho," said the wolf, "you *must* have been looking, or you would not have got hurt." "No, no," he replied again, "I was not. I will repay the saucy wolf this," thought he to himself. So, next day, taking up a bone to obtain the marrow, he said to the wolf, "Cover your head and don't look at me, for I fear a piece may fly in your eye." The wolf did so. He then took the legbone of the moose, and looking first to see if the wolf was well covered, he hit him a blow with all his might. The wolf jumped up, cried out, and fell prostrate from the effects of the blow. "Why," said he, "do you strike me so?" "Strike you!" he replied; "no, you must have been looking at me." "No," answered the wolf, "I say I have not." But he persisted in the assertion, and the poor magician had to give up.

Manabozho was an expert hunter when he earnestly undertook it. He went out one day and killed a fat moose. He was very hungry, and sat down to eat. But immediately he fell into great doubts as to the proper point to begin. "Well," said he, "I do not know where to commence. At the head? No! People will laugh and say 'he ate him backward.' " He went to the side. "No!" said he, "they will say I ate him sideways." He then went to the hind-quarter. "No!" said he, "they will say I ate him forward. I will commence *here,* say what they will." He took a delicate piece from the rump, and was just ready to put it in his mouth, when a tree close by made a creaking noise, caused by the rubbing of one large branch against another. This annoyed him. "Why!" he exclaimed, "I cannot eat when I hear such a noise. Stop! stop!" said he to the tree. He was putting the morsel again to his mouth, when the noise was repeated. He put it down, exclaiming, "*I cannot eat* with such a noise;" and immediately left the meat, although very hungry, to go and put a stop to the noise. He climbed the tree and was pulling at the limb, when his arm was caught between the two branches so that he could not extricate himself. While thus held fast, he saw a pack of wolves coming in the direction towards his meat. "Go that way! go that way!" he cried out; "what would you come to get here?" The wolves talked among themselves and said, "Manabozho must have something there, or he would not tell us to go another way." "I begin to know him," said an old wolf, "and all his tricks. Let us go forward and see." They came on, and finding the moose, soon made away with the whole carcass. Manabozho looked on wishfully to see them eat till they were fully satisfied, and they left him nothing but the bare bones. The next heavy blast of wind opened the branches and liberated him. He went home, thinking to himself, "See the effect of meddling with frivolous things when I had certain good in my possession."

Next day the old wolf addressed him thus: "My brother, I am going to separate from you, but I will leave behind me one of the young wolves to be your hunter." He then departed. In the act Manabozho was disenchanted, and again resumed his mortal shape. He was sorrowful and dejected, but soon resumed his wonted air of cheerfulness. The young wolf who was left with him was a good hunter, and never failed to keep the lodge well supplied with meat. One day he addressed him as follows: "My grandson, I had a dream last night, and it does not portend good. It is of the large lake which lies in *that* direction (pointing). You must be careful never to cross it, even if the ice should appear good. If you should come to it at night weary or hungry, you must make the circuit of it." Spring commenced, and the snow was melting fast before the rays of the sun, when one evening the wolf came to this lake, weary with the day's chase. He disliked to go so far to make the circuit of it. "Hwooh!" he exclaimed, "there can be no great harm in trying the ice, as it appears to be sound.

Nesho[16] is overcautious on this point." But he had not got halfway across when the ice gave way and he fell in, and was immediately seized by the serpents, who knew it was Manabozho's grandson, and were thirsting for revenge upon him. Manabozho sat pensively in his lodge.

Night came on, but no son returned. The second and third night passed, but he did not appear. He became very desolate and sorrowful. "Ah!" said he, "he must have disobeyed me, and has lost his life in that lake I told him of. Well!" said he at last, "I must mourn for him." So he took coal and blackened his face. But he was much perplexed as to the right mode. "I wonder," said he, "how I must do it? I will cry 'Oh! my grandson! Oh! my grandson!" He burst a-laughing. "No! no! that won't do. I will try so—'Oh! my heart! Oh! my heart! ha! ha! ha!' That won't do either. I will cry 'Oh my grandson *obiquadj!*"[17] This satisfied him, and he remained in his lodge and fasted, till his days of mourning were over. "Now," said he, "I will go in search of him." He set out and traveled some time. At last he came to a great lake. He then raised the same cries of lamentation for his grandson which had pleased him. He sat down near a small brook that emptied itself into the lake, and repeated his cries. Soon a bird called *Ke-ske-mun-i-see*[18] came near to him. The bird inquired, "What are you doing here?" "Nothing," he replied; "but can you tell me whether any one lives in this lake, and what brings you here yourself?" "Yes!" responded the bird; "the Prince of Serpents lives here, and I am watching to see whether the obiquadj of Manabozho's grandson will not drift ashore, for he was killed by the serpents last spring. But are you not Manabozho himself?" "No," he answered, with his usual deceit; "how do you think *he* could get to this place? But tell me, do the serpents ever appear? when? and where? Tell me all about their habits." "Do you see that beautiful white sandy beach?" said the bird. "Yes!" he answered. "It is there," continued the Kingfisher, "that they bask in the sun. Before they come out, the lake will appear perfectly calm; not even a ripple will appear. After midday (na-wi-qua) you will see them."

"Thank you," he replied; "I am Manabozho himself. I have come in search of the body of my son, and to seek my revenge. Come near me that I may put a medal round your neck as a reward for your information." The bird unsuspectingly came near, and received a white medal, which can be seen to this day.[19] While bestowing the medal, he attempted slyly to wring the bird's head off, but it escaped him, with only a disturbance of the crown feathers of its head, which are rumpled backward. He had found out all he wanted to know, and then desired to conceal the knowledge of his purposes by killing his informant.

He went to the sandy beach indicated, and transformed himself into an oak stump. He had not been there long before he saw the lake perfectly calm. Soon hundreds of monstrous serpents came crawling on the beach. One of the number was beautifully white. He was the prince. The others were red and yellow. The prince spoke to those about him as follows: "I never saw that black stump standing there before. It may be Manabozho. There is no knowing but he may be somewhere about here. He has the

power of an evil genius, and we should be on our guard against his wiles."
One of the large serpents immediately went and twisted himself around it
to the top, and pressed it very hard. The greatest pressure happened to be
on his throat; he was just ready to cry out when the serpent let go. Eight
of them went in succession and did the like, but always let got at the
moment he was ready to cry out. "It cannot be him," they said. "He is too
great a weak-heart[20] for that." They then coiled themselves in a circle about
their prince. It was a long time before they fell asleep. When they did so,
Manabozho took his bow and arrows, and cautiously stepping over the
serpents till he came to the prince, drew up his arrow with the full strength
of his arm, and shot him in the left side. He then gave a saw-saw-quan and
ran off at full speed. The sound uttered by the snakes on seeing their prince
mortally wounded, was horrible. They cried, "Manabozho has killed our
prince; go in chase of him." Meantime he ran over hill and valley, to gain
the interior of the country, with all his strength and speed, treading a mile
at a step. But his pursuers were also spirits, and he could hear that something was approaching him fast. He made for the highest mountain, and
climbed the highest tree on its summit, when, dreadful to behold, the
whole lower country was seen to be overflowed, and the water was gaining
rapidly on the high lands. He saw it reach to the foot of the mountain,
and at length it came up to the foot of the tree, but there was no abate-
ment. The flood rose steadily and perceptibly. He soon felt the lower part
of his body to be immersed in it. He addressed the tree: "Grandfather,
stretch yourself." The tree did so. But the waters still rose. He repeated
his request, and was again obeyed. He asked a third time, and was again
obeyed; but the tree replied, "It is the last time; I cannot get any higher."
The waters continued to rise till they reached up to his chin, at which
point they stood, and soon began to abate. Hope revived in his heart.
He then cast his eyes around the illimitable expanse, and spied a loon.
"Dive down, my brother," he said to him, "and fetch up some earth, so
that I can make a new earth." The bird obeyed, but rose up to the surface
a lifeless form. He then saw a muskrat. "Dive!" said he, "and if you succeed, you may hereafter live either on land or water, as you please; or I
will give you a chain of beautiful little lakes, surrounded with rushes, to
inhabit." He dove down, but he floated up senseless. He took the body
and breathed in his nostrils, which restored him to life. "Try again," said
he. The muskrat did so. He came up senseless the second time, but clutched
a little earth in one of his paws, from which, together with the carcass of
the dead loon, he created a new earth as large as the former had been, with
all living animals, fowls, and plants.

As he was walking to survey the new earth, he heard some one singing.
He went to the place, and found a female spirit, in the disguise of an old
woman, singing these words, and crying at every pause:

	Literal translation.
Ma nau bo sho,	Manabozho.
O do' zheem un,	His nephew.

Ogeem' au wun,   The king (or chief).
Onis' sa waun,   He killed him.
          Hee-Ub bub ub bub (crying).

"Noko," said he, "what is the matter?" "Matter!" said she, "where have
you been, not to have heard how Manabozho shot my son, the prince of
serpents, in revenge for the loss of his nephew, and how the earth was
overflowed, and created anew? So I brought my son here, that he might
kill and destroy the inhabitants, as he did on the former earth. But," she
continued, casting a scrutinizing glance, "N'yau! indego Manabozho! hub!
ub! ub! ub! Oh, I am afraid you are Manabozho!" He burst out into a
laugh to quiet her fears. "Ha! ha! ha! how can that be? Has not the old
earth perished, and all that was in it?" "Impossible! impossible!" "But,
Noko," he continued, "what do you intend doing with all that cedar cord on
your back?" "Why," said she, "I am fixing a snare for Manabozho, if he
should be on this earth; and, in the meantime, I am looking for herbs to heal
my son. I am the only person that can do him any good. He always gets
better when I sing,

        " 'Manabozho a ne we guawk,
          Koan dan mau wah, ne we guawk,
        " 'Manabozho a ne we guawk,

          Manabozho's dart,
          I try to get his dart,
          I try to get his dart.[21]

     Having found out, by conversation with her, all he wished, he put her to
death. He then took off her skin, and assuming this disguise, took the
cedar cord on his back, and limped away singing her songs. He completely
aped the gait and voice of the old woman. He was met by one who told
him to make haste; that the prince was worse. At the lodge, limping and
muttering, he took notice that they had his grandson's hide to hang over
the door. "Oh dogs!" said he; "the evil dogs!" He sat down near the door,
and commenced sobbing like an aged woman. One observed, "Why don't
you attend the sick, and not sit there making such a noise?" He took up
the poker and laid it on them, mimicking the voice of the old woman. "Dogs
that you are! why do you laugh at me? You know very well that I am so
sorry that I am nearly out of my head." With that he approached the
prince, singing the songs of the old woman, without exciting any suspicion.
He saw that his arrow had gone in about one half its length. He pretended
to make preparations for extracting it, but only made ready to finish his
victim; and giving the dart a sudden thrust, he put a period to the prince's
life. He performed this act with the power of a giant, bursting the old
woman's skin, and at the same moment rushing through the door. The
serpents followed him, hissing and crying out, "Perfidy! murder! vengeance! it is Manabozho." He immediately transformed himself into a
wolf, and ran over the plain with all his speed, aided by his father the West

wind. When he got to the mountains he saw a badger. "Brother," said he, "make a hole quick, for the serpents are after me." The badger obeyed. They both went in, and the badger threw all the earth backward, so that it filled up the way behind.

The serpents came to the badger's wauzh,[22] and decided to watch. "We will starve him out," said they; so they continued watching. Manabozho told the badger to make an opening on the other side of the mountain, from which he could go out and hunt, and bring meat in. Thus they lived some time. One day the badger came in his way and displeased him. He immediately put him to death, and threw out his carcass, saying, "I don't like you to be getting in my way so often."

After living in this confinement for some time alone, he decided to go out. He immediately did so; and after making the circuit of the mountain, came to the corpse of the prince, who had been deserted by the serpents to pursue his destroyer. He went to work and skinned him. He then drew on his skin, in which there were great virtues, took up his war-club, and set out for the place where he first went in the ground. He found the serpents still watching. When they saw the form of their dead prince advancing towards them, fear and dread took hold of them. Some fled. Those who remained Manabozho killed. Those who fled went towards the South.

Having accomplished the victory over the reptiles, Manabozho returned to his former place of dwelling, and married the arrow-maker's daughter.[23]

Concluding Note.—(The story of this northern Hercules[24] is dropped at this point of his triumph over the strongest of the reptile race. But his feats and adventures, by land and sea, do not terminate here. There is scarcely a prominent lake, mountain, precipice, or stream in the northern part of America, which is not hallowed in Indian story by his fabled deeds. Further accounts will be found in several of the subsequent tales, which are narrated by the Indians in an independent form, and may be now appropriately left as they are found, as episodes, detached from the original story. To collect all these and arrange them in order would be an arduous labor; and, after all, such an arrangement would lack consistency and keeping, unless much of the thread necessary to present them in an English dress were supplied by invention,[25] alteration, and transposition. The portions above narrated present a beginning and an end, which could hardly be said of the loose and disjointed fragmentary tales referred to. How long Manabozho lived on earth is not related. We hear nothing more of his grandmother; every mouth is filled with his queer adventures, tricks, and sufferings. He was everywhere present where danger presented itself, power was required, or mischief was going forward. Nothing was too low or trivial for him to engage in, nor too high or difficult for him to attempt. He affected to be influenced by the spirit of a god, and was really actuated by the malignity of a devil. The period of his labors and adventures having expired, he withdrew to dwell with his brother in the North, where he is understood to direct those storms which proceed from points west of the pole. He is regarded as the spirit of the northwest tempests, but receives no worship from the present race of Indians. It is believed by them that he is again to appear, and to exercise an important power in the final disposition of the human race.

In this singular tissue of incongruities will be perceived several ideas probably derived from Asiatic sources. It will be found, in the tale of the visitors to the Sun and Moon, that Manabozho was met on the way, and he is represented as expressing a deep repentance for the sins he had committed while on earth. He is, however, found exercising the vocation of a necromancer; has a pointed lodge, from which he utters oracles; and finally transforms on the spot two of the party, who had consulted him, and asked the gift of immortality, the one into a cedar-tree, and the other into a block of granite.

Manabozho is regarded by the Indians as a god and a benefactor, and is admired and extolled as the personification of strength and wisdom. Yet he constantly presents the paradox of being a mere mortal; is driven to low and common expedients; and never utters a sentiment wiser or better than the people among whom he appears. The conception of a divinity, pure, changeless, and just, as well as benevolent, in the distribution of its providences, has not been reached by any traits exhibited in the character of this personage. And if such notions had ever been conceived by the ancestors of the present race of Indians in the East, they have been obscured, if not obliterated, in the course of their long, dark, and hopeless pilgrimage in the forests of America.) [The prevalence of this legend, among the Indian tribes, is extensive. The character, the place, which he holds in the Indian mythology are further denoted in the 5th vol. of my *Hist.*, p. 417, where he is represented as giving passage to souls on their way through regions of space, to the Indian paradise; and also in the legend of the White Stone Canoe. The general myth is recognized in the legend of the Iroquois, under the name of Hiawatha, and Tarenyawazon. See *Notes on the Iroquois*, p. 270 (1846), and also in the 3rd vol. *Hist.*, p. 314. Mr. Longfellow has given prominence to it, and to its chief episodes, by selecting and generalizing such traits as appeared best susceptible of poetic uses.] That the tribes themselves are of Oriental origin, is probable, from the grammatical structure of their languages, and their mode of expressing thought. But it is apparent that their separation took place at a very ancient period. Whether this event is of a date prior to the organization of the Hebrew theocracy, or whether the American tribes have originated, as some writers suppose, in a separation from the latter sub-stock, there is not, at this time, sufficient data, stamped with the character of sound investigation, to determine; but is rendered manifest, by the present investigation into Indian opinions, that, although they probably had, at the epoch of their expatriation, a knowledge of the Creator and a tradition of the creation, and also of the subsequent destruction of men by the deluge, this knowledge was already corrupted and mixed with notions of materialism and carnality, somewhat after the comparatively recent and grosser manner exhibited in the existing legend of Manabozho.[26]

NOTES

1. In *M. H.* this story is titled "Hiawatha; or, Manabozho." As the differences in the two versions are significant to the legend, they have been indicated at the appropriate places. Bracketed material has been inserted from *M. H.* Parentheses indicate a section found in both versions.

2. An abbreviated term for "my grandmother," derived from *no-kó-miss*. [H. R. S.] Note Longfellow's use of the word.

3. This is a term for the west wind. It is a derivative from *Ka-bian-oong*, the proper appellation for the occident. [H. R. S.] Cf. Kabeyun.

4. An interjection indicating pain. [H. R. S.]

5. The Scirpus or bulrush. [H. R. S.]

6. Do not—do not. [H. R. S.]

7. The Northern Indians, when traveling in company with each other, or with white persons who possess their confidence, so as to put them at ease, are in the habit of making frequent allusions to Manabozho and his exploits. "There," said a young Chippewa, pointing to some huge boulders of greenstone, "are pieces of the rock broken off in Manabozho's combat with his father." "This is the duck," said an Indian interpreter on the sources of the Mississippi, "that Manabozho kicked." "Under that island," said a friend conversant with their language, "under that island Manabozho lost a beaver." [H. R. S.]

8. The term .weendigo, translated here monster, is commonly applied, at this time, by the Indians, to cannibals. Its ancient use appears, however, to have embraced giants and anomalous voracious beasts of the land, to the former existence of which, on this Continent, their traditions refer.

The word genábik, rendered serpent, appears likewise to have been used in a generic sense for amphibious animals of large and venomous character. When applied to existing species of serpents, it requires an adjective prefix or qualifying term. [H. R. S.]

9. The wampum or pearl feather. [H. R. S.]

10. An interjection equivalent to shame! shame! [H. R. S.]

11. Animal tail, or bottom upward. [H. R. S.]

12. A free translation of this expression might be rendered, noble scratchers, or grabbers. [H. R. S.]

13. The conaus is the most ancient garment known to these tribes, being a simple extended single piece, without folds. The word is the apparent root of godaus, a female garment. Waub-e-wion, a blanket, is a comparatively modern phrase for a wrapper, signifying, literally, a white skin with the wool on. [H. R. S.]

14. Fasts. The rite of fasting is one of the most deep-seated and universal in the Indian ritual. It is practiced among all the American tribes, and is deemed by them essential to their success in life in every situation. No young man is fitted and prepared to begin the career of life until he has accomplished his great fast. Seven days appear to have been the ancient maximum limit of endurance, and the success of the devotee is inferred from the length of continued abstinence to which he is known to have attained. These fasts are anticipated by youth as one of the most important events of life. They are awaited with

interest, prepared for with solemnity, and endured with a self-devotion border-
ing on the heroic. Character is thought to be fixed from this period, and the
primary fast, thus prepared for and successfully established, seems to hold that
relative importance to subsequent years that is attached to a public profession
of religious faith in civilized communities. It is at this period that the young
men and the young women "see visions and dream dreams," and fortune or
misfortune is predicted from the guardian spirit chosen during this, to them,
religious ordeal. The hallucinations of the mind are taken for divine inspiration.
The effect is deeply felt and strongly impressed on the mind; too deeply, indeed,
to be ever obliterated in after life. The father in the circle of his lodge, the
hunter in the pursuit of the chase, and the warrior in the field of battle, think
of the guardian genius which they fancy to accompany them, and trust to his
power and benign influence under every circumstance. This genius is the
absorbing theme of their silent meditations, and stands to them in all respects
in place of the Christian's hope, with the single difference that, however deeply
mused upon, the *name* is never uttered, and every circumstance connected with
its selection, and the devotion paid to it, is most studiously and professedly
concealed even from their nearest friends.

Fasts in subsequent life appear to have for their object a renewal of the
powers and virtues which they attribute to the rite. And they are observed
more frequently by those who strive to preserve unaltered the ancient state of
society among them, or by men who assume austere habits for the purpose
of acquiring influence in the tribe, or as preparatives for war or some extraordinary feat. It is not known that there is any fixed day observed as a general
fast. So far as a rule is followed, a general fast seems to have been observed
in the spring, and to have *preceded* the general and customary feasts at that
season.

It will be inferred from these facts, that the Indians believe fasts to be very
meritorious. They are deemed most acceptable to the Manitoes or spirits whose
influence and protection they wish to engage or preserve. And it is thus clearly
deducible, that a very large proportion of the time devoted by the Indians to
secret worship, so to say, is devoted to these guardian or intermediate spirits,
and not to the Great Spirit or Creator. [H. R. S.]

15. The tuft feathers of the red-headed woodpecker are used to ornament
the stems of the Indian pipe, and are symbolical of valour. [H. R. S.]

16. Abbreviated from Neshomiss, my grandfather. [H. R. S.]

17. That part of the intestines of a fish, which, by its expansion from air in
the first stage of decomposition, causes the body to rise and float. The expression here means float. [H. R. S.]

18. The Alcedo or Kingfisher. [H. R. S.]

19. This bird has a white spot on the breast, and a tufted head. [H. R. S.]

20. Shau-go-dai-a, i.e., a Coward. [H. R. S.]

21. Schoolcraft's literal translations gave place in *M. H.* to these artistic
attempts:

> "Dread Manabozho in revenge,
> For his grandson lost—
> Has killed the chief—the king."

> "It is Manabozho's dart,
> I try my magic power to withdraw."

22. A burrow. [H. R. S.]

23. Schoolcraft dealt with the Manabozho-Hiawatha material frequently. The above tale and that of "The Moose and the Woodpecker" were reprinted together under the title, "Hiawatha; or Manabozho," in *M. H.*, pp. 12-51. A short account of Manabozho's exploits was published in *H. S. I.*, I, 317-319. In both *C. M.*, pp. 215-251, and *C-C*, pp. 7-41, the story, much abbreviated, is called "Manabozho, the Mischief Maker."

24. In *M. H.* "this northern Hercules" is changed to "this chief of northern myths is dropped in my notes at this point of his triumph. . . ."

25. This word omitted from *M. H.* It was *invention* that Longfellow employed in order to supply the "necessary thread."

26. This passage on the Hebrew origins was dropped in *M. H.*, no doubt because of the repudiation of the lost tribe theory.

BOKWEWA

OR

THE HUMPBACK

FROM THE ODJIBWA

BOKWEWA AND HIS BROTHER LIVED in a secluded part of the country. They were considered as Manitoes, who had assumed mortal shapes. Bokwewa was the most gifted in supernatural endowments, although he was deformed in person. His brother partook more of the nature of the present race of beings. They lived retired from the world, and undisturbed by its cares, and passed their time in contentment and happiness.

Bokwewa,[1] owing to his deformity, was very domestic in his habits, and gave his attention to household affairs. He instructed his brother in the manner of pursuing game, and made him acquainted with all the accomplishments of a sagacious and expert hunter. His brother possessed a fine form, and an active and robust constitution; and felt a disposition to show himself off among men. He was restive in his seclusion, and showed a fondness for visiting remote places.

One day he told his brother that he was going to leave him; that he wished to visit the habitations of men, and procure a wife. Bokwewa objected to his going; but his brother overruled all that he said, and he finally departed on his travels. He traveled a long time. At length he fell in with the footsteps of men. They were moving by encampments, for he saw several places where they had encamped. It was in the winter. He came to a place where one of their number had died. They had placed the corpse on a scaffold. He went to it and took it down. He saw that it was the corpse of a beautiful young woman. "She shall be my wife!" he exclaimed.

He took her up, and placing her on his back, returned to his brother. "Brother," he said, "cannot you restore her to life? Oh, do me that favor!" Bokwewa said he would try. He performed numerous ceremonies, and at last succeeded in restoring her to life. They lived very happily for some time. Bokwewa was extremely kind to his brother, and did everything to render his life happy. Being deformed and crippled, he always remained at home, while his brother went out to hunt. And it was by following his directions, which were those of a skillful hunter, that he always succeeded in returning with a good store of meat.

One day he had gone out as usual, and Bokwewa was sitting in his lodge, on the opposite side of his brother's wife, when a tall, fine young man entered, and immediately took the woman by the hand and drew her

84

to the door. She resisted and called on Bokwewa, who jumped up to her assistance. But their joint resistance was unavailing; the man succeeded in carrying her away. In the scuffle, Bokwewa had his humpback much bruised on the stones near the door. He crawled into the lodge and wept very sorely, for he knew that it was a powerful Manito who had taken the woman.

When his brother returned he related all to him exactly as it had happened. He would not taste food for several days. Sometimes he would fall to weeping for a long time, and appeared almost beside himself. At last he said he would go in search of her. Bokwewa tried to dissuade him from it, but he insisted.

"Well!" said he, "since you are bent on going, listen to my advice. You will have to go south. It is a long distance to the residence of your captive wife, and there are so many charms and temptations in the way, I am afraid you will be led astray by them, and forget your errand. For the people whom you will see in that country do nothing but amuse themselves. They are very idle, gay, and effeminate, and I am fearful they will lead you astray. Your journey is beset with difficulties. I will mention one or two things, which you must be on your guard against. In the course of your journey, you will come to a large grapevine lying across your way. You must not even taste its fruit, for it is poisonous. Step over it. It is a snake. You will next come to something that looks like bear's fat, transparent and tremulous. Don't taste it, or you will be overcome by the pleasures of those people. It is frog's eggs. These are snares laid by the way for you."

He said he would follow the advice, and bid farewell to his brother. After traveling a long time, he came to the enchanted grapevine. It looked so tempting, he forgot his brother's advice and tasted the fruit. He went on till he came to the frog's eggs. The substance so much resembled bear's fat that he tasted it. He still went on. At length he came to a very extensive plain. As he emerged from the forest the sun was setting, and cast its scarlet and golden shades over all the plain. The air was perfectly calm, and the whole prospect had the air of an enchanted land. The most inviting fruits and flowers spread out before the eye. At a distance he beheld a large village, filled with people without number, and as he drew near he saw women beating corn in silver mortars. When they saw him approaching, they cried out, "Bokwewa's brother has come to see us." Throngs of men and women, gaily dressed, came out to meet him. He was soon overcome by their flatteries and pleasures, and he was not long afterward seen beating corn with their women (the strongest proof of effeminacy), although his wife, for whom he had mourned so much, was in that Indian metropolis.

Meantime Bokwewa waited patiently for the return of his brother. At length, after the lapse of several years, he set out in search of him, and arrived in safety among the luxurious people of the South. He met with the same allurements on the road, and the same flattering reception that his brother did. But he was above all temptations. The pleasures he saw had no other effect upon him than to make him regret the weakness of mind of those who were led away by them. He shed tears of pity to see that his brother had laid aside the arms of a hunter, and was seen beating corn with the women.

He ascertained where his brother's wife remained. After deliberating some time, he went to the river where she usually came to draw water. He there changed himself into one of those hair-snakes which are sometimes seen in running water. When she came down, he spoke to her, saying, "Take me up; I am Bokwewa." She then scooped him out and went home. In a short time the Manito who had taken her away asked her for water to drink. The lodge in which they lived was partitioned. He occupied a secret place, and was never seen by any one but the woman. She handed him the water containing the hair-snake, which he drank, with the snake, and soon after was a dead Manito.

Bokwewa then resumed his former shape. He went to his brother, and used every means to reclaim him. But he would not listen. He was so much taken up with the pleasures and dissipations into which he had fallen, that he refused to give them up, although Bokwewa, with tears, tried to convince him of his foolishness, and to show him that those pleasures could not endure for a long time. Finding that he was past reclaiming, Bokwewa left him, and disappeared forever.[2]

NOTES

1. I.e., the sudden stopping of a voice. [H. R. S.]
2. As "Bokwewa, or the Humpback Magician" this tale was reprinted in *M. H.*, pp. 269-273. It also was published in *C. M.*, pp. 315-323 and *C-C*, pp. 276-284.

IENA

OR

THE MAGIC BUNDLE

A MASKEGO ALLEGORY[1]

THERE WAS ONCE a poor man called Iena,[2] who was in the habit of wandering about from place to place, forlorn, without relations and almost helpless. One day, as he went on a hunting excursion, he hung up his bundle on the branch of a tree, to relieve himself from the burden of carrying it, and then went in quest of game. On returning to the spot in the evening, he was surprised to find a small but neat lodge built in the place where he had left his bundle; and on looking in, he beheld a beautiful female sitting in the lodge, with his blanket lying beside her. During the day he had been fortunate in killing a deer, which he laid down at the lodge door. But, to his surprise, the woman, in her attempt to bring it in, broke both her legs. He looked at her with astonishment, and thought to himself, "I supposed I was blessed, but I find my mistake. Gweengweeshee,"[3] said he, "I will leave my game with you, that you may feast on it."

He then took up his bundle and departed. After walking some time he came to another tree, on which he suspended his bundle as before, and went in search of game. Success again rewarded his efforts, and he returned bringing a deer, but found, as before, that a lodge had sprung up in the place where he had suspended his bundle. He looked in, and saw, as before, a beautiful female sitting alone, with his bundle by her side. She arose, and came out to bring in the deer, which he had deposited at the door, and he immediately went into the lodge and sat by the fire, as he felt fatigued with the day's labors. Wondering, at last, at the delay of the woman, he arose, and peeping through the door of the lodge, beheld her eating all the fat of the deer. He exclaimed, "I thought I was blessed, but I find I am mistaken." Then addressing the women, "Poor Wabizhas,"[4] said he, "feast on the game that I have brought." He again took up his bundle and departed, and, as usual, hung it up on the branch of a tree, and wandered off in quest of game. In the evening he returned with his customary good luck, bringing in a fine deer, and again found a lodge occupying the place of his bundle. He gazed through an aperture in the side of the lodge, and saw a beautiful woman sitting alone, with a bundle by her side. As soon as he entered the lodge, she arose with alacrity, brought in the carcass, cut it up, and hung up the meat to dry. After this, she prepared a portion of it for the supper of the weary hunter. The man thought to himself:

87

"Now I am certainly blessed." He continued his practice of hunting every day, and the woman, on his return, always readily took care of the meat, and prepared his meals for him. One thing, however, astonished him; he had never, as yet, seen her eat anything, and kindly said to her, "Why do you not eat?" She replied, "I have food of my own, which I eat."

On the fourth day he brought home with him a branch of uzadi[5] as a cane, which he placed, with his game, at the door of the lodge. His wife, as usual, went out to prepare and bring in the meat. While thus engaged, he heard her laughing to herself, and saying, "This is very acceptable." The man, in peeping out to see the cause of her joy, saw her, with astonishment, eating the bark of the poplar cane in the same manner that beavers gnaw. He then exclaimed, "Ho, ho! Ho, ho! this is Amik;"[6] and ever afterward he was careful at evening to bring in a bough of the poplar or the red willow, when she would exclaim, "Oh, this is very acceptable; this is a change, for one gets tired eating white fish always (meaning the poplar); but the carp (meaning the red willow) is a pleasant change."

On the whole, Iena was much pleased with his wife for her neatness and attention to the things in the lodge, and he lived a contented and happy man. Being industrious, she made him beautiful bags from the bark of trees, and dressed the skins of the animals he killed, in the most skillful manner. When spring opened, they found themselves blessed with two children, one of them resembling the father and the other the mother. One day the father made a bow and arrows for the child that resembled him, who was a son, saying, "My son, you will use these arrows to shoot at the little beavers when they begin to swim about the rivers." The mother, as soon as she heard this, was highly displeased; and taking her children, unknown to her husband, left the lodge in the night. A small river ran near the lodge, which the woman approached with her children. She built a dam across the stream, erected a lodge of earth, and lived after the manner of the beavers.

When the hunter awoke, he found himself alone in his lodge, and his wife and children absent. He immediately made diligent search after them, and at last discovered their retreat on the river. He approached the place of their habitation, and throwing himself prostrate on the top of the lodge, exclaimed, "Shingisshenaun tshee neeboyaun."[7] The woman allowed the children to go close to their father, but not to touch him; for, as soon as they came very near, she would draw them away again, and in this manner she continued to torment him a long time. The husband laid in this situation until he was almost starved, when a young female approached him, and thus accosted him: "Look here; why are you keeping yourself in misery, and thus starving yourself? Eat this," reaching him a little mokuk containing fresh raspberries which she had just gathered. As soon as the beaveress, his former wife, beheld this, she began to abuse the young woman, and said to her, "Why do you wish to show any kindness to that *animal* that has but two legs? you will soon repent it." She also made sport of the young woman, saying, "Look at her; she has a long nose, and she is just like a bear." The young woman, who was all the time a bear in disguise, hearing herself thus reproached, broke down the dam of the beaver, let the water run out, and nearly killed the beaver herself. Then turning to the man, she thus addressed him: "Follow me; I will be kind to you. Follow me closely. You must be courageous, for there are three persons who are desirous of marrying me, and will oppose you. Be careful of yourself. Follow me nimbly, and, just as we approach the lodge, put your feet in the prints of mine, for I have eight sisters who will do their utmost to divert your attention and make you lose the way. Look neither to the right nor the left, but enter the lodge just as I do, and take your seat where I do." As they proceeded they came in sight of a large lodge, when he did as he had been directed, stepping in her tracks. As they entered the lodge the eight sisters clamorously addressed him. "Oh, Ogidahkumigo[8] has lost his way," and each one invited him to take his seat with her, desiring to draw him from their sister. The old people also addressed him as he entered, and said, "Oh, make room for our son-in-law." The man, however, took his seat by the side of his protectress, and was not farther importuned.

As they sat in the lodge, a great rushing of waters, as of a swollen river, came through the center of it, which also brought in its course a large stone, and left it before the man. When the water subsided, a large white bear came in, and taking up the stone, bit it, and scratched it with his paws, saying, "This is the manner in which I would handle Ogidahkumigo if I was jealous." A yellow bear also entered the lodge and did the same. A black bear followed and did the same. At length the man took up his bow and arrows, and prepared to shoot at the stone, saying, "This is the way I would treat ODANAMEKUMIGO[9] if I was jealous." He then drew up his bow and drove his arrow into the stone. Seeing this, the bears turned around, and with their eyes fixed on him, stepped backward and left the lodge, which highly delighted the woman. She exulted to think that her husband had conquered them.

Finally, one of the old folks made a cry, and said, "Come, come! there must be a gathering of provisions for the winter." So they all took their *cossoes,* or bark dishes, and departed to gather acorns for the winter. As they departed, the old man said to his daughter, "Tell Ogidahkumigo to go to the place where your sisters have gone, and let him select one of them, so that, through her aid, he may have some food for himself during the winter; but be sure to caution him to be very careful, when he is taking the skin from the animal, that he does not cut the flesh." No sooner had the man heard this message, than he selected one of his sisters-in-law; and when he was taking the skin from her, for she was all the while an enchanted female bear, although careful, he cut her a little upon one of her arms, when she jumped up, assumed her natural form, and ran home. The man also went home, and found her with her arm bound up, and quite unwell.

A second cry was then made by the master of the lodge: "Come, come! seek for winter quarters;" and they all got ready to separate for the season. By this time the man had two children, one resembling himself and the

other his wife. When the cry was made, the little boy who resembled his
father was in such a hurry in putting on his moccasins, that he misplaced
them, putting the moccasin of the right foot upon the left. And this is the
reason why the foot of the bear is turned in.

They proceeded to seek their winter quarters, the wife going before to
point the way. She always selected the *thickest* part of the forest, where
the child resembling the father found it difficult to get along; and he never
failed to cry out and complain. Iena then went in the advance, and sought
the open plain, whereupon the child resembling the mother would cry out
and complain, because she disliked an *open* path. As they were encamping,
the woman said to her husband, "Go and break branches for the lodge for
the night." He did so; but when she looked at the *manner* in which her
husband broke the branches, she was very much offended, for he broke
them *upward* instead of *downward*. "It is not only very awkward," said
she, "but we will be found out; for the Ogidahkumigoes will see where
we have passed by the branches we have broken." To avoid this they
agreed to change their route and were finally well established in their winter quarters. The wife had sufficient food for her child and would now and
then give the dry berries she had gathered in the summer to her husband.

One day, as spring drew on, she said to her husband, "I must boil you
some meat," meaning her own paws, which bears suck in the month of
April. She had all along told him during the winter that she meant to resume
her real shape of a female bear and to give herself up to the Ogidahkumigoes to be killed by them and that the time of their coming was near at
hand. It came to pass, soon afterward, that a hunter discovered her retreat. She told her husband to move aside, "for," she added, "I am now
giving myself up." The hunter fired and killed her.

Iena then came out from his hiding-place, and went home with the
hunter. As they went, he instructed him what he must hereafter do when
he killed bears. "You must," said he, "never cut the flesh in taking off the
skin, nor hang up the feet with the flesh when drying it. But you must take
the head and feet, and decorate them handsomely, and place tobacco on
the head, for these animals are very fond of this article, and on the *fourth
day* they come to life again."[10]

NOTES

1. As Schoolcraft later changed the tribal identification to "Odjibwa," he
probably meant that he heard the tale in the Muskegon (Michigan) or the Mus-
kigo (Wisconsin) regions. Certainly, he does not refer to either the Muskogee of
the South or to the Maskegon-Cree groups of Lake Winnepeg.

2. From Ienawdizzi, a wanderer. [H. R. S.]

3. The night-hawk. [H. R. S.]

4. A marten. [H. R. S.]

5. The common poplar, or P. tremuloides. [H. R. S.]

6. The beaver. [H. R. S.]

7. Here I will lie until I die. [H. R. S.]

8. This term means a man that lives on the surface of the earth, as contra-distinguished from beings living under ground. [H. R. S.]

9. He who lives in the city under ground. [H. R. S.]

10. In 1856 Schoolcraft republished this story as "Iena, The Wanderer; or Magic Bundle. A Chippewa Allegory." *M. H.,* pp. 194-201. The *C. M.* version is called "The Magic Bundle," pp. 135-137; the *C-C* story is called "The Magic Packet," pp. 189-191.

SHEEM[1]

OR

THE FORSAKEN BOY

FROM THE ODJIBWA

A SOLITARY LODGE stood on the banks of a remote lake. It was near the hour of sunset. Silence reigned within and without. Not a sound was heard but the low breathing of the dying inmate and head of this poor family. His wife and three children surrounded his bed. Two of the latter were almost grown up; the other was a mere child. All their simple skill in medicine had been exhausted to no effect. They moved about the lodge in whispers, and were waiting the departure of the spirit. As one of the last acts of kindness, the skin door of the lodge had been thrown back to admit the fresh air. The poor man felt a momentary return of strength, and, raising himself a little, addressed his family.

"I leave you in a world of care, in which it has required all my strength and skill to supply you food, and protect you from the storms and cold of a severe climate. For you, my partner in life, I have less sorrow in parting, because I am persuaded you will not remain long behind me, and will therefore find the period of your sufferings shortened. But you, my children! my poor and forsaken children, who have just commenced the career of life, who will protect you from its evils? Listen to my words! Unkindness, ingratitude, and every wickedness is in the scene before you. It is for this cause that, years ago, I withdrew from my kindred and my tribe, to spend my days in this lonely spot. I have contented myself with the company of your mother and yourselves during seasons of very frequent scarcity and want, while your kindred, feasting in a scene where food is plenty, have caused the forests to echo with the shouts of successful war. I gave up these things for the enjoyment of peace. I wished to shield you from the bad examples you would inevitably have followed. I have seen you, thus far, grow up in innocence. If we have sometimes suffered bodily want, we have escaped pain of mind.[2] We have been kept from scenes of rioting and bloodshed.

"My career is now at its close. I will shut my eyes in peace, if you, my children, will promise me to cherish each other. Let not your mother suffer during the few days that are left to her; and I charge you, on no account, to forsake your youngest brother. Of him I give you both my dying charge to take a tender care." He sank exhausted on his pallet. The family waited a moment, as if expecting to hear something farther; but, when they came to his side, the spirit had taken its flight.

The mother and daughter gave vent to their feelings in lamentations. The elder son witnessed the scene in silence. He soon exerted himself to supply, with the bow and net, his father's place. Time, however, wore away heavily. Five moons had filled and waned, and the sixth was near its full, when the mother also died. In her last moments she pressed the fulfillment of their promise to their father, which the children readily renewed, because they were yet free from selfish motives.

The winter passed; and the spring, with its enlivening effects in a northern hemisphere, cheered the drooping spirits of the bereft little family. The girl, being the eldest, dictated to her brothers, and seemed to feel a tender and sisterly affection for the youngest, who was rather sickly and delicate. The other boy soon showed symptoms of restlessness and ambition, and addressed the sister as follows: "My sister, are we always to live as if there were no other human beings in the world? Must I deprive myself of the pleasure of associating with my own kind? I have determined this question for myself. I shall seek the villages of men, and you cannot prevent me."

The sister replied: "I do not say no, my brother, to what you desire. We are not prohibited the society of our fellow-mortals; but we are told to cherish each other, and to do nothing independent of each other. Neither pleasure nor pain ought, therefore, to separate us, especially from our younger brother, who, being but a child, and weakly withal, is entitled to a double share of our affection. If we follow our separate gratifications, it will surely make us neglect him, whom we are bound by vows, both to our father and mother, to support." The young man received this address in silence. He appeared daily to grow more restive and moody, and one day, taking his bow and arrows, left the lodge and never returned.

Affection nerved the sister's arm. She was not so ignorant of the forest arts as to let her brother want. For a long time she administered to his necessities, and supplied a mother's cares. At length, however, she began to be weary of solitude and of her charge. No one came to be a witness of her assiduity, or to let fall a single word in her native language. Years, which added to her strength and capability of directing the affairs of the household, brought with them the irrepressible desire of society, and made solitude irksome. At this point, selfishness gained the ascendancy of her heart; for, in meditating a change in her mode of life, she lost sight of her younger brother, and left him to be provided for by contingencies.

One day, after collecting all the provisions she had been able to save for emergencies, after bringing a quantity of wood to the door, she said to her little brother: "My brother, you must not stray from the lodge. I am going to seek our elder brother. I shall be back soon." Then, taking her bundle, she set off in search of habitations. She soon found them, and was so much taken up with the pleasures and amusements of social life, that the thought of her brother was almost entirely obliterated. She accepted proposals of marriage; and, after that, thought still less of her hapless and abandoned relative.

Meantime her elder brother had also married, and lived on the shores of the same lake whose ample circuit contained the abandoned lodge of his father and his forsaken brother. The latter was soon brought to the pinching turn of his fate. As soon as he had eaten all the food left by his sister, he was obliged to pick berries and dig up roots. These were finally covered by the snow. Winter came on with all its rigors. He was obliged to quit the lodge in search of other food. Sometimes he passed the night in the clefts of old trees or caverns, and ate the refuse meals of the wolves. The latter, at last, became his only resource; and he became so fearless of these animals that he would sit close by them while they devoured their prey. The wolves, on the other hand, became so familiar with his face and form, that they were undisturbed by his approach; and, appearing to sympathize with him in his outcast condition, would always leave something for his repast. In this way he lived till spring. As soon as the lake was free from ice, he followed his new-found friends to the shore. It happened, the same day, that his elder brother was fishing in his canoe, a considerable distance out in the lake, when he thought he heard the cries of a child on the shore, and wondered how any could exist on so bleak and barren a part of the coast. He listened again attentively, and distinctly heard the cry repeated. He made for shore as quick as possible, and, as he approached land, discovered and recognized his little brother, and heard him singing, in a plaintive voice,

> Neesia—neesia,
> Shyegwuh goosuh!
> Ni my een gwun iewh!
> Ni my een gwun iewh!
> > Heo hwooh.

> Ke ge wai bin im
> She gwuh dush
> Ni my een gwun iewh!
> Ni my een gwun iewh!
> > Heo hwooh.

> Tyau, tyau! sunaagud,
> Nin dininee wun aubun
> She gwuh dush
> Ni my een gwun iewh!
> > Heo hwooh.

> Listen, brother—elder brother!
> Now my fate is near its close;
> Soon my state shall be another,
> Soon shall cease my day of woes.

Left by friends I loved the dearest,
    All who knew and loved me most;
Woes the darkest and severest,
    Bide me on this barren coast.

Pity! ah, that manly feeling,
    Fled from hearts where once it grew,
Now in wolfish forms revealing,
    Glows more warmly than in you.

Stony hearts! that saw me languish,
    Deaf to all a father said,
Deaf to all a mother's anguish,
    All a brother's feelings fled.

Ah, ye wolves, in all your ranging,
    I have found you kind and true;
More than man—and now I'm changing,
    And will soon be one of you.[3]

At the termination of his song, which was drawn out with a peculiar cadence, he howled like a wolf. The elder brother was still more astonished, when, getting nearer shore, he perceived his poor brother partly transformed into that animal. He immediately leaped on shore, and strove to catch him in his arms, soothingly saying, "My brother, my brother, come to me." But the boy eluded his grasp, crying as he fled, "Neesia, neesia," etc., and howling in the intervals.

The elder brother, conscience stricken, and feeling his brotherly affection strongly return, with redoubled force exclaimed, in great anguish, "My brother! my brother! my brother!"

But, the nearer he approached, the more rapidly the transformation went on; the boy alternately singing and howling, and calling out the name, first of his brother, and then of his sister, till the change was completely accomplished, when he exclaimed, "I am a wolf!" and bounded out of sight.

[The moral of this tale may be said to rebuke a species of cruelty, which is not peculiar to the tribe from whose traditions it has been obtained. The truth it indicates is impressed upon the minds of the young, to warn them against the perpetration of similar barbarities—barbarities which claim pity even from wild animals.

But while we know of no recorded instance of abandonment of *children of either sex* by any North American tribes, it is attested by travelers that *the very aged and helplessly superannuated,* among some of the more northerly tribes, have been thus left. This remark was made at an early day, and has been repeated in modern times, as practiced among bands on the borders of the Arctic Ocean. Certainly no practice of this kind has been found to prevail among the Odjibwas, Ottowas, and other more well-known existing branches of the Algic stock.][4]

NOTES

1. Abbreviated from *Nee Sheema,* my younger brother or younger sister. [H. R. S.]

2. Wesugaindum, meaning pain or bitterness of mind, is a single expression in the original. It is a trinary compound. [H. R. S.]

3. Stanzas 2, 3, 4, and 5 of the translation are the same as stanzas 3, 4, 5, and 6 in "Song of the Wolf-brother" in "Wild Notes of the Pibbigwun," *M. H.,* pp. 339-44. In the later poem there are nine stanzas. In *M. H.,* only the first stanza of the Algonquin is retained, p. 140.

4. This postscript was omitted from "Sheem, the Forsaken Boy, or Wolf Brother," printed in *M. H.,* pp. 136-141. G. R. Gilman copied this tale from Schoolcraft's notebook and printed it under the title, "The Forsaken Brother," in *Life on the Lakes* (New York, 1836) II, pp. 216-224. There are a few insignificant differences. Mrs. Jameson next used the story in *Winter Studies and Summer Rambles,* III, pp. 88-95. Since her version is closer to Gilman than to *Algic Researches,* it is safe to assume that their versions were nearly exact reproductions of Schoolcraft's original notebook. "The Wolf Brother" was printed in *H. S. I.* (1852) II, pp. 202-204. Both *C. M.,* pp. 115-134, and *C-C,* pp. 159-177, print the story as "Sheem, the Forsaken Boy."

PAUP-PUK-KEEWISS[1]

FROM THE ALGIC

A MAN OF LARGE STATURE, and great activity of mind and body, found himself standing alone on a prairie. He thought to himself, "How came I here? Are there no beings on this earth but myself? I must travel and see. I must walk till I find the abodes of men." So soon as his mind was made up, he set out, he knew not where, in search of habitations. No obstacles could divert him from his purpose. Neither prairies, rivers, woods, nor storms had the effect to daunt his courage or turn him back. After traveling a long time he came to a wood, in which he saw decayed stumps of trees, as if they had been cut in ancient times, but no other traces of men. Pursuing his journey, he found more recent marks of the same kind; and after this, he came to fresh traces of human beings; first their footsteps, and then the wood they had cut, lying in heaps. Continuing on, he emerged towards dusk from the forest, and beheld at a distance a large village of high lodges, standing on rising ground. He said to himself, "I will arrive there on a run." Off he started with all his speed; on coming to the first large lodge, he jumped over it. Those within saw something pass over the opening, and then heard a thump on the ground.

"What is that?" they all said.

One came out to see, and invited him in. He found himself in company with an old chief and several men, who were seated in the lodge. Meat was set before him, after which the chief asked him where he was going and what his name was. He answered, that he was in search of adventures, and his name was Paup-Puk-Keewiss. A stare followed.

"Paup-Puk-Keewiss!"[2] said one to another, and a general titter went round.

He was not easy in his new position; the village was too small to give him full scope for his powers, and after a short stay he made up his mind to go farther, taking with him a young man who had formed a strong attachment for him, and might serve him as his mesh-in-au-wa.[3] They set out together, and when his companion was fatigued with walking, he would show him a few tricks, such as leaping over trees, and turning round on one leg till he made the dust fly, by which he was mightily pleased, although it sometimes happened that the character of these tricks frightened him.

One day they came to a very large village, where they were well received. After staying in it some time, they were informed of a number of manitoes who lived at a distance, and who made it a practice to kill all who came to their lodge. Attempts had been made to extirpate them, but the war-parties who went out for this purpose were always unsuccessful.

Paup-Puk-Keewiss determined to visit them, although he was advised not to do so. The chief warned him of the danger of the visit; but, finding him resolved,

"Well," said he, "if you will go, being my guest, I will send twenty warriors to serve you."

He thanked him for the offer. Twenty young men were ready at the instant, and they went forward, and in due time descried the lodge of the manitoes. He placed his friend and the warriors near enough to see all that passed, while he went alone to the lodge. As he entered he saw five horrid-looking manitoes in the act of eating. It was the father and his four sons. They looked hideous; their eyes were swimming low in their heads, as if half starved. They offered him something to eat, which he refused.

"What have you come for?" said the old one.

"Nothing," Paup-Puk-Keewiss answered.

They all stared at him.

"Do you not wish to wrestle?" they all asked.

"Yes," he replied.

A hideous smile came over their faces.

"*You* go," they said to the eldest brother.

They got ready, and were soon clinched in each other's arms for a deadly throw. He knew their object—his death—his *flesh* was all they wanted, but he was prepared for them.

"Haw! haw!"[4] they cried, and soon the dust and dry leaves flew about as if driven by a strong wind.

The manito was strong, but Paup-Puk-Keewiss soon found that he could master him; and, giving him a trip, he threw him with a giant's force head foremost on a stone, and he fell like a puffed thing.

The brothers stepped up in quick succession, but he put a number of tricks in force, and soon the whole four lay bleeding on the ground. The old manito got frightened and ran for his life. Paup-Puk-Keewiss pursued him for sport; sometimes he was before him, sometimes flying over his head. He would now give him a kick, then a push or a trip, till he was almost exhausted. Meantime his friend and the warriors cried out, "Ha! ha! a! ha! ha! a! Paup-Puk-Keewiss is driving him before him." The manito only turned his head now and then to look back; at last, Paup-Puk-Keewiss gave him a kick on his back, and broke his backbone; down he fell, and the blood gushing out of his mouth prevented him from saying a word. The warriors piled all the bodies together in the lodge, and then took fire and burned them. They all looked with deep interest at the quantity of human bones scattered around.

Paup-Puk-Keewiss then took three arrows, and, after having performed a ceremony to the Great Spirit, he shot one into the air, crying, with a loud voice,

"*You* who are lying down, rise up, or you will be hit!" The bones all moved to one place. He shot the second arrow, repeating the same words, when each bone drew towards its fellow-bone; the third arrow brought forth to life the whole multitude of people who had been killed by the

Manitoes. Paup-Puk-Keewiss then led them to the chief of the village who had proved his friend, and gave them up to him. Soon after the chief came with his counselors.

"Who is more worthy," said he, "to rule than you? *You* alone can defend them."

Paup-Puk-Keewiss thanked him, and told him he was in search of more adventures. The chief insisted. Paup-Puk-Keewiss told him to confer the chieftainship on his friend, who, he said, would remain while he went on his travels. He told them that he would, some time or other, come back and see them.

"Ho! ho! ho!" they all cried, "come back again and see us," insisting on it. He promised them he would, and then set out alone.

After traveling some time he came to a large lake; on looking about, he discovered a very large otter on an island. He thought to himself, "His skin will make me a fine pouch," and immediately drew up, at long shots, and drove an arrow into his side. He waded into the lake, and with some difficulty dragged him ashore. He took out the entrails, and even then the carcass was so heavy that it was as much as he could do to drag it up a hill overlooking the lake. As soon as he got him up into the sunshine, where it was warm, he skinned him, and threw the carcass some distance, thinking the war-eagle would come, and he should have a chance to get his skin and feathers as head ornaments. He soon heard a rushing noise in the air, but could see nothing; by-and-by, a large eagle dropped, as if from the air, on the otter's carcass. He drew his bow, and the arrow passed through under both his wings. The bird made a convulsive flight upward with such force, that the heavy carcass (which was nearly as big as a moose) was borne up several feet. Fortunately, both claws were fastened deeply into the meat, the weight of which soon brought the bird down. He skinned him, crowned his head with the trophy, and next day was on his way, on the lookout for something new.

After walking a while he came to a lake, which flooded the trees on its banks; he found it was only a lake made by beavers. He took his station on the elevated dam, where the stream escaped, to see whether any of the beavers would show themselves. He soon saw the head of one peeping out of the water to see who disturbed them.

"My friend," said Paup-Puk-Keewiss, "could you not turn me into a beaver like yourself?" for he thought, if he could become a beaver, he would see and know how these animals lived.

"I do not know," replied the beaver; "I will go and ask the others."

Soon all the beavers showed their heads above the water, and looked to see if he was armed; but he had left his bow and arrows in a hollow tree at a short distance. When they were satisfied, they all came near.

"Can you not, with all your united power," said he, "turn me into a beaver? I wish to live among you."

"Yes," answered their chief; "lie down;" and he soon found himself changed into one of them.

"You must make me *large*," said he; "*larger* than any of you."

"Yes, yes!" said they. "By-and-by, when we get into the lodge, it shall be done."

In they all dove into the lake; and, in passing large heaps of limbs and logs at the bottom, he asked the use of them; they answered, "It is for our winter's provisions." When they all got into the lodge, their number was about one hundred. The lodge was large and warm.

"Now we will make you large," said they. "Will *that* do?" exerting their power.

"Yes," he answered, for he found he was ten times the size of the largest.

"You need not go out," said they. "We will bring your food into the lodge, and you will be our chief."

"Very well," Paup-Puk-Keewiss answered. He thought, "I will stay here and grow fat at their expense. But, soon after, one ran into the lodge out of breath, saying, "We are visited by Indians." All huddled together in great fear. The water began to *lower,* for the hunters had broken down the dam, and they soon heard them on the roof of the lodge, breaking it up. Out jumped all the beavers into the water, and so escaped. Paup-Puk-Kee-wiss tried to follow them; but, alas! they had made him so large that he could not creep out of the hole. He tried to call them back, but to no effect; he worried himself so much in trying to escape, that he looked like a bladder. He could not turn himself back into a man, although he heard and understood all the hunters said. One of them put his head in at the top of the lodge.

"Ty-au!" cried he; *"Tut Ty-au!* Me-shau-mik—king of the beavers is in." They all got at him, and knocked his skull till it was as soft as his brains. He thought, as well as ever he did, although he was a beaver. Seven or eight of them then placed his body on poles and carried him home. As they went, he reflected in this manner: "What will become of me? my ghost or shadow will not die after they get me to their lodges." Invitations were immediately sent out for a grand feast. The women took him out into the snow to skin him; but, as soon as his flesh got cold, his *Jee-bi* went off.

Paup-Puk-Keewiss found himself standing near a prairie, having re-assumed his mortal shape. After walking a distance, he saw a herd of elk feeding. He admired the apparent ease and enjoyment of their life, and thought there could be nothing pleasanter than the liberty of running about and feeding on the prairies. He asked them if they could not turn him into their shape.

"Yes," they answered, after a pause. "Get down on your hands and feet." And he soon found himself an elk.

"I want big horns, big feet," said he; "I wish to be very large."

"Yes! yes!" they said.

"There!" exerting their power; "are you big enough?"

"Yes!" he answered, for he saw that he was very large. They spent a good time in grazing and running. Being rather cold one day, he went into a thick wood for shelter, and was followed by most of the herd. They had not been long there before some elks from behind passed the others like a strong wind. All took the alarm, and off they ran, he with the rest.

"Keep out on the plains," they said.

But he found it was too late, as they had already got entangled in the thick woods. Paup-Puk-Keewiss soon smelled the hunters, who were closely following his trail, for they had left all the others and followed him. He jumped furiously, and broke down saplings in his flight, but it only served to retard his progress. He soon felt an arrow in his side; he jumped over trees in his agony, but the arrows clattered thicker and thicker upon his sides, and at last one entered his heart. He fell to the ground, and heard the whoop of triumph sounded by the hunters. On coming up, they looked on the carcass with astonishment, and with their hands up to their mouths exclaimed Ty-au! Ty-au! There were about sixty in the party, who had come out on a special hunt, as one of their number had, the day before, observed his *large tracks* on the plains. After skinning him and his flesh getting cold, his *Jee-bi* took its flight from the carcass, and he again found himself in human shape, with a bow and arrows.

But his passion for adventure was not yet cooled; for, on coming to a large lake with a sandy beach, he saw a large flock of brant, and, speaking to them, asked them to turn him into a brant.

"Yes," they replied.

"But I want to be very large," he said.

"Very well," they answered; and he soon found himself a large brant, all the others standing gazing in astonishment at his large size.

"You must fly as leader," they said.

"No," answered Paup-Puk-Keewiss, "I will fly behind."

"Very well," they said. "One thing more we have to say to you. You must be careful, in flying, not to look *down,* for something may happen to you."

"Well! it is so," said he; and soon the flock rose up into the air, for they were bound north. They flew very fast, he behind. One day, while going with a strong wind, and as swift as their wings could flap, while passing over a large village, the Indians raised a great shout on seeing them, particularly on Paup-Puk-Keewiss's account, for his wings were broader than two large aupukwa.[5] They made such a noise, that he forgot what had been told him, about looking down. They were now going as swift as arrows; and, as soon as he brought his neck in and stretched it down to look at the shouters, his tail was caught by the wind, and over and over he was blown. He tried to right himself, but without success. Down, down he went, making more turns than he wished for, from a height of several miles. The first thing he knew was, that he was jammed into a large hollow tree. To get back or forward was out of the question, and there he remained till his brant life was ended by starvation. His *Jee-bi* again left the carcass, and he once more found himself in the shape of a human being.

Traveling was still his passion; and, while traveling, he came to a lodge in which were two old men with heads white from age. They treated him well, and he told them that he was going back to his village to see his friends and people. They said they would aid him, and pointed out the direction he should go; but they were deceivers. After walking all day, he came to a lodge looking very much like the first, with two old men in it with white heads. It was, in fact, the very same lodge, and he had been walking in a circle; but they did not undeceive him, pretending to be strangers, and saying, in a kind voice, "We will show you the way." After walking the third day, and coming back to the same place, he found them out in their tricks, for he had cut a notch on the doorpost.

"Who are you," said he to them, "to treat me so?" and he gave one a kick and the other a slap, which killed them. Their blood flew against the rocks near the lodge, and this is the reason there are red streaks in them to this day. He then burned their lodge down, and freed the earth of two pretended good men, who were manitoes.

He then continued his journey, not knowing exactly which way to go. At last he came to a big lake. He got on the highest hill to try and see the opposite side, but he could not. He then made a canoe, and took a sail into the lake. On looking into the water, which was very clear, before he got to the abrupt depth, he saw the bottom covered with dark fishes, numbers of which he caught. This inspired him with a wish to return to his village and bring his people to live near this lake. He went on, and towards evening came to a large island, where he encamped and ate the fish he had speared.

Next day he returned to the mainland, and, in wandering along the shore, he encountered a more powerful manito than himself, called Manabozho. He thought best, after playing him a trick, to keep out of his way. He again thought of returning to his village; and, transforming himself into a partridge, took his flight towards it. In a short time he reached it, and his return was welcomed with feasting and songs. He told them of the lake and the fish, and persuaded them all to remove to it, as it would be easier for them to live there. He immediately began to remove them by short encampments, and all things turned out as he had said. They caught abundance of fish. After this, a messenger came for him in the shape of a bear, who said that their king wished to see him immediately at his village. Paup-Puk-Keewiss was ready in an instant; and, getting onto the messenger's back, off he ran. Towards evening they went up a high mountain, and came to a cave where the bear-king lived. He was a very large person, and made him welcome by inviting him into his lodge. As soon as propriety allowed, he spoke, and said that he had sent for him on hearing that he was the chief who was moving a large party towards his hunting-grounds.

"You must know," said he, "that you have no right there. And I wish you would leave the country with your party, or else the strongest force will take possession."

"Very well," replied Paup-Puk-Keewiss. "So be it." He did not wish to do anything without consulting his people; and besides, he saw that the bear-king was raising a war-party. He then told him he would go back that night. The bear-king left him to do as he wished, but told him that one of his young men was ready at his command; and, immediately jumping on his back, Paup-Puk-Keewiss rode home. He assembled the village, and told the young men to kill the bear, make a feast of it, and hang the head outside the village, for he knew the bear spies would soon see it, and carry the news to their chief.

Next morning Paup-Puk-Keewiss got all his young warriors ready for a fight. After waiting one day the bear war-party came in sight, making a tremendous noise. The bear-chief advanced, and said that he did not wish to shed the blood of the young warriors; but that if he, Paup-Puk-Keewiss, consented, they two would have a race, and the winner should kill the losing chief, and all his young men should be slaves to the other. Paup-Puk-Keewiss agreed, and they ran before all the warriors. He was victor, and came in first; but, not to terminate the race too soon, he gave the bear-chief some specimens of his skill and swiftness by forming eddies and whirlwinds with the sand, as he leaped and turned about him. As the bear-chief came up, he drove an arrow through him, and a great chief fell. Having done this, he told his young men to take all those blackfish (meaning the bears), and tie them at the door of each lodge, that they might remain in future to serve as servants.

After seeing that all was quiet and prosperous in the village, Paup-Puk-Keewiss felt his desire for adventure returning. He took a kind leave of his friends and people, and started off again. After wandering a long time, he came to the lodge of Manabozho, who was absent. He thought he would play him a trick, and so turned everything in the lodge upside down, and killed his chickens. Now Manabozho calls all the fowls of the air his chickens; and among the number was a raven, the meanest of birds, which Paup-Puk-Keewiss killed and hung up by the neck to insult him. He then went on till he came to a very high point of rocks running out into the lake, from the top of which he could see the country back as far as the eye could reach. While sitting there, Manabozho's mountain chickens flew round and past him in great numbers. So, out of spite, he shot them in great numbers, for his arrows were sure and the birds very plenty and he amused himself by throwing the birds down the rocky precipice. At length a wary bird cried out, "Paup-Puk-Keewiss is killing us. Go and tell our father." Away flew a delegation of them, and Manabozho soon made his appearance on the plain below. Paup-Puk-Keewiss made his escape on the opposite side. Manabozho cried out from the mountain,

"The earth is not so large but I can get up to you." Off Paup-Puk-Keewiss ran, and Manabozho after him. He ran over hills and prairies with all his speed, but still saw his pursuer hard after him. He thought of this expedient. He stopped and climbed a large pine-tree, stripped it of all its green foliage, and threw it to the winds, and then went on. When Manabozho reached the spot, the tree addressed him.

"Great chief," said the tree, "will you give me my life again? Paup-Puk-Keewiss has killed me."

"Yes," replied Manabozho; and it took him some time to gather the scattered foliage, and then renewed the pursuit. Paup-Puk-Keewiss repeated the same thing with the hemlock, and with various other trees, for

Manabozho would always stop to restore what he had destroyed. By this means he got in advance; but Manabozho persevered, and was fast over-taking him, when Paup-Puk-Keewiss happened to see an elk. He asked him to take him on his back, which the elk did, and for some time he made great progress, but still Manabozho was in sight. Paup-Puk-Keewiss dis-mounted, and, coming to a large sandstone rock, he broke it in pieces and scattered the grains. Manabozho was so close upon him at this place that he had almost caught him; but the foundation of the rock cried out,

"Haye! Ne-me-sho, Paup-Puk-Keewiss has spoiled me. Will you not re-store me to life?"

"Yes," replied Manabozho; and he restored the rock to its previous shape. He then pushed on in the pursuit of Paup-Puk-Keewiss, and had got so near as to put out his arm to seize him; but Paup-Puk-Keewiss dodged him, and immediately raised such a dust and commotion by whirlwinds as made the trees break, and the sand and leaves dance in the air. Again and again Manabozho's hand was put out to catch him; but he dodged him at every turn, and kept up such a tumult of dust, that in the thickest of it, he dashed into a hollow tree which had been blown down, and changed himself into a snake, and crept out at the roots. Well that he did; for at the moment he had got out, Manabozho, who is Ogee-bau-ge-mon,[6] struck it with his power, and it was in fragments. Paup-Puk-Keewiss was again in human shape; again Manabozho pressed him hard. At a distance he saw a very high bluff of rock jutting out into the lake, and ran for the foot of the precipice, which was abrupt and elevated. As he came near, the local manito of the rock opened his door and told him to come in. The door was no sooner closed than Manabozho knocked.

"Open it!" he cried, with a loud voice.

The manito was afraid of him, but he said to his guest,

"Since I have sheltered you, I would sooner die with you than open the door."

"Open it!" Manabozho again cried.

The manito kept silent. Manabozho, however, made no attempt to open it by force. He waited a few moments. "Very well," he said; "I give you only till night to live." The manito trembled, for he knew he would be shut up under the earth.

Night came. The clouds hung low and black, and every moment the forked lightning would flash from them. The black clouds advanced slowly, and threw their dark shadows afar, and behind there was heard the rum-bling noise of the coming thunder. As they came near to the precipice, the thunders broke, the lightning flashed, the ground shook, and the solid rocks split, tottered, and fell. And under their ruins were crushed the mortal bodies of Paup-Puk-Keewiss and the manito.

It was only then that Paup-Puk-Keewiss found he was really dead. He had been killed in different animal shapes; but now his body, in human shape, was crushed. Manabozho came and took their Jee-bi-ug or spirits.

"You," said he to Paup-Puk-Keewiss, "shall not be again permitted to

live on the earth. I will give you the shape of the war-eagle, and you will be
the chief of all fowls, and your duty shall be to watch over their destinies."[7]

NOTES

1. In *M. H.* this tale is linked with another, "The Storm Fool," which
appears in the second volume of *Algic Researches.*

2. This word appears to be derived from the same root as *Paup-puk-ke-nay,*
a grasshopper, the inflection *iss* making it personal. The Indian idea is that of
harum scarum. He is regarded as a foil to Manabozho, with whom he is frequently brought in contact in aboriginal story craft. [H. R. S.]

3. This is an official who bears the pipe for the ruling chief, and is an
inferior dignity [dignitary] in councils. [H. R. S.]

4. This is a studied perversion of the interjection *Ho.* In another instance,
in "Wassamo," it is rendered *Hoke.* [H. R. S.]

5. Mats. [H. R. S.]

6. A species of lightning. [H. R. S.]

7. In *M. H.,* pp. 55-70, the tale is entitled simply "Paup-Puk-Keewiss."
Both *C. M.,* pp. 34-67, and *C-C,* pp. 104-135, give it the title "The Wonderful
Exploits of Grasshopper."

IADILLA

OR

THE ORIGIN OF THE ROBIN

FROM THE ODJIBWA

AN OLD MAN HAD AN ONLY SON named *Iadilla*,[1] who had come to that age which is thought to be most proper to make the long and final fast, that is to secure through life a guardian genius or spirit. In the influence of this choice, it is well known, our people have relied for their prosperity in after life; it was, therefore, an event of deep importance.

The old man was ambitious that his son should surpass all others in whatever was deemed most wise and great among his tribe; and, to fulfill his wishes, he thought it necessary that he should fast a much longer time than any of those persons, renowned for their prowess or wisdom, whose fame he coveted. He therefore directed his son to prepare, with great ceremony, for the important event. After he had been in the sweating lodge and bath several times, he ordered him to lie down upon a clean mat, in a little lodge expressly prepared for him; telling him, at the same time, to endure his fast like a man, and that, at the expiration of *twelve* days, he should receive food and the blessing of his father.

The lad carefully observed this injunction, lying with perfect composure, with his face covered, awaiting those mystic visitations which were to seal his good or evil fortune. His father visited him regularly every morning, to encourage him to perseverance, expatiating at length on the honor and renown that would attend him through life if he accomplished the full term prescribed. To these admonitions and encouragements the boy never replied, but lay, without the least sign of discontent or murmuring, until the ninth day, when he addressed his father as follows:

"My father, my dreams forebode evil. May I break my fast now, and at a more propitious time make a new fast?" The father answered,

"My son, you know not what you ask. If you get up now, all your glory will depart. Wait patiently a little longer. You have but three days yet to accomplish your desire. You know it is for your own good, and I encourage you to persevere."

The son assented; and, covering himself closer, he lay till the eleventh day, when he repeated his request. Very nearly the same answer was given him by his father, who added that the next day he would himself prepare his first meal, and bring it to him. The boy remained silent, but lay as motionless as a corpse. No one would have known he was living but by the gentle heaving of his breast.

The next morning, the father, elated at having gained his end, prepared a repast for his son, and hastened to set it before him. On coming to the door, he was surprised to hear his son talking to himself. He stooped to listen; and, looking through a small aperture, was more astonished when he beheld his son painted with vermilion over all his breast, and in the act of finishing his work by laying on the paint as far back on his shoulders as he could reach with his hands, saying, at the same time, to himself, "My father has destroyed my fortune as a man. He would not listen to my requests. He will be the loser. I shall be forever happy in my new state, for I have been obedient to my parent; he alone will be the sufferer, for my guardian spirit is a just one; though not propitious to me in the manner I desired, he has shown me pity in another way; he has given me another shape; and now I must go."

At this moment the old man broke in, exclaiming, "My son! my son! I pray you leave me not." But the young man, with the quickness of a bird, had flown to the top of the lodge, and perched himself on the highest pole, having been changed into a beautiful robin redbreast.

He looked down upon his father with pity beaming in his eyes, and addressed him as follows: "Regret not, my father, the change you behold. I shall be happier in my present state than I could have been as a man. I shall always be the friend of men, and keep near their dwellings. I shall ever be happy and contented; and although I could not gratify your wishes as a warrior, it will be my daily aim to make you amends for it as a harbinger of peace and joy. I will cheer you by my songs, and strive to inspire in others the joy and lightsomeness I feel in my present state. This will be some compensation to you for the loss of the glory you expected. I am now free from the cares and pains of human life. My food is spontaneously furnished by the mountains and fields, and my pathway of life is in the bright air." Then stretching himself on his toes, as if delighted with the gift of wings, he caroled one of his sweetest songs, and flew away into a neighboring grove.

IADILLA'S SONG

In the boundless woods there are berries of red,
  And fruits of a beautiful blue,
Where, by nature's own hand, the sweet singers are fed,
  And to nature they ever are true.

We go not with arrow and bow to the field,
  Like men of the fierce ruddy race,
To take away lives which they never can give,
  And revel the lords of the chase.

If danger approaches, with instant alarm
  We fly to our own leafy woods,

And there, with an innocent carol and charm,
  We sing to our dear little broods.

At morning we sally in quest of the grain
  Kind nature in plenty supplies,
We skip o'er the beautiful wide-stretching plain,
  And sport in the vault of the skies.

At evening we perch in some neighbouring tree
  To carol our evening adieu,
And feel, although man may assert he is free,
  We only have liberty true.

We sing out our praises to God and to man,
  We live as heaven taught us to live,
And I would not change back to mortality's plan
  For all that the mortal can give.

Here ceased the sweet singer; then pluming his breast,
  He winged the blue firmament free,
Repeating, as homeward he flew to his rest,
  Tshee-ree-lee—Tshee-ree-lee—Tshee-ree-lee![2]

NOTES

1. The son's name is changed to Opeechee in *M. H.*
2. The poem is transferred in *M. H.* from the text to "Wild Notes of the Pibbigwun," pp. 310-311. In *M. H.* the title is changed to "Opeechee, or the Origin of the Robin." Both Gilman, I, pp. 165-169, and Jameson, III, pp. 114-118, print the story without title. In *H. S. I.*, II, pp. 229-230, the tale is called "Transformation of a Hunter's Son into a Bird." *C. M.*, pp. 98-101, and *C-C,* pp. 143-146, entitle the story "The Origin of the Robin."

ENCHANTED MOCCASINS

A MASKEGO TALE[1]

THERE ONCE LIVED A LITTLE BOY with his sister, entirely alone, in an un-inhabited country. He was called the Boy that carries the Ball on his Back, from an idea of his having supernatural powers. This boy was constantly in the habit of meditating, and asking within himself whether there were other and similar beings to themselves on the earth. When he grew up to manhood, he asked his sister if she knew of any human beings besides themselves. She replied that she did; and that there was, at a great dis-tance, a large village. As soon as he heard this, he said to his sister, "I am now a young man, and very much in want of a partner;" and he asked his sister to make him several pairs of moccasins. She complied with his re-quest; and, as soon as he received the moccasins, he took up his war-club and set out in quest of the distant village. He traveled on, till at length he came to a small wigwam, and, on looking into it, discovered a very old woman sitting alone by the fire. As soon as she saw the stranger, she in-vited him in, and thus addressed him: "My poor grandchild, I suppose you are one of those who seek for the distant village, from which no person has ever yet returned. Unless your guardian is more powerful than the guardian of your predecessors, you too will share a similar fate to theirs. Be careful to provide yourself with the Ozhebahguhnun—the bones they use in the medicine dance,[2] without which you cannot succeed." After she had thus spoken, she gave him the following directions for his journey. "When you come near to the village which you seek, you will see in the center a large lodge, in which the chief of the village, who has two daughters, resides. Before the door you will see a great tree, which is smooth and destitute of bark. On this tree, about the height of a man from the ground, a small lodge is suspended, in which these two daughters dwell. It is here so many have been destroyed. Be wise, my grandchild, and abide strictly by my directions." The old woman then gave him the Ozhebahguhnun, which would cause his success. Placing them in his bosom, he continued his jour-ney, till at length he arrived at the sought-for village; and, as he was gazing around him, he saw both the tree and the lodge which the old woman had mentioned. Immediately he bent his steps for the tree, and approaching, he endeavored to reach the suspended lodge. But all his efforts were vain; for as often as he attempted to reach it, the tree began to tremble, and soon shot up so that the lodge could hardly be perceived. Foiled as he was in all his attempts, he thought of his guardian, and changed himself into a small squirrel, that he might more easily accomplish his design. He then mounted the tree in quest of the lodge. After climbing for some time, he became fatigued and panted for breath; but, remembering the instructions which the old woman had given him, he took from his bosom one of the bones, and thrust it into the trunk of the tree on which he sat. In this way he quickly found relief; and, as often as he became fatigued, he repeated this; but whenever he came near the lodge and attempted to touch it, the tree would shoot up as before, and place the lodge beyond his reach. At length, the bones being exhausted, he began to despair, for the earth had long since vanished from his sight. Summoning all resolution, he determined to make another effort to reach the object of his wishes. On he went; yet, as soon as he came near the lodge and attempted to touch it, the tree again shook, but it had reached the arch of heaven, and could go no higher; so now he entered the lodge, and beheld the two sisters sitting opposite each other. He asked their names. The one on his left hand called herself Azhabee, and the one on the right Negahnahbee.[3] Whenever he addressed the one on his left hand, the tree would tremble as before, and settle down to its former position. But when he addressed the one on his right hand, it would again shoot upward as before. When he thus discovered that, by addressing the one on his left hand, the tree would descend, he continued to do so until it had resumed its former position; then seizing his war-club, he thus addressed the sisters: "You, who have caused the death of so many of my brothers, I will now put an end to, and thus have revenge for the numbers you have destroyed." As he said this he raised the club and laid them dead at his feet. He then descended, and learning that these sisters had a brother living with their father, who would pursue him for the deed he had done, he set off at random, not knowing whither he went. Soon after, the father and mother of the young women visited their residence and found their remains. They immediately told their son Mudjikewis that his sisters had been slain. He replied, "The person who has done this must be the Boy that carries the Ball on his Back. I will pursue him, and have revenge for the blood of my sisters." "It is well, my son," replied the father. "The spirit of your life grant you success. I counsel you to be wary in the pursuit. It is a strong spirit who has done this injury to us, and he will try to deceive you in every way. Above all, avoid tasting food till you succeed; for if you break your fast before you see his blood, your power will be destroyed." So saying, they parted.

His son instantly set out in search of the murderer, who, finding he was closely pursued by the brother of the slain, climbed up into one of the tallest trees and shot forth his magic arrows. Finding that his pursuer was not turned back by his arrows, he renewed his flight; and when he found himself hard pressed, and his enemy close behind him, he transformed himself into the skeleton of a moose that had been killed, whose flesh had come off from his bones. He then remembered the moccasins which his sister had given him, which were enchanted. Taking a pair of them, he placed them near the skeleton. "Go," said he to them, "to the end of the earth."

The moccasins then left him and their tracks remained. Mudjikewis at length came to the skeleton of the moose, when he perceived that the track he had long been pursuing did not end there, so he continued to follow it up, till he came to the end of the earth, where he found only a pair of moccasins. Mortified that he had been outwitted by following a pair of moccasins instead of the object of his revenge, he bitterly complained, resolving not to give up the pursuit, and to be more wary and wise in scrutinizing signs. He then called to mind the skeleton he met with on his way, and concluded that *it* must be the object of his search. He retraced his steps towards the skeleton, but found, to his surprise, that it had disappeared, and that the tracks of *Onwee Bahmondung,* or he who carries the Ball,[4] were in another direction. He now became faint with hunger, and resolved to give up the pursuit; and when he remembered the blood of his sisters, he determined again to pursue.

The other, finding he was closely pursued, now changed himself into a very old man, with two daughters, who lived in a large lodge in the center of a beautiful garden, which was filled with everything that could delight the eye or was pleasant to the taste. He made himself appear so very old as to be unable to leave his lodge, and had his daughters to bring him food and wait on him. The garden also had the appearance of ancient occupancy, and was highly cultivated.

His pursuer contined on till he was nearly starved and ready to sink. He exclaimed, "Oh! I will forget the blood of my sisters, for I am starving." But again he thought of the blood of his sisters, and again he resolved to pursue, and be satisfied with nothing but the attainment of his right to revenge.

He went on till he came to the beautiful garden. He approached the lodge. As soon as the daughters of the owner perceived him, they ran and told their father that a stranger approached the lodge. Their father replied, "Invite him in, my children, invite him in." They quickly did so; and, by the command of their father, they boiled some corn and prepared other savory food. Mudjikewis had no suspicion of the deception. He was faint and weary with travel, and felt that he could endure fasting no longer. Without hesitancy, he partook heartily of the meal, and in so doing was overcome. All at once he seemed to forget the blood of his sisters, and even the village of his nativity. He ate so heartily as to produce drowsiness, and soon fell into a profound sleep. Onwee Bahmondung watched his opportunity, and, as soon as he found his slumbers sound, resumed his youthful form. He then drew the magic ball from his back, which turned out to be a heavy war-club, with one blow of which he put an end to his pursuer, and thus vindicated his title as the Wearer of the Ball.[5]

NOTES

1. Maskego is changed to Odjibwa, in *M. H.* This title was used once by Cornelius Matthews for the entire collection of Schoolcraft's Indian stories. According to Schoolcraft's *Personal Memoirs* (1851), p. 548, this story was told him by Rev. William McMurray, his brother-in-law, who had it from Charlotte Johnston.

2. The idea attached to the use of these bones in the medicine dance is, that, by their magical influence, the actor can penetrate and go through any substance. [H. R. S.]

3. One who sits behind [and] one who sits before. [H. R. S.]

4. The boy's name is given in the *first* paragraph in *M. H.* Except for the addition of a few trifling details about life in the forest, the stories are the same.

5. The mention of the "beautiful garden" suggests that this story might have derived from the Algonquin Mascoutens, supposedly the creators of the famous "garden beds" in southwestern Michigan. Reprinted in *M. H.*, pp. 293-298; in *C. M.*, pp. 190-206; in *C-C*, pp. 212-217.

THE BROKEN WING

AN ALLEGORY

THERE WERE SIX YOUNG FALCONS living in a nest, all but one of whom were still unable to fly, when it so happened that both the parent birds were shot by the hunters in one day. The young brood waited with impatience for their return; but night came, and they were left without parents and without food. Meeji-geeg-wona, or the Gray Eagle, the eldest, and the only one whose feathers had become stout enough to enable him to leave the nest, assumed the duty of stilling their cries and providing them with food, in which he was very successful. But, after a short time had passed, he, by an unlucky mischance, got one of his wings broken in pouncing upon a swan. This was the more unlucky, because the season had arrived when they were soon to go off to a southern climate to pass the winter, and they were only waiting to become a little stouter and more expert for the journey. Finding that he did not return, they resolved to go in search of him, and found him sorely wounded and unable to fly.

"Brothers," he said, "an accident has befallen me, but let not this prevent your going to a warmer climate. Winter is rapidly approaching, and you cannot remain here. It is better that I alone should die than for you all to suffer miserably on my account." "No! no!" they replied, with one voice, "we will not forsake you; we will share your sufferings; we will abandon our journey, and take care of you, as you did of us, before we were able to take care of ourselves. It the climate kills you, it shall kill us. Do you think we can so soon forget your brotherly care, which has surpassed a father's, and even a mother's kindness? Whether you live or die, we will live or die with you."

They sought out a hollow tree to winter in, and contrived to carry their wounded nestmate there; and, before the rigors of winter set in, they had stored up food enough to carry them through its severities. To make it last the better, two of the number went off south, leaving the other three to watch over, feed, and protect the wounded bird. Meeji-geeg-wona in due time recovered from his wound, and he repaid their kindness by giving them such advice and instruction in the art of hunting as his experience had qualified him to impart. As spring advanced, they began to venture out of their hiding-place, and were all successful in getting food to eke out their winter's stock, except the youngest, who was called Peepigeewi-zains, or the Pigeon Hawk. Being small and foolish, flying hither and yon, he always came back without anything. At last the Gray Eagle spoke to him, and demanded the cause of his ill luck. "It is not my smallness or weakness of body," said he, "that prevents my bringing home flesh

113

as well as my brothers. I kill ducks and other birds every time I go out; but, just as I get to the woods, a large Ko-ko-ko-ho[1] robs me of my prey." "Well! don't despair, brother," said Meeji-geeg-wona. "I now feel my strength perfectly recovered, and I will go out with you tomorrow," for he was the most courageous and warlike of them all.

Next day they went forth in company, the elder seating himself near the lake. Peepi-geewi-zains started out, and soon pounced upon a duck.

"Well done!" thought his brother, who saw his success; but, just as he was getting to land with his prize, up came a large white owl from a tree, where he had been watching, and laid claim to it. He was about wresting it from him, when Meeji-geeg-wona came up, and, fixing his talons in both sides of the owl, flew home with him.

The little pigeon hawk followed him closely, and was rejoiced and happy to think he had brought home something at last. He then flew in the owl's face, and wanted to tear out his eyes, and vented his passion in abundance of reproachful terms. "Softly," said the Gray Eagle; "do not be in such a passion, or exhibit so revengeful a disposition; for this will be a lesson to him not to tyrannize over any one who is weaker than himself for the future." So, after giving him good advice, and telling him what kind of herbs would cure his wounds, they let the owl go.

While this act was taking place, and before the liberated owl had yet got out of view, two visitors appeared at the hollow tree. They were the two nestmates, who had just returned from the south after passing the winter there, and they were thus all happily reunited, and each one soon chose a mate and flew off to the woods. Spring had now revisited the north. The cold winds had ceased, the ice had melted, the streams were open, and the forest began rapidly to put on its vernal hue. "But it is in vain," said the old man who related this story, "it is in vain that spring returns, if we are not thankful to the Master of Life who has preserved us through the winter. Nor does that man answer the end for which he was made who does not show a kind and charitable feeling to all who are in want or sickness, especially to his blood relations. These six birds only represent one of our impoverished northern families of children, who had been deprived of both their parents and the aid of their elder brother nearly at the same time."[2]

NOTES

1. Owl. [H. R. S.]
2. This tale is called "The Six Hawks or Broken Wing. An Allegory of Fraternal Affection" in *M. H.*, pp. 258-261. In the later collections it bears the title "Gray Eagle and His Five Brothers," *C. M.*, pp. 83-89; *C-C*, pp. 80-86.

THE THREE CRANBERRIES

A CHIPPEWA FABLE

THREE CRANBERRIES WERE LIVING IN A LODGE together. One was green, one white, and one red. They were sisters. There was snow on the ground; and as the men were absent, they felt afraid, and began to say to each other, "What shall we do if the wolf comes?" "I," said the green one, "will climb up a shingoub[1] tree." "I," said the white one, "will hide myself in the kettle of boiled hominy;" "and I," said the red one, "will conceal myself under the snow." Presently the wolves came, and each one did as she had said. But only one of the three had judged wisely. The wolves immediately ran to the kettle and ate up the corn, and, with it, the white cranberry. The red one was trampled to pieces by their feet, and her blood spotted the snow. But she who had climbed the thick spruce tree escaped notice, and was saved.[2]

NOTES

1. Spruce. [H. R. S.]
2. Nowhere else does Schoolcraft retell this fable, not even in the delightful little series that he calls "Nursery Cradle Songs of the Forest," *The Indian and his Wigwam* (1848), pp. 390-398.

115

PARADISE OPENED TO THE INDIANS[1]

Historical Note.—The following is a literal translation of the story related by the noted Algic chief Pontiac, to the Indian tribes whom he wished to bring into his views in forming his general confederacy against the Anglo-Saxon race in the last century. It is taken from an ancient manuscript journal now in the possession of the Michigan Historical Society. This journal, the preservation of which is due to one of the French families at Detroit, appears to have been kept by a person holding an official station, or intimate with the affairs of the day,[2] during the siege of the fort of Detroit by the confederate Indians in 1763. It is minute in its details of the transactions of every day, from the investment of the fort until the disaster of the sortie made by the English garrison in the direction of Bloody Run. And its authenticity has never been brought into question. There is no air of exaggeration in the narrative. There is nothing recorded in the process of the negotiations, the siege, or the disclosure of the plot preceding it, which was not perfectly reasonable under the circumstances, and in keeping with the character of the tribes and their means of action.

That a document of so much historical interest might be the better preserved, the society took measures, about a twelvemonth since, for its translation; and the tale here furnished is a transcript of this particular portion of the journal. The only addition to the text consists of the insertion of four or five words of ordinary use in the narrative, which appear to have been obliterated by a chemical change in the ink in a few places.

Without entering into the moral bearing of this curious specimen of Indian fiction, it may be regarded as no equivocal testimony of the sagacity and foresight of its celebrated author. To turn the mythology and superstitious belief of his auditors to political account, was certainly a capital stroke of policy. And no stronger proof could, perhaps, be adduced of the existence of the popular belief on this head, and the prevalence, at that time, of oral tales and fanciful legends among the tribes.

AN INDIAN OF THE LENAPEE[3] TRIBE, anxious to know the Master of Life, resolved, without mentioning his design to anyone, to undertake a journey to Paradise, which he knew to be God's residence. But, to succeed in his project, it was necessary for him to know the way to the celestial regions. Not knowing any person who, having been there himself, might aid him in finding the road, he commenced juggling [conjuring], in the hope of drawing a good augury from his dream.

The Indian, in his dream, imagined that he had only to commence his journey, and that a continued walk would take him to the celestial abode. The next morning very early, he equipped himself as a hunter, taking a gun, powder-horn, ammunition, and a boiler to cook his provisions. The first part of his journey was pretty favorable; he walked a long time without being discouraged, having always a firm conviction that he should attain his aim. Eight days had already elapsed without his meeting with anyone to oppose his desire. On the evening of the eighth day, at sunset, he stopped as usual on the bank of a brook, at the entrance of a little prairie, a place which he thought favorable for his night's encampment. As he was preparing his lodging, he perceived at the other end of the prairie three very wide and well-beaten paths; he thought this somewhat singular; he, however, continued to prepare his wigwam, that he might shelter himself from the weather. He also lighted a fire. While cooking, he found that, the darker it grew, the more distinct were those paths. This surprised, nay, even frightened him; he hesitated a few moments. Was it better for him to remain in his camp, or seek another at some distance? While in this incertitude, he remembered his juggling, or rather his dream. He thought that his only aim in undertaking his journey was to see the Master of Life. This restored him to his senses. He thought it probable that one of those three roads led to the place which he wished to visit. He therefore resolved upon remaining in his camp until the morrow, when he would, at random, take one of them. His curiosity, however, scarcely allowed him time to take his meal; he left his encampment and fire, and took the widest of the paths. He followed it until the middle of the day without seeing anything to impede his progress; but, as he was resting a little to take breath, he suddenly perceived a large fire coming from under ground. It excited his curiosity; he went towards it to see what it might be; but, as the fire appeared to increase as he drew nearer, he was so overcome with fear, that he turned back and took the widest of the other two paths. Having followed it for the same space of time as he had the first, he perceived a similar spectacle. His fright, which had been lulled by the change of road, awoke, and he was obliged to take the third path, in which he walked a whole day without seeing anything. All at once, a mountain of a marvelous whiteness burst upon his sight. This filled him with astonishment; nevertheless, he took courage and advanced to examine it. Having arrived at the foot, he saw no signs of a road. He became very sad, not knowing how to continue his journey. In this conjuncture, he looked on all sides and perceived a female seated upon the mountain; her beauty was dazzling, and the whiteness of her garments surpassed that of snow. The woman said to him in his own language, "You appear surprised to find no longer a path to reach your wishes. I know that you have for a long time longed to see and speak to the Master of Life; and that you have undertaken this journey purposely to see him. The way which leads to his abode is upon this mountain. To ascend it, you must undress yourself completely, and leave all your accouterments and clothing at the foot. No person shall injure them. You will then go and wash yourself in the river which I am now showing you, and afterward ascend the mountain."

The Indian obeyed punctually the woman's words; but one difficulty remained. How could he arrive at the top of the mountain, which was steep, without a path, and as smooth as glass? He asked the woman how he was to accomplish it. She replied, that if he really wished to see the Master of Life, he must, in mounting, only use his left hand and foot. This appeared almost impossible to the Indian. Encouraged, however, by the female, he commenced ascending, and succeeded after much trouble. When at the top, he was astonished to see no person, the woman having disappeared. He found himself alone, and without a guide. Three unknown villages were in sight; they were constructed on a different plan from his own, much handsomer, and more regular. After a few moments' reflection, he took his way towards the handsomest. When about halfway from the top of the mountain, he recollected that he was naked, and was afraid to proceed; but a voice told him to advance, and have no apprehensions; that, as he had washed himself, he might walk in confidence. He proceeded without hesitation to a place which appeared to be the gate of the village, and stopped until someone came to open it. While he was considering the exterior of the village, the gate opened, and the Indian saw coming towards him a handsome man dressed all in white, who took him by the hand, and said he was going to satisfy his wishes by leading him to the presence of the Master of Life.

The Indian suffered himself to be conducted, and they arrived at a place of unequaled beauty. The Indian was lost in admiration. He there saw the Master of Life, who took him by the hand, and gave him for a seat a hat bordered with gold. The Indian, afraid of spoiling the hat, hesitated to sit down; but, being again ordered to do so, he obeyed without reply.

The Indian being seated, God said to him, "I am the Master of Life, whom thou wishest to see, and to whom thou wishest to speak. Listen to that which I will tell thee for thyself and for all the Indians. I am the Maker of Heaven and earth, the trees, lakes, rivers, men, and all that thou seest or hast seen on the earth or in the heavens; and because I love you, you must do my will; you must also avoid that which I hate; I hate you to drink as you do, until you lose your reason; I wish you not to fight one another; you take two wives, or run after other people's wives; you do wrong; I hate such conduct; you should have but one wife, and keep her until death. When you go to war, you juggle,[4] you sing the medicine song, thinking you speak to me; you deceive yourselves; it is to the Manito that you speak; he is a wicked spirit who induces you to evil, and, for want of knowing me, you listen to him.

"The land on which you are, I have made for you, not for others: wherefore do you suffer the whites to dwell upon your lands? Can you not do without them? I know that those whom you call the children of your great Father supply your wants. But, were you not wicked as you are, you would not need them. You might live as you did before you knew them. Before those whom you call your brothers had arrived, did not your bow and arrow maintain you? You needed neither gun, powder, nor any other object. The flesh of animals was your food, their skins your raiment. But when I saw you inclined to evil, I removed the animals into the depths of the forest, that you might depend on your brothers for your necessaries, for your clothing. Again become good and do my will, and I will send animals for your sustenance. I do not, however, forbid suffering among you your Father's children; I love them, they know me, they pray to me; I supply their own wants, and give them that which they bring to you. Not so with those who are come to trouble your possessions. Drive them away; wage war against them. I love them not. They know me not. They are my enemies, they are your brothers' enemies. Send them back to the lands I have made for them. Let them remain there.

"Here is a written prayer which I give thee; learn it by heart, and teach it to all the Indians and children." (The Indian, observing here that he could not read, the Master of Life told him that, on his return upon earth, he should give it to the chief of his village, who would read it, and also teach it to him, as also to all the Indians.) "It must be repeated," said the Master of Life, "morning and evening. Do all that I have told thee, and announce it to all the Indians as coming from the Master of Life. Let them drink but one draught, or two at most, in one day. Let them have but one wife, and discontinue running after other people's wives and daughters. Let them not fight one another. Let them not sing the medicine song, for in singing the medicine song they speak to the evil spirit. Drive from your lands," added the Master of Life, "those dogs in red clothing; they are only an injury to you. When you want anything, apply to me, as your brothers do, and I will give to both. Do not sell to your brothers that which I have placed on the earth as food. In short, become good, and you shall want nothing. When you meet one another, bow, and give one another the . . . hand of the heart. Above all, I command thee to repeat, morning and evening, the prayer which I have given thee."

The Indian promised to do the will of the Master of Life, and also to recommend it strongly to the Indians; adding that the Master of Life should be satisfied with them.

His conductor then came, and, leading him to the foot of the mountain, told him to take his garments and return to his village; which was immediately done by the Indian.

His return much surprised the inhabitants of the village, who did not know what had become of him. They asked him whence he came; but, as he had been enjoined to speak to no one until he saw the chief of the village, he motioned to them with his hand that he came from above. Having entered the village, he went immediately to the chief's wigwam, and delivered to him the prayer and laws entrusted to his care by the Master of Life.[5]

NOTES

1. For the story of the manuscript and Francis Parkman's use of it see *Journal of Pontiac's Conspiracy* (Detroit, 1912) edited by Agnes Burton. Professor R. Clyde Ford of Michigan State Normal College translated the French for Mrs. Burton.

2. Parkman had conjectured that the journal had been written by a French priest. Ford, however, agreed with Schoolcraft that it was the work of a professional record keeper, probably Robert Navarre.

3. Delawares. [H. R. S.]

4. Schoolcraft's translator thus rendered *"vous jonglez"*; more properly "you conjure."

5. This legend is printed, with parallel French text, on pages 22-32 of the Burton edition. As "Eroneniera, or An Indian Visit to the Great Spirit. An Algonquin Legend," it was reprinted in *M. H.*, pp. 251-257.

END OF VOL. I.

ALGIC RESEARCHES,

COMPRISING

INQUIRIES RESPECTING THE MENTAL CHARACTERISTICS

OF THE

NORTH AMERICAN INDIANS

FIRST SERIES

INDIAN TALES AND LEGENDS

IN TWO VOLUMES

VOL. II

BY HENRY ROWE SCHOOLCRAFT

Author of a Narrative Journal of Travels to the Sources of the Mississippi;
Travels in the Central Portions of the Mississippi Valley;
An Expedition to Itasca Lake, &c.

NEW-YORK:

HARPER & BROTHERS, 82 CLIFF-STREET

1839

CONTENTS

Volume II

THE RED SWAN

FROM THE ALGIC[1]

THREE BROTHERS WERE LEFT DESTITUTE, by the death of their parents, at an early age. The eldest was not yet able to provide fully for their support, but did all he could in hunting, and with his aid, and the stock of provisions left by their father, they were preserved and kept alive, rather, it seems, by miraculous interposition, than the adequacy of their own exertions. For the father had been a hermit,[2] having removed far away from the body of the tribe, so that when he and his wife died they left their children without neighbors and friends, and the lads had no idea that there was a human being near them. They did not even know who their parents had been, for the eldest was too young, at the time of their death, to remember it. Forlorn as they were, they did not, however, give up to despondency, but made use of every exertion they could, and in process of time, learned the art of hunting and killing animals. The eldest soon became an expert hunter, and was very successful in procuring food. He was noted for his skill in killing buffalo, elk, and moose, and he instructed his brothers in the arts of the forest as soon as they became old enough to follow him. After they had become able to hunt and take care of themselves, the elder proposed to leave them, and go in search of habitations, promising to return as soon as he could procure them wives. In this project he was overruled by his brothers, who said they could not part with him. Maujeekewis, the second eldest, was loud in his disapproval, saying, "What will you do with *those you propose to get*—we have lived so long without them, and we can still do without them." His words prevailed, and the three brothers continued together for a time.

One day they agreed to kill, each, a male of those kind of animals each was most expert in hunting, for the purpose of making quivers from their skins. They did so, and immediately commenced making arrows to fill their quivers, that they might be prepared for any emergency. Soon after, they hunted on a wager, to see who should come in first with game, and prepare it so as to regale the others. They were to shoot no other animal, but such as each was in the habit of killing. They set out different ways; Odjibwa, the youngest, had not gone far before he saw a bear, an animal he was not to kill, by the agreement. He followed him close and drove an arrow through him, which brought him to the ground. Although contrary to the bet, he immediately commenced skinning him, when suddenly something red tinged all the air around him. He rubbed his eyes, thinking he was perhaps deceived, but without effect, for the red hue continued. At length he heard a strange noise at a distance. It first appeared like a human voice, but after following the sound for some distance, he reached the shores of a lake, and soon saw the object he was looking for. At a distance out in the lake, sat a most beautiful Red Swan, whose plumage glittered in the sun, and who would, now and then, make the same noise he had heard. He was within long bow shot, and pulling the arrow from the bow-string up to his ear, took deliberate aim and shot. The arrow took no effect; and he shot and shot again till his quiver was empty. Still the swan remained, moving round and round, stretching its long neck and dipping its bill into the water, as if heedless of the arrows shot at it. Odjibwa ran home, and got all his own and his brothers' arrows, and shot them all away. He then stood and gazed at the beautiful bird. While standing, he remembered his brother's saying that in ·their deceased father's medicine sack were three magic arrows. Off he started, his anxiety to kill the swan overcoming all scruples. At any other time, he would have deemed it sacrilege to open his father's medicine sack, but now he hastily seized the three arrows and ran back, leaving the other contents of the sack scattered over the lodge. The swan was still there. He shot the first arrow with great precision, and came very near to it. The second came still closer; as he took the last arrow, he felt his arm firmer, and drawing it up with vigor, saw it pass through the neck of the swan a little above the breast. Still it did not prevent the bird from flying off, which it did, however, at first slowly, flapping its wings and rising gradually into the air, and then flying off toward the sinking of the sun.[3] Odjibwa was disappointed; he knew that his brothers would be displeased with him; he rushed into the water and rescued the two magic arrows, the third was carried off by the swan; but he thought that it could not fly very far with it, and let the consequences be what they might, he was bent on following it.

Off he started on the run; he was noted for speed, for he would shoot an arrow, and then run so fast that the arrow always fell behind him. I can run fast, he thought, and I can get up with the swan sometime or other. He thus ran over hills and prairies, toward the west, till near night, and was only going to take one more run, and then seek a place to sleep for the night, when suddenly he heard noises at a distance, which he knew were from people; for some were cutting trees, and the strokes of their axes echoed through the woods. When he emerged from the forest, the sun was just falling below the horizon, and he felt pleased to find a place to sleep in, and get something to eat, as he had left home without a mouthful. All these circumstances could not damp his ardor for the accomplishment of his object, and he felt that if he only persevered, he could succeed. At a distance, on a rising piece of ground, he could see an extensive town. He went toward it, but soon heard the watchman, MUDJEE-KOKOKOHO, who was placed on some height, to overlook the place, and give notice of the approach of friends or foes—crying out, "We are visited;" and a loud holla indicated that they all heard it. The young man advanced, and was pointed by the watchman to the lodge of the chief, "It is there you must go in," he said, and left him. "Come in, come in," said the chief, "take a seat there," pointing to the side where his daughter sat. "It is there you must sit." Soon they gave him something to eat, and very few questions were asked him, being a stranger. It was only when he spoke, that the others answered him. "Daughter," said the chief, after dark, "take our son-in-law's moccasins, and see if they be torn; if so, mend them for him, and bring in his bundle." The young man thought it strange that he should be so warmly received, and married instantly, without his wishing it, although the young girl was pretty. It was sometime before she would take his moccasins, which he had taken off. It displeased him to see her so reluctant to do so, and when she did reach them, he snatched them out of her hand and hung them up himself. He laid down and thought of the swan, and made up his mind to be off by dawn. He awoke early, and spoke to the young woman, but she gave no answer. He slightly touched her. "What do you want?" she said, and turned her back toward him. "Tell me," he said, "what time the swan passed. I am following it, and come out and point the direction." "Do you think you can catch up to it?" she said. "Yes," he answered. "Naubesah," (foolishness) she said. She, however, went out and pointed in the direction he should go. The young man went slowly till the sun arose, when he commenced traveling at his accustomed speed. He passed the day in running, and when night came, he was unexpectedly pleased to find himself near another town; and when at a distance, he heard the watchman crying out, "We are visited;" and soon the men of the village stood out to see the stranger. He was again told to enter the lodge of the chief, and his reception was, in every respect, the same as he met the previous night; only that the young woman was more beautiful, and received him very kindly, and although urged to stay, his mind was fixed on the object of his journey. Before daylight he asked the young woman what time the Red Swan passed, and to point out the way. She did so, and said it passed yesterday when the sun was between midday and *pungishemoo*—its falling place. He again set out rather slowly, but when the sun had arisen he tried his speed by shooting an arrow ahead, and running after it; but it fell behind him. Nothing remarkable happened in the course of the day, and he went on leisurely. Toward night, he came to the lodge of an old man. Sometime after dark he saw a light emitted from a small low lodge. He went up to it very slyly, and peeping through the door, saw an old man alone, warming his back before the fire, with his head down on his breast. He thought the old man did not know that he was standing near the door, but in this he was disappointed; for so soon as he looked in, "Walk in, Nosis,"[4] he said, "take a seat opposite to me, and take off your things and dry them, for you must be fatigued; and I will prepare you something to eat." Odjibwa did as he was requested. The old man, whom he perceived to be a magician, then said, "My kettle with water stands near the fire," and immediately a small earthen or a kind of metallic pot with legs appeared by the fire. He then took one grain of corn, also one whortleberry, and put them in the pot. As the young man was very hungry, he thought that his chance for a supper was but small. Not a word or a look, however, revealed his feelings. The pot soon boiled, when the old man spoke, commanding it to stand some distance from the fire; "Nosis," said he, "feed yourself," and he handed him a dish and ladle made out of the same metal as the pot. The young man helped himself to all that was in the pot; he felt ashamed to think of his having done so, but before he could speak, the old man said, "Nosis, eat, eat;" and soon after he again said, "help yourself from the pot." Odjibwa was surprised on looking into it to see it full, he kept on taking *all out,* and as soon as it was done, it was again filled, till he had amply satisfied his hunger. The magician then spoke, and the pot occupied its accustomed place in one part of the lodge. The young man then leisurely reclined back, and listened to the predictions of his entertainer who told him to keep on, and he would obtain his object. "To tell you more," said he, "I am not permitted; but go on as you have commenced, and you will not be disappointed; tomorrow you will again reach one of my fellow old men; but the one you will see after him will tell you all, and the manner in which you will proceed to accomplish your journey. Often has this Red Swan passed, and those who have followed it have never returned: but you must be firm in your resolution, and be prepared for all events." "So will it be," answered Odjibwa, and they both laid[5] down to sleep. Early in the morning, the old man had his magic kettle prepared, so that his guest should eat before leaving. When leaving, the old man gave him his parting advice.

Odjibwa set out in better spirits than he had done since leaving home. Night again found him in company with an old man, who received him kindly, and directed him on his way in the morning. He traveled with a light heart, expecting to meet the one who was to give him directions how to proceed to get the Red Swan. Toward nightfall, he reached the third old man's lodge. Before coming to the door, he heard him saying, "Nosis, come in," and going in immediately, he felt quite at home. The old man prepared him something to eat, acting as the other magicians had done, and his kettle was of the same dimensions and material. The old man waited till he had done eating, when he commenced addressing him. "Young man, the errand you are on is very difficult. Numbers of young men have passed with the same purpose, but never returned. Be careful, and if your guardian spirits are powerful, you may succeed. This Red Swan you are following, is the daughter of a magician, who has plenty of everything, but he values his daughter but little less than wampum. He wore a cap of wampum, which was attached to his scalp; but powerful Indians—warriors of a distant chief, came and told him, that their chief's daughter was on the brink of the grave, and she herself requested his scalp of wampum to effect a cure. If I can only see it, I will recover, she said, and it was for this reason they came, and after long urging the magician, he at last consented to part with it, only from the idea of restoring the young woman to health; although when he took it off, it left his head bare and bloody. Several years have passed since, and it has not healed. The warriors' coming for it was only a cheat, and they are now constantly making sport of it, dancing it about from village to village; and on every insult it receives the old man groans from pain. Those Indians are too powerful for the magician, and numbers have sacrificed themselves to recover it for him, but without success. The Red Swan has enticed many a young man, as she has done you, in order to get them to procure it, and whoever is the fortunate one that succeeds, will receive the Red Swan as his reward. In the morning you will proceed on your way, and toward evening you will come to the magician's lodge, but before you enter you will hear his groans; he will immediately ask you in, and you will see no one but himself; he will make inquiries of you, as regards your dreams, and the powers of your guardian spirits; he will then ask you to attempt the recovery of his scalp; he will show you the direction, and if you feel inclined, as I dare say you do, go forward, my son, with a strong heart, persevere, and I have a presentiment you will succeed." The young man answered, "I will try." Early next morning after having eaten from the magic kettle, he started off on his journey. Toward evening he came to the lodge as he was told, and soon heard the groans of the magician. "Come in," he said, even before the young man reached the door. On entering he saw his head all bloody, and he was groaning most terribly. "Sit down, sit down," he said, "while I prepare you something to eat," at the same time doing as the other magicians had done, in preparing food—"You see," he said, "how poor I am; I have to attend to all my wants." He said this to conceal the fact that the Red Swan was there, but Odjibwa perceived that the lodge was partitioned, and he heard a rustling noise, now and then, in that quarter, which satisfied him that it was occupied. After having taken his leggings and moccasins off, and eaten, the old magician commenced telling him how he had lost his scalp—the insults it was receiving—the pain he was suffering in consequence—his wishes to regain it—the unsuccessful attempts that had already been made, and the numbers and power of those who detained it; stated the best and most probable way of getting it; touching the young man on his pride and ambition, by the proposed adventure, and last, he spoke of such things as would make an Indian rich. He would interrupt his discourse by now and then groaning, and saying, "Oh, how shamefully they are treating it!" Odjibwa listened with solemn attention. The old man then asked him about his dreams. His dreams (or as *he saw when asleep*[6]), at the particular time he had fasted and blackened his face to procure guardian spirits.

The young man then told him one dream; the magician groaned; "No, that is not it," he said. The young man told him another. He groaned again; "That is not it," he said. The young man told him of two or three others. The magician groaned at each recital, and said, rather peevishly, "No, those are not they." The young man then thought to himself, Who are you? you may groan as much as you please; I am inclined not to tell you any more dreams. The magician then spoke in rather a supplicating tone. "Have you no more dreams of another kind?" "Yes," said the young man, and told him one. "That is it, that is it," he cried; "you will cause me to live. That was what I was wishing you to say;" and he rejoiced greatly. "Will you then go and see if you cannot procure my scalp?" "Yes," said the young man. "I will go; and the day after tomorrow,[7] when you hear the cries of the Kakak,[8] you will know, by this sign, that I am successful, and you must prepare your head, and lean it out through the door, so that the moment I arrive, I may place your scalp on." "Yes, yes," said the magician; "as you say, it will be done." Early next morning, he set out on his perilous adventure, and about the time that the sun hangs toward home, (afternoon) he heard the shouts of a great many people. He was in a wood at the time, and saw, as he thought, only a few men; but the farther he went, the more numerous they appeared. On emerging into a plain, their heads appeared like the hanging leaves for number. In the center he perceived a post, and something waving on it, which was the scalp. Now and then the air was rent with the sau-sau-quan, for they were dancing the war dance around it. Before he could be perceived, he turned himself into a No-noskau-see (humming bird), and flew toward the scalp.

As he passed some of those who were standing by he flew close to their ears, making the humming noise which this bird does when it flies. They jumped on one side and asked each other what it could be. By this time he had nearly reached the scalp, but fearing he should be perceived while untying it, he changed himself into a Me-sau-be-wau-aun (the down of anything that floats lightly on the air), and then floated slowly and lightly onto the scalp. He untied it, and moved off slowly, as the weight was almost too great. It was as much as he could do to keep it up, and prevent the Indians from snatching it away. The moment they saw it was moving, they filled the air with their cries of "It is taken from us; it is taken from us." He continued moving a few feet above them: the rush and hum of the people was like the dead beating surges after a storm. He soon gained on them, and they gave up the pursuit. After going a little farther he changed himself into a Kakak, and flew off with his prize, making that peculiar noise which this bird makes.

In the meantime, the magician had followed his instructions, placing his head outside of the lodge, as soon as he heard the cry of the Kakak, and soon after he heard the rustling of its wings. In a moment Odjibwa stood before him. He immediately gave the magician a severe blow on the head with the wampum scalp: his limbs extended and quivered in agony from the effects of the blow: the scalp adhered, and the young man walked in and sat down, feeling perfectly at home. The magician was so long in recovering from the stunning blow, that the young man feared he had killed him. He was however pleased to see him show signs of life; he first commenced moving, and soon sat up. But how surprised was Odjibwa to see, not an aged man, far in years and decrepitude, but one of the handsomest young men he ever saw stand up before him.

"Thank you, my *friend*," he said; "you see that your kindness and bravery has restored me to my former shape. It was so ordained, and you have now accomplished the victory." The young magician urged the stay of his deliverer for a few days; and they soon formed a warm attachment for each other. The magician never alluded to the Red Swan in their conversations.

At last, the day arrived when Odjibwa made preparations to return. The young magician amply repaid him for his kindness and bravery, by various kinds of wampum, robes, and all such things as he had need of to make him an influential man. But though the young man's curiosity was at its height about the Red Swan, he controlled his feelings, and never so much as even hinted of her; feeling that he would surrender a point of propriety in so doing; while the one he had rendered such service to, whose hospitality he was now enjoying, and who had richly rewarded him, had never so much as even mentioned anything about her, but studiously concealed her.

Odjibwa's pack for traveling was ready, and he was taking his farewell smoke, when the young magician thus addressed him: "Friend, you know for what cause you came thus far. You have accomplished your object, and conferred a lasting obligation on me. Your perseverance shall not go unrewarded; and if you undertake other things with the same spirit you have this, you will never fail to accomplish them. My duty renders it necessary for me to remain where I am, although I should feel happy to go with you. I have given you all you will need as long as you live; but I see you feel backward to speak about the Red Swan. I vowed that whoever procured me my scalp, should be rewarded by possessing the Red Swan." He then spoke, and knocked on the partition. The door immediately opened, and the Red Swan met his eager gaze. She was a most beautiful female, and as she stood majestically before him, it would be impossible to describe her charms, for she looked as if she did not belong to earth. "Take her," the young magician said; "she is my sister, treat her well; she is worthy of you, and what you have done for me merits more. She is ready to go with you to your kindred and friends, and has been so ever since your arrival, and my good wishes go with you both." She then looked very kindly on her husband, who now bid farewell to his friend indeed, and accompanied by the object of his wishes, he commenced retracing his footsteps.

They traveled slowly, and after two or three days reached the lodge of the third old man, who had fed him from his small magic pot. He was very kind, and said, "You see what your perseverance has procured you; do so always and you will succeed in all things you undertake."

On the following morning when they were going to start, he pulled from the side of the lodge a bag, which he presented to the young man, saying, "Nosis, I give you this; it contains a present for you; and I hope you will live happily till old age." They then bid farewell to him and proceeded on.

They soon reached the second old man's lodge. Their reception there was the same as at the first; he also gave them a present, with the old man's wishes that they would be happy. They went on and reached the first town, which the young man had passed in his pursuit. The watchman gave notice, and he was shown into the chief's lodge. "Sit down there, son-in-law," said the chief, pointing to a place near his daughter. "And you also," he said to the Red Swan.

The young woman of the lodge was busy in making something, but she tried to show her indifference about what was taking place, for she did not even raise her head to see who was come. Soon the chief said, "Let someone bring in the bundle of our son-in-law." When it was brought in, the young man opened one of the bags, which he had received from one of the old men; it contained wampum, robes, and various other articles; he presented them to his father-in-law, and all expressed their surprise at the value and richness of the gift. The chief's daughter then only stole a glance at the present, then at Odjibwa and his beautiful wife; she stopped working, and remained silent and thoughtful all the evening. They conversed about his adventures; after this the chief told him that he should take his daughter along with him in the morning—the young man said "Yes." The chief then spoke out, saying, "Daughter, be ready to go with him in the morning."

There was a Maujeekewis in the lodge, who thought to have got the young woman to wife; he jumped up, saying, "Who is he (meaning the young man), that he should take her for a few presents? I will kill him," and he raised a knife which he had in his hand. But he only waited till someone held him back, and then sat down, for he was too great a coward to do as he had threatened. Early they took their departure, amid the greetings of their new friends, and toward evening reached the other town. The watchman gave the signal, and numbers of men, women, and children stood out to see them. They were again shown into the chief's lodge, who welcomed them by saying, "Son-in-law, you are welcome," and requested him to take a seat by his daughter; and the two women did the same.

After the usual formalities of smoking and eating, the chief requested the young man to relate his travels in the hearing of all the inmates of the lodge, and those who came to see. They looked with admiration and astonishment at the Red Swan, for she was so beautiful. Odjibwa gave them his whole history. The chief then told him that his brothers had been to their town in search of him, but had returned, and given up all hopes of ever seeing him again. He concluded by saying that since he had been so fortunate and so manly, he should take his daughter with him; "For although your brothers," said he, "were here, they were too timid to enter any of our lodges, and merely inquired for you and returned. You will take my daughter, treat her well, and that will bind us more closely together."

It is always the case in towns, that someone in it is foolish or clownish. It happened to be so here; for a Maujeekewis was in the lodge; and after the young man had given his father-in-law presents, as he did to the first, this Maujeekewis jumped up in a passion, saying, "Who is this stranger, that he should have her? I want her myself." The chief told him to be quiet, and not to disturb or quarrel with one who was enjoying their hospitality. "No, no," he boisterously cried, and made an attempt to strike the stranger. Odjibwa was above fearing his threats, and paid no attention to him. He cried the louder, "I will have her; I will have her." In an instant he was laid flat on the ground from a blow of a war-club given by the chief. After he came to himself, the chief upbraided him for his foolishness, and told him to go out and tell stories to the old women.

Their arrangements were then made, and the stranger invited a number of families to go and visit their hunting grounds, as there was plenty of game. They consented, and in the morning a large party were assembled to accompany the young man; and the chief with a large party of warriors escorted them a long distance. When ready to return the chief made a speech, and invoked the blessing of the great good Spirit on his son-in-law and party.

After a number of days' travel, Odjibwa and his party came in sight of his home. The party rested while he went alone in advance to see his brothers. When he entered the lodge he found it all dirty and covered with ashes: on one side was his eldest brother, with his face blackened, and sitting amid ashes, crying aloud. On the other side was Maujeekewis, his other brother; his face was also blackened, but his head was covered with feathers and swan's down; he looked so odd, that the young man could not keep from laughing, for he appeared and pretended to be so absorbed with grief that he did not notice his brother's arrival. The eldest jumped up and shook hands with him and kissed him, and felt very happy to see him again.

Odjibwa, after seeing all things put to rights, told them that he had brought each of them a wife. When Maujeekewis heard about the wife, he jumped up and said, "Why, is it just now that you have come?" and made for the door and peeped out to see the women. He then commenced jumping and laughing, saying, "Women! women!" That was the only reception he gave his brother. Odjibwa then told them to wash themselves and prepare, for he would go and fetch them in. Maujeekewis jumped and washed himself, but would every now and then go and peep out to see the women. When they came near he said, I will have this one, and that one, he did not exactly know which—he would go and sit down for an instant, and then go and peep and laugh; he acted like a madman.

As soon as order was restored, and all seated, Odjibwa presented one of the women to his eldest brother, saying, "These women are given to me; I now give one to each; I intended so from the first." Maujeekewis spoke, and said, "I think three wives would have been *enough* for you." The young man led one to Maujeekewis, saying, "My brother, here is one for you, and live happily." Maujeekewis hung down his head as if he was ashamed, but would every now and then steal a glance at his wife, and also at the other women. By and by he turned toward his wife, and acted as if he had been married for years. "Wife," he said, "I will go and hunt," and off he started.

All lived peaceably for some time, and their town prospered, the inhabitants increased, and everything was abundant among them. One day dissatisfaction was manifested in the conduct of the two elder brothers, on account of Odjibwa's having taken their deceased father's magic arrows: they upbraided and urged him to procure others if he could. Their object was to get him away, so that one of them might afterward get his wife. One day, after listening to them, he told them he would go. Maujeekewis and himself went together into a sweating lodge to purify themselves. Even there, although it was held sacred, Maujeekewis upbraided him for the arrows. He told him again he would go; and next day, true to his word, he left them. After traveling a long way he came to an opening in the earth, and descending, it led him to the abode of departed spirits. The country appeared beautiful, the extent of it was lost in the distance: he saw animals of various kinds in abundance. The first he came near to were buffaloes; his surprise was great when these animals addressed him as human beings. They asked him what he came for, how he descended, why he was so bold as to visit the abode of the dead. He told them he was in search of magic arrows to appease his brothers. "Very well," said the leader of the buffaloes, whose whole form was nothing but bone. "Yes, we know it," and he and his followers moved off a little space as if they were afraid of him. "You have come," resumed the Buffalo Spirit, "to a place where a living man has never before been. You will return immediately to your tribe, for your brothers are trying to dishonor your wife; and you will live to a very old age, and live and die happily; you can go no farther in these abodes of ours." Odjibwa looked, as he thought, to the west, and saw a bright light, as if the sun was shining in its splendor, but he saw no sun. "What light is that I see yonder?" he asked. The all-boned buffalo answered, "It is the place where those who were good dwell." And that dark cloud?" Odjibwa again asked. "Mudjee-izzhi-wabezewin" (wickedness), answered the buffalo. He asked no more questions, and with the aid of his guardian spirits, again stood on this earth and saw the sun giving light as usual, and breathed the pure air. All else he saw in the abodes of the dead and his travels and actions previous to his return, are unknown. After wandering a long time in quest of information to make his people happy, he one evening drew near to his village or town, passing all the other lodges and coming to his own, he heard his brothers at high words with each other; they were quarreling for the possession of his wife. She had, however, remained constant and mourned the absence and probable loss of her husband; but she had mourned him with the dignity of virtue. The noble youth listened till he was satisfied of the base principles of his brothers. He then entered the lodge, with the stern air and conscious dignity of a brave and honest man. He spoke not a word, but placing the magic arrows to his bow, drew them to their length and laid the brothers dead at his feet. Thus ended the contest between the hermit's sons, and a firm and happy union was consummated between ODJIBWA,[9] or him of the primitive or gathered voice, and the Red Swan.[10]

NOTES

1. Subtitle omitted in *M. H.*
2. Pai-gwud-aw-diz-zid. [H. R. S.]
3. Pungish-e-moo, falling or sinking to a position of repose. [H. R. S.]
4. My grandchild. [H. R. S.]
5. Many seeming flaws in grammatical construction are attributable to linguistic changes since Schoolcraft wrote. "Laid" for "lay" was common usage in the early nineteenth century, before the school grammarians proscribed it.
6. Enaw-bandum. [H. R. S.]

7. The Indian expression is Awuss-Waubung—the day *beyond* tomorrow. [H. R. S.]

8. A species of hawk. [H. R. S.]

9. This word may be a derivative from Ojeebik, a root, etc. and maidwa, voice, or from odjeebwuh, to gather, v. a. [H. R. S.] Note omitted from *M. H.*

10. "The Red Swan," pp. 161-179, *M. H.*, was later reprinted by *C. M.*, pp. 138-169, and *C-C*, pp. 42-71.

AGGO DAH GAUDA

THE MAN WITH HIS LEG TIED UP[1]

AGGO DAH GAUDA HAD ONE LEG LOOPED up to his thigh, so that he was obliged to get along by hopping. He had a beautiful daughter, and his chief care was to secure her from being carried off by the king of the buffaloes. It was a peculiarity in which he differed from other Indians, that he lived in a log house, and he advised his daughter to keep in doors and never go out into the neighborhood for fear of being stolen away.

One sunshiny morning Aggo Dah Gauda prepared to go out a-fishing, but before he left the lodge reminded his daughter of her strange and persecuting lover. "My daughter," said he, "I am going out to fish, and as the day will be a pleasant one, you must recollect that we have an enemy near, who is constantly going about, and do not expose yourself out of the lodge." When he had reached his fishing ground, he heard a voice singing at a distance the following strains, in derision of him.

> Aggo Dah Gauda
> Aggo Dah Gauda
> Ke anne po—po—
> Ko no gun a.

> Aggo Dah Gauda
> Aggo Dah Gauda
> Ke anne po—po—
> Ko gau da.

> Man with the leg tied up,
> Man with the leg tied up,
> Broken hip—hip—
> > Hipped.

> Man with the leg tied up,
> Man with the leg tied up,
> Broken leg—leg—
> > Legged.[2]

He saw no one, but suspecting it to come from his enemies the buffaloes, he hastened his return.

Let us now see what happened to the daughter. Her father had not been

135

long absent from the lodge, when she thought in her mind [*ke in ain dum*],
it is hard to be thus forever kept indoors. The spring is now coming on,
and the days are so sunny and warm, that it would be very pleasant to sit
outdoors. But my father says it would be dangerous. I know what I will
do. I will get on the top of the house, and there I can comb and dress my
hair. She accordingly got up on the roof of the small house, and busied
herself in untying and combing her beautiful hair. For her hair was not
only of a fine glossy quality, but was so long that it reached down on the
ground, and hung over the eaves of the house, as she sat dressing it. She
was so intent upon this, that she forgot all ideas of danger, till it was too
late to escape. For, all of a sudden, the king[3] of the buffaloes came dashing
on, with his herd of followers, and taking her between his horns, away he
cantered over the plains, plunged into a river that bounded his land, and
carried her safely to his lodge, on the other side. Here he paid every attention to gain her affections, but all to no purpose, for she sat pensively and
disconsolate in the lodge among the other females, and scarcely ever spoke,
and took no part in the domestic cares of her lover the king. He, on the
contrary did everything he could think of to please her and win her affections. He told the others in his lodge to give her everything she wanted,
and to be careful not to displease her. They set before her the choicest food.
They gave her the seat of honor in the lodge. The king himself went out
hunting to obtain the most dainty bits of meat, both of animals and wild
fowl. And not content with these proofs of his attachment he fasted himself,
and would often take his pib be gwun,[4] and sit near the lodge indulging his
mind in repeating a few pensive notes.

> Ne ne moo sha
> Ne ne moo sha
>   We yea.
>
> Ma kow
> We au nin
>   We yea.
>
> Azhe—azhe
> Sau gee naun ih
>   We yea.
>
> Ka-go ka-go
> Dush ween e
> Shing gain—
> E me she kain
>   We yea.
>
> My sweetheart,
> My sweetheart,
>   Ah me!

When I think of you,
When I think of you,
Ah me!

How I love you,
How I love you,
Ah me!

Do not hate me,
Do not hate me,
Ah me![5]

In the meantime Aggo Dah Gauda came home, and finding his daughter had been stolen, determined to get her back. For this purpose he immediately set out. He could easily track the king, until he came to the banks
of the river, and saw that he had plunged in and swam over. But there
had been a frosty night or two since, and the water was so covered with
thin ice, so that he could not walk on it. He determined to encamp till it
became solid, and then crossed over and pursued the trail. As he went
along he saw branches broken off and strewed behind, for these had been
purposely cast along by the daughter, that the way might be found. And
the manner in which she had accomplished it, was this. Her hair was all
untied when she was caught up, and being very long, it caught on the
branches as they darted along, and it was these twigs that she broke off for
signs to her father. When he came to the king's lodge it was evening. Carefully approaching it, he peeped through the sides and saw his daughter
sitting disconsolately. She immediately caught his eye, and knowing that it
was her father come for her, she all at once appeared to relent in her heart,
and asking for the dipper, said to the king, "I will go and get you a drink
of water." This token of submission delighted him, and he waited with
impatience for her return. At last he went out with his followers, but nothing could be seen or heard of the captive daughter. They sallied out in the
plains, but had not gone far, by the light of the moon, when a party of
hunters, headed by the father-in-law of Aggo Dah Gauda, set up their yells
in their rear, and a shower of arrows was poured in upon them. Many of
their numbers fell, but the king being stronger and swifter than the rest,
fled toward the west, and never again appeared in that part of the country.

While all this was passing Aggo Dah Gauda, who had met his daughter
the moment she came out of the lodge, and being helped by his guardian
spirit, took her on his shoulders and hopped off, a hundred steps in one,
till he reached the stream, crossed it, and brought back his daughter in
triumph to his lodge.[6]

NOTES

1. In *M. H.*, p. 274, the title reads, "Aggodaguada and his Daughter; or,
the Man with his Leg Tied Up." In the later version the situation is more
clearly outlined. The father, Aggodaguada, is compared to Pauppukkewiss.

2. The Indian words of this song were omitted from the *M. H.* version.

3. In our Indian languages the highest terms for men in power are KOSI-NAUN, our father, and OGIMAU, chief. Both admit of a prefixed adjective to indicate great, and of a diminutive inflection to denote inferiority in size, power, or excellence. The term "king" is retained here, from the verbal narration of the interpreters. [H. R. S.]

4. Indian flute. [H. R. S.]

5. In *M. H.* the Indian words of this song are reduced to:

> Ne ne mo sha makow
> Aghi saw ge naun

which are translated:

> My sweetheart—my bosom is true,
> You only—it is you that I love.

6. Although A. I. Hallowell does not list this story in his "Concordance of Schoolcraft's Ojibwa Narratives," *J. Am. Folklore,* Vol. 59 (1946), pp. 136-153, its context indicates that it belongs to the legends that arose from the constant warfare between the Ojibwas and the plains Indians. The tale was reprinted in *M. H.,* pp. 274-277; in *C. M.,* pp. 170-178, and in *C-C,* pp. 192-199.

IOSCO

OR

A VISIT TO THE SUN AND MOON

A TALE OF INDIAN COSMOGONY, FROM THE OTTOWA[1]

ONE DAY five young men and a boy of about ten years of age, went out a-shooting with their bows and arrows. They left their lodges with the first appearance of daylight, and having passed through a long reach of woods, had ascended a lofty eminence before the sun arose. While standing there in a group, the sun suddenly burst forth in all the effulgence of a summer's morning. It appeared to them to be at no great distance from the position they occupied. "How very near it is!" they all said. "It cannot be far," said Iosco, the eldest, "and if you will accompany me, we will see if we cannot reach it." "I will go! I will go!" burst from every lip. Even the boy said he would also go. They told him he was too young; but he replied, "If you do not permit me to go with you, I will mention your design to each of your parents." They then said to him, "you shall also go with us, so be quiet."

They then fell upon the following arrangement. It was resolved that each one should obtain from his parents as many pairs of moccasins as he could, and also new clothing of leather. They fixed on a spot where they would conceal all their articles, until they were ready to start on their journey, and which would serve, in the meantime, as a place of rendezvous, where they might secretly meet and consult. This being arranged, they returned home.

A long time passed before they could put their plan into execution. But they kept it a profound secret, even to the boy. They frequently met at the appointed place, and discussed the subject. At length everything was in readiness, and they decided on a day to set out. That morning the boy shed tears for a pair of new leather leggings. "Don't you see," said he to his parents, "how my companions are dressed?" This appeal to their pride and envy prevailed. He obtained the leggings. Artifices were also resorted to by the others, under the plea of going out on a special hunt. They said to one another, but in a tone that they might be overheard, "we will see who will bring in the most game." They went out in different directions, but soon met at the appointed place, where they had hid the articles for their journey, and as many arrows as they had time to make. Each one took something on his back, and they began their march. They traveled day after day, through a thick forest, but the sun was always at the same distance. "We must," said they, "travel toward Waubunong,[2] and we shall get to the object, some time or other." No one was discouraged, although winter

139

overtook them. They built a lodge and hunted, till they obtained as much dried meat as they could carry, and then continued on. This they did several times; season followed season. More than one winter overtook them. Yet none of them became discouraged, or expressed dissatisfaction.

One day the travelers came to the banks of a river, whose waters ran toward Waubunong. They followed it down many days. As they were walking, one day, they came to rising grounds, from which they saw something white or clear through the trees. They encamped on this elevation. Next morning they came, suddenly, in view of an immense body of water. No land could be seen as far as the eye could reach. One or two of them laid down on the beach to drink. As soon as they got the water into their mouths, they spit it out, and exclaimed with surprise, Shewetagon awbo! [salt water.] It was the sea. While looking on the water, the sun arose as if from the deep, and went on in its steady course through the heavens, enlivening the scene with his cheering and animating beams. They stood in fixed admiration, but the object appeared to be as distant from them as ever. They thought it best to encamp, and consult whether it were advisable to go on, or return. "We see," said the leader, "that the sun is still on the opposite side of this great water, but let us not be disheartened. We can walk around the shore." To this they all assented.

Next morning they took the northerly shore, to walk around it, but had only gone a short distance when they came to a large river. They again encamped, and while sitting before the fire, the question was put, whether any one of them had ever dreamed of water, or of walking on it. After a long silence, the eldest said he had. Soon after they laid down to sleep. When they arose the following morning, the eldest addressed them: "We have done wrong in coming north. Last night my spirit appeared to me, and told me to go south, and that but a short distance beyond the spot we left yesterday, we should come to a river with high banks. That by looking off its mouth, we should see an island, which would approach to us. He directed that we should all get on it. He then told me to cast my eyes toward the water. I did so, and I saw all he had declared. He then informed me that we must return south, and wait at the river until the day after tomorrow. I believe all that was revealed to me in this dream, and that we shall do well to follow it."

The party immediately retraced their footsteps in exact obedience to these intimations. Toward the evening they came to the borders of the indicated river. It had high banks, behind which they encamped, and here they patiently awaited the fulfillment of the dream. The appointed day arrived. They said, "we will see if that which has been said will be seen. Midday is the promised time." Early in the morning two had gone to the shore to keep a lookout. They waited anxiously for the middle of the day, straining their eyes to see if they could discover anything. Suddenly they raised a shout. "Ewaddee suh neen! There it is! There it is!" On rushing to the spot they beheld something like an *island* steadily advancing toward the shore. As it approached, they could discover that something was moving on it in various directions. They said, "it is a Manito, let us be off into the woods." "No, no," cried the eldest, "let us stay and watch." It now became stationary, and lost much of its imagined height. They could only see *three* trees, as they thought, resembling trees in a pinery that had been burnt. The wind, which had been off the sea, now died away into a perfect calm. They saw something leaving the fancied island and approaching the shore, throwing and flapping its wings, like a loon when he attempts to fly in calm weather. It entered the mouth of the river. They were on the point of running away, but the eldest dissuaded them. "Let us hide in this hollow," he said, "and we will see what it can be." They did so. They soon heard the sounds of chopping, and quickly after they heard the falling of trees. Suddenly a man came.up to their place of concealment. He stood still and gazed at them. They did the same in utter amazement. After looking at them for some time, the person advanced and extended his hand toward them. The eldest took it, and they shook hands. He then spoke, but they could not understand each other. He then cried out for his comrades. They came, and examined very minutely their dresses. They again tried to converse. Finding it impossible, the strangers then motioned to the Naubequon, and to the Naubequon-ais,[3] wishing them to embark. They consulted with each other for a short time. The eldest then motioned that they should go on board. They embarked on board the boat, which they found to be loaded with wood. When they reached the side of the supposed island, they were surprised to see a great number of people, who all came to the side and looked at them with open mouths. One spoke out, above the others, and appeared to be the leader. He motioned them to get on board. He looked [at] and examined them, and took them down into the cabin, and set things before them to eat. He treated them very kindly.

When they came on deck again all the sails were spread, and they were fast losing sight of land. In the course of the night and the following day they were sick at the stomach, but soon recovered. When they had been out at sea ten days, they became sorrowful, as they could not converse with those who had hats on.[4]

The following night Iosco dreamed that his spirit appeared to him. He told him not to be discouraged, that he would open his ears, so as to be able to understand the people with hats. I will not permit you to understand much, said he, only sufficient to reveal your wants, and to know what is said to you. He repeated this dream to his friends, and they were satisfied and encouraged by it. When they had been out about thirty days, the master of the ship told them, and motioned them to change their dresses of leather, for such as his people wore; for if they did not, his master would be displeased. It was on this occasion that the elder first understood a few words of the language. The first phrase he comprehended was *La que notte,* and from one word to another he was soon able to speak it.

One day the men cried out, "land!" and soon after they heard a noise resembling thunder, in repeated peals. When they had got over their fears, they were shown the large guns which made this noise. Soon after they saw a vessel smaller than their own, sailing out of a bay, in the direction toward them. She had flags on her masts, and when she came near she fired a gun.

The large vessel also hoisted her flags, and the boat came alongside. The master told the person who came in it, to tell his master or king, that he had six strangers on board, such as had never been seen before, and that they were coming to visit him. It was .some time after the departure of this messenger before the vessel got up to the town. It was then dark, but they could see people, and horses, and odawbons[5] ashore. They were landed and placed in a covered vehicle, and driven off. When they stopped, they were taken into a large and splendid room. They were here told that the great chief wished to see them. They were shown into another large room, filled with men and woman. All the room was Shoneancauda.[6] The chief asked them their business, and the object of their journey. They told him where they were from, and where they were going, and the nature of the enterprise which they had undertaken. He tried to dissuade them from its execution, telling them of the many trials and difficulties they would have to undergo: that so many days' march from his country dwelt a bad spirit, or Manito, who foreknew and foretold the existence and arrival of all who entered into his country. It is impossible, he said, my children, for you ever to arrive at the object you are in search of.

Iosco replied; "Nosa," and they could see the chief blush in being called *father,* "we have come so far on our way, and we will continue it: we have resolved firmly that we will do so. We think our lives are of no value, for we have given them up for this object. Nosa," he repeated, "do not then prevent us from going on our journey." The chief then dismissed them with valuable presents, after having appointed the next day to speak to them again, and provided everything that they needed or wished for.

Next day they were again summoned to appear before the king. He again tried to dissuade them. He said he would send them back to their country in one of his vessels: but all he said had no effect. "Well," said he, "if you will go, I will furnish you all that is needed for your journey." He had everything provided accordingly. He told them, that three days before they reached the Bad Spirit he had warned them of, they would hear his Shéshegwun.[7] He cautioned them to be wise, for he felt that he should never see them all again.

They resumed their journey, and traveled sometimes through villages, but they soon left them behind and passed over a region of forests and plains, without inhabitants. They found all the productions of a new country: trees, animals, birds, were entirely different from those they were accustomed to, on the other side of the great waters. They traveled, and traveled, till they wore out all of the clothing that had been given to them, and had to take to their leather clothing again.

The three days the chief spoke of meant three years, for it was only at the end of the third year, that they came within the sound of the spirit's shéshegwun. The sound appeared to be near, but they continued walking on, day after day, without apparently getting any nearer to it. Suddenly they came to a very extensive plain; they could see the blue ridges of distant mountains rising on the horizon beyond it: they pushed on, thinking to get over the plain before night, but they were overtaken by darkness:

they were now on a stony part of the plain, covered by about a foot's depth of water: they were weary and fatigued: some of them said, let us lie down; no, no, said the others, let us push on. Soon they stood on firm ground, but it was as much as they could do to stand, for they were very weary. They, however, made an effort to encamp, lighted up a fire, and refreshed themselves by eating. They then commenced conversing about the sound of the spirit's shéshegwun, which they had heard for several days. Suddenly the instrument commenced; it sounded as if it were subterraneous, and it shook the ground: they tied up their bundles and went toward the spot. They soon came to a large building, which was illuminated. As soon as they came to the door, they were met by a rather elderly man. "How do ye do," said he, "my grandsons? Walk in, walk in; I am glad to see you: I knew when you started: I saw you encamp this evening: sit down, and tell me the news of the country you left, for I feel interested in it." They complied with his wishes, and when they had concluded, each one presented him with a piece of tobacco. He then revealed to them things that would happen in their journey, and predicted its successful accomplishment. "I do not say that all of you," said he, "will successfully go through it. You have passed over three-fourths of your way, and I will tell you how to proceed after you get to the edge of the earth. Soon after you leave this place, you will hear a deafening sound: it is the sky descending on the edge, but it keeps moving up and down; you will watch, and when it moves up, you will see a vacant space between it and the earth. You must not be afraid. A chasm of awful depth is there, which separates the unknown from this earth, and a veil of darkness conceals it. Fear not. You must leap through; and if you succeed you will find yourselves on a beautiful plain, and in a soft and mild light emitted by the moon." They thanked him for his advice. A pause ensued.

"I have told you the way," he said; "now tell me again of the country you left; for I committed dreadful ravages while I was there: does not the country show marks of it? and do not the inhabitants tell of me to their children? I came to this place to mourn over my bad actions, and am trying, by my present course of life, to relieve my mind of the load that is on it." They told him that their fathers spoke often of a celebrated personage called Manabozho, who performed great exploits. "I am he," said the Spirit. They gazed with astonishment and fear. "Do you see this pointed house?"[8] asked he, pointing to one that resembled a sugar-loaf; "you can now each speak your wishes and will be answered from that house. Speak out, and ask what each wants, and it shall be granted." One of them, who was vain, asked with presumption, that he might live forever, and never be in want. He was answered, "Your wish shall be granted." The second made the same request, and received the same answer. The third asked to live longer than common people, and to be always successful in his war excursions, never losing any of his young men. He was told, "Your wishes are granted." The fourth joined in the same request, and received the same reply. The fifth made an humble request, asking to live as long as men generally do, and that he might be crowned with such success in hunting as to be able to provide for his parents and relatives. The sixth made the same request, and it was granted to both, in pleasing tones, from the pointed house.

After hearing these responses they prepared to depart. They were told by Manabozho, that they had been with him but one day, but they afterward found that they had remained there upward of a year. When they were on the point of setting out, Manabozho exclaimed, "Stop! you two, who asked me for eternal life, will receive the boon you wish immediately." He spake, and one was turned into a stone called Shingauba-wossin,[9] and the other into a cedar-tree. "Now," said he to the others, "you can go." They left him in fear, saying, "we were fortunate to escape so, for the king told us he was wicked, and that we should not probably escape from him." They had not proceeded far, when they began to hear the sound of the beating sky. It appeared to be near at hand, but they had a long interval to travel before they came near, and the sound was then stunning to their senses; for when the sky came down, its pressure would force gusts of wind from the opening, so strong that it was with difficulty they could keep their feet, and the sun passed but a short distance above their heads. They, however, approached boldly, but had to wait some time before they could muster courage enough to leap through the dark veil that covered the passage. The sky would come down with violence, but it would rise slowly and gradually. The two who had made the humble request, stood near the edge, and with no little exertion, succeeded, one after the other, in leaping through, and gaining a firm foothold. The remaining two were fearful and undecided: the others spoke to them through the darkness saying, "leap! leap! the sky is on its way down." These two looked up and saw it descending, but fear paralyzed their efforts; they made but a feeble attempt, so as to reach the opposite side with their hands; but the sky at the same time struck on the earth with great violence and a terrible sound, and forced them into the dreadful black chasm.

The two successful adventurers found themselves in a beautiful country, lighted by the moon, which shed around a mild and pleasant light. They could see the moon approaching as if it were from behind a hill. They advanced, and an aged woman spoke to them; she had a white face and pleasing air, and looked rather old, though she spoke to them very kindly: they knew from her first appearance that she was the moon: she asked them several questions: she told them that she knew of their coming, and was happy to see them: she informed them that they were halfway to her brother's, and that from the earth to her abode was half the distance. "I will, by and by, have leisure," said she, "and will go and conduct you to my brother, for he is now absent on his daily course: you will succeed in your object, and return in safety to your country and friends, with the good wishes, I am sure, of my brother." While the travelers were with her, they received every attention. When the proper time arrived, she said to them, "My brother is now rising from below, and we shall see his light as he comes over the distant edge: come," said she, "I will lead you up." They went forward, but in some mysterious way, they hardly knew how:

they rose almost directly up, as if they had ascended steps. They then came upon an immense plain, declining in the direction of the sun's approach. When he came near, the moon spake—"I have brought you these persons, whom we knew were coming;" and with this she disappeared. The sun motioned with his hand for them to follow him. They did so, but found it rather difficult, as the way was steep: they found it particularly so from the edge of the earth till they got halfway between that point and midday: when they reached this spot, the sun stopped, and sat down to rest. "What, my children," he asked, "has brought you here? I could not speak to you before: I could not stop at any place but this, for this is my first resting-place—then at the center, which is at midday, and then halfway from that to the western edge.[10] "Tell me," he continued, "the object of your undertaking this journey and all the circumstances which have happened to you on the way." They complied. Iosco told him their main object was to see him. They had lost four of their friends on the way, and they wished to know whether they could return in safety to the earth, that they might inform their friends and relatives of all that had befallen them. They concluded by requesting him to grant their wishes. He replied, "Yes, you shall certainly return in safety; but your companions were vain and presumptuous in their demands. They were Gug-ge-baw-diz-ze-wug.[11] They aspired to what Manitoes only could enjoy. But you two, I said, shall get back to your country, and become as happy as the hunter's life can make you. You shall never be in want of the necessaries of life, as long as you are permitted to live; and you will have the satisfaction of relating your journey to your friends, and also of telling them of me. Follow me, follow me," he said, commencing his course again. The ascent was now gradual, and they soon came to a level plain. After traveling some time he again sat down to rest, for he had arrived at Nau-we-qua.[12] "You see," said he, "it is level at this place, but a short distance onwards, my way descends gradually to my last resting place, from which there is an abrupt descent." He repeated his assurance that they should be shielded from danger, if they relied firmly on his power. "Come here quickly," he said, placing something before them on which they could descend; "keep firm," said he, as they resumed the descent. They went downward as if they had been let down by ropes.

In the meantime the parents of these two young men dreamed that their sons were returning, and that they should soon see them. They placed the fullest confidence in their dreams. Early in the morning they left their lodges for a remote point in the forest, where they expected to meet them. They were not long at the place before they saw the adventurers returning, for they had descended not far from that place. The young men knew they were their fathers. They met, and were happy. They related all that had befallen them. They did not conceal anything; and they expressed their gratitude to the different Manitoes who had preserved them, by feasting and gifts, and particularly to the sun and moon, who had received them as their children.

[The foregoing tale was related by Chusco,[13] an Ottowa chief, converted to Christianity a few years ago. He was born at L'Arbre Croche, in Michigan, some years after the taking of Fort Mackinac, in 1763—an event of such notoriety in Indian tradition, that it is generally referred to by them as an era. He was present at the treaty of Greenville, in 1793, and received an annuity during the last few years of his life in consequence of a promise understood to have been made to him by General Wayne.

Chusco was a man of small stature; he appears to have possessed great bodily activity in his youth, united to a mind of quick observation. He embraced, at an early period of his life, the profession of a seer, and practiced it with the approbation of his tribe till within a few years. About 1827 his mind was arrested by the truths of revelation, which were first brought to his notice by his wife, who had been instructed at a mission on the island of Mackinac. He made a profession of religion within a year or two after, renounced his idolatry, gave up the use of ardent spirits and every species of fermented drink, and exhibited a consistent Christian life, to the period of his death, in 1837. He is buried at Round Island, in Lake Huron, where a neat paling has been placed over his grave. The story itself, so far as respects the object, is calculated to remind the reader of South American history, of the alleged descent of Manco Capac and the Children of the Sun.[14] But I am not prepared to say, that an examination of the traditional history of the Algics will sustain the comparison.

The tale does not appear to be of great comparative antiquity. The introduction of ships, and guns, and axes, is sufficient to indicate this. It is interesting, however, as revealing their notions of cosmogony, the division of the day into quartads, and their impressions of general geography. It would appear that they believe the earth to be *globular;* they speak of but a single sea. The tradition of Manabozho is attested, and he is here represented, as in all other known instances, to be a Bad, and not a Good Spirit, and there is no countenance given to the verbal opinion, sometimes expressed, that this personage partakes of any of the characters of a Saviour.[15]

The moral bearing of the story is, perhaps, to indicate the danger of ambition. Ambition and presumption, in human wishes, are very clearly rebuked by the results of the oracular response, and by the immediate fulfillment of the predictions.][16]

NOTES

1. For *M. H.*, Schoolcraft changed the title to: "Iosco; or, the Prairie Boys' Visit to the Sun and Moon. An Ottawa Legend."

2. The East—i.e., place of light. [H. R. S.]

3. Ship and boat. These terms exhibit the simple and the diminutive forms of the name for ship or vessel. It is also the term for a woman's needlework, and seems to imply a tangled thready mass, and was perhaps transferred in allusion to a ship's ropes. [H. R. S.]

4. Wewaquonidjig, a term early and extensively applied to the white man, by our Indians, and still frequently used. [H. R. S.]

5. Odawbon comprehends all vehicles between a dog train and a coach, whether on wheels or runners. The term is nearest allied to vehicle. [H. R. S.]

6. Massive silver. [H. R. S.]

7. A rattle. [H. R. S.]

8. All "jossakeeds," or seers and diviners, lived in pointed-roofed dwellings.

9. A hard primitive stone, frequently found along the borders of the lakes and water-courses, generally fretted into image shapes. Hardness and indestructibility are regarded as its characteristics by the Indians. It is often granite. [H. R. S.] For a discussion of the stones see Schoolcraft's article "Shingeba-Woosin, or Image Stones" in *The Red Race of America* (1847), pp. 291-293. (This title was one of the many given *Oneóta,* published in eight installments, 1844-45.) Hereafter referred to as *R. R. A.*

10. This computation of time separates the day into four portions of six hours each—two of which, from 1 to 6, and from 6 to 12, A. M. compose the *morning,* and the other two, from 1 to 6, and from 6 to 12, P. M. compose the *evening.* [H. R. S.]

11. This is a verbal form, plural number, of the transitive adjective—foolish. [H. R. S.]

12. Midday, or middle line. [H. R. S.]

13. Zachariah Chusco (Wauzhusko or the muskrat) was an Ottowa jossakeed converted to Christianity at the Mackinac mission. He died September 30, 1837. See Schoolcraft's *Personal Memoirs of a Residence of Thirty Years with the Indian Tribes* (1851), pp. 449, 477, 478. Hereafter referred to as *P. M.* See also *R. R. A.,* p. 290.

14. Manco Capac, according to some Spanish historians, was the "first" Inca, a child of the sun. See Garcilasso de la Vega's *Commentarios Reales* (1609) for the story of the dynasty "founded" by this mythical personage. There are frequent references in *P. M.* and *Oneóta* to the "antiquities" of Mexico and Peru.

15. Nevertheless, it is apparent that Chusco's Christianity colored his memory of the legend.

16. This tailpiece was omitted from *M. H.* The story, with slight verbal changes, was reprinted in *M. H.,* pp. 278-292.

THE TWO JEEBI-UG[1]

OR

A TRIAL OF FEELING

FROM THE ODJIBWA

THERE LIVED A HUNTER in the north who had a wife and one child. His lodge stood far off in the forest, several days' journey from any other. He spent his days in hunting, and his evenings in relating to his wife the incidents that had befallen him. As game was very abundant he found no difficulty in killing as much as they wanted. Just in all his acts, he lived a peaceful and happy life.

One evening during the winter season, it chanced that he remained out later than usual, and his wife began to feel uneasy, for fear some accident had befallen him. It was already dark. She listened attentively and at last heard the sound of approaching footsteps. Not doubting it was her husband, she went to the door and beheld two strange females. She bade them enter, and invited them to remain.

She observed that they were total strangers in the country. There was something so peculiar in their looks, air, and manner, that she was uneasy in their company. They would not come near the fire; they sat in a remote part of the lodge, were shy and taciturn, and drew their garments about them in such a manner as nearly to hide their faces. So far as she could judge, they were pale, hollow-eyed, and long-visaged, very thin and emaciated. There was but little light in the lodge, as the fire was low, and served by its fitful flashes, rather to increase than dispel their fears. "Merciful spirit!" cried a voice from the opposite part of the lodge, "there are two corpses clothed with garments." The hunter's wife turned around, but seeing nobody, she concluded the sounds were but gusts of wind. She trembled, and was ready to sink to the earth.

Her husband at this moment entered and dispelled her fears. He threw down the carcass of a large fat deer. "Behold what a fine and fat animal," cried the mysterious females, and they immediately ran and pulled off pieces of the whitest fat,[2] which they ate with greediness. The hunter and his wife looked on with astonishment, but remained silent. They supposed their guests might have been famished. Next day, however, the same unusual conduct was repeated. The strange females tore off the fat and devoured it with eagerness. The third day the hunter thought he would anticipate their wants by tying up a portion of the fattest pieces for them, which he placed on the top of his load. They accepted it, but still appeared

148

dissatisfied, and went to the wife's portion and tore off more. The man and his wife felt surprised at such rude and unaccountable conduct, but they remained silent, for they respected their guests and had observed that they had been attended with marked good luck during the residence of these mysterious visitors.

In other respects the deportment of the females was strictly unexceptionable. They were modest, distant, and silent. They never uttered a word during the day. At night they would occupy themselves in procuring wood, which they carried to the lodge, and then returning the implements exactly to the places in which they had found them, resume their places without speaking. They were never known to stay out until daylight. They never laughed or jested.

The winter had nearly passed away, without anything uncommon happening, when, one evening the hunter stayed out very late. The moment he entered and laid down his day's hunt as usual before his wife, the two females began to tear off the fat, in so unceremonious a way, that her anger was excited. She constrained herself, however, in a measure, but did not conceal her feelings, although she said but little. The guests observed the excited state of her mind, and became unusually reserved and uneasy. The good hunter saw the change, and carefully inquired into the cause, but his wife denied having used any hard words. They retired to their couches, and he tried to compose himself to sleep, but could not, for the sobs and sighs of the two females were incessant. He arose on his couch and addressed them as follows:

"Tell me," said he, "what is it that gives you pain of mind, and causes you to utter those sighs. Has my wife given you offense, or trespassed on the rights of hospitality?"

They replied in the negative. "We have been treated by you with kindness and affection. It is not for any slight we have received, that we weep. Our mission is not to you only. We come from the land of the dead to test mankind, and to try the sincerity of the living. Often we have heard the bereaved by death say that if the dead could be restored, they would devote their lives to make them happy. We have been moved by the bitter lamentations which have reached the place of the dead, and have come to make proof of the sincerity of those who have lost friends. Three moons were allotted us by the Master of life to make the trial. More than half the time had been successfully past, when the angry feelings of your wife indicated the irksomeness you felt at our presence, and has made us resolve on our departure."

They continued to talk to the hunter and his wife, gave them instructions as to a future life, and pronounced a blessing upon them.

"There is one point," they added, "of which we wish to speak. You have thought our conduct very strange in rudely possessing ourselves of the choicest parts of your hunt. *That* was the point of trial selected to put you to. It is the wife's peculiar privilege. For another to usurp it, we knew to be the severest trial of her, and consequently of your temper and feelings. We know your manners and customs, but we came to prove you, not by a compliance with them, but a violation of them. Pardon us. We are the agents of him who sent us. Peace to your dwelling, adieu!"

When they ceased total darkness filled the lodge. No object could be seen. The inmates heard the door open and shut, but they never saw more of the two JEEBI-UG.

The hunter found the success which they had promised. He became celebrated in the chase, and never wanted for anything. He had many children, all of whom grew up to manhood, and health, peace, and long life were the rewards of his hospitality.[3]

NOTES

1. Ghosts. [H. R. S.] In *M. H.* the title contained its own translation: "The Jeebi; or, Two Ghosts. From the Odjibwa."

2. The fat of animals is esteemed by the N. A. Indians among the choicest parts. [H. R. S.]

3. This tale was first published, with many figurative and moral adornments, in *Travels in the Central Mississippi Valley* (1825), pp. 412-421. Jones next purloined it for his book, II, pp. 285-302. In *M. H.* it appears as the fifth tale, pp. 81-84. *C. M.* selected it for his volume, pp. 68-73, but *C-C* ignored it.

PAH-HAH-UNDOOTAH

OR

THE RED HEAD

A SIOUX TALE[1]

AS SPRING APPROACHES, the Indians return from their wintering grounds to their villages, engage in feasting, soon exhaust their stock of provisions, and begin to suffer for the want of food. Such of the hunters as are of an active and enterprising cast of character, take the occasion to separate from the mass of the population, and remove to some neighboring locality in the forest, which promises the means of subsistence during this season of general lassitude and enjoyment.

Among the families who thus separated themselves, on a certain occasion, there was a man called ODSHEDOPH WAUCHEENTONGAH, or the Child of Strong Desires, who had a wife and one son. After a day's travel he reached an ample wood with his family, which was thought to be a suitable place to encamp. The wife fixed the lodge, while the husband went out to hunt. Early in the evening he returned with a deer. Being tired and thirsty he asked his son to go to the river for some water. The son replied that it was dark and he was afraid. He urged him to go, saying that his mother, as well as himself, was tired, and the distance to the water was very short. But no persuasion was of any avail. He refused to go. "Ah, my son," said the father, at last, "if you are afraid to go to the river you will never kill the Red Head."

The boy was deeply mortified by this observation. It seemed to call up all his latent energies. He mused in silence. He refused to eat, and made no reply when spoken to.

The next day he asked his mother to dress the skin of the deer, and make it into moccasins for him, while he busied himself in preparing a bow and arrows. As soon as these things were done, he left the lodge one morning at sunrise, without saying a word to his father or mother. He fired one of his arrows into the air, which fell westward. He took that course, and at night coming to the spot where the arrow had fallen, was rejoiced to find it piercing the heart of a deer. He refreshed himself with a meal of the venison, and the next morning fired another arrow. After traveling all day, he found it also in another deer. In this manner he fired four arrows, and every evening found that he had killed a deer. What was very singular, however, was, that he left the arrows sticking in the carcasses, and passed on without withdrawing them. In consequence of this, he had no arrow for the

151

fifth day, and was in great distress at night for the want of food. At last he threw himself upon the ground in despair, concluding that he might as well perish there as go farther. But he had not lain long before he heard a hollow, rumbling noise, in the ground beneath him. He sprang up, and discovered at a distance the figure of a human being, walking with a stick. He looked attentively and saw that the figure was walking in a wide beaten path, in a prairie, leading from a lodge to a lake. To his surprise this lodge was at no great distance. He approached a little nearer and concealed himself. He soon discovered that the figure was no other than that of the terrible witch, WOK-ON-KAHTOHN-ZOOEYAH′PEE-KAH-HAITCHEE, or the little old woman who makes war. Her path to the lake was perfectly smooth and solid, and the noise our adventurer had heard, was caused by the striking of her walking staff upon the ground. The top of this staff was decorated with a string of the toes and bills of birds of every kind, who at every stroke of the stick, fluttered and sung their various notes in concert.

She entered her lodge and laid off her mantle, which was entirely composed of the scalps of women. Before folding it, she shook it several times, and at every shake the scalps uttered loud shouts of laughter, in which the old hag joined. Nothing could have frightened him more than this horrific exhibition. After laying by the cloak she came directly to him. She informed him that she had known him from the time he left his father's lodge, and watched his movements. She told him not to fear or despair, for she would be his friend and protector. She invited him into her lodge, and gave him a supper. During the repast, she inquired of him his motives for visiting her. He related his history, stated the manner in which he had been disgraced, and the difficulties he labored under. She cheered him with the assurance of her friendship, and told him he would be a brave man yet.

She then commenced the exercise of her power upon him. His hair being very short she took a large leaden comb, and after drawing it through his hair several times, it became of a handsome feminine length. She then proceeded to dress him as a female, furnishing him with the necessary garments, and decorated his face with paints of the most beautiful dye. She gave him a bowl of shining metal. She directed him to put in his girdle a blade of scented sword-grass, and to proceed the next morning to the banks of the lake, which was no other than that over which the Red Head reigned. Now PAH-HAH-UNDOOTAH, or the Red Head, was a most powerful sorcerer and the terror of all the country, living upon an island in the center of the lake.

She informed him that there would be many Indians on the island, who as soon as they saw him use the shining bowl to drink with, would come and solicit him to be their wife, and to take him over to the island. These offers he was to refuse, and say that he had come a great distance to be the wife of the Red Head, and that if the chief could not come for her in his own canoe, she should return to her village. She said that as soon as the Red Head heard of this, he would come for her in his own canoe, in which she must embark. On reaching the island he must consent to be his wife, and in the evening induce him to take a walk out of the village, when he was to take the first opportunity to cut off his head with the blade of grass. She also gave him general advice how he was to conduct himself to sustain his assumed character of a woman. His fear would scarcely permit him to accede to this plan, but the recollection of his father's words and looks decided him.

Early in the morning, he left the witch's lodge, and took the hard beaten path to the banks of the lake. He reached the water at a point directly opposite the Red Head's village. It was a beautiful day. The heavens were clear, and the sun shone out in the greatest effulgence. He had not been long there, having sauntered along the beach, when he displayed the glittering bowl, by dipping water from the lake. Very soon a number of canoes came off from the island. The men admired his dress, and were charmed with his beauty, and a great number made proposals of marriage. These he promptly declined, agreeably to the concerted plan. When the facts were reported to the Red Head, he ordered his canoe to be put in the water by his chosen men, and crossed over to see this wonderful girl. As he came near the shore, he saw that the ribs of the sorcerer's canoe were formed of living rattlesnakes, whose heads pointed outward to guard him from enemies. Our adventurer had no sooner stepped into the canoe than they began to hiss and rattle, which put him in a great fright. But the magician spoke to them, after which they became pacified and quiet, and all at once they were at the landing upon the island. The marriage immediately took place, and the bride made presents of various valuables which had been furnished by the old witch.

As they were sitting in the lodge surrounded by friends and relatives, the mother of the Red Head regarded the face of her new daughter-in-law for a long time with fixed attention. From this scrutiny she was convinced that this singular and hasty marriage augured no good to her son. She drew her husband aside and disclosed to him her suspicions: This can be no female, said she, the figure and manners, the countenance, and more especially the expression of the eyes, are, beyond a doubt, those of a man. Her husband immediately rejected her suspicions, and rebuked her severely for the indignity offered to her daughter-in-law. He became so angry, that seizing the first thing that came to hand, which happened to be his pipe stem, he beat her unmercifully. This act requiring to be explained to the spectators, the mock bride immediately rose up, and assuming an air of offended dignity, told the Red Head that after receiving so gross an insult from his relatives he could not think of remaining with him as his wife, but should forthwith return to his village and friends. He left the lodge followed by the Red Head, and walked until he came upon the beach of the island, near the spot where they had first landed. Red Head entreated him to remain. He pressed him by every motive which he thought might have weight, but they were all rejected. During this conference they had seated themselves upon the ground, and Red Head, in great affliction, reclined his head upon his fancied wife's lap. This was the opportunity ardently sought for, and it was improved to the best advantage. Every means was taken to lull him to sleep, and partly by a soothing manner, and partly by a seeming compliance with his request, the object was at last attained. Red Head fell into a sound sleep. Our aspirant, for the glory of a brave man, then drew his blade of grass, and drawing it once across the neck of the Red Head completely severed the head from the body.

He immediately stripped off his dress, seized the bleeding head, and plunging into the lake, swam safely over to the main shore. He had scarcely reached it, when looking back he saw amid the darkness, the torches of persons come out in search of the new-married couple. He listened till they had found the headless body, and he heard their piercing shrieks of sorrow, as he took his way to the lodge of his kind adviser.

She received him with rejoicing. She admired his prudence, and told him his bravery could never be questioned again. Lifting up the head, she said he need only have brought the scalp. She cut off a small piece for herself, and told him he might now return with the head, which would be evidence of an achievement that would cause the Indians to respect him. "In your way home," she said, "you will meet with but one difficulty. MAUNKAH KEESH WOCCAUNG, or the Spirit of the Earth, requires an offering from those who perform extraordinary achievements. As you walk along in a prairie, there will be an earthquake. The earth will open and divide the prairie in the middle. Take this partridge and throw it into the opening, and instantly spring over it." All this happened precisely as it had been foretold. He cast the partridge into the crevice and leaped over it. He then proceeded without obstruction to a place near his village, where he secreted his trophy. On entering the village he found his parents had returned from the place of their spring encampment, and were in great sorrow for their son, whom they supposed to be lost. One and another of the young men had presented themselves to the disconsolate parents, and said, "Look up, I am your son." Having been often deceived in this manner, when their own son actually presented himself, they sat with their heads down, and with their eyes nearly blinded with weeping. It was some time before they could be prevailed upon to bestow a glance upon him. It was still longer before they recognized him for their son; when he recounted his adventures they believed him mad. The young men laughed at him. He left the lodge and soon returned with his trophy. It was soon recognized. All doubts of the reality of his adventures now vanished. He was greeted with joy and placed among the first warriors of the nation. He finally became a chief, and his family were ever after respected and esteemed.[2]

NOTES

1. This tale was given the subtitle "A Dacotah Legend" in *M. H.*
2. The tale, without variation, was reprinted in *M. H.*, pp. 216-222. It was also included in *C. M.*, pp. 22-33, and in *C-C*, pp. 178-188, much altered, under the title "Strong Desire and the Red Sorcerer."

LEELINAU

OR

THE LOST DAUGHTER

AN ODJIBWA TALE[1]

LEELINAU was the favorite daughter of an able hunter who lived near the base of the lofty highlands called Kaug Wudjoo, on the shore of Lake Superior. From her earliest youth she was observed to be pensive and timid, and to spend much of her time in solitude and fasting. Whenever she could leave her father's lodge she would fly to remote haunts and recesses in the woods, or sit upon some high promontory of rock overlooking the lake. In such places she was supposed to invoke her guardian spirit. But amid all the sylvan haunts, so numerous in a highly picturesque section of country, none had so great attractions for her mind as a forest of pines, on the open shore, called Manitowak, or the Sacred Grove. It was one of those consecrated places which are supposed to be the residence of the PUK WUDJ ININEE, or little wild men of the woods, and MISHEN IMO- KINAKOG, or turtle-spirits, two classes of minor spirits or fairies who love romantic scenes. Owing to this notion, it was seldom visited by Indians, who attribute to these imaginary beings a mischievous agency. And whenever they were compelled by stress of weather to make a landing on this part of the coast, they never failed to leave an offering of tobacco, or some other article.[2]

To this fearful spot Leelinau had made her way at an early age, gathering strange flowers or plants, which she would bring home to her parents, and relate to them all the little incidents that had occurred in her rambles. Although they discountenanced her visits to the place, they were unable to restrain them, for they did not wish to lay any violent commands upon her. Her attachment to the spot, therefore, increased with her age. If she wished to propitiate her spirits to procure pleasant dreams, or any other favor, she repaired to the Manitowok. If her father remained out later than usual, and it was feared he had been overwhelmed by the tempest, or met with some other accident, she offered up her prayers at the Manitowok. It was there that she fasted, supplicated, and strolled. And she spent so much of her time there, that her parents began to suspect some bad spirit had enticed her to its haunts, and thrown a charm around her which she was unable to resist. This conjecture was confirmed by her mother (who had secretly followed her) overhearing her repeat sentiments like these.

155

Spirit of the dancing leaves
Hear a throbbing heart that grieves,
Not for joys this world can give,
But the life that spirits live:
Spirit of the foaming billow,
Visit thou my nightly pillow,
Shedding o'er it silver dreams,
Of the mountain brooks and streams,
Sunny glades, and golden hours,
Such as suit thy buoyant powers:
Spirit of the starry night,
Pencil out thy fleecy light,
That my footprints still may lead
To the blush-let Miscodeed,[3]
Or the flower to passion true
Yielding free its carmine hue:
Spirit of the morning dawn,
Waft thy fleecy columns on,
Snowy white, or tender blue
Such as brave men love to view.
Spirit of the green wood plume
Shed around thy leaf perfume
Such as spring from buds of gold
Which thy tiny hands unfold.
Spirits hither quick repair,
Hear a maiden's evening prayer.

The effect of these visits was to render the daughter dissatisfied with the realities of life, and to disqualify her for an active and useful participation in its duties. She became melancholy and taciturn. She had permitted her mind to dwell so much on imaginary scenes, that she at last mistook them for realities, and sighed for an existence inconsistent with the accidents of mortality. The consequence was, a disrelish for all the ordinary sources of amusement and employment which engaged her equals in years. When the girls of the neighboring lodges assembled to play at the favorite game of pappus-e-kowaun,[4] before the lodge door, Leelinau would sit vacantly by, or enter so feebly into the spirit of the play, as to show plainly that it was irksome to her. Again, in the evening, when the youths and girls formed a social ring around the lodge, and the piepeendjigun[5] passed rapidly from hand to hand, she either handed it along without attempting to play, or if she played, it was with no effort to swell her count. Her parents saw that she was a prey to some secret power, and attempted to divert her in every way they could. They favored the attentions paid to her by a man much her senior in years, but who had the reputation of great activity, and was the eldest son of a neighboring chief. But she could not be persuaded to listen to the proposal. Supposing her aversion merely the result of natural timidity, her objections were not deemed of a serious character;

and in a state of society where matches are left very much in the hands of the parents, they proceeded to make the customary arrangements for the union. The young man was informed, through his parents, that his offer had been favorably received. The day was fixed for the marriage visit to the lodge, and the persons who were to be present were invited. As the favorable expression of the will of the parents had been explicitly given, and compliance was as certainly expected, she saw no means of frustrating the object, but by a firm declaration of her sentiments. She told her parents that she could never consent to the match, and that her mind was unalterably made up.

It had been her custom to pass many of her hours in her favorite place of retirement, under a low, broad-topped young pine, whose leaves whispered in the wind. Thither she now went, and while leaning pensively against its trunk, she fancied she heard articulate sounds. Very soon they became more distinct, and appeared to address her.

> Maiden, think me not a tree
> But thine own dear lover free,
> Tall and youthful in my bloom
> With the bright green nodding plume.
> Thou art leaning on my breast,
> Lean for ever there, and rest!
> Fly from man, that bloody race,
> Pards, assassins, bold and base;
> Quit their din, and false parade
> For the quiet lonely shade.
> Leave the windy birchen cot
> For my own, light happy lot,
> O'er thee I my veil will fling,
> Light as beetle's silken wing;
> I will breathe perfume of flowers,
> O'er thy happy evening hours;
> I will in my shell canoe
> Waft thee o'er the waters blue;
> I will deck thy mantle fold,
> With the sun's last rays of gold.
> Come, and on the mountain free
> Rove a fairy bright with me.[6]

Her fancy confirmed all she heard as the words of sober truth. She needed nothing more to settle her purpose.

On the evening preceding the day fixed for her marriage, she dressed herself in her best garments. She arranged her hair according to the fashion of her tribe, and put on the ornaments she possessed. Thus robed, she assumed an air of unwonted gaiety, as she presented herself before her parents. "I am going," said she, "to meet my little lover, the chieftain of the green plume, who is waiting for me at the Spirit Grove;" and her countenance expressed a buoyant delight, which she had seldom evinced.

They were quite pleased with these evidences of restored cheerfulness, supposing she was going to act some harmless freak. "I am going," said she, to her mother, as she left the lodge, "from one who has watched my infancy, and guarded my youth; who has given me medicine when I was sick, and prepared me food when I was well. I am going from a father who has ranged the forest to procure the choicest skins for my dress, and kept his lodge supplied with the best food of the chase. I am going from a lodge which has been my shelter from the storms of winter, and my shield from the heats of summer. Adieu! adieu!" she cried as she skipped lightly over the plain.

So saying she hastened to the confines of the fairy haunted grove. As it was her common resort, no alarm was entertained, and the parents confidently waited her return with the sunset hour. But as she did not arrive, they began to feel uneasy. Darkness approached, and no daughter returned. They now lighted torches of pine wood, and proceeded to the gloomy forest of pines, but were wholly unsuccessful in the search. They called aloud upon her name, but the echo was their only reply. Next day the search was renewed, but with no better success. Suns rose and set, but they rose and set upon a bereaved father and mother, who were never afterward permitted to behold a daughter whose manners and habits they had not sufficiently guarded, and whose inclinations they had, in the end, too violently thwarted.

One night a party of fishermen, who were spearing fish near the Spirit Grove, descried something resembling a female figure standing on the shore. As the evening was mild, and the waters calm, they cautiously paddled their canoe ashore, but the slight ripple of the water excited alarm. The figure fled, but they recognized, in the shape and dress, as she ascended the bank, the lost daughter, and they saw the green plumes of her lover waving over his forehead, as he glided lightly through the forest of young pines.[7]

NOTES

1. "Leelinau. A Chippewa Tale" in *M. H.*
2. Schoolcraft overemphasized the Puk Wudj Ininee in *M. H.*, again for obvious association with *Hiawatha,* and changed Kaug Wudjoo to Naigow Wudjoo or the Grand Sablé. Kaug Wudjoo is now known as the Porcupine Mountains.
3. Claytonia Virginica, or the spring beauty.
4. A game played with sticks and two small blocks on a string by females. [H. R. S.]
5. A game played with a piece of perforated leather and a bone. [H. R. S.]
6. This, and the preceding poem, are printed together as invocation and response in "Fairy Whisperings," Wild Notes of the Pibbigwun, *M. H.*, pp. 309-310. Here, Schoolcraft equals or surpasses many of the poets of the famed collections of R. W. Griswold in sentimentalism.

7. From the fact that this story was severely pruned in *M. H.*, pp. 299-301, one suspects that it was chiefly Schoolcraft's invention. The geography (Leelanau—western Michigan, Manitowoc—eastern Wisconsin, La Grand Sable—upper Michigan) links it to contemporary Indian tales in popular magazines rather than to an authentic Indian source. Retold in *C. M.*, pp. 252-260, and *C-C*, pp. 200-208.

PUK WUDJ ININEE

AN ODJIBWA TALE[1]

THERE WAS A TIME when all the inhabitants of the earth had died, excepting two helpless children, a baby boy, and a little girl. When their parents died, these children were asleep. The little girl, who was the elder, was the first to awake. She looked around her, but seeing nobody besides her little brother, who lay asleep, she quietly resumed her bed. At the end of ten days her brother moved without opening his eyes. At the end of ten days more he changed his position, lying on the other side.

The girl soon grew up to woman's estate, but the boy increased in stature very slowly. It was a long time before he could even creep. When he was able to walk, his sister made him a little bow and arrows, and suspended around his neck a small shell, saying, you shall be called WA-DAIS-AIS-IMID, or He of the Little Shell. Every day he would go out with his little bow shooting at the small birds. The first bird he killed was a tomtit. His sister was highly pleased when he took it to her. She carefully skinned and stuffed it, and put it away for him. The next day he killed a red squirrel. His sister preserved this too. The third day he killed a partridge (Peéna), which she stuffed and set up. After this, he acquired more courage, and would venture some distance from home. His skill and success as a hunter daily increased, and he killed the deer, bear, moose, and other large animals inhabiting the forest. In fine he became a great hunter.

He had now arrived to maturity of years, but remained a perfect infant in stature. One day walking about he came to a small lake. It was in the winter season. He saw a man on the ice killing beavers. He appeared to be a giant. Comparing himself to this great man he appeared no bigger than an insect. He seated himself on the shore, and watched his movements. When the large man had killed many beavers, he put them on a hand sled, which he had, and pursued his way home. When he saw him retire, he followed him, and wielding his magic shell, cut off the tail of one of the beavers, and ran home with his trophy. When the tall stranger reached his lodge, with his sled load of beavers, he was surprised to find the tail of one of them gone, for he had not observed the movements of the little hero of the shell.

The next day WA-DAIS-AIS-IMID, went to the same lake. The man had already fixed his load of beavers on his *odaw'bon* or sled, and commenced his return. But he nimbly ran forward, and overtaking him, succeeded, by the same means, in securing another of the beaver's tails. When the man saw that he had lost another of this most esteemed part of the animal, he was very angry. I wonder, said he, what dog it is, that has thus cheated

160

me. Could I meet him, I would make his flesh quiver at the point of my lance. Next day he pursued his hunting at the beaver dam near the lake, and was followed again by the little man of the shell. On this occasion the hunter had used so much expedition, that he had accomplished his object, and nearly reached his home, before our tiny hero could overtake him. He nimbly drew his shell and cut off another beaver's tail. In all these pranks, he availed himself of his power of invisibility, and thus escaped observation. When the man saw that the trick had been so often repeated, his anger was greater than ever. He gave vent to his feelings in words. He looked carefully around to see whether he could discover any tracks. But he could find none. His unknown visitor had stepped so lightly as to leave no track.

Next day he resolved to disappoint him by going to his beaver pond very early. When WA-DAIS-AIS-IMID reached the place, he found the fresh traces of his work, but he had already returned. He followed his tracks, but failed to overtake him. When he came in sight of the lodge the stranger was in front of it, employed in skinning his beavers. As he stood looking at him, he thought, I will let him see me. Presently the man, who proved to be no less a personage than Manabozho, looked up and saw him. After regarding him with attention, "Who are you, little man?" asked Manabozho. "I have a mind to kill you." The little hero of the shell replied, "If you were to try to kill me you could not do it."

When he returned home he told his sister that they must separate. "I must go away," said he, "it is my fate. You too," he added, "must go away soon. Tell me where you would wish to dwell." She said, "I would like to go to the place of the breaking of daylight. I have always loved the east. The earliest glimpses of light are from that quarter, and it is, to my mind, the most beautiful part of the heavens. After I get there, my brother, whenever you see the clouds in that direction of various colors, you may think that your sister is painting her face."

"And I," said he, "my sister, shall live on the mountains and rocks. There I can see you at the earliest hour, and there the streams of water are clear, and the air pure. And I shall ever be called PUK WUDJ ININEE, or the little wild man of the mountains.

"But," he resumed, "before we part forever, I must go and try to find some Manitoes." He left her and traveled over the surface of the globe, [sic] and then went far down into the earth. He had been treated well wherever he went. At last he found a giant Manito, who had a large kettle, which was forever boiling. The giant regarded him with a stern look, and then took him up in his hand, and threw him unceremoniously into the kettle. But by the protection of his personal spirit, he was shielded from harm, and with much ado got out of it and escaped. He returned to his sister, and related his rovings and misadventures. He finished his story by addressing her thus: "My sister, there is a Manito, at each of the four corners of the earth.[2] There is also one above them, far in the sky, and last," continued he, "there is another, and wicked one, who lives deep down in the earth. We must now separate. When the winds blow from the four corners of the earth you must then go. They will carry you to the place you wish. I go to the rocks and mountains, where my kindred will ever delight to dwell." He then took his ball stick, and commenced running up a high mountain, whooping as he went. Presently the winds blew, and as he predicted, his sister was borne by them to the eastern sky, where she has ever since been, and her name is the Morning Star.

> Blow, winds, blow! my sister lingers
> For her dwelling in the sky,
> Where the morn, with rosy fingers,
> Shall her cheeks with vermil dye.
>
> There, my earliest views directed,
> Shall from her their colour take,
> And her smiles, through clouds reflected,
> Guide me on, by wood or lake.
>
> While I range the highest mountains,
> Sport in valleys green and low,
> Or beside our Indian fountains
> Raise my tiny hip holla.[3]

NOTES

1. In *M. H.* the title is shifted to the plural: "Puk Wudj Ininees; or, the Vanishing Little Men. An Odjibwa Myth of Fairies."

2. The opinion that the earth is a square and level plain, and that the winds blow from its four corners, is a very ancient eastern opinion. [H. R. S.] As the reader will have noticed, Schoolcraft was a rapid and often careless writer. A "square and level plain" could hardly be a "globe."

3. This poem is another of Schoolcraft's inventions. The tale was reprinted unchanged in *M. H.*, pp. 90-94. In both *C. M.*, pp. 252-260, and *C-C*, pp. 87-94, the story is called "He of the Little Shell."

MISHOSHA

OR

THE MAGICIAN OF THE LAKES[1]

IN AN EARLY AGE of the world, when there were fewer inhabitants than there now are, there lived an Indian, in a remote place, who had a wife and two children. They seldom saw anyone out of the circle of their own lodge. Animals were abundant in so secluded a situation, and the man found no difficulty in supplying his family with food.

In this way they lived in peace and happiness, which might have continued if the hunter had not found cause to suspect his wife. She secretly cherished an attachment for a young man whom she accidentally met one day in the woods. She even planned the death of her husband for his sake, for she knew if she did not kill her husband, her husband, the moment he detected her crime, would kill her.

The husband, however, eluded her project by his readiness and decision. He narrowly watched her movements. One day he secretly followed her footsteps into the forest, and having concealed himself behind a tree, he soon beheld a tall young man approach and lead away his wife. His arrows were in his hands, but he did not use them. He thought he would kill her the moment she returned.

Meantime, he went home and sat down to think. At last he came to the determination of quitting her forever, thinking that her own conscience would punish her sufficiently, and relying on her maternal feelings to take care of the two children, who were boys, he immediately took up his arms and departed.

When the wife returned she was disappointed in not finding her husband, for she had now concerted her plan, and intended to have dispatched him. She waited several days, thinking he might have been led away by the chase, but finding he did not return, she suspected the true cause. Leaving her two children in the lodge, she told them she was going a short distance and would return. She then fled to her paramour and came back no more.

The children, thus abandoned, soon made away with the food left in the lodge, and were compelled to quit it in search of more. The eldest boy, who was of an intrepid temper, was strongly attached to his brother, frequently carrying him when he became weary, and gathering all the wild fruit he saw. They wandered deeper and deeper into the forest, losing all traces of their former habitation, until they were completely lost in its mazes.

The eldest boy had a knife, with which he made a bow and arrows, and

163

was thus enabled to kill a few birds for himself and brother. In this manner they continued to pass on, from one piece of forest to another, not knowing whither they were going. At length they saw an opening through the woods, and were shortly afterward delighted to find themselves on the borders of a large lake. Here the elder brother busied himself in picking the seed pods of the wild rose, which he preserved as food. In the meantime, the younger brother amused himself by shooting arrows in the sand, one of which happened to fall into the lake. PANIGWUN,[2] the elder brother, not willing to lose the arrow, waded in the water to reach it. Just as he was about to grasp the arrow, a canoe passed up to him with great rapidity. An old man, sitting in the center, seized the affrighted youth and placed him in the canoe. In vain the boy addressed him—"My grandfather (a term of respect for old people), pray take my little brother also. Alone, I cannot go with you; he will starve if I leave him." Mishosha (the old man) only laughed at him. Then uttering the charm, CHEMAUN POLL, and giving his canoe a slap, it glided through the water with inconceivable swiftness. In a few moments they reached the habitation of the magician, standing on an island in the center of the lake.[3] Here he lived with his two daughters, who managed the affairs of his household. Leading the young man up to the lodge, he addressed his eldest daughter. "Here," said he, "my daughter, I have brought a young man to be your husband." Husband! thought the young woman; rather another victim of your bad arts, and your insatiate enmity to the human race. But she made no reply, seeming thereby to acquiesce in her father's will.

The young man thought he saw surprise depicted in the eyes of the daughter, during the scene of this introduction, and determined to watch events narrowly. In the evening he overheard the two daughters in conversation. "There," said the eldest daughter, "I told you he would not be satisfied with his last sacrifice. He has brought another victim, under the pretense of providing me a husband. Husband, indeed! The poor youth will be in some horrible predicament before another sun has set. When shall we be spared the scenes of vice and wickedness which are daily taking place before our eyes?"

Panigwun took the first opportunity of acquainting the daughters how he had been carried off, and been compelled to leave his little brother on the shore. They told him to wait until their father was asleep, then to get up and take his canoe, and using the charm he had obtained, it would carry him quickly to his brother; that he could carry him food, prepare a lodge for him, and be back before daybreak. He did, in every respect, as he had been directed—the canoe obeyed the charm, and carried him safely over, and after providing for the subsistence of his brother, told him that in a short time he should come for him. Then returning to the enchanted island, he resumed his place in the lodge, before the magician awoke. Once, during the night, Mishosha awoke, and not seeing his destined son-in-law, asked his daughter what had become of him. She replied that he had merely stepped out, and would be back soon. This satisfied him. In the morning, finding the young man in the lodge, his suspicions were completely lulled. "I see, my daughter," said he, "you have told the truth."

As soon as the sun arose, Mishosha thus addressed the young man. "Come, my son, I have a mind to gather gulls' eggs. I know an island where there are great quantities, and I wish your aid in getting them." The young man saw no reasonable excuse; and getting into the canoe, the magician gave it a slap, and uttering a command, they were in an instant at the island. They found the shores strewn with gulls' eggs, and the island full of birds of this species. "Go, my son," said the old man, "and gather the eggs, while I remain in the canoe."

But Panigwun had no sooner got ashore, than Mishosha pushed his canoe a little from the land, and exclaimed—"Listen, ye gulls! you have long expected an offering from me. I now give you a victim. Fly down and devour him." Then striking his canoe, he left the young man to his fate.

The birds immediately came in clouds around their victim, darkening the air with their numbers. But the youth, seizing the first that came near him, and drawing his knife, cut off its head. He immediately skinned the bird, and hung the feathers as a trophy on his breast. "Thus," he exclaimed, "will I treat every one of you who approaches me. Forbear, therefore, and listen to my words. It is not for you to eat human flesh. You have been given by the Great Spirit as food for man. Neither is it in the power of that old magician to do you any good. Take me on your backs and carry me to his lodge, and you shall see that I am not ungrateful." The gulls obeyed; collected in a cloud for him to rest upon, and quickly flew to the lodge, where they arrived before the magician. The daughters were surprised at his return, but Mishosha, on entering the lodge, conducted himself as if nothing extraordinary had taken place.

The next day he again addressed the youth:—"Come, my son," said he, "I will take you to an island covered with the most beautiful stones and pebbles, looking like silver. I wish you to assist me in gathering some of them. They will make handsome ornaments, and possess great medicinal virtues." Entering the canoe, the magician made use of his charm, and they were carried in a few moments to a solitary bay in an island, where there was a smooth sandy beach. The young man went ashore as usual, and began to search. "A little farther, a little farther," cried the old man. "Upon that rock you will get some fine ones." Then pushing his canoe from land —"Come, thou great king of fishes," cried the old man; "you have long expected an offering from me. Come, and eat the stranger whom I have just put ashore on your island." So saying, he commanded his canoe to return, and it was soon out of sight.

Immediately, a monstrous fish thrust his long snout from the water,[4] crawled partially on the beach, and opened wide his jaws to receive his victim. "When!" exclaimed the young man, drawing his knife and putting himself in a threatening attitude, "when did you ever taste human flesh? Have a care of yourself. You were given by the Great Spirit to man, and if you, or any of your tribe eat human flesh, you will fall sick and die.

Listen not to the words of that wicked man, but carry me back to his island, in return for which I will present you a piece of red cloth." The fish complied, raising his back out of the water, to allow the young man to get on. Then taking his way through the lake, he landed his charge safely on the island before the return of the magician. The daughters were still more surprised to see that he had escaped the arts of their father the second time. But the old man on his return maintained his taciturnity and self-composure. He could not, however, help saying to himself—"What manner of boy is this, who is ever escaping from my power. But his spirit shall not save him. I will entrap him tomorrow. Ha, ha, ha!"

Next day the magician addressed the young man as follows: "Come, my son," said he, "you must go with me to procure some young eagles. I wish to tame them. I have discovered an island where they are in great abundance." When they had reached the island, Mishosha led him inland until they came to the foot of a tall pine, upon which the nests were. "Now, my son," said he, "climb up this tree and bring down the birds." The young man obeyed. When he had with great difficulty got near the nest, "Now," exclaimed the magician, addressing the tree, "stretch yourself up and be very tall." The tree rose up at the command. "Listen, ye eagles," continued the old man, "you have long expected a gift from me. I now present you this boy, who has had the presumption to molest your young. Stretch forth your claws and seize him." So saying he left the young man to his fate, and returned.

But the intrepid youth drawing his knife, and cutting off the head of the first eagle that menaced him, raised his voice and exclaimed, "Thus will I deal with all who come near me. What right have you, ye ravenous birds, who were made to feed on beasts, to eat human flesh? Is it because that cowardly old canoe-man has bid you do so? He is an old woman. He can neither do you good nor harm. See, I have already slain one of your number. Respect my bravery, and carry me back that I may show you how I shall treat you."

The eagles, pleased with his spirit, assented, and clustering thick around him formed a seat with their backs, and flew toward the enchanted island. As they crossed the water they passed over the magician, lying half asleep in his canoe.

The return of the young man was hailed with joy by the daughters, who now plainly saw that he was under the guidance of a strong spirit. But the ire of the old man was excited, although he kept his temper under subjection. He taxed his wits for some new mode of ridding himself of the youth, who had so successfully baffled his skill. He next invited him to go a-hunting.

Taking his canoe, they proceeded to an island and built a lodge to shelter themselves during the night. In the meanwhile the magician caused a deep fall of snow, with a storm of wind and severe cold. According to custom, the young man pulled off his moccasins and leggings and hung them before the fire to dry. After he had gone to sleep the magician, watching his opportunity, got up, and taking one moccasin and one legging, threw them into the fire. He then went to sleep. In the morning, stretching himself as he arose and uttering an exclamation of surprise, "My son," said he, "what has become of your moccasin and legging? I believe this is the moon in which fire attracts, and I fear they have been drawn in." The young man suspected the true cause of his loss, and rightly attributed it to a design of the magician to freeze him to death on the march. But he maintained the strictest silence, and drawing his conaus over his head thus communed with himself: "I have full faith in the Manito who has preserved me thus far, I do not fear that he will forsake me in this cruel emergency. Great is his power, and I invoke it now that he may enable me to prevail over this wicked enemy of mankind."

He then drew on the remaining moccasin and legging, and taking a dead coal from the fireplace, invoked his spirit to give it efficacy, and blackened his foot and leg as far as the lost garment usually reached. He then got up and announced himself ready for the march. In vain Mishosha led him through snows and over morasses, hoping to see the lad sink at every moment. But in this he was disappointed, and for the first time they returned home together.

Taking courage from this success, the young man now determined to try his own power, having previously consulted with the daughters. They all agreed that the life the old man led was detestable, and that whoever would rid the world of him, would entitle himself to the thanks of the human race.

On the following day the young man thus addressed his hoary captor. "My grandfather, I have often gone with you on perilous excursions and never murmured. I must now request that you will accompany me. I wish to visit my little brother, and to bring him home with me." They accordingly went on a visit to the mainland, and found the little lad in the spot where he had been left. After taking him into the canoe, the young man again addressed the magician: "My grandfather, will you go and cut me a few of those red willows on the bank? I wish to prepare some smoking mixture." "Certainly, my son," replied the old man, "what you wish is not very hard. Ha, ha, ha! do you think me too old to get up there?" No sooner was Mishosha ashore, than the young man, placing himself in the proper position struck the canoe with his hand, and pronouncing the charm, N'CHIMAUN POLL, the canoe immediately flew through the water on its return to the island. It was evening when the two brothers arrived, and carried the canoe ashore. But the elder daughter informed the young man that unless he sat up and watched the canoe, and kept his hand upon it, such was the power of their father, it would slip off and return to him. Panigwun watched faithfully till near the dawn of day, when he could no longer resist the drowsiness which oppressed him, and he fell into a short doze. In the meantime the canoe slipped off and sought its master, who soon returned in high glee. "Ha, ha, ha! my son," said he; "you thought to play me a trick. It was very clever. But you see I am too old for you."

A short time after, the youth again addressed the magician. "My grandfather, I wish to try my skill in hunting. It is said there is plenty of game on an island not far off, and I have to request that you will take me there in your canoe." They accordingly went to the island and spent the day in hunting. Night coming on they put up a temporary lodge. When the magician had sunk into a profound sleep, the young man got up, and taking one of Mishosha's leggings and moccasins from the place where they hung, threw them into the fire, thus retaliating the artifice before played upon himself. He had discovered that the foot and leg were the only vulnerable parts of the magician's body. Having committed these articles to the fire, he besought his Manito that he would raise a great storm of snow, wind, and hail, and then laid himself down beside the old man. Consternation was depicted on the countenance of the latter, when he awoke in the morning and found his moccasin and legging missing. "I believe, my grandfather," said the young man, "that this is the moon in which fire attracts, and I fear your foot and leg garments have been drawn in." Then rising and bidding the old man follow him, he began the morning's hunt, frequently turning to see how Mishosha kept up. He saw him faltering at every step, and almost benumbed with cold, but encouraged him to follow, saying, we shall soon get through and reach the shore; although he took pains, at the same time, to lead him in roundabout ways, so as to let the frost take complete effect. At length the old man reached the brink of the island where the woods are succeeded by a border of smooth sand. But he could go no farther; his legs became stiff and refused motion, and he found himself fixed to the spot. But he still kept stretching out his arms and swinging his body to and fro. Every moment he found the numbness creeping higher. He felt his legs growing downward like roots, the feathers of his head turned to leaves, and in a few seconds he stood a tall and stiff sycamore, leaning toward the water.

Panigwun leaped into the canoe, and pronouncing the charm, was soon transported to the island, where he related his victory to the daughters. They applauded the deed, agreed to put on mortal shapes, become wives to the two young men, and forever quit the enchanted island. And passing immediately over to the mainland, they lived lives of happiness and peace.[5]

NOTES

1. "Mishosha; or, the Magician of Lake Superior" in *M. H.*

2. The end wing feather. [H. R. S.]

3. Grand Island in Lake Superior was the traditional home of Mishosha as well as of Kaubina ("The Charmed Arrow"). See *P. M.*, p. 102.

4. One of the gigantic sturgeon that once filled Lake Superior. Compare with the sturgeon in *Hiawatha*.

5. Reprinted in *M. H.*, pp. 202-212. Mrs. Jameson also used this story in her book, *op. cit.*, III, pp. 96-113. Compare with "Owasso and Wagoond."

THE WEENDIGOES[1]

A SAGINAW STORY

ONCE THERE LIVED in a lonely forest, a man and his wife, who had a son. The father went out every day, according to the custom of the Indians, to hunt for food, to support his family. One day while he was absent, his wife, on going out of the lodge, looked toward the lake that was near, and saw a very large man walking on the water, and coming fast toward the lodge. He had already advanced so near that flight was useless. She thought to herself, what shall I say to the monster that will please him. As he came near, she ran in, and taking the hand of her son, a boy of three or four years old, led him out. Speaking very loud, "See, my son," said she, "your grandfather," and then added in a conciliatory tone, "he will have pity on us." The giant advanced, and said sneeringly, "Yes, my son." And then addressing the woman asked, "Have you anything to eat?" Fortunately the lodge was filled with meat of various kinds. The woman thought to please him by handing him some cooked meat, but he pushed it away in a dissatisfied manner, and took up the raw carcass of a deer, which he *glutted* up, sucking the bones, and drinking the blood.

When the hunter came home, he was surprised to see the monster, for he looked very frightful. He had again brought home the whole carcass of a deer, which he had no sooner put down than the cannibal seized it, tore it to pieces, and devoured it, as if it had been a mere mouthful. The hunter looked at him with fear and astonishment, telling his wife that he was afraid for their lives, as this monster was one whom Indians call Weendigo. He did not even dare to speak to him, nor did the cannibal say a word, but as soon as he had finished his meal, he laid himself down and fell asleep.

Early next morning he told the hunter that he should also go out hunting, and they went together. Toward evening they returned, the man bringing a deer, but the Weendigo brought home the bodies of two Indians, whom he had killed. He very composedly sat down and commenced tearing the limbs apart, breaking the bones with his teeth, and despatching them as easily as if they had been soft pieces of flesh. He was not even satisfied with that, but again took up the deer which the hunter had brought, to finish his supper, while the hunter and his family had to live on their dried meat.

In this manner the hunter and the Weendigo lived for some time, and it is remarkable that the monster never made an attempt on their lives although the ground outside the lodge was white with the human bones he had cast out. He was always still and gloomy, and seldom spake to them. One evening he told the hunter that the time had now arrived for him to

169

take his leave, but before doing so he would give him a charm that would always make him successful in killing moose. This charm consisted of two arrows, and after giving them to the hunter he thanked him and his wife for their kindness, and departed, saying that he had all the world to travel over.

The hunter and his wife felt happy when freed from his presence, for they had expected, at every moment, to have been devoured by him. He tried the virtues of his arrows, and never failed to be successful in their use. They had lived in this manner for a year, when a great evil befell them. The hunter was absent one day when his wife, on going out of the lodge, saw something like a black cloud approaching. She looked till it came near, when she perceived that it was another Weendigo. She apprehended no danger, thinking he would treat them as the first one had done. In this she was wholly mistaken. Unluckily they had but a small portion of moose meat in the lodge. The Weendigo looked around for something to eat, and being disappointed he took the lodge and threw it to the winds. He hardly seemed to notice the woman, for she was but a morsel for him. However, he grasped her by the waist. Her cries and entreaties, with those of her son, had no effect—the monster tore out her entrails, and taking her body at one mouthful, started off without noticing the boy, probably thinking it was not worth his while to take half a mouthful.

When the hunter returned from the forest, he did not know what to think. His lodge was gone, and he saw his son sitting near the spot where it had stood, shedding tears. On a nearer approach he saw a few remains of his wife, and his son related all the circumstances of her death. The man blackened his face and vowed in his heart he would have revenge. He built another lodge, and collecting the remains of his wife, placed them in the hollow part of a dry tree. He left his boy to take care of the lodge while he was absent, hunting, and would roam about from place to place, trying to forget his misfortune. He made a bow and arrows for his son, and did everything in his power to please him.

One day, while he was absent, his son shot his arrows out, through the top of the lodge, but when he went out to look for them he could not find them. His father made him some more, and when he was again left alone, he shot one of them out, but although he paid particular attention to the spot where it fell, he could not find it. He shot another, and immediately ran out of the lodge to see where it fell. He was surprised to see a beautiful boy, just in the act of taking it up, and running with it toward a large tree, where he disappeared. He followed, and having come to the tree, he beheld the face of the boy, looking out through an opening in the hollow part. "Nha-ha[2] (oh dear)," he said, "my friend, come out and play with me." And he urged him till he consented. They played and shot their arrows by turns. Suddenly the younger boy said, "your father is coming. We must stop. Promise me that you will not tell him." The elder promised, and the other disappeared in the tree. The elder boy then went home, and when his father returned from the chase, sat demurely by the fire. In the course of the evening he asked his father to make him a new bow. To an inquiry of his father as to the use he meant to make of two bows, he replied, that one might break, or get lost; he then consented. Next day, after his father had gone, he went to his friend, and invited him to come out and play, and at the same time presented him the new bow. They went and played in the lodge together, and raised the ashes all over it. Suddenly again the youngest said, "your father is coming, I must leave." He again exacted a promise of secrecy, and went back to his tree. The eldest took his seat near the fire. When the hunter came in, he was surprised to see the ashes scattered about. "Why, my son," said he, "you must have played very hard today, to raise such a dust, all alone." "Yes," said the boy, "I was lonesome, and ran round and round—*that* is the cause of it."

Next day the hunter made ready for the chase as usual. The boy said, "Father, try and hunt all day, and see what you can kill." As soon as he had gone, the boy called his friend, and they played and chased each other round the lodge. The man was returning and came to a rising piece of ground, when he heard his son laughing and making a noise, but the sounds appeared as if they arose from *two* persons playing. At the same instant the young boy of the tree stopped, and after saying, "your father is coming," ran off to the tree, which stood near the lodge. The hunter, on entering found his son sitting near the fire, very quiet, but he was much surprised to see all the articles of the lodge lying in various directions. "Why, my son," said he, "you must play *very* hard, every day, and what do you do, all alone to throw about all our things in this manner, and cause the ashes to spread about the lodge?" The boy again made excuse. "Father," said he, "I play in *this* manner—I chase and drag my coat around the lodge, and that is the reason you see ashes spread about." The hunter was not satisfied until he saw his son play with the coat, which he did so adroitly as to deceive him. Next day the boy repeated his request that the father would be absent all day, and see if he could not kill *two* deer. He thought it strange for his son to make such a request, and rather suspected something. He, however, went into the forest, and when out of sight, his son went for his young companion to the tree, and they resumed their sports. The father, on coming home at evening, when he reached the rising ground, which almost overlooked the lodge, heard again the sounds of laughing and playing, and could not be mistaken; he was now certain there were two voices. The boy from the tree had barely time to escape, when he entered and found his son, sitting as usual, near the fire. When he was seated and cast his eyes around, he saw the lodge was in worse confusion than before. "My son," said he, "you must be very foolish, when alone, to play so. But tell me—I heard two voices I am certain," and he looked closely on the prints of the footsteps in the ashes. "True," he said, "here is the print of a foot that is smaller than my son's," which satisfied him that his suspicions were well founded, and that some very young person had played with his son. The boy, at this time, thought best to tell his father all that had been done. "Why, father," said he, "I found a boy in the hollow of the tree, near the lodge, where you put my mother's bones." Strange thoughts came over the man; he thought that this little boy might have been created from the remains of his deceased wife. But as Indians are generally fearful of disturbing the dead, he did not dare to go near the place where he had placed her remains. He thought best to tell his son, and make him promise, that he would entice his friend to a dead tree, that was near their lodge, by telling him that they could kill many flying squirrels by setting fire to it. He said he would conceal himself near by, and take the boy. Next day the hunter went into the woods, and his son went and insisted on his friend's going with him to kill the squirrels. He objected that his father was near, but was, at length, persuaded to go, and, after they had set fire to the tree, and while they were busy in killing the squirrels, the father suddenly made his appearance and clasped the boy in his arms. He cried out, "Kago! Kago! (don't, don't) you will tear my clothes"—which appeared to have been made of a fine transparent skin. The father tried to reassure him by every means in his power. By long-continued kindness, he, at last, succeeded, and the boy was reconciled to his new situation; but it was owing principally to the society of his friend. The father now knew that it was the Great Spirit who had thus miraculously raised him a son from the remains of his wife; and he felt persuaded that the boy would, in time, become a great man, and aid him in his revenge on the Weendigoes.

The hunter was now more reconciled to the loss of his wife, and spent as much time as he could spare from the chase, in attending to his sons. But what was very remarkable, both his sons retained their low stature, although they were well formed and beautiful.

One day he advised his sons not to go near a certain lake, which, he said, was inhabited by foul birds, who were vicious and dangerous. In the course of one of their rambles, the boys had wandered near it, and they came out and stood on its banks. They saw, on one side, a mountain, rising precipitously from the water, and reaching apparently to the sky. They stood and looked for some time with astonishment at the sight. The youngest spoke and said, "I see no harm in climbing the rock to see what is to be discovered on its top." They ascended, and had got up, with difficulty, halfway, when the rumbling noise of thunder was heard, and lightning began to play near them. But they were undaunted, and reached the top, where they beheld an enormous bird's nest, and in it two very large young birds. Although they had only the soft down, as yet, on their bodies, they appeared to be monsters, and when the young men put a stick near their eyes, which they opened and shut very quick, the flashes they emitted broke the stick in pieces. They, however, took the young birds, and with great difficulty reached the lodge with them. When their father came home, they told him what fine birds they had, and requested him to tame them, and bring them up as pets, "for," said they, "when we took them we intended them for you." They told him where they had procured them, saying, that he need not have given them the caution respecting the dangers of the lake. The father was now convinced that both his sons were gifted with supernatural powers. He, however, advised them not to go near another lake he told them of, which was inhabited by *Mishe-genabigoes.*[3] When he was again absent, the boys wandered near that lake, and as they were talking, they heard some one ordering them away, and telling them not to make so much noise. "Who are you?" they answered. "I am Mishegenabig," cried the same voice; "and who are you that dare to disobey me?" The youngest boy told his brother to sing some magic words, while he went in search of the one who had so insultingly spoken to them; and while he waded into the water, the other sang these words:

	Literal translation.
O pau neence	Little slave—
In de go wish	Bad monster—
Se nau bun	I spy him—
Opunai sun	His diminutive liver—
Mau moke e sagin.	Peeping out (as a mushroom suddenly

shooting out of the ground, or a thing appearing from beneath the water, and applied generally to a person, or noun animate, unexpectedly appearing as a mushroom, etc.).

He continued singing as he was directed, and he soon saw pieces of liver floating on the water. Soon after his brother returned from under the water with a mishegenabig, whom he dragged by his horns. "Brother," said he, "this is the one who was so insolent to us. We will now go home and make a pet of him." When they reached home they told their father that they had brought him another pet. Their father was thoughtful. He was surprised to see his son overcome all manner of monsters; he, however, kept silent, and rejoiced in spirit to think that his sons were so fortunate in commencing life.

One day, after musing for a long time, he told his sons that his time was come, and that he should have to follow his forefathers to the land of the west. "But," he continued, "before I leave this earth, my sons, listen to my advice." He proceeded to speak to them, and when he had done, the youngest said, "Father, you must remember the Weendigoes, and the misery they brought on you. You will now leave earth, with your two feathered favorites; but first we will feed them with the flesh of the mishegenabig." They did so, and their father departed amid thunder and lightnings, for the two birds were the offspring of thunder. He fixed his residence as directed by the Great Manito in the sky toward the north, and he retains his name to the present day, which is, The Thunder commencing in the north, and going south.[4]

(This story exhibits the mind of the Saginaws in a characteristic light. This tribe are emphatically the Seminoles of the North, consisting originally of individuals who were refugees from the great Odjibwa family. Their origin, as a distinct band, is comparatively recent, dating no farther back than the time of the flight of the Sauks from the district or country which is now, in allusion to them, denominated Saginaw. The principal town of that adventurous and warlike tribe, was, and is still, called by the natives SAUKINONG (i.e. Sauk-town), and the Chippewa refugees who succeeded, took their denomination of Saginaws from the term. Without further allusion to their history, it may be observed, that the Saginaws have never made the least advances in education or religion. Cruelty, deception, intemperance, and a blind adherence to the idolatrous customs and superstitions of the nation from which they sprang, have been their characteristics. Up to·this day, there is not a. school, or teacher, or preacher, among them. There is not one individual of unmixed blood in the tribe, who can read, or has any pretense to the knowledge of Christianity. Most of their lore is of murders and thefts committed, or vicious adventures of some sort. They have been, emphatically, a band of plunderers. They bore a conspicuous part in the depredations committed on the frontiers of Virginia and Pennsylvania, during the Revolutionary War, and Wayne's war. Their late leader and head chief, KISHKAKO, was a perfect Abaellino in purpose, who spent a long life in iniquities, private and public, and would, at last, have paid the forfeit of his life on the gallows, had he not committed suicide in jail.

The tales of this tribe, of which there are three specimens furnished, partake strongly of the character of the tribe. They have less originality, less moral[ity], and less adherence to the ancient manners and customs of the original stock, than any other of the traditionary fictions yet examined. There is also less purity of language in the original, and a strong dash of vulgarity, which it has required some care to keep out of the translation.)[5]

NOTES

1. The radix of this word is not apparent. The term is used to signify cannibal, giant, monster. The plural termination in *es* is in accordance with the rule of number in English orthography, applied to originally foreign substantives ending in *o,* as in potatoes, mulattoes, etc., and previously applied in relation to Indian words, in Winnebagoes, Otoes, etc. [H. R. S.]

2. This phrase is peculiar to boys and girls, and is sung repeating it several times. [H. R. S.]

3. Monstrous serpents. [H. R. S.]

4. Thunder from this part of the heavens is called, by the Indians, the autumnal thunder. It is the last generally heard for the season, and they say, speaking of it in the plural, that "they are hollaing on their way home." [H. R. S.]

5. This story is not reprinted in *M. H.* A shorter and less gruesome version was presented in *C. M.,* pp. 288-298, and *C-C,* pp. 228-237, with the title "The Weendigoes and the Bone-Dwarf."

THE RACCOON AND CRAWFISH

A FABLE

FROM THE ODJIBWA

THE RACCOON searches the margins of streams for shell-fish, where he is generally sure of finding the AS-SHOG-AISH-I, or crawfish. Indian story says, that the enmity between these two species, and the consequent wariness of each for the other, was such, that the poor raccoon, with all his stealthiness, was at last put to great straits for a meal. The crawfish would no longer venture near the shore, and the raccoon was on the point of starvation. At length he fixed on this expedient to decoy his enemy.

Knowing the crawfish to feed on worms, he procured a quantity of old rotten wood (filled with these worms) and stuffing it in his mouth and ears, and powdering it over his body, he lay down by the water's edge, to induce the belief that he was dead.

An old crawfish came out warily from the water, and crawled around and over his apparently deceased enemy. He rejoiced to find an end put to his murderous career, and cried out to his fellows, "Come up my brothers and sisters, Aissibun[1] is dead, come up and eat him." When a great multitude had gathered around, the raccoon suddenly sprung up, and set to killing and devouring them in such a way that not one was left alive.

While he was still engaged with the broken limbs, a little female crawfish, carrying her infant sister on her back, came up, seeking her relations. Finding they had all been devoured by the raccoon, she resolved not to survive the destruction of her kindred, but went boldly up to the enemy and said, "Here, Aissibun, you behold me and my little sister. We are all alone. You have eaten up our parents, and all our friends, eat us too." And she continued plaintively singing her chant.

> Raccoon, raccoon, monster thin!
> You have murdered all my kin:
> Leave not one to pine alone
> On those shores so late our own.
> You have glutted not a few,
> Stealthy monster, eat us too—
> Let the work be finished soon,
>   Aissibun amoon.[2]

> Here, behold us! linger not,
> Sad and lone is now my lot:

One poor sister, young and small,
Now makes up my little all—
She a baby—faint and weak,
Who cannot yet "mother" speak—
Come, you monster, eat us soon,
                    Aissibun amoon.

Once my people, lodge and band,
Stretched their numbers through the land;
Roving brooks and limpid streams,
By the moon's benignant beams.
First in revel, dance, and play,
Now, alas! ah! where are they?
Clutch us, monster,—eat us soon,
                    Aissibun amoon.

The raccoon felt reproached by this act of courage and magnanimity. "No," said he, "I have banqueted on the largest and the fattest,—I will not dishonor myself by such little prey."

At this moment Manabozho happened to pass by. Seeing how things were, "Tyau!" said he to the raccoon, "thou art a thief and an unmerciful dog. Get thee up into trees, lest I change thee into one of these same worm-fish, for thou wast thyself originally a shell, and bearest in thy name the influence of my transforming hand."[3]

He then took up the little supplicant crawfish and her infant sister and cast them into the stream. "There," said he, "you may dwell. Hide yourselves under the stones, and hereafter you shall be playthings for little children."[4]

NOTES

1. The Raccoon. [H. R. S.]
2. Raccoon, eat us. [H. R. S.]
3. The name of the raccoon in the Chippewa language, appears to be a derivation from *Ais* a shell, with the inflection for the perfect past tense (bun) united with the copulative vowel *i*. But no tale of such transformation as is here alluded to, has been met with. [H. R. S.]
4. This tale does not appear in any other published work of Schoolcraft. The plaintive song is obviously another Schoolcraft fabrication.

LA POUDRE

OR

THE STORM-FOOL

FROM THE ODJIBWA

THE VERNAL EQUINOX in America, north of the 44° of north latitude, generally takes place while the ground is covered with snow, and winter still wears a polar aspect. Storms of wind and light drifting snow, expressively called *poudre* by the French of the upper Lakes, fill the atmosphere, and render it impossible to distinguish objects at a short distance. The fine powdery flakes of snow are driven into the smallest crannies of buildings and fixtures, and seem to be endowed with a subtile power of insinuation, which renders northern joinerwork but a poor defense. It is not uncommon for the sleeper on waking up in the morning, to find heaps of snow, where he had supposed himself quite secure on lying down.

Such seasons are, almost invariably, times of scarcity and hunger with the Indians, for the light snows have buried up the traps of the hunters, and the fishermen are deterred from exercising their customary skill in decoying fish through the ice. They are often reduced to the greatest straits, and compelled to exercise their utmost ingenuity to keep their children from starving. Abstinence, on the part of the elder members of the family, is regarded both as a duty and a merit. Every effort is made to satisfy the importunity of the little ones for food, and if there be a story-teller in the lodge, he is sure to draw upon his cabin lore, to amuse their minds, and beguile the time.

In these storms, when each inmate of the lodge has his *conaus,* or wrapper, tightly drawn around him, and all are cowering around the cabin fire, should some sudden puff of wind drive a volume of light snow into the lodge, it would scarcely happen, but that some one of the group would cry out "Ah, Pauppukeewiss is now gathering his harvest," an expression which has the effect to put them all into good humor.

Pauppukeewiss was a crazy brain, who played many queer tricks, but took care, nevertheless, to supply his family and children with food. But, in this, he was not always successful. Many winters have passed since he was overtaken, at this very season of the year, with great want, and he, with his whole family, was on the point of starvation. Every resource seemed to have failed. The snow was so deep, and the storm continued so long, that he could not even find a partridge or a hare. And his usual resource of fish had entirely failed. His lodge stood in a point of woods, not

177

far back from the shores of the Gitchiguma,[1] or great water, where the autumnal storms had piled up the ice into high pinnacles, resembling castles.

"I will go," said he to his family one morning, "to these castles, and solicit the pity of the spirits, who inhabit them, for I know that they are the residence of some of the spirits of Kabiboonoka. He did so, and found that his petition was not disregarded. They told him to fill his mushkemoots, or sacks, with the ice and snow, and pass on toward his lodge, without looking back, until he came to a certain hill. He must then drop his sacks, and leave them till morning, when he would find them filled with fish.

They cautioned him, that he must by no means look back, although he would hear a great many voices crying out to him, in abusive terms, for these voices were nothing but the wind playing through the branches of the trees. He faithfully obeyed the injunction, although he found it hard to avoid turning round, to see who was calling out to him. And when he visited his sacks in the morning, he found them filled with fish.

It chanced that Manabozho visited him on the morning that he brought home the sacks of fish. He was invited to partake of a feast, which Pauppukeewiss ordered to be prepared for him. While they were eating, Manabozho could not help asking him, by what means he had procured such an abundance of food, at a time when they were all in a state of starvation.

Pauppukeewiss frankly told him the secret, and repeated the precautions which were necessary to ensure success. Manabozho determined to profit by his information, and as soon as he could, he set out to visit the icy castles. All things happened as he had been told. The spirits seemed propitious, and told him to fill and carry. He accordingly filled his sacks with ice and snow, and proceeded rapidly toward the hill of transmutation. But as he ran he heard voices calling out behind him, "thief!" "thief! He has stolen fish from Kabiboonoka," cried one. "Mukumik! mukumik! Take it away! Take it away!" cried another.

In fine his ears were so assailed by all manner of opprobrious terms, that he could not avoid turning his head, to see who it was that thus abused him. But his curiosity dissolved the charm. When he came to visit his bags next morning, he found them filled with ice and snow.

In consequence, he is condemned every year, during the month of March, to run over the hills, with Pauppukeewiss following him, with the cries of mukumik! mukumik!

(NOTE. This trick seems put, with allegoric justice, on Manabozho, on account of his vain-glorious boasting, and imitation of others; for there was nothing done by any one, which he did not deem himself adequate to, and immediately set about to perform. Story-tellers say, he was once rebuked for this spirit, by a little child, who picking up his foot put his great toe in his mouth, which Manabozho tried, but could not do. The Odjibwas apply the term PEEWUN to the kind of finely granulated snow-storm, above alluded to.[2])

NOTES

1. Note the word Longfellow made famous.
2. The substance of this tale is incorporated in "Paup Puk Kewiss," *M. H.*, pp. 52-54.

GIT-CHEE-GAU-ZINEE

THE TRANCE

(THE FOLLOWING STORY is related by the Odjibwas, as semi-traditionary. Without attaching importance to it, in that light, it may be regarded as indicating Indian opinion on the temporary suspension of nervous action in trance, and on the (to them) great unknown void of a future state. The individual, whose name it bears, is vouched to have been an actual personage living on the shores of Lake Superior, where he exercised the authority of a village chief.

In former times, it is averred, the Chippewas followed the custom of interring many articles with the dead, including, if the deceased was a male, his gun, trap, pipe, kettle, war club, clothes, wampum, ornaments, and even a portion of food. This practice has been gradually falling into disuse until at present, it is rare to see the Indians deposit any articles of value with adults. What effect tales like the following may have had, in bringing this ancient pagan custom into discredit, we will not undertake to decide. Much of the change of opinion which has supervened, within the last century, may be fairly attributable to the intercourse of the Indians with white men, and in some situations, to the gradual and almost imperceptible influence of Christianity on their external manners and customs. Still, more is probably due to the keen observation of a people, who have very little property, and may be naturally judged to have ascertained the folly of burying any valuable portion of it with the dead.)

GIT-CHEE-GAU-ZINEE, after a few days' illness, suddenly expired in the presence of his friends, by whom he was beloved and lamented. He had been an expert hunter, and left, among other things, a fine gun, which he had requested might be buried with his body. There were some who thought his death a suspension and not an extinction of the animal functions, and that he would again be restored. His widow was among the number, and she carefully watched the body for the space of four days. She thought that by laying her hand upon his breast she could discover remaining indications of vitality. Twenty-four hours had elapsed, and nearly every vestige of hope had departed, when the man came to life. He gave the following narration to his friends:

"After death, my Jeebi traveled in the broad road of the dead toward the happy land, which is the Indian paradise. I passed on many days with-

180

out meeting with anything of an extraordinary nature. Plains of large extent, and luxuriant herbage, began to pass before my eyes. I saw many beautiful groves, and heard the songs of innumerable birds. At length I began to suffer for the want of food. I reached the summit of an elevation. My eyes caught the glimpse of the city of the dead. But it appeared to be distant, and the intervening space, partly veiled in silvery mists, was spangled with glittering lakes and streams. At this spot I came in sight of numerous herds of stately deer, moose, and other animals, which walked near my path, and appeared to have lost their natural timidity. But having no gun I was unable to kill them. I thought of the request I had made to my friends, to put my gun in my grave, and resolved to go back and seek for it.

"I found I had the free use of my limbs and faculties, and I had no sooner made this resolution, than I turned back. But I now beheld an immense number of men, women, and children, traveling toward the city of the dead, every one of whom I had to face in going back. I saw, in this throng, persons of every age, from the little infant—the sweet and lovely *Penaisee*,[1] to the feeble gray-headed man, stooping with the weight of years. All whom I met, however, were heavily laden with implements, guns, pipes, kettles, meats, and other articles. One man stopped me and complained of the great burdens he had to carry. He offered me his gun, which I however refused, having made up my mind to procure my own. Another offered me a kettle. I saw women who were carrying their basket work and painted paddles, and little boys, with their ornamented war clubs and bows and arrows—the presents of their friends.

"After encountering this throng for two days and nights, I came to the place where I had died. But I could see nothing but a great fire, the flames of which rose up before me, and spread around me. Whichever way I turned to avoid them, the flames still barred my advance. I was in the utmost perplexity, and knew not what to do. At length I determined to make a desperate leap, thinking my friends were on the other side, and in this effort, I awoke from my trance." Here the chief paused, and after a few moments concluded his story with the following admonitory remarks:

"My chiefs and friends," said he, "I will tell you of one practice, in which our forefathers have been wrong. They have been accustomed to deposit too many things with the dead. These implements are burthensome to them. It requires a longer time for them to reach the peace of repose, and almost every one I have conversed with, complained bitterly to me of the evil. It would be wiser to put such things only, in the grave, as the deceased was particularly attached to, or made a formal request to have deposited with him. If he has been successful in the chase, and has abundance of things in his lodge, it would be better that they should remain for his family, or for division among his friends and relatives."

Advice which comes in this pleasing form of story and allegory, can give offense to no one. And it is probably the mode which the northern Indians have employed, from the earliest times, to rebuke faults and instill instruction. The old men, upon whom the duty of giving advice uniformly falls, may have found this the most efficacious means of molding opinion and forming character.[2]

NOTES

1. The term of endearment for a young son. [H. R. S.]
2. First printed in *Travels* (1825), pp. 410-412. The two versions are basically the same though the details differ; e.g., the "twenty-four hours" were four days in the earlier story. Also printed in Jones, *op. cit.,* II, pp. 181-187.

WASSAMO

OR

THE FIRE PLUME

FROM THE OTTOWA

WASSAMO WAS LIVING with his parents on the shores of a large bay on the east coast of Lake Michigan. It was at a period when nature spontaneously furnished everything that was wanted, when the Indian used skins for clothing, and flints for arrow heads. It was long before the time that the flag of the white man had been first seen in these lakes, or the sound of an iron axe had been heard. The skill of our people supplied them with weapons to kill game, and instruments to procure bark for their canoes, and to dress and cook their victuals.

One day, when the season had commenced for fish to be plenty near the shore of the lake, Wassamo's mother said to him, "My son, I wish you would go to yonder point, and see if you cannot procure me some fish, and ask your cousin to accompany you." He did so. They set out, and in the course of the afternoon arrived at the fishing ground. His cousin attended to the nets, for he was grown up to manhood, but Wassamo had not quite reached that age. They put their nets in the water and encamped near them, using only a few pieces of birch bark for a lodge to shelter them at night. They lit up a fire, and while they sat conversing with each other, the moon arose. Not a breath of wind disturbed the smooth and bright surface of the lake. Not a cloud was seen. Wassamo looked out on the water toward their nets, and saw that almost all the floats had disappeared. "Cousin," he said, "let us visit our nets, perhaps we are fortunate." They did so, and were rejoiced, as they drew them up, to see the meshes white, here and there, with fish. They landed in fine spirits, and put away their canoe in safety from the winds. "Wassamo," said his cousin, "you cook, that we may eat." He set about it immediately, and soon got his kettle on the fire, while his cousin was lying at his ease on the opposite side of the fire. "Cousin," said Wassamo, "tell me stories, or sing me some love songs." The other obeyed and sung his plaintive songs. He would frequently break off, and tell parts of stories, and then sing again, as suited his feelings or fancy. While thus employed, he unconsciously fell asleep. Wassamo had scarcely noticed it, in his care to watch the kettle, and when the fish were done, he took the kettle off. He spoke to his cousin, but received no answer. He took the wooden ladle and skimmed off the oil, for the fish were very fat. He had a flambeau of twisted bark in one hand to give light, but when he came to take

183

out the fish he did not know how to manage to hold the light. He took off his garters and tied them around his head, and then placed the lighted flambeau above his forehead, so that it was firmly held by the bandage, and threw its light brilliantly around him. Having both hands thus at liberty, he began to take out the fish, every now and then moving his head, as he blew off the oil from the broth. He again spoke to his cousin, but he now perceived by his breathing, that he was asleep. He hastened to finish the removal of the fish, and while he blew over the broth repeatedly, the plume of fire over his forehead waved brilliantly in the air. Suddenly he heard a laugh. There appeared to be one or two persons, at no great distance. "Cousin," he said, to the sleeping boy, "some person is near us. I hear a laugh; awake and let us look out." But his cousin was in a profound sleep. Again he heard the laughing. Looking out as far as the reflection of the fire threw light, he beheld two beautiful young females smiling on him. Their countenances appeared to be perfectly white, and were exceedingly beautiful. He crouched down and pushed his cousin, saying, in a low voice, "awake! awake! here are two young women." But he received no answer. His cousin seemed locked up in one of the deepest slumbers. He started up alone, and went toward the females. He was charmed with their looks, but just as he was about to speak to them, he suddenly fell senseless, and both he and they vanished together.

Some short time afterward the cousin awoke. He saw the kettle near him. Some of the fish were in the bowl. The fire still cast its glare faintly around, but he could discover no person. He waited and waited, but Wassamo did not appear. Perhaps, thought he, he is gone out again to visit the nets. He looked, but the canoe was still in the place where it had been left. He searched and found his footsteps on the ashes. He became uneasy— "NETAWIS! NETAWIS! (cousin, cousin)," he cried out, but there was no answer. He cried out louder and louder, "NETAWIS, NETAWIS, where are you gone?" but still no answer. He started for the edge of the woods, crying "NETAWIS, NETAWIS." He ran in various directions repeating the same words. The dark woods echoed "NETAWIS, NETAWIS." He burst into tears and sobbed aloud.

He returned to the fire and sat down, but he had no heart to eat. Various conjectures passed in his mind respecting his cousin. He thought, he may have been playing me a trick. No, impossible! or he may have become deranged and run into the woods. He hoped the morning would bring with it some discovery. But he was oppressed by the thought that the Indians would consider him the murderer of the lost man. "Although," reasoned he, "his parents are my relations, and they know that we are inseparable friends, they will not believe me, if I go home with a report that he is lost. They will say I killed him, and will require blood for blood."

These thoughts weighed upon his mind. He could not sleep. Early in the morning he got up and took in the nets, and set out on foot for the village, running all the way. When they saw him coming, they said, "some accident has happened." When he got in, he told them how his cousin had disappeared. He stated all the circumstances. He kept back nothing. He declared all he knew. Some said, "he has killed him treacherously." Others said, "it is impossible, they were like brothers; sooner than do that they would have given up their lives for each other." He asserted his innocence and asked them to go and look at the spot of their encampment. Many of the men accordingly went, and found all as he had stated. No footsteps showed that any scuffle had taken place. There were no signs of blood. They came to the conclusion that the young man had got deranged, and strayed away, and was lost. With this belief they returned to the village. But the parents still waited and hoped he would return. Spring came on and the Indians assembled from various quarters. Among them was Wassamo's cousin. He continued to say that he had done nothing to hurt his friends. Anxiety and fear had, however, produced a visible change in his features. He was pale and emaciated. The idea of the blood of his friend and relation being laid to his charge, caused a continual pain of mind.

The parents of Wassamo now demanded the life of Netawis. The village was in an uproar. Some sided with the parents, some with the young man. All showed anxiety in the affair. They at last, however, decided to give the young man's life to the parents. They said they had waited long enough for the return of their son. A day was appointed on which the young man should give his life for his friend's. He still went at large. He said he was not afraid to die, for he had never committed what they laid to his charge. A day or two before the time set to take his life, he wandered in a melancholy mood from the village, following the beach. His feelings were wrought to such a pitch, that he thought once or twice to throw himself into the lake. But he reflected, they will say I was guilty, or I would not have done so. No, I will not, I would prefer dying under their hands. He walked on, thinking of his coming fate, till he reached the sand banks, a short distance from the village. Here we will dismiss him for the present.

When Wassamo fell senseless before the two young women, it must have been some minutes before he recovered, for when he came to himself, he did not know where he was, and had been removed to a distant scene. On recovering his senses he heard persons conversing. One spoke in a tone of authority, saying, "You foolish girls, is this the way you go about at nights, without our knowing it? Put that person you brought on that bed of yours, and let him not lie on the ground." After this Wassamo felt himself moved and placed on a bed. Sometime after he opened his eyes fully, and was surprised to find himself in a spacious and superb lodge, extending as far as the eye could reach. One spoke to him, saying, "Stranger, awake, and take something to eat." He arose and sat up. On each side of the lodge he beheld rows of people sitting in regular order. At a distance he could see two prominent persons who looked rather older than the rest, and who appeared to command obedience from all around them. One of them, the Old Spirit man, addressed him. "My son," said he, "those foolish girls brought you here. They saw you at the fishing ground. When you attempted to approach them, you fell senseless, and they conveyed you underground to this place. But be satisfied. We will make your stay with us pleasant. I am the guardian Spirit of NAGOW WUDJOO.[1] I have wished frequently to

get one of your race to intermarry with us. If you can make up your mind
to remain, I will give you one of my daughters—the one who brought you
away from your parents and friends."[2] The young man dropped his head
and made no answer. His silence they construed into an assent to their
wishes.

"Your wants," continued the Old Spirit, "will all be supplied, only be
careful not to stray away far from this. I am afraid of that Spirit who rules
all islands lying in the Lakes. For he demanded my daughter in marriage,
and I refused him: when he hears that you are my guest, it may be an
inducement for him to harm you. There is my daughter (he pointed).
Take her, she shall be your wife." And forthwith they sat near each other
in the lodge, and were considered as married.

"Son-in-law," said the Old Spirit, "I am in want of tobacco. You shall
return to visit your parents, and can make known my wishes. For it is very
seldom that those few who pass these Sand Hills, offer a piece of tobacco.
When they do it, it immediately comes to me. Just so," he added, putting
his hand out of the side of the lodge, and drawing in several pieces of
tobacco, which some one at that moment happened to offer to the Spirit,
for a smooth lake and prosperous voyage. "You see," he said, "everything offered me on earth, comes immediately to the side of my lodge."
Wassamo saw the women also putting their hands to the side of the lodge,
and then handing something around, of which all partook. This he found
to be offerings of food made by mortals on earth.

"Daughter," said the Old Spirit Woman, "NAUONGUISK[3] cannot eat what
we eat, so you can procure him what he is accustomed to." "Yes," she replied, and immediately pushed her hand through the side of the lodge,
and took a white fish out of the lake, which she prepared for him. She daily
followed the same practice, giving every variety of fish he expressed a wish
for. Sometimes it was trout, pike, sturgeon, or any other fish the lake
furnished. She did the same with regard to meats, or the flesh of any animal
or fowl he asked for. For the animals walked over the roof of the lodge,
the birds sat upon its poles, and the waters came so near to its side, that the
Spirits had only to extend their hands to the outside to procure whatever
they wanted.

One day the Old Spirit said (although it was perpetual day with them),
"son-in-law, you must not be surprised at what you will see, for since you
have been with us, you have never seen us go to sleep. It was on account of
its being summer, which is constant daylight with us. But now what *you*
call winter is approaching. It is six months night with us, you will soon see
us lie down, and we shall not get up, but for a moment, throughout the
whole winter. Take my advice. Leave not the lodge, but try and amuse
yourself. You will find all you wish there," raising his arm slowly and
pointing. Wassamo said he would obey, and act as he recommended.

On another occasion a thunder storm came on, when every spirit instantly disappeared. When the storm was over, they all again re-entered
the lodge. This scene was repeated during every tempest. "You are surprised," said the Old Spirit, "to see us disappear whenever it thunders.

The reason is this. A greater Spirit, who lives above, makes those thunders sound and sends his fire. We are afraid, and hide ourselves."

The season of sleep approached, and they, one after another, laid themselves down to their long sleep. In the meantime Wassamo amused himself in the best way he could. His relations got up but once during the whole winter, and they then said it was midnight, and laid down again. "Son-in-law," said the Old Spirit, "you can now, in a few days, start with your wife to visit your relations. You can be absent one year, but after that time you must return. When you get to the village you must first go in alone. Leave your wife a short distance from the lodge, and when you are welcome then send for her.[4] When there, do not be surprised at her disappearance whenever you hear it thunder. You will also prosper in all things, for she is very industrious. All the time that you pass in sleep she will be at work. The distance is short to your village. A road leads directly to it, and when you get there do not forget my wants, as I stated to you before."

Wassamo promised obedience to their directions, and then set out in company with his wife. They traveled in a good road, his wife leading the way, till they got to a rising ground. At the highest point of this, she said, we will soon get to your country. After reaching the summit, they passed, for a short distance, under the lake, and emerged from the water at certain sand banks on the bay of WEKUADONG.[5]

Wassamo left his wife concealed in a thicket, while he went toward the village alone. On turning the first point of land, who should he meet but his cousin. "Oh Netawis, Netawis," said his cousin, "you have just come in time to save me. They accuse me of having killed you." Words cannot express their joy. The cousin ran off in haste for the village and entered the lodge where Wassamo's mother was. "Hear me," he said, "I have seen him whom you accuse me of having killed. He will be here in a few moments." The village was in instant commotion. All were anxious to see him whom they had thought dead. While the excitement was at its height Wassamo entered the lodge of his parents. All was joy at the happy meeting. He related all that had happened to him from the moment of his leaving their temporary night lodge with the flame on his head. He told them where he had been, and that he was married. As soon as the excitement of his reception had abated, he told his mother that he had left his wife a short distance from the village. She went immediately in search of her, and soon found her. All the women of the village conducted her to the lodge of her relations. They were astonished at her beauty, at the whiteness of her skin, and more so, at her being able to converse with them in their own language. All was joy in the village; nothing but feasting could be seen while they had the means of doing so. The Indians came from different quarters, to offer them welcome, and to present their tobacco to the Spirit's daughter.

Thus passed the summer and the fall, and Wassamo's parents and relations, and the Indians around were prospered in all things. But his cousin would never leave him, he was constantly near him, and asking him questions. They took notice that at every thunderstorm his wife disappeared, and that at night, as well as during the day, she was never idle. Winter was drawing on, and she told her husband to prepare a lodge for her to pass the season in, and to inform the Indians beforehand of her father's request. He did so, and all now began to move off to their winter quarters. Wassamo also prepared for the season. He gave one half of his lodge to his wife. Before lying down, she said, "no one but yourself must pass on the side of the lodge I am on." Winter passed slowly away, and when the sap of the maple began to run, she awoke and commenced her duties as before. She also helped to make sugar. It was never known before or since that so much sugar was made during the season. As soon as the Indians had finished their sugar-making, they left the woods and encamped at their village. They offered tobacco profusely at the lodge of Wassamo, asking for the usual length of life, for success as hunters, and for a plentiful supply of food. Wassamo replied, that he would mention each of their requests to his father-in-law. So much tobacco had been offered, that they were obliged to procure two sacks, made of dressed mooseskin, to hold it. On the outside of these skins the different totems[6] of the Indians, who had given the tobacco, were painted and marked, and also those of all persons who had made any request.

When the time arrived for their departure, they told their relatives not to follow them, or see how they disappeared. They then took the two sacks of mooseskin filled with tobacco, and bade adieu to all but Netawis. He insisted on going with them a distance, and when they got to the sand banks he expressed the strongest wish to proceed with them on their journey. Wassamo told him it was impossible, that it was only spirits who could exert the necessary power. They then took an affectionate leave of each other. The young man saw them go into the water and disappear. He returned home and told his friends that he had witnessed their disappearance.

Wassamo and his wife soon reached their home at the grand Sand Hills. The Old Spirit was delighted to see them, and hailed their return with open arms. They presented him with the tobacco, and told him all the requests of the people above. He replied that he would attend to all, but he must first invite his friends to smoke with him. He then sent his MEZHINAUWA,[7] to invite his friends the Spirits, and named the time for their reception. Before the time arrived he spoke to his son-in-law. "My son," said he, "some of those Manitoes I have invited are very wicked, and I warn you particularly of the one who wished to marry my daughter. Some of them you will, however, find to be friendly. Take my advice, and when they come in, sit close to your wife—so close you must touch her. If you do not you will be lost, for those who are expected to come in are so powerful, that they will draw you from your seat. You have only to observe my words closely, and all will be well." Wassamo said he would obey.

About midday they commenced coming in. There were spirits from all parts of the country. One entered who smiled on him. He was the guardian Spirit of the Ottowas, and he lived near the present GITCHY WEKUADONG.[8]

Soon after, he heard the sounds of the roaring and foaming of waters. Presently they rushed in, and passed through the lodge like a raging tempest. Tremendous pieces of rocks, whole trees, logs, and stumps rolled past, and were borne away by the strong current, with the noise and foaming of some mighty cataract in the spring. It was the guardian spirit of Water-Falls. Again, they heard the roaring of waves, as if beating against a rocky shore. The sounds came rapidly on. In a few moments in rolled the waves of Lake Superior. They were mountain high, and covered with silver-sparkling foam. Wassamo felt their pressure and with difficulty clung to his seat, for they were of frightful appearance, and each one seemed as if it would overwhelm them. This was the last spirit who entered. It was the Guardian of Islands in the surrounding lake.

Soon after, the Old Spirit arose and addressed the assembly. "Brothers," he said, "I have invited you to partake with me of the offerings made by the mortals on earth, which have been brought by our relative (pointing to Wassamo). Brothers, you see their wishes and desires (pointing to the figured mooseskins). Brothers, the offering is worthy of our consideration. Brothers, I see nothing on my part to prevent our granting their requests; they do not appear to be unreasonable. Brothers, the offering is gratifying. Our wants for this article are urgent. Shall we grant their requests? One thing more I would say—Brothers, it is this. There is my son-in-law; he is a mortal. I wish to detain him with me, and it is with us jointly to make him one of us." "Hoke! Hoke!" ran through the whole company of Spirits.[9]

The tobacco was then divided equally among them all. They decided to grant the requests of the people on earth, and also respecting the spirit's son-in-law. When the Spirit of Islands passed Wassamo, he looked angrily at him. The guardian spirit of the Ottowa bands said, "it is very strange that he can never appear anywhere without showing his bad disposition."

When the company was dispersed, the Old Spirit told Wassamo that he should once more visit his parents and relatives, and then it should be only for a short time. "It is merely to go and tell them that their wishes are granted, and then to bid them farewell forever." Sometime after, Wassamo and his wife made this visit. Having delivered his message, he said, "I must now bid you all farewell forever." His parents and friends raised their voices in loud lamentation. They accompanied him to the Sand Banks, where they all seated themselves to see them make their final departure. The day was mild; the sky clear; not a cloud appeared, nor a breath of wind to disturb the bright surface of the water. The most perfect silence reigned throughout the company. They gazed intently on Wassamo and his wife as they waded out into the water, waving their hands. They saw them go into deeper and deeper water. They saw the waves close over their heads. All at once they raised a loud and piercing wail. They looked again; a red flame, as if the sun had glanced on a billow, marked the spot for an instant, but the Feather of Flames and his wife had disappeared forever.[10]

(The preceding tale opens a chapter in Indian demonology, which was narrated by the late chief Chusco, an Ottowa. This individual had performed the office of a seer and necromancer for his tribe for a long series of years, and had acquired notoriety and power among them from the successful display of these arts. The story was related after his conversion to Christianity,[11] but he continued to affirm to the last, that his power as a JOSSAKEED, or juggler, was derived from a *direct energy* communicated by the Great Evil Spirit.)

NOTES

1. Sand mountains, usually called *La Grandes Sables,* a noted range of SAND DOWNS, of oceanic formation, on the south shores of Lake SUPERIOR. [H. R. S.]

2. This speech was commenced by throwing the blame of his captivity upon the daughters. But the Spirit soon reveals, that he had long wished for such an event, and leaves it to be inferred that it was brought about by his direct agency. This subterfuge, to call it by its lightest name, shows that plain truth is not a point of character most strenuously sought after by the OLD SPIRIT. [H. R. S.]

3. This is a term applied by women to a son-in-law, etc. [H. R. S.]

4. This is the present ceremonious custom of visiting among the northern Indians, for strangers of their own, or other tribes. Friends proceed directly to the lodges, but it is the privilege of relations only to enter them without invitation at the door. [H. R. S.]

5. Little Traverse Bay of Lake Michigan. [H. R. S.]

6. Family marks, or arms. This institution has been noticed among the Algonquin tribes from an early day. It is a link in the genealogical chain by which the bands are held together—and a curious trait, whether it be regarded of ancient or modern usage. It has no reference to personal names, but indicates the family or tribal name. All the individuals of a particular family, as the deer, crane, beaver, etc. when called upon for their signature, affix their respective family mark, without regard to specific names. And it is precisely analogous to the existing feudal institutions of coats of arms. *Totame,* or *totem* is the term, and it is a word appealed to by them with pride, and as furnishing evidence of blood relationship. Whatever the institution may be derived from, it is certain that a Benjaminite or an Ephraimite, could not appeal to his tribal appellation with more emphasis and dogmatism than do our northern Indians to their *totems.* [H. R. S.]

7. This is an official personage, standing in the light of an aid, or office help, to the chiefs. He carves at feasts, and lights the pipe at councils or ceremonial occasions. He is the verbal messenger of state messages, but not a messenger in the common acceptation of the term. He is an important functionary in all formal business, or negotiations with the chiefs. [H. R. S.]

8. Grand Traverse Bay of Lake Michigan. [H. R. S.]

9. The interjection Hoh! is used by these tribes to imply approbation and assent. The change in the word here indicated, is to be regarded as one of the points of invention, in their tales of demonology. [H. R. S.]

10. "The Fire Plume," *C. M.,* pp. 263-287, and *C-C,* pp. 238-260, is some-

what modified, e.g., the Old Spirit claims not to be afraid of the thunder; he hides to avoid asking him in to dinner! Schoolcraft did not reprint the story again.

11. Chief Chusco's Christianity seems to be on a par with that of Browning's Caliban. Both the Old Spirit and Setebos fear a higher and malevolent deity.

OSSEO

THE SON OF THE EVENING STAR

AN ALGONQUIN TALE

THERE ONCE LIVED an Indian in the north, who had ten daughters, all of whom grew up to womanhood. They were noted for their beauty, but especially Oweenee, the youngest, who was very independent in her way of thinking. She was a great admirer of romantic places, and paid very little attention to the numerous young men who came to her father's lodge for the purpose of seeing her. Her elder sisters were all solicited in marriage from their parents, and one after another, went off to dwell in the lodges of their husbands, or mothers-in-law, but she would listen to no proposals of the kind. At last she married an old man called OSSEO, who was scarcely able to walk, and was too poor to have things like others. They jeered and laughed at her, on all sides, but she seemed to be quite happy, and said to them, "It is my choice, and you will see in the end, who has acted the wisest." Soon after, the sisters and their husbands and their parents were all invited to a feast, and as they walked along the path, they could not help pitying their young and handsome sister, who had such an unsuitable mate. Osseo often stopped and gazed upwards, but they could perceive nothing in the direction he looked, unless it was the faint glimmering of the evening star. They heard him muttering to himself as they went along, and one of the elder sisters caught the words, "Sho-wain-ne-me-shin-nosa."[1] "Poor old man," said she, "he is talking to his father, what a pity it is, that he would not fall and break his neck, that our sister might have a handsome young husband." Presently they passed a large hollow log, lying with one end toward the path. The moment Osseo, who was of the turtle totem, came to it, he stopped short, uttered a loud and peculiar yell, and then dashing into one end of the log, he came out at the other, a most beautiful young man, and springing back to the road, he led off the party with steps as light as the reindeer. But on turning round to look for his wife, behold, she had been changed into an old, decrepit woman, who was bent almost double, and walked with a cane. The husband, however, treated her very kindly, as she had done him during the time of his enchantment, and constantly addressed her by the term of ne-ne-moosh-a, or my sweetheart.

When they came to the hunter's lodge with whom they were to feast, they found the feast ready prepared, and as soon as their entertainer had finished his harangue (in which he told them his feasting was in honor of the Evening, or Woman's Star), they began to partake of the portion dealt out, according to age and character, to each one. The food was very delicious, and they were all happy but Osseo, who looked at his wife and then gazed upward, as if he was looking into the substance of the sky. Sounds were soon heard, as if from far-off voices in the air, and they became plainer and plainer, till he could clearly distinguish some of the words.

"My son—my son," said the voice, "I have seen your afflictions and pity your wants. I come to call you away from a scene that is stained with blood and tears. The earth is full of sorrows. Giants and sorcerers, the enemies of mankind, walk abroad in it, and are scattered throughout its length. Every night they are lifting their voices to the Power of Evil, and everyday they make themselves busy in casting evil in the hunter's path. You have long been their victim, but shall be their victim no more. The spell you were under is broken. Your evil genius is overcome. I have cast him down by my superior strength, and it is this strength I now exert for your happiness. Ascend, my son—ascend into the skies, and partake of the feast I have prepared for you in the stars, and bring with you those you love.

"The food set before you is enchanted and blessed. Fear not to partake of it. It is endowed with magic power to give immortality to mortals, and to change men to spirits. Your bowls and kettles shall be no longer wood and earth. The one shall become silver, and the other wampum. They shall shine like fire, and glisten like the most beautiful scarlet. Every female shall also change her state and looks, and no longer be doomed to laborious tasks. She shall put on the beauty of the starlight, and become a shining bird of the air, clothed with shining feathers. She shall dance and not work —she shall sing and not cry."

"My beams," continued the voice, "shine faintly on your lodge, but thy have a power to transform it into the lightness of the skies, and decorate it with the colors of the clouds. Come, Osseo, my son, and dwell no longer on earth. Think strongly on my words, and look steadfastly at my beams. My power is now at its height. Doubt not—delay not. It is the voice of the Spirit of the stars that calls you away to happiness and celestial rest."

The words were intelligible to Osseo, but his companions thought them some far-off sounds of music, or birds singing in the woods. Very soon the lodge began to shake and tremble, and they felt it rising into the air. It was too late to run out, for they were already as high as the tops of the trees. Osseo looked around him as the lodge passed through the topmost boughs, and behold! their wooden dishes were changed into shells of a scarlet color, the poles of the lodge to glittering wires of silver, and the bark that covered them into the gorgeous wings of insects. A moment more, and his brothers and sisters, and their parents and friends, were transformed into birds of various plumage. Some were jays, some partridges and pigeons, and others gay singing birds, who hopped about displaying their glittering feathers, and singing their songs. But OWEENEE still kept her earthly garb, and exhibited all the indications of extreme age. He again cast his eyes in the direction of the clouds, and uttered that peculiar yell, which had given him the victory at the hollow log. In a moment the youth and beauty of his wife returned; her dingy garments assumed the shining appearance of green silk, and her cane was changed into a silver feather. The lodge again shook and trembled, for they were now passing through the uppermost clouds, and they immediately after found themselves in the Evening Star, the residence of Osseo's father.

"My son," said the old man, "hang that cage of birds, which you have brought along in your hand, at the door, and I will inform you why you and your wife have been sent for." Osseo obeyed the directions, and then took his seat in the lodge. "Pity was shown to you," resumed the king of the star, "on account of the contempt of your wife's sister, who laughed at her ill fortune, and ridiculed you while you were under the power of that wicked spirit, whom you overcame at the log. That spirit lives in the next lodge, being a small star you see on the left of mine, and he has always felt envious of my family, because we had greater power than he had, and especially on account of our having had the care committed to us of the female world. He failed in several attempts to destroy your brothers-in-law and sisters-in-law, but succeeded at last in transforming yourself and your wife into decrepit old persons. You must be careful and not let the light of his beams fall on you, while you are here, for therein is the power of his enchantment; a ray of light is the bow and arrows he uses."

Osseo lived happy and contented in the parental lodge, and in due time his wife presented him with a son, who grew up rapidly, and was the image of his father. He was very quick and ready in learning everything that was done in his grandfather's dominions, but he wished also to learn the art of hunting, for he had heard that this was a favorite pursuit below. To gratify him his father made him a bow and arrows, and he then let the birds out of the cage that he might practice in shooting. He soon became expert, and the very first day brought down a bird, but when he went to pick it up, to his amazement, it was a beautiful young woman with the arrow sticking in her breast. It was one of his younger *aunts*. The moment her blood fell upon the surface of that pure and spotless planet, the charm was dissolved. The boy immediately found himself sinking, but was partly upheld, by something like wings, till he passed through the lower clouds, and he then suddenly dropped upon a high, romantic island in a large lake. He was pleased on looking up, to see all his aunts and uncles following him in the form of birds, and he soon discovered the silver lodge, with his father and mother, descending with its waving barks looking like so many insects' gilded wings. It rested on the highest cliffs of the island, and here they fixed their residence. They all resumed their natural *shapes,* but were diminished to the *size* of fairies, and as a mark of homage to the King of the Evening Star, they never failed on every pleasant evening, during the summer season, to join hands, and dance upon the top of the rocks. These rocks were quickly observed by the Indians to be covered, in moonlight evenings, with a larger sort of PUK WUDJ ININEES, or little men, and were called Mish-in-e-mok-in-ok-ong, or turtle spirits, and the island is named from them to this day.[2] Their shining lodge can be seen in the summer evenings when the moon shines strongly on the pinnacles of the rocks, and the fishermen, who go near those high cliffs at night, have even heard the voices of the happy little dancers.[3]

NOTES

1. Pity me, my father. [H. R. S.]

2. Michilimackinac, the term alluded to, is the original French orthography of MISH EN I MOK IN ONG, the *local* form (sing. and plu.), of Turtle Spirits. [H. R. S.]

3. The tale was published in *M. H.*, pp. 71-76; in *C. M.*, pp. 74-82, and in *C-C*, pp. 95-103.

KWASIND

THE FEARFULLY STRONG MAN

PAUWATING[1] WAS A VILLAGE where the young men amused themselves very much in ancient times, in sports and ball-playing.

One day as they were engaged in their sports, one of the strongest and most active, at the moment he was about to succeed in a trial of lifting, slipped and fell upon his back. "Ha! ha! ha!" cried the lookers on, "you will never rival Kwasind." He was deeply mortified, and when the sport was over, these words came to his mind. He could not recollect any man of this name. He thought he would ask the old man, the story-teller of the village, the next time he came to the lodge. The opportunity soon occurred.

"My grandfather," said he, "who was Kwasind? I am very anxious to know what he could do."

Kwasind, the old man replied, was a listless idle boy. He would not play when the other boys played, and his parents could never get him to do any kind of labor. He was always making excuses. His parents took notice, however, that he fasted for days together, but they could not learn what spirit he supplicated, or had chosen as the guardian spirit to attend him through life. He was so inattentive to his parents' requests, that he, at last, became a subject of reproach.

"Ah," said his mother to him one day, "is there any young man of your age, in all the village, who does so little for his parents? You neither hunt nor fish. You take no interest in anything, whether labor or amusement, which engages the attention of your equals in years. I have often set my nets[2] in the coldest days of winter, without any assistance from you. And I have taken them up again, while you remained inactive at the lodge fire. Are you not ashamed of such idleness? Go, I bid you, and wring out that net, which I have just taken from the water."

Kwasind saw that there was a determination to make him obey. He did not therefore make any excuses, but went out and took up the net. He carefully folded it, doubled and redoubled it, forming it into a roll, and then with an easy twist of his hands wrung it short off, with as much ease as if every twine had been a thin brittle fiber. Here, they at once saw, the secret of his reluctance. He possessed supernatural strength.

After this, the young men were playing one day on the plain, where there was lying one of those large, heavy, black pieces of rock, which Manabozho is said to have cast at his father. Kwasind took it up with much ease, and threw it into the river. After this, he accompanied his father on a hunting

196

excursion into a remote forest. They came to a place where the wind had thrown a great many trees into a narrow pass. "We must go the other way," said the old man, "it is impossible to get the burdens through this place." He sat down to rest himself, took out his smoking apparatus, and gave a short time to reflection. When he had finished, Kwasind had lifted away the largest pine trees, and pulled them out of the path.

Sailing one day in his canoe, Kwasind saw a large furred animal, which he immediately recognized to be the king of beavers. He plunged into the water in pursuit of it. His companions were in the greatest astonishment and alarm, supposing he would perish. He often dove down and remained a long time under water, pursuing the animal from island to island; and at last returned with the kingly prize. After this, his fame spread far and wide, and no hunter would presume to compete with him.[3]

He performed so many feats of strength and skill, that he excited the envy of the Puk-wudj In-in-ee-sug, or fairies, who conspired against his life. "For," said they, "if this man is suffered to go on, in his career of strength and exploits, we shall presently have no work to perform. Our agency in the affairs of men must cease. He will undermine our power, and drive us, at last, into the water, where we must all perish, or be devoured by the wicked Neebanawbaig."[4]

The strength of Kwasind was all concentrated in the crown of his head. This was, at the same time, the only vulnerable part of his body; and there was but one species of weapon which could be successfully employed in making any impression upon it. The fairies carefully hunted through the woods to find this weapon. It was the burr or seed vessel of the white pine. They gathered a quantity of this article, and waylaid Kwasind at a point on the river, where the red rocks jut into the water, forming rude castles— a point which he was accustomed to pass in his canoe. They waited a long time, making merry upon these rocks, for it was a highly romantic spot. At last the wished-for object appeared. Kwasind came floating calmly down the stream, on the afternoon of a summer's day, languid with the heat of the weather, and almost asleep. When his canoe came directly beneath the cliff, the tallest and stoutest fairy began the attack. Others followed his example. It was a long time before they could hit the vulnerable part, but success at length crowned their efforts, and Kwasind sunk, never to rise more.

Ever since this victory, the Puk Wudj Ininee have made that point of rock a favorite resort. The hunters often hear them laugh, and see their little plumes shake as they pass this scene on light summer evenings.

"My son," continued the old man, "take care that you do not imitate the faults of Kwasind. If he had not so often exerted his strength merely for the sake of *boasting,* he would not, perhaps, have made the fairies feel jealous of him. It is better to use the strength you have, in a quiet useful way, than to sigh after the possession of a giant's power. For if you run, or wrestle, or jump, or fire at a mark, only as well as your equals in years, nobody will envy you. But if you would needs be a Kwasind, you must expect a Kwasind's fate."[5]

NOTES

1. i.e. Place of shallow cataract, named *Sault de Ste Marie* on the arrival of the French. This is the *local* form of the word, the substantive proper terminates in EEG. [H. R. S.]

2. Nets are set in winter, in high northern latitudes, through orifices cut in the ice. [H. R. S.]

3. In *M. H.* this sentence was added: "He helped Manabozho to clear away the obstructions in the streams, and to remove the great wind-falls of trees from the valleys, the better to fit them for the residence of man."

4. A kind of water spirits. [H. R. S.]

5. Reprinted with no further change in *M. H.*, pp. 77-80.

MUDJEE MONEDO AND MINNO MONEDO

OR

THE SPIRIT OF EVIL AND THE SPIRIT

OF GOOD

A SAGINAW TALE

IN A BEAUTIFUL PORTION OF THE COUNTRY, which was part forest and part prairie, there lived a bloodthirsty Manito in the guise of an Indian, who made use of all his arts to decoy men into his power for the purpose of killing them. Although the country yielded an abundance of game, and every other production to satisfy his wants, yet it was the study of his life to destroy human beings, and subsist upon their blood. The country had once been thickly populated, but he had thinned it off by his wickedness, and his lodge was surrounded by the bleached bones of his victims.

The secret of his success lay in his great speed. He had the power to assume the shape of any quadruped, and it was his custom to challenge persons to run with him. He had a beaten path on which he ran, leading around a large lake, and he always ran around this circle, so that the starting and winning point were the same. At this point stood a post, having a sharp and shining knife tied to it, and whoever lost the race lost his life. The winner immediately took up the knife and cut off his competitor's head. No man was ever known to beat this evil Manito in the race, although he ran everyday; for whenever he was pressed hard, he changed himself into a fox, wolf, or deer, or other swift-footed animal, and thus left his competitor behind.

The whole country was in dread of him, and yet, such was the folly and rashness of the young men, that they were continually running with him; for if they refused, he called them cowards, which was a taunt they could not bear. They would rather die than be called cowards. In other respects, the Manito had pleasing manners, and visited the lodges around the country, like others; but his secret object in these visits was to see whether the young boys were getting to be old enough to run with him, and he was careful to keep a watch upon their growth, and never failed to challenge them to run on his race ground. There was no family which had not lost some of its most active members in this way, and the Manito was execrated by all the Indian mothers in the country.

There lived near him a widow, whose husband and ten sons he had killed in this way, and she was now left with an only daughter and a son of ten

199

or twelve years old. She was very poor and feeble, and suffered so much for the want of food, that she would have been glad to die, had it not been for her daughter and her little son, who was not yet able to hunt. The Manito had already visited her lodge to see whether the boy was not sufficiently grown to challenge him. And the mother saw there was a great probability that he would be decoyed and killed as his father and brothers had been. Still, she hoped a better fate would attend him, and strove, in the best way she could, to instruct him in the maxims of a hunter's and a warrior's life. To the daughter she also taught all that could make her useful as a wife, and instructed her in the arts of working with porcupine quills on leather, and various other things, which the Indian females regard as accomplishments. She was also neat and tasteful in arranging her dress according to their customs, and possessing a tall and graceful person, she displayed her national costume to great advantage. She was kind and obedient to her mother, and never neglected to perform her appropriate domestic duties. Her mother's lodge stood on an elevation on the banks of a lake, which gave them a fine prospect of the country for many miles around, the interior of which was diversified with groves and prairies. It was in this quarter that they daily procured their fuel. One day the daughter had gone out to these open groves to pick up dry limbs for their fire, and while admiring the scenery, she strolled farther than usual, and was suddenly startled by the appearance of a young man near her. She would have fled, but was arrested by his pleasing smile, and by hearing herself addressed in her own language. The questions he asked were trivial, relating to her place of residence and family, and were answered with timidity. It could not be concealed, however, that they were mutually pleased with each other, and before parting, he asked her to get her mother's consent to their marriage. She returned home later than usual, but was too timid to say anything to her mother on the subject. The meetings, however, with her admirer on the borders of the prairie, were frequent, and he every time requested her to speak to her mother on the subject of their marriage, which, however, she could not muster the resolution to do. At last the widow suspected something of the kind, from the tardiness of her daughter in coming in, and from the scanty quantity of fuel she sometimes brought. In answer to inquiries, she revealed the circumstance of her meeting the young man, and of his request. After reflecting upon her lonely and destitute situation, the mother gave her consent. The daughter went with a light step to communicate the answer, which her lover heard with delight, and after saying that he would come to the lodge at sunset, they separated. He was punctual to his engagement, and came at the precise time, dressed out as a warrior with every customary decoration, and approached the lodge with a mild and pleasing, yet manly air and commanding step. On entering it, he spoke affectionately to his mother-in-law, whom he called (contrary to the usage), NEEJEE, or *friend*.[1] She directed him to sit down beside her daughter, and from this moment they were regarded as man and wife.

Early the following morning, he asked for the bow and arrows of those who had been slain by the Manito, and went out a-hunting. As soon as he had got out of sight of the lodge, he transformed himself into a PEENA, or partridge, and took his flight in the air. Where or how he procured his food, is unknown; but he returned at evening with the carcasses of two deer. This continued to be his daily practice, and it was not long before the scaffolds near the lodge were loaded with meat. It was observed, however, that he ate but little himself, and that of a peculiar kind of meat which, added to some other particulars, convinced the family of his mysterious character. In a few days his mother-in-law told him that the Manito would come to pay them a visit, to see how the young man prospered. He told her that he should be away that day purposely, but would return the moment the visitor left them. On the day named he flew upon a tall tree, overlooking the lodge, and took his stand there to observe the movement of the Manito. This wicked spirit soon appeared, and as he passed the scaffolds of meat, cast suspicious glances toward them. He had no sooner entered the lodge, stopping first to look, before he went in, than he said—"Why, woman, who is it that is furnishing you meat so plentifully?" "No one," she answered, "but my son—he is just beginning to kill deer." "No, no," said he, "some one is living with you." "Kaween,"² said the old woman, dissembling again, "you are only jesting on my destitute situation. Who do you think would come and trouble themselves about *me*?" "Very well," replied the Manito, "I will go; but on such a day, I will again visit you, and see who it is that furnishes the meat, and whether it is your son or not." He had no sooner left the lodge and got out of sight, than the son-in-law made his appearance with two more deer. On being told of the particulars of the visit, "Very well," said he, "I will be at home next time and see him." They remonstrated against this, telling him of his cruelties, and the barbarous murders he had committed. "No matter," said he, "if he invites me to the race ground, I will not be backward. The result will teach him to show pity on the vanquished, and not to trample on the widow, and those who are without fathers." When the day of the expected visit arrived, he told his wife to prepare certain pieces of meat, which he pointed out and handed to her, together with two or three buds of the birch-tree which he requested her to put in the pot; and he directed that nothing should be wanting to show the usual hospitality to their guest, although he knew that his only object was to kill him. He then dressed himself as a warrior, putting tints of red on his visage and dress, to show that he was prepared for either war or peace.

As soon as the Manito arrived, he eyed this, to him, strange warrior, but dissembled his feelings, and spoke laughingly to the old woman, saying, "Did I not tell you that some one was staying with you, for I knew your son was too young to hunt!" She turned it off by saying that she did not think it necessary to tell him, as he was a Manito and knew before asking. He then conversed with the son-in-law on different topics, and finished by inviting him to the race ground, saying it was a manly amusement—that it would give him an opportunity of seeing other men, and he should himself be pleased to run with him. The young man said he knew nothing of running. "Why," he replied, "don't you see how old I look, while you are

young and active? We must at least run to amuse others." "Be it so, then,"
replied the young man, "I will go in the morning." Pleased with his success,
the Manito now wished to return, but he was pressed to remain and partake
of the customary hospitalities, although he endeavored to excuse himself.
The meal was immediately spread. But one dish was used. The young man
partook of it first, to show his guest that he need not fear to partake, and
saying at the same time to him, "It is a feast, and as we seldom meet, we
must eat all that is placed on the dish, as a mark of gratitude to the Great
Spirit for permitting me to kill the animals, and for the pleasure of seeing
you, and partaking of it with you." They ate and conversed until they had
eaten nearly all, when the Manito took up the dish and drank the broth.
On setting it down, he immediately turned his head and commenced
coughing violently, having, as the young man expected, swallowed a grain
of the birch tops, which had lodged in his windpipe. He coughed incessantly, and found his situation so unpleasant, that he had to leave, saying,
as he quit the lodge, that he should expect the young man at the race
ground in the morning.

MONEDOWA prepared himself early in the morning by oiling his limbs,
and decorating himself so as to appear to advantage, and having procured
leave for his brother to attend him, they repaired to the Manito's race
ground. The Manito's lodge stood on an eminence, and a row of other
lodges stood near it, and as soon as the young man and his companion
came near it, the inmates cried out, "We are visited." At this cry he came
out, and descended with them to the starting post on a plain. From this,
the course could be seen, as it wound around the lake, and as soon as the
people assembled, he began to speak of the race, then belted himself up,
and pointed to the knife which hung on the post, and said it was to be used
by the winner. "But before we start," said the old man, "I wish it to be
understood, that when men run with me, I make a bet, and expect them to
abide by it. Life against life." He then gave a yell, casting a triumphant
glance on the piles of human bones that were scattered about the stake. "I
am ready," replied the stranger, as he was called, (for no one knew the
widow's son-in-law), and they all admired the symmetry and beauty of his
limbs, and the fine and bold air which he assumed before his grim antagonist. The shout was given, and they went off with surprising speed,
and were soon out of sight. The old man began to show his power by
changing himself into a fox, and passing the stranger with great ease, went
leisurely along. Monedowa now exerted his magic powers by assuming the
shape of a partridge, and lighting a distance ahead of his antagonist, resumed his former shape. When the Manito spied his opponent ahead,
"Whoa! whoa!" he exclaimed involuntarily, "this is strange," and immediately changed himself into a wolf, and repassed him. As he went by, he
[Monedowa] heard a whistling noise in the Manito's throat. He again took
flight as a partridge, ascending some distance into the air, and then suddenly
coming down with great velocity, as partridges do, lit in the path far ahead.
As he passed the wolf, he addressed him thus: "My friend, is this the extent

of your speed?" The Manito began to have strong forebodings, for, on looking ahead, he saw the stranger in his natural shape, running along very leisurely. He then assumed alternately the shapes of various animals noted for
speed. He again passed the stranger in the shape of a reindeer.[3] They had
now got round the circle of the lake, and were approaching the point of
starting, when the stranger again took his flight as a partridge, and lit some
distance in advance. To overtake him, the Manito at last assumed the shape
of a buffalo, and again got ahead; but it appears this was the last form he
could assume, and it was that, in which he had most commonly conquered.
The stranger again took his flight as a partridge, and in the act of passing his
competitor saw his tongue hanging out from fatigue, "My friend," said he,
"is this all your speed?" The Manito answered not. The stranger had now
got within a flight of the winning post, when the fiend had nearly caught
up to him. "Bakah! bakah! neejee," he vociferated. "Stop, my friend, I
wish to talk to you," for he felt that he should be defeated and lose his life,
and it was his purpose to beg for it. The stranger laughed, as he replied, "I
will speak to you at the starting post. When men run with me, I make a bet,
and expect them to abide by it. Life against life." And immediately taking
his flight, alighted so near to the goal, that he could easily reach it in his
natural form. The Manito saw the movement, and was paralyzed. The
people at the stake shouted. The stranger ran with his natural speed, his
limbs displaying to great advantage, and the war eagle's feathers waving on
his head. The shouts were redoubled, hope added to his speed, and amid
the din, he leaped to the post, and grasping the shining blade, stood ready
to dispatch his adversary the moment of his arrival. The Manito came, with
fear and cowardice depicted in his face. "My friend," said he, "spare my
life," and then added in a low voice, as if he did not wish others to hear it,
"give me to live," and began to move off, as if the request was granted. "As
you have done to others," replied the noble youth, "so shall it be done to
you;" and his bleeding head rolled down the sloping hill. The spectators
then drew their knives, and cut his body into numberless pieces. The conqueror then asked to be led to the Manito's lodge, the interior of which
had never been seen. Few had ever dared even to ascend the eminence on
which it stood. On entering, they saw that it consisted of several apart-
ments. The first was arranged and furnished as Indian lodges usually are.
But horror struck upon his mind as they entered the second—it was entirely surrounded by a wall of human skulls and bones, with pieces of
human flesh scattered about. Upon a scaffold, the dead bodies of two
human beings were hanging, cut open, for the purpose of drying the flesh.
The third apartment had its sides beautifully decorated, but horrid to behold, two monsters in the form of black snakes, lay coiled up, one on each
side of the lodge. It appears that one of them was the wife, and the other
the child of the Manito. They were MISHEGENABIKOES, or Devils. This was
also the natural shape of the Manito, but he had assumed the human form
only to deceive. The orifice by which they had originally come out of the
earth was closed, and escape for them was impossible. The magic knife

still glittered in the stranger's hand, and without a moment's delay, he severed both their heads. He then commanded the people to bring together combustibles, which they set fire to, and consumed their remains. When the fire reached their carcasses, a dark smoke ascended from the lodge, and the hideous forms of fiery serpents were seen curling amid the flames.

The mysterious stranger, who had thus proved their deliverer, then commanded them to bring together all the human bones scattered around, and after making due preparations, he chose three magic arrows, and shooting the first into the air, cried, "Arise!" He then shot the second, repeating the cry, and immediately shot the third, uttering aloud, "Arise!" And the bones arose, and stood up covered with flesh, in their natural forms. And they instantly raised a loud and joyous shout of thanks to their deliverer.

The Genius of Benevolence (for such we must now regard him), motioned to all the people to keep silence, and addressed them as follows;[4] "My friends, the Great Spirit who lives above the skies, seeing the cruelties of the Manito I have destroyed, was moved with pity for you, and determined to rid the earth of such a monster. I am the creation of His thinking mind, and therein first appeared, and he gave me such power, that when the word was spoken, it was done. When I wished to have the swiftness of a bird, I flew, and whatever power I wanted was given me. You are witnesses of it, and have seen the Mudjee Monedo killed and burned, and the bones of his victims get up and shout. This is as nothing with Him. It was done to restore your friends. And this will be the way when the earth has an end, for all people will arise again, and friends unite in going to the happy hunting grounds, when they will see who directs all things. My stay with you will be short, for I must return whence I came. During this brief time, I will, however, instruct you, and teach you to live happy."

The whole multitude then followed him to the widow's lodge, where he taught them what to do. They built their lodges around him, forming a very large town. They dug up the earth and planted—they built large houses, and learned many new arts, and were happy. Not as it is now—for all the Indians have forgotten it. Having done this, he ascended into the clouds, leaving his wife the future mother of a son, to whom he referred the people assembled to witness his departure, for subsequent counsel.[5]

NOTE.—How much of the present fiction is due to ideas communicated to the Indian mind, since the discovery of America, it would be impossible to determine.

It has been found by the examination of the skull of a Saginaw [made by Mr. J. Toulmin Smith], that the organ of destructiveness is very largely developed, exceeding by an inch, in the posterior breadth of the head, that of exhibited specimens of the Caucasian race. This skull, however, exhibited benevolence strongly marked, and the entire groups of the anterior organs, exceeded as 6 to 5½ those of the posterior groups, indicating, so far as the theory is followed, that favorable effects might be anticipated to result from education.[6]

NOTES

1. The term Neejee, is restricted in its use by males to males, and cannot, with propriety, be applied by males to females, or by females to males. [H. R. S.]

2. No indeed! [H. R. S.]

3. The CERVUS SYLVESTRIS, or American species of Reindeer, is confined in its range, north of Lake Huron. No traces of it have been observed south of the parallel of the straits of Michilimackinac, although it is found in the peninsular area between those straits and the south shores of Lake Superior. This animal is called ADDICK by the Algic race, and is the CARABOO of the Canadian. [H. R. S.]

4. The echoes of Christian phraseology in this paragraph cause one to suspect Schoolcraft (or his Christianized wife) of tampering with the original legend. Deliverers and instructors of divine origin, however, were common to both Algonquin and Iroquois tribes.

5. Not reprinted in *M. H.* As "The Bird Lover," where the youth, Monedowa, appeared to his sweetheart as a bird, the story was included in *C. M.*, pp. 299-314, and in *C-C*, pp. 261-275.

6. Schoolcraft's reference to phrenology reflects the excitement of the thirties over that pseudo-science. Mr. J. Toulmin Smith, of Boston, lectured in Detroit during the winter of 1837-38. Schoolcraft heard the lectures and corresponded with Smith for some time. The Saginaw skull, supplied by Schoolcraft, was that of Etowigezhig. *P. M.*, pp. 594, 614.

THE PIGEON HAWK AND TORTOISE

FROM THE ODJIBWA

THE PIGEON HAWK BANTERED the tortoise for a race, but the tortoise declined it, unless he would consent to run several days' journey. The hawk very quickly consented, and they immediately set out. The tortoise knew, that if he obtained the victory it must be by great diligence, so he went down into the earth, and taking a straight line, stopped for nothing. The hawk, on the contrary, knowing that he could easily beat his competitor, kept carelessly flying this way and that way in the air, stopping now to visit one, and then another, till so much time had been lost, that when he came in sight of the winning point, the tortoise had just come up out of the earth, and gained the prize.[1]

NOTE

1. This universal type fable was never used again by Schoolcraft nor by those in his debt for stories.

THE CHARMED ARROW

FROM THE OTTOWA

[THIS TALE IS SEPARATED from a mass of traditionary matter, relating to the origin and wars of the northern Indians, with which, however, it appears to have no historical connection beyond the existence of a few actual proper names of men and places.]

SAGIMAU had performed great feats against the enemies of his tribe. He had entirely routed and driven off one of the original tribes from the lakes, and came back to his residence on Lake Huron a conqueror. He was also regarded as a Manito. But, he could not feel easy while he heard of the fame and exploits of Kaubina, a great Chippewa chief and Manito in the north. Kaubina lived on a large island in Lake Superior, and was not only versed in magic himself, but had an aged female coadjutor who was a witch, and went under the name of his grandmother. She lived under Lake Superior, and took care to inform him of everything that threatened him.

Sagimau determined to measure strength with him. He accordingly thought much about him. One night he dreamed that there was a certain head of a lance,[1] which, if it could be procured, would give him sway over other tribes. This treasure was in the possession of a certain beautiful and majestic eagle, to whom all other birds owed obedience, and who, in consequence of having this weapon, was acknowledged king of birds. The lance was, however, seldom seen, even by those most intimate with the owner. The seer of the village dreamed the same dream. It was much talked about, and made much noise. Sagimau determined to seek for it, as it would make him the greatest hero in the world. He thought he would first go and see Kaubina, and endeavor to deceive him, or try his skill in necromancy. But he resolved to proceed by stratagem. After several days' travel he crossed the neck of land separating the two great waters, and reached the banks of Lake Superior, opposite a large island, which is now called Grand Island. Here Kaubina lived. Some days before this visit, the witch came into Kaubina's lodge and requested some tobacco. But he happened to be in an ill humor, and refused her, telling her he had none. "Very well," said she, "you will see the time when you may wish you had given me some."

Meantime Sagimau was plotting against him. He resolved to carry off his youngest wife. Having no canoe to cross to the island, he asked his companions whether any of them had ever dreamed of walking in the water. One of the men answered yes. He was therefore selected to accompany him. They went into the water until it came breast high. "You must not have

207

the least doubt," said he to the young man, "but resolve that you can walk under water. If you doubt, you will fail. They both thought strong of it,[2] and disappeared. When about halfway through the strait, they met two monsters, who looked as long as pine trees, and had glistening eyes. But they appeased them by giving them tobacco, and went on. On getting near the island, Sagimau said to his friend, you must turn yourself into a white stone on the shore, near the path where the women come to dip water. I will assume the shape of a black log of driftwood, and be floating, and thumping on the shore near by.

Kaubina had attended a feast that day, and after he got home to his lodge, complained of thirst. He requested his old wife to get him some water. "My! My!" said she, "it is dark, and why not let that one go, whom you think so much of?" He then spoke to the youngest, who immediately got a flambeau, and prepared to go, having first asked the elder wife to accompany her. She declined. Dark as it was, and alone, she pursued the path to the edge of the water. She noticed the white stone, and the wood near it, and thought she had never seen them before; but if I return, thought she to herself, with such a story, without the water, they will laugh at me. She made a quick motion to dip the water, but was instantly seized by Sagimau and his companion. They drew her under the water, carried her to the main land, and proceeded one day's journey homeward, when they encamped. Meantime Kaubina waited for his expected drink of water. He at last got up and searched for her on the shore, and in the lodges, but could get no intelligence. He was distressed, and could not rest. Next morning he renewed his search, but in vain. He invoked the name of his grandmother, with due ceremony, making the customary present of tobacco. At length she appeared, and after reminding him of his neglect of her, in her last application for the sacred weed, she revealed to him the whole plot, and also told him the means he must use to recover his lost wife. If you follow my advice, said she, you will get her back in a friendly way, and without bloodshed. Kaubina obeyed the injunctions of the witch. He carried with him a number of young men, and overtook Sagimau at his first night's encampment. When the latter saw him, he assumed a smiling aspect, and came forward and offered his hand. It was accepted. They then sat down and smoked. After this Kaubina said, "Why did you take my wife?" "It was only," Sagimau replied, "to see how great a Manito you were. Here she is— take her. Now that I know your qualities, we will live in peace." Each concealed the deep hostility he entertained for the other. They parted in peace.

After the interview, Sagimau sent his warriors home to Lake Michigan. He determined to remain in the country and seek the charmed arrow. For this purpose he retired to a remote wood, and transformed himself into a dead moose, which appeared as if the carcass had lain a long period, for worms were in its eyes and nostrils. Very soon eagles, hawks, crows, and other birds of prey, flocked to the carcass. But the skin was so hard and tough that they could not penetrate it with their bills. At length they said, "Let us go and call WAUB WE NONGA to come and cut a hole for us with his lance." Ze Ghe Nhiew offered to go, but having been told that the dead moose was Sagimau, flew back affrighted. The birds renewed their attempt to pierce the hide, but without success. They then repeated their request to the white vulture-eagle. The latter returned the same wary reply, fearful it was the stratagem of the Manito Sagimau; but when appealed to the third time, with the assurance that worms were in the eyes and nostrils of the carcass, he consented. All the birds were seated around the carcass, eager for the feast. When they heard the sweeping noise of the wings of Waub-we-nonga, the king of the birds, they made a cry of joy. He viewed the carcass from a distance. Two birds older than the rest, screamed out to him to come and cut the skin. He advanced cautiously, and gave a blow, but to no effect, the lance bounded back from the tough hide. The birds set up a loud scream, desiring that he would renew the effort. He did so, and drove the lance in, about a foot. Sagimau immediately caught hold of it and wrenched it from the bird. He instantly resumed his human form and commenced his return to his country. The great bird followed him, entreating him to give it back, and promising, on compliance, that he would grant him anything that he might desire. Sagimau sternly refused. He knew that it contained magic virtues by which he could accomplish all his purposes, one of the first of which was, to overthrow Kaubina. This resolution he firmly maintained, although the bird followed him all the way back, flying from tree to tree, and renewing its solicitations.

Sagimau had no sooner reached his village with this trophy, than he commenced gathering all the tobacco he could, as presents to the different spirits of the land, whom he deemed it necessary to appease, in consequence of the deception he had used in wrongfully getting possession of the arrow. This sacred offering he carefully put up in cedar bags, and then commenced a journey to such places as he knew they inhabited, to leave his offering, and to obtain the permission of the Manitoes to retain his trophy. He traveled the whole circuit of Lake Michigan, and then went across to Lake Huron, visiting every high place and waterfall, celebrated as the residence of spirits. But he was unfavorably received. None of the spirits would accept his offerings. Every spirit he asked replied, "Waub-we-nonga has passed before you with his complaints, accusing you of a theft, and requesting that the arrow be returned to its lawful owner. We cannot, therefore, hear you. He who has stolen shall again be stolen from." The very same words were used by each. The last spirit he applied to lived in a cleft, on a high point of rock, surrounded by woods, on the summit of the island called Mishinimakinong.[3] He added this sentence. "Hlox has cursed you." Thus foiled at every point, he returned home with all his tobacco. He called all his *jossakeeds*,[4] and medicine-men, and jugglers together, and laid the gift before them, requesting their advice in this emergency. He asked each one to tell him whether his skill could designate the spirit which was meant by that outlandish word uttered on the island. One of the oldest men said, "It has been revealed to me, by my guardian spirit, in a dream. It is the name of a witch living in the bottom of Lake Superior;

she is a relative of Waub-we-nonga." Not another word was uttered in the
council. Silently they smoked out their pipes, and silently they returned
to their lodges.

We must now return to Kaubina. When he had recovered his wife, he
went back directly to his lodge on the island, and with due ceremony invoked the counsel and aid of his grandmother. For this purpose he erected
a *pointed* lodge,[5] and covered it close around with bark. He took nothing
in with him but his drum, medicine sack, and rattles. After singing for
some time, he heard a noise under ground, and the woman appeared. "My
grandson," said she, "I am made acquainted with your wishes. Your enemy
seeks your blood. Sagimau has obtained the great war bird's arrow, and is
preparing the sacred gift of our country[6] to appease the spirits, and obtain
their permission to use it. If he obtains his wishes, he will prevail. But I
will use all my power to circumvent him. I have a firm friend among the
guardian spirits of our nation, who lives on an island toward the south.
Waub-we-nonga himself is my relation. You may rely upon my power. In
nine days I shall reappear." At the end of that time she fulfilled her promise, and told him to watch, and that at such a time his enemy would come
against him with a large war party in canoes.

In the meantime, Sagimau had visited the spirits, and failed in his design. He would have remained at home, after the result of his council with
the old men and sages, had he not continued to hear of the exploits of
Kaubina, who was making excursions toward the southwest, and driving
back all the tribes who lived on the great lake. He was not only goaded on
by envy of his fame, but he thought him the cause of the spirits not accept-
ing his tobacco, and thus rendering useless in his hands the sacred arrow.
He mustered a large war party and set off in canoes for the north, for the
purpose of attacking the Odjibwas. His old men tried to dissuade him from
this expedition, but were not heeded. When the party reached the Great
Sand Dunes, Sagimau dreamed that he saw Kaubina on an island, and took
him prisoner. He was, therefore, assured of success, and went boldly on.
They crossed over to the island to watch the movements of Kaubina, who,
at this time, had his village on the mainland. This was revealed to the latter
by his grandmother, who declared the bloody intentions of the enemy.
Kaubina appeared in a moment to forget this advice, for he said to his wife,
"Come, let us go over to the island for basswood bark." "Why," said she,
"have you not just told me that Sagimau was watching there?" "Well,"
said he, "I am not afraid. I would have gone if I had not heard this account,
and I will go now." While crossing the bay in his canoe, he directed his wife
to land him alone, and push out her canoe from the shore, and rest there,
so that if any accident occurred, she might immediately cross and arouse
the warriors. He directed her, the moment she reached his lodge, to take
out his medicine sack, and his fighting skin (which was made out of a
large bear skin), and to spread out the latter ready for him, when he
arrived, so that he could slip it on in an instant, as he relied on its magic
virtues to ensure him an easy victory. Shortly after landing him, while

resting on her paddles, she heard the sa-sa-kwan, or war whoop. She immediately paddled for the village, and gave the alarm.

It turned out that when Kaubina landed from the canoe, he stepped ashore near the ambush of Sagimau's party, who arose to a man and instantly made him a prisoner. They immediately tied him to a tree, and pushed over to the mainland to secure the village before the alarm spread. They landed very expeditiously, and getting behind the village, approached from that part. The fight had but just commenced when Kaubina appeared. He had been released by Hlox, and invoking his spirit, flew to the rescue of his people. He found his fighting skin ready, and slipping it on hastily, he now felt himself invulnerable. He then cried out to his adversary and challenged him to single combat. Sagimau did not decline. "Here am I," said he. "I defy you." They closed instantly. Blow was answered with blow, without any apparent advantage to either, till about midday, when Sagimau began to give out. He appealed to Kaubina, saying, "My elder brother, it is enough!" (nesia me-a-me-nik.) No answer was returned, but the reinvigorated blows of his rival and adversary. Kaubina fought with the rage of a demon, and soon after the scalp of Sagimau was flying in the air. Nearly the whole Ottowa party fell with him. It is said the arrow which Sagimau either forgot to use, or was mysteriously withheld from using, was lost in this combat, and returned to the spirit of the King of the Birds who owned it.[7]

NOTES

1. Meaning "the charmed arrow."

2. This phraseology is peculiar to the Indian language, and is in accordance with the Indian plan of thought. To think strong of a thing, implies resolution to the enterprising, and confidence to the doubting. [H. R. S.]

3. Mackinac Island.

4. Magicians.

5. A high pointed pyramidal lodge is appropriated to the Indian priesthood or magicians. [H. R. S.]

6. Tobacco.

7. This tale is an example of the mixture of legend and fact. It was not included in later collections.

ADDIK KUM MAIG[1]

OR

THE ORIGIN OF THE WHITE FISH

A LONG TIME AGO, there lived a famous hunter in a remote part of the north. He had a handsome wife and two sons, who were left in the lodge every day, while he went out in quest of the animals, upon whose flesh they subsisted. Game was very abundant in those days, and his exertions in the chase were well rewarded. The skins of animals furnished them with clothing, and their flesh with food. They lived a long distance from any other lodge, and very seldom saw any one. The two sons were still too young to follow their father to the chase, and usually diverted themselves within a short distance of the lodge. They noticed that a young man visited the lodge during their father's absence, and these visits were frequently repeated. At length the elder of the two said to his mother; "my mother, who is this tall young man that comes here so often during our father's absence?"

"Does he wish to see him? Shall I tell him when he comes back this evening?" "Bad boy," said the mother, pettishly, "mind your bow and arrows, and do not be afraid to enter the forest in search of birds and squirrels, with your little brother. It is not manly to be ever about the lodge. Nor will you become a warrior if you tell all the little things you see and hear to your father. Say not a word to him on the subject." The boys obeyed, but as they grew older, and still saw the visits of this mysterious stranger, they resolved to speak again to their mother, and told her that they meant to inform their father of all they had observed, for they frequently saw this young man passing through the woods, and he did not walk in the path, nor did he carry anything to eat. If he had any message to deliver, they had observed that messages were always addressed to the men, and not to the women. At this, the mother flew into a rage. "I will kill you," said she, "if you speak of it." They were again intimidated to hold their peace. But observing the continuance of an improper intercourse, kept up by stealth, as it were, they resolved at last to disclose the whole matter to their father. They did so. The result was such as might have been anticipated. The father, being satisfied of the infidelity of his wife, watched a suitable occasion, when she was separated from the children, that they might not have their feelings excited, and with a single blow of his war club dispatched her. He then buried her under the ashes of his fire, took down the lodge, and removed, with his two sons, to a distant position.

But the spirit of the woman haunted the children, who were now grown up to the estate of young men. She appeared to them as they returned from hunting in the evening. They were also terrified in their dreams, which they attributed to her. She harassed their imaginations wherever they went. Life became a scene of perpetual terrors. They resolved, together with their father, to leave the country, and commenced a journey toward the south. After traveling many days along the shores of Lake Superior, they passed around a high promontory of rock where a large river issued out of the lake, and soon after came to a place called PAUWATEEG.[2]

They had no sooner come in sight of these falls, than they beheld the skull of the woman rolling along the beach. They were in the utmost fear, and knew not how to elude her. At this moment one of them looked out, and saw a stately crane sitting on a rock in the middle of the rapids. They called out to the bird. "See, grandfather, we are persecuted by a spirit. Come and take us across the falls, so that we may escape her."

This crane was a bird of extraordinary size and great age. When first descried by the two sons, he sat in a state of stupor, in the midst of the most violent eddies. When he heard himself addressed he stretched forth his neck with great deliberation, and lifting himself by his wings, flew across to their assistance. "Be careful," said the crane, "that you do not touch the back part of my head. It is sore, and should you press against it, I shall not be able to avoid throwing you both into the rapids." They were, however, attentive on this point, and were safely landed on the south shore of the river.

The crane then resumed his former position in the rapids. But the skull now cried out. "Come, my grandfather, and carry me over, for I have lost my children, and am sorely distressed." The aged bird flew to her assistance. He carefully repeated the injunction that she must by no means touch the back part of his head, which had been hurt, and was not yet healed. She promised to obey, but soon felt a curiosity to know where the head of her carrier had been hurt, and how so aged a bird could have received so bad a wound. She thought it strange, and before they were halfway over the rapids, could not resist the inclination she felt to touch the affected part. Instantly the crane threw her into the rapids. "There," said he, "you have been of no use during your life, you shall now be changed into something for the benefit of your people, and it shall be called Addik Kum Maig." As the skull floated from rock to rock, the brains were strewed in the water, in a form resembling roes, which soon assumed the shape of a new species of fish, possessing a whiteness of color, and peculiar flavor, which have caused it, ever since, to be in great repute with the Indians.

The family of this man, in gratitude for their deliverance, adopted the crane as their totem, or mark; and this continues to be the distinguishing tribal sign of the band to this day.[3]

NOTES

1. This term appears to be a derivative from ADDIK, the reindeer, and the

plural form of the generic GUMEE water, implying deer of the waters. To facilitate the reading of this, and other compound derivatives, a capital letter is placed at the head of syllables. [H. R. S.]

2. Sault Ste Marie. [H. R. S.]

3. First published in Schoolcraft's *Narrative of an Expedition . . . to Itasca Lake* (1834), "Origin of the White Fish," pp. 147-149. It was printed without change in *M. H.*, pp. 264-268. In *C. M.*, pp. 324-329, it is titled "The Crane that Crossed the River." Mrs. Jameson referred to it (III, p. 131) but did not reproduce it. Compare with "Mash-Kwa-Sha-Kwong" in Appendix A. There is a brief reference to the legend in *P. M.*, p. 124.

OWASSO AND WAYOOND

THE MANITO FOILED

A SAGINAW TALE

OWASSO AND WAYOOND WERE SONS of the Thunder that rules in the northern hemisphere.[1] Their father had left them at an early age, after having suffered greatly from the power of some horrid Weendigoes, or man-eaters, against whom he prevailed at last. Wayoond[2] was the youngest of the two, and was but a mere boy when his father left them, and ascended into the skies; but he was entrusted to the care of his elder brother. And he left them his parting advice. They lived in a large country, where there were lakes and open fields, and often amused themselves in playing ball. Game was very plenty at that time, and they had no difficulty in killing as many animals and birds as they wanted. For their father had been a great medicine man, and had given them powerful spirits to aid them in all they undertook.

Sometime after the father's ascent, the young men went to amuse themselves by playing ball near the shores of a beautiful lake. They played and laughed with great spirit, and the ball was seldom allowed to touch the ground. In this lake happened to be a wicked old Manito, who looked at them playing, and was very much pleased with their beauty and activity. He thought to himself, what shall I do to get them to accompany me—he willed that one of them should hit the ball sideways, and that it should fall into his canoe. It so happened. When the boys saw the old man they were surprised, as they had not noticed him before. "Bring the ball to us," they both cried out, "come to the shore." "No," answered the old man. He, however, came near enough for either of them to wade out to him. "Come, come," he said, "come and get your ball." They insisted on his coming ashore, but he would not consent. "Very well," said the eldest, "I will go and get it," and he jumped into the water and approached the old man. "Hand it to me," he said, touching the canoe. "Ha," answered the old man, "reach over and get it yourself." The young man did so, and as he was in the act of reaching, the old Manito pushed him into the canoe, and uttering the words, *maujaun chemaun!* off they flew, cutting the water so fast, that the spray fell over them. In a short time they reached the old man's lodge.

He then took the young man by the arm and led him to his lodge. "My daughter," he said, to his eldest, as they entered the lodge, "I have brought

215

you a husband." The young woman smiled, for she soon saw what a fine looking young man he was. The old man told him to take his seat near her, and the ceremony was soon ended that made them man and wife.

The young man felt for his poor brother, but it was out of his power, at that time, to render him any assistance. He remained very happy with his wife, and they were blessed with a son. She told him that her father was a magician, and had a magic canoe, and was wicked. He, one day, asked his son-in-law to go out a-fishing with him. They started, for the magician had only to speak, and off went the canoe. They reached a rocky island and fished round it. The young man had fastened his spear in a very large sturgeon, who was making violent efforts to extricate himself from the barbs. The old man thought this a very favorable opportunity to drown his son-in-law, and by aiding the canoe as it rocked outwards, plunged the young man head foremost into the lake. He then spoke to his canoe, and in a very few moments was out of sight. The young man knew that this would happen, but being gifted with limited magic powers, he knew also how to relieve himself. He spoke to the fish and told him to swim toward the lodge, while he carried him along, which he did with great velocity. Once he told the sturgeon to rise near the surface of the water, so that he might catch a glimpse of the magician. He did so, and the young man saw him busy, in another direction, fishing. He proceeded and reached the beach, near the magician's lodge, in advance of him. He then spoke to the fish, not to be angry for his having speared him, as he was created to be meat for man. He then drew the fish on shore, and went up and told his wife to dress it and pull out the gristly part and cook it immediately. She did so, and when it was cooked the magician arrived. "Your grandfather is arrived," said the woman to her son, "go and see what he brings, and eat this as you go," handing him some of the gristle. The boy went, and the magician immediately asked him, "What are you eating? and who brought it?" He replied, "My father brought it." The magician had his doubts and felt perplexed; he, however, put on a grave face, and entering the lodge, acted as if nothing unusual had transpired.

Some days elapsed when he again requested his son-in-law to accompany him. The young man said, "Yes!" His wife had then told him the true character of her father, and the number of times he could exercise his magic powers. They went out, and arrived at a solitary island composed entirely of rocks. The magician said, "go on shore and pick up all the gulls' eggs you can find." The rocks were covered with them, and the air resounded with the cry of the gulls, who saw the robbery committed on them. The magician took the opportunity to speak to the gulls. "I have long wished," said he, "to offer you something. I now give you this young man for food." He then uttered the charm to his canoe, and it shot out of sight, abandoning the young man to his fate. The gulls flew in immense numbers around him, and were ready to devour him. He addressed them and said—"Gulls, you know you were not formed to eat human flesh, and man was not made to be the prey of birds; obey my words. Fly close together, a sufficient number of you, and carry me on your backs to the magician's lodge." They obeyed him, and he soon found himself swiftly gliding toward home.

It appears that the magician in telling his canoe to go, often limited it, in point of time, or distance, till he ordered it forward again. In this instance he fell asleep, and the canoe stood still, for the young man in his flight over the lake saw him lying on his back in the canoe, taking a nap, as the day was calm and delightful. The gulls, as they passed over him, treated him with great disrespect. He jumped up and exclaimed, "It is always so with these double pierced birds!" Owasso reached the lodge in safety, and killed two or three of the gulls for the sake of their feathers to ornament his son's head. When the magician arrived, his grandson met him with his head covered with feathers. "Where did you get these?" he asked. "My father brought them," he answered. He felt perplexed and uneasy, but said nothing. He entered the lodge in silence, and sat down to meditate upon some new plan for destroying his son-in-law. He reflected that he had tried two of his charms without effect, and had but two more left. He again asked the young man to go with him to get young eagles, he said he wished to tame them, and keep them as pets. They started on the trip, and after traversing an immense waste of water, at length reached a desolate island in the center of the lake. They landed and soon found an eagle's nest. The young man obeyed his father-in-law's wishes, by climbing up to get the young ones. He had nearly reached the nest, when he heard the magician's voice addressing the tree, saying, "Grow up," and the tree instantly reached an extraordinary height. "Now, eagles!" said he, "I promised you food, and I give you this young man to feed upon." Then he said to the canoe, "Go!" and away he went, leaving the young man at the mercy of the eagles. The birds were enraged at seeing their young in danger—they flew round him with their beaks open, and their claws distended, ready to tear him in pieces. His power, however, extended to them also, and he got them to fly back with him to the lodge. His wife was rejoiced to think that he had escaped the third charm, and told him it was now his turn to ask the magician to go out, fearing that the old man would not repeat the invitation himself. She gave him all necessary directions, which he promised to follow.

When the magician arrived, his surprise and consternation was at its height, finding that his third effort had failed, and that he had but a single charm more in his power.

One evening as Owasso and his wife were sitting on the banks of the lake, and the soft breeze swept over it, they heard a song, as if sung by someone at a great distance. The sound continued sometime and then died away in perfect stillness. "Oh! 'tis the voice of my brother," cried the young man. "If I could only see him!" and he hung down his head in deep anguish. His wife felt for him, and to console him, she proposed that they should attempt to make their escape on the morrow. The plan was laid. The younger sister was to offer to comb her father's hair during the warm and sultry part of the day, and pick the hairs clean, and in so doing, it was supposed he would fall asleep. The plan succeeded, and as soon as he slept, the young man and family embarked in the magic canoe, then saying *majaun chemaun!* off the canoe started. They had nearly reached the land, and could distinctly hear the voice of the young man, singing, as before, when the magician awoke. He suspected something, and looking for his canoe immediately found it gone. He spoke his magic words, extended his sinewy arm in the air, and drew it in. The charm was irresistible—the young man and his wife saw, with anguish, when almost within reach of the shore, that the canoe suddenly turned back. They soon reached the lodge. The magician stood on the beach, and drew up his canoe. He did not utter a word. The young couple entered the lodge in silence.[3] Autumn was now near its close, and winter soon set in. Soon after the first fall of snow, the young man asked the magician to go out hunting deer, as they could now easily be tracked. They set out together, and after several days' journey, arrived at a fit place for their object. They busied themselves in hunting all day, but without success. At evening they built themselves a lodge of pine branches to sleep in. The night was bitterly cold, but the young man took off his leggings and moccasins and hung them up to dry. The magician did the same, carefully hanging his own in a separate place, and they laid down to sleep. During the night the magician got up and went out, remaining some time. As the young man suspected him, and knew, indeed, what kind of a trick the old man meant to play him, he took this opportunity to get up and change the moccasins and leggings, putting his own in the place of the magician's, depending on the darkness of the lodge to impose on him. Afterward they both laid down and slept. Near daylight the magician got up to rekindle the fire, and slyly reached down his own leggings and moccasins with a stick, thinking they were the young man's, and dropped them into the fire, at the same instant throwing himself down, pretending he still wanted to sleep.

The leather leggings and moccasins soon drew up and were burnt. Instantly jumping up, and rubbing his eyes, the magician cried out, "Son-in-law, your moccasins are burning." Owasso got up deliberately and unconcerned. "No, my friend," said he, "here are *mine,*" taking them down and putting them on. "It is *your* moccasins that are burning." The magician dropped his head in vexation to think that he had been foiled in all his attempts. Nothing was now left, and he knew that no mercy would be shown him. The young man left him to meditate on all his crimes of blood, and to meet that fate from the want of covering for his feet and legs, which he had prepared for him. He reached home in safety in a few days, notwithstanding the cold, and resolved to quit the place forever, and go in search of his brother. Although the weather was cold, the lake had not yet frozen over, and the young hunter and his family resolved to embark immediately, the younger sister went with them in the hope of getting a husband. Word was given to the magic canoe, and they went swiftly on their way to the opposite shore. Owasso soon heard his younger brother's well-known voice, as the sounds were wafted on the breeze, singing the following words:

Ni si ai
Ni si ai
A ko nau gud dau o un
A ko nau gud dau o un
Ash i gun ai a he ee
Ni mau en gun e wee
Ash i gun ai a he ee
Ni mau en gun e wee.

"My brother—my brother! since you left me going in the canoe, a-hee-ee, I am half changed into a wolf, E-wee—I am half changed into a wolf, E-wee." This he kept repeating as they neared the shore. The sounds were very distinct. On the sand they saw the tracks of a wolf, as if departing. They also saw the prints of human hands; and they soon saw Wayoond himself, half man and half wolf, running along shore. Owasso ran after him, crying, Ni she ma! Ni she ma! but the partly transformed object, jumped on the bank and looked back for some time, repeating the former words, and disappeared in the woods.

The women built a lodge at the spot, and got everything comfortable for a long stay. The man was, however, very uneasy, and exerted his power to regain his brother—for he kept near the lodge at night, singing in a most pitiful strain. They always left food for him some distance from the lodge, which he eat[4] in the night.

The unmarried woman, who was something of a mud-jee-kee-kuá-wis, proposed to dig a pit and cover it with light sticks and leaves, for the purpose of placing the meat on, that when he came to eat it he might fall in. Her plan succeeded, and when they came next morning to examine it, they were rejoiced to find the half wolf in the pit. The man had been fasting previously, and he brought his medicines and charms, and threw some over his brother, who, after sometime, resumed his human shape. He was taken to the lodge, but it was sometime before the change was perfect, and still longer before he was restored to health. His disposition, however, was soured, for he always sat and looked very gloomy, and felt no pleasure in the society of his friends. He recommended hunting, in which he was very successful, for he always hung the tail of a wolf to his girdle at his back, or at his leg-bands or garters, which gave him great speed and vigor in overtaking animals of the deer kind.

MAUJEEKIKUAWIS was forward in her advances toward him. He, however, paid no attention to it, and shunned her. She continued to be very assiduous in attending to his wants, such as cooking, and mending his moccasins. She felt hurt and displeased at his indifference, and resolved to play him a trick. Opportunity soon offered. The lodge was spacious, and she dug a hole in the ground, where the young man usually sat, covering it very carefully. When the brothers returned from the chase, the young man threw himself down carelessly at the usual place, and fell into the cavity, his head and feet remaining out, so that he was unable to extricate himself. "Ha! Ha!" cried Maujeekikuawis, as she helped him out, "you are mine,

I have caught you at last, and I did it on purpose." A smile came over the young man's face, and he said, "So be it, I will be yours": and from that moment they lived happily as man and wife.

They all lived contented and happy after this, for a length of time. The elder brother's son grew up to manhood, and was noted for his beauty, bravery, and manliness. He was very expert in the chase, and supplied them abundantly with food.

One evening the brothers mentioned their desire of visiting a very high mountain in the vicinity, in order, as they said, to gratify their curiosity, and see the country which lay beyond it. The women tried to dissuade them, and expressed their fears lest some accident might befall them; but their opposition was unavailing. The men prepared to depart, and gave their parting advice to their wives and children, telling them, that should anything serious happen, Owasso's elder son was now fully capable of supporting them, and that the time was not far distant when they should all meet each other in those happy hunting grounds toward the setting sun.

The night after this parting address they left the lodge. It was very dark, still not a breath of air could be felt—when lo! flashes of lightning appeared, and the noise of rumbling thunder was suddenly heard advancing from the north (where their father had gone) and the quietude of the night gave place to one of the most terrible tempests. The dark air was lit up with flashes of vivid and forked lightning, and the roar of that ear-stopping thunder was incessant. At the same time the south wind rushed on with a tremendous noise, laying the most stately trees level with the earth.

The young men never returned, but tradition says that they were taken up by their father from the mountain's top, and aided him in wreaking just vengeance on all Weendigoes and magicians. For it appears that after he was fixed in his ethereal abode, he beheld with horror the bad actions of these wicked men. And he resolved to destroy them, and rid the earth of such monsters, as well as to take vengeance for what he had himself suffered from them. To this end he exerted the power the Great Spirit had given him, by sending thunder and lightning to destroy them all. From this period the Indian world has been free from them. Still the imaginations of our old and young men often dwell upon their former power, and they are led to believe that the hills, and caves, and forests, occupied by these once visible, are still possessed by invisible demons.[5]

NOTE. This story, it will be perceived, very much resembles, in some of its incidents, one previously inserted from the Odjibwa. ["Mishosha."] It also embraces one of the principal incidents in the allegory of the "Forsaken Boy," from the same source. [H. R. S.]

NOTES

1. Thunder is invariably *personified* by the Algic Indians. There is no other mode of describing it in their vocabulary. [H. R. S.]

2. Wayoond was also the name of an Indian who died of drunkenness and exposure in July 1828. *P. M.*, p. 297.

3. This taciturnity is characteristic of the American Indians, who seldom speak or manifest any emotion when events of this nature take place in actual life, especially if hard feelings have been excited in either party. [H. R. S.]

4. Eat, pronounced et, as past tense was common usage in the last century. Today, of course, it is considered a vulgarism.

5. This version of "Mishosha, the Magician of Lake Superior" is not re-printed elsewhere.

SHAWONDASEE

FROM THE MYTHOLOGY OF THE ODJIBWAS

MUDJEKEWIS AND NINE BROTHERS conquered the Mammoth Bear,[1] and obtained the Sacred Belt of Wampum, the great object of previous warlike enterprise, and the great means of happiness to men. The chief honor of this achievement was awarded to Mudjekewis, the youngest of the ten, who received the government of the West Winds. He is therefore called KABEYUN, the father of the winds. To his son, WABUN, he gave the East; to SHAWONDASEE, the South, and to KABIBONOKKA, the North. Manabozho, being an illegitimate son, was left unprovided. When he grew up, and obtained the secret of his birth, he went to war against his father, KABEYUN, and having brought the latter to terms, he received the government of the Northwest Winds, ruling jointly with his brother KABIBONOKKA the tempests from that quarter of the heavens.

Shawondasee is represented as an affluent, plethoric old man, who has grown unwieldy from repletion, and seldom moves. He keeps his eyes steadfastly fixed on the north. When he sighs, in autumn, we have those balmy southern airs, which communicate warmth and delight over the northern hemisphere, and make the *Indian Summer*.

One day, while gazing toward the north, he beheld a beautiful young woman of slender and majestic form, standing on the plains. She appeared in the same place for several days, but what most attracted his admiration, was her bright and flowing locks of yellow hair. Ever dilatory, however, he contented himself with gazing. At length he saw, or fancied he saw, her head enveloped in a pure white mass like snow. This excited his jealousy toward his brother Kabibonokka, and he threw out a succession of short and rapid sighs—when lo! the air was filled with light filaments of a silvery hue, but the object of his affections had forever vanished. In reality, the southern airs had blown off the fine-winged seed-vessels of the prairie dandelion.

"My son," said the narrator, "it is not wise to differ in our tastes from other people; nor ought we to put off, through slothfulness, what is best done at once. Had Shawondasee conformed to the tastes of his countrymen, he would not have been an admirer of *yellow* hair; and if he had evinced a proper activity in his youth, his mind would not have run flower-gathering in his age."[2]

NOTES

1. See "Iamo, or the Undying Head."
2. Reprinted in *M. H.*, pp. 88-89.

THE LINNET AND EAGLE

FROM THE ODJIBWA

THE BIRDS MET TOGETHER one day, to try which could fly the highest. Some flew up very swift, but soon got tired, and were passed by others of stronger wing. But the eagle went up beyond them all, and was ready to claim the victory, when the gray linnet, a very small bird, flew from the eagle's back, where it had perched unperceived, and being fresh and unexhausted, succeeded in going the highest. When the birds came down, and met in council to award the prize, it was given to the eagle, because that bird had not only gone up nearer to the sun than any of the larger birds, but it had carried the linnet on its back.

Hence the feathers of the eagle are esteemed the most honorable marks for a warrior, as it is not only considered the bravest bird, but also endowed with strength to soar the highest.[1]

NOTE

1. This totemic fable is not found in any other collection of Schoolcraft tales.

THE MOOSE AND WOODPECKER

FROM THE PILLAGERS[1]

AFTER MANABOZHO HAD KILLED the Prince of Serpents, he was living in a state of great want, completely deserted by his powers, as a deity, and not able to procure the ordinary means of subsistence. He was at this time living with his wife and children, in a remote part of the country, where he could get no game. He was miserably poor. It was winter, and he had not the common Indian comforts.

He said to his wife, one day, "I will go out a-walking, and see if I cannot find some lodges." After walking some time he saw a lodge at a distance. The children were playing at the door. When they saw him approaching they ran into the lodge, and told their parents that Manabozho was coming. It was the residence of the large red-headed Woodpecker. He came to the lodge door and asked him to enter. He did so. After some time, the Wood-pecker, who was a magician, said to his wife, "Have you nothing to give Manabozho; he must be hungry." She answered, "No." In the center of the lodge stood a large white tamarack tree. The Woodpecker flew onto it, and commenced going up, turning his head on each side of the tree, and every now and then driving in his bill. At last he drew something out of the tree, and threw it down, when, behold! a fine, fat raccoon on the ground. He drew out six or seven more. He then descended, and told his wife to prepare them. "Manabozho," he said, "this is the only thing we eat. What else can we give you?" "It is very good," replied Manabozho. They smoked their pipes and conversed with each other. After eating, the great spirit-chief got ready to go home. The Woodpecker said to his wife, "Give him the remaining raccoons to take home for his children." In the act of leaving the lodge he dropped intentionally one of his mittens, which was soon after observed. "Run," said the Woodpecker to his eldest son, "and give it to him. But don't give it into his hand; throw it at him, for there is no knowing him, he acts so curiously." The boy did as he was bid. "Nemesho (my grandfather)," said he, as he came up to him, "you have left one of your mittens—here it is." "Yes," said he, affecting to be ignorant of the circum-stance, "it is so. But don't throw it, you will soil it on the snow." The lad, however, threw it, and was about to return. "List," said Manabozho, "is that all you eat—do you eat nothing else with the raccoon?" "No," replied the young Woodpecker. "Tell your father, he answered, "to come and visit me, and let him bring a sack. I will give him what he shall eat with his raccoon meat." When the young one reported this to his father, the old man turned up his nose at the invitation. "What does the old fellow think he has got!" exclaimed he.

Sometime after the Woodpecker went to pay a visit to Manabozho. He was received with the usual attention. It had been the boast of Manabozho, in former days, that he could do what any other being in the creation could, whether man or animal. He affected to have the sagacity of all animals, to understand their language, and to be capable of exactly imitating it. And in his visits to men, it was his custom to return, exactly, the treatment he had received. He was very ceremonious in following the very voice and manner of his entertainers. The Woodpecker had no sooner entered his lodge, therefore, than he commenced playing the mimic. He had previously directed his wife to change his lodge, so as to enclose a large dry tamarack tree. "What can I give you?" said he to the Woodpecker; "but as we eat, so shall you eat." He then put a long piece of bone in his nose, in imitation of the bill of this bird, and jumping on the tamarack tree, attempted to climb it, doing as he had seen the Woodpecker do. He turned his head first on one side, then on the other. He made awkward efforts to ascend, but continually slipped down. He struck the tree with the bone in his nose, until at last he drove it so far up his nostrils that the blood began to flow, and he fell down senseless at the foot of the tree. The Woodpecker started after his drum and rattle to restore him, and having got them, succeeded in bringing him to. As soon as he came to his senses, he began to lay the blame of his failure to his wife, saying to his guest, "Nemesho, it is this woman relation of yours—*she* is the cause of my not succeeding. She has rendered me a worthless fellow. Before I took her I could also get raccoons." The Woodpecker said nothing, but flying on the tree, drew out several fine raccoons. "Here," said he, "this is the way *we* do," and left him with apparent contempt.

Severe weather continued, and Manabozho still suffered for the want of food. One day he walked out, and came to a lodge, which was occupied by the Moose (Möz.) The young Mozonsug[2] saw him and told their father Manabozho was at the door. He told them to invite him in. Being seated they entered into conversation. At last the Moose, who was a Meeta, said, "What shall we give Manabozho to eat? We have nothing." His wife was seated with her back toward him, making garters. He walked up to her, and untying the covering of the armlet from her back, cut off a large piece of flesh from the square of her shoulder.[3] He then put some medicine on it, which immediately healed the wound. The skin did not even appear to have been broken, and his wife was so little affected by it, that she did not so much as leave off her work, till he told her to prepare the flesh for eating. "Manabozho," said he, "this is all we eat, and it is all we can give you."

After they had finished eating Manabozho set out for home, but intentionally, as before, dropped one of his *minjekawun,* or mittens. One of the young Moose took it to him, telling him that his father had sent him with it. He had been cautioned not to hand it to him, but to throw it at him. Having done so, contrary to the remonstrance of Manabozho, he was going back when the latter cried out "BAKAH! BAKAH![4] Is *that*[5] the only kind of meat you eat? Tell me." "Yes," answered the young man, "that is all, we have nothing else." "Tell your father," he replied, "to come and visit me, and I will give him what you shall eat with your meat." The old Moose listened to this message with indignity. I wonder what he thinks he has got, poor fellow!

He was bound, however, to obey the invitation, and went accordingly, taking along a cedar sack, for he had been told to bring one. Manabozho received him in the same manner he had himself been received—repeating the same remarks, and attempted to supply the lack of food in the same manner. To this end he had requested his wife to busy herself in making garters. He arose and untied the covering of her back as he had seen the Moose do. He then cut her back shockingly, paying no attention to her cries or resistance, until he saw her fall down, from the loss of blood. "Manabozho," said the Moose, "you are killing your wife." He immediately ran for his drum and rattle, and restored her to life by his skill. He had no sooner done this than Manabozho began to lay the blame of his ill success on his wife. "Why, Nemesho," said he, "this woman, this relation of yours—she is making me a most worthless fellow. Formerly, I procured my meat in this way. But now I can accomplish nothing."

The Moose then cut large pieces of flesh off his own thighs, without the least injury to himself, and gave them to Manabozho, saying with a contemptuous air, "this is the way *we* do." He then left the lodge.

After these visits Manabozho was sitting pensively in his lodge one day, with his head down. He heard the wind whistling around it, and thought, by attentively listening, he could hear the voice of someone speaking to him. It seemed to say to him: "Great chief, why are you sorrowful? Am not I your friend—your guardian Spirit?" He immediately took up his rattle, and without leaving his sitting posture, began to sing the chant which at the close of every stanza has the chorus of "Whaw Lay Le Aw." When he had devoted a long time to this chant, he laid his rattle aside, and determined to fast. For this purpose he went to a cave, and built a very small fire near which he laid down, first telling his wife, that neither she nor the children must come near him, till he had finished his fast. At the end of seven days he came back to the lodge, pale and emaciated. His wife in the meantime had dug through the snow, and got a small quantity of the root called truffles. These she boiled and set before him. When he had finished his repast, he took his large bow and bent it. Then placing a strong arrow to the string, he drew it back, and sent the arrow, with the strength of a giant, through the side of his bark lodge. "There," said he to his wife, "go to the outside, and you will find a large bear, shot through the heart." She did so, and found one as he had predicted.

He then sent the children out to get red willow sticks. Of these he cut off as many pieces, of equal length, as would serve to invite his friends to a feast. A red stick was sent to each one, not forgetting the Moose and the Woodpecker.

When they arrived they were astonished to see such a profusion of meat cooked for them, at such a time of scarcity. Manabozho understood their glances and felt a conscious pride in making such a display. "Akewazi," said he, to one of the oldest of the party, "the weather is very cold, and the snow lasts a long time. We can kill nothing now but small squirrels. And I have sent for you to help me eat some of them." The Woodpecker was the first to put a mouthful of the bear's meat to his mouth, but he had no sooner begun to taste it, than it changed into a dry powder, and set him coughing. It appeared as bitter as ashes. The Moose felt the same effect, and began to cough. Each one, in turn, was added to the number of coughers. But they had too much sense of decorum, and respect for their entertainer, to say anything. The meat looked very fine. They thought they would try more of it. But the more they ate, the faster they coughed and the louder became the uproar, until Manabozho, exerting his former power, which he now felt to be renewed, transformed them all into the ADJIDAMO, or squirrel, an animal which is still found to have the habit of barking, or coughing, whenever it sees anyone approach its nest.[6]

NOTES

1. A warlike tribe of the Algic stock located at the sources of the Mississippi. [H. R. S.]

2. Diminutive form, plural number, of the noun Möz. [H. R. S.]

3. The dress of the females in the Odjibwa nation consists of sleeves, open on the inner side of the arm from the elbow up, and terminating in large square folds, falling from the shoulders, which are tied at the back of the neck with ribbon or binding. The sleeves are separately made, and not attached to the breast garment, which consists of square folds of cloth, ornamented and sustained by shoulder straps. To untie the sleeves or armlets, as is here described, is therefore to expose the shoulders, but not the back—a simple device, quickly accomplished, by which the magician could readily exercise his art almost imperceptibly to the object. [H. R. S.]

4. Stop! stop! [H. R. S.]

5. It is difficult to throw into the English pronoun the whole of the meaning of the Indian. Pronouns in this language being, like other parts of speech, transitive; they are at once indicative both of the actor, personal, and relative, and the nature of the object, or subject of the action, or relation. This, and that, are not used in the elementary form these pronouns invariably possess in the English. Inflections are put to them indicating the class of natural objects to which they refer. A noun masculine or feminine, requiring an animate pronoun, a noun inanimate, a pronoun inanimate. [H. R. S.]

6. This fragment of the Manabozho cycle was incorporated with "Hiawatha" in *M. H.*, pp. 43-49.

WEENG[1]

SLEEP IS PERSONIFIED by the Algic race, under the name of Weeng.[2] But the power of the Indian Morpheus is executed in a peculiar manner, and by a novel agency. Weeng seldom acts directly in inducing sleep, but he exercises dominion over hosts of gnome-like beings, who are everywhere present, and are constantly on the alert. These beings are invisible to common eyes. Each one is armed with a tiny puggamaugon, or club, and when he observes a person sitting or reclining under circumstances favorable to sleep, he nimbly climbs upon his forehead and inflicts a blow. The first blow only creates drowsiness, the second makes the person lethargic, so that he occasionally closes his eyelids, the third produces sound sleep. It is the constant duty of these little emissaries to put everyone to sleep whom they encounter—men, women, and children. And they are found secreted around the bed, or on small protuberances of the bark of the Indian lodges. They hide themselves in the GUSHKEEPITAUGUN, or smoking pouch of the hunter, and when he sits down to light his pipe in the woods, are ready to fly out and exert their sleep-compelling power. If they succeed, the game is suffered to pass, and the hunter obliged to return to his lodge without a reward.

In general, however, they are represented to possess friendly dispositions, seeking constantly to restore vigor and elasticity to the exhausted body. But being without judgment, their power is sometimes exerted at the hazard of reputation, or even life. Sleep may be induced in a person carelessly floating in his canoe, above a fall; or in a war party, on the borders of an enemy's country; or in a female, without the protection of the lodge circle. Although their peculiar season of action is in the night, they are also alert during the day.

While the forms of these gnomes are believed to be those of *ininees,* little or fairy men, the figure of Weeng himself is unknown, and it is not certain that he has ever been seen. Most of what is known on this subject, is derived from Iagoo, who related, that going out one day with his dogs to hunt, he passed through a wide range of thicket, where he lost his dogs. He became much alarmed, for they were faithful animals, and he was greatly attached to them. He called out, and made every exertion to recover them in vain. At length he came to a spot where he found them asleep, having incautiously ran near the residence of Weeng. After great exertions he aroused them, but not without having felt the power of somnolency himself. As he cast up his eyes from the place where the dogs were lying, he saw the Spirit of Sleep sitting upon a branch of a tree. He was in the

228

shape of a giant insect, or *monetoas,* with many wings from his back, which made a low deep murmuring sound, like distant falling water. But Iagoo himself, being a very great liar and braggart, little credit was given to his narration.

Weeng is not only the dispenser of sleep, but it seems he is also the author of dullness, which renders the word susceptible of an ironical use. If an orator fails, he is said to be struck by Weeng. If a warrior *lingers,* he has ventured too near the sleepy god. If children begin to nod or yawn, the Indian mother looks up smilingly, and says, "they have been struck by Weeng," and puts them to bed.[3]

NOTES

1. This word has the *g* sounded hard, as if it were followed by a half sound of *k*—a common sound for *g* final in the Odjibwa. [H. R. S.]

2. There is a discussion of Weeng in *P. M.,* p. 154.

3. Reprinted in *M. H.,* pp. 262-264, with minor changes, chiefly in the first paragraph.

IAGOO

FROM THE MYTHOLOGY OF THE CHIPPEWAS

IAGOO IS THE NAME of a personage noted in Indian lore for having given extravagant narrations of whatever he had seen, heard, or accomplished. It seems that he always saw extraordinary things, made extraordinary journeys, and performed extraordinary feats. He could not look out of his lodge and see things as other men did. If he described a bird, it had a most singular variety of brilliant plumage. The animals he met with were all of the monstrous kind; they had eyes like orbs of fire, and claws like hooks of steel, and could step over the top of an Indian lodge. He told of a serpent he had seen, which had hair on its neck like a mane, and feet resembling a quadruped; and if one were to take his own account of his exploits and observations, it would be difficult to decide whether his strength, his activity, or his wisdom should be most admired.

Iagoo did not appear to have been endowed with the ordinary faculties of other men. His eyes appeared to be magnifiers, and the tympanum of his ears so constructed that what appeared to common observers to be but the sound of a zephyr, to him had a far closer resemblance to the noise of thunder. His imagination appeared to be of so exuberant a character, that he scarcely required more than a drop of water to construct an ocean, or a grain of sand to form an earth. And he had so happy an exemption from both the restraints of judgment and moral accountability, that he never found the slightest difficulty in accommodating his facts to the most enlarged credulity. Nor was his ample thirst for the marvelous ever quenched by attempts to reconcile statements the most strange, unaccountable, and preposterous.

Such was Iagoo, the Indian story-teller, whose name is associated with all that is extravagant and marvelous, and has long been established in the hunter's vocabulary as a perfect synonym for liar, and is bandied about as a familiar proverb. If a hunter or warrior, in telling his exploits, undertakes to embellish them; to overrate his merits, or in any other way to excite the incredulity of his hearers, he is liable to be rebuked with the remark, "So here we have Iagoo come again." And he seems to hold the relative rank in oral narration which our written literature awards to Baron Munchausen, Jack Falstaff, and Captain Lemuel Gulliver.

Notwithstanding all this, there are but a few scraps of his actual stories to be found. He first attracted notice by giving an account of a water lilly, a single leaf of which, he averred, was sufficient to make a petticoat and upper garments for his wife and daughter. One evening he was sitting in his lodge, on the banks of a river, and hearing the quacking of ducks on the stream, he fired through the lodge door at a venture. He killed a swan that happened to be flying by, and twenty brace of ducks in the stream. But this did not check the force of his shot; they passed on, and struck the heads of two loons, at the moment they were coming up from beneath the water, and even went beyond and killed a most extraordinary large fish called Moshkeenozha.[1] On another occasion he had killed a deer, and after skinning it, was carrying the carcass on his shoulders, when he spied some stately elks on the plain before him. He immediately gave them chase, and had run, over hill and dale, a distance of half a day's travel, before he recollected that he had the deer's carcass on his shoulders.

One day, as he was passing over a tract of *mushkeeg,* or bog-land, he saw mosquitoes of such enormous size, that he staked his reputation on the fact that a single wing of one of the insects was sufficient for a sail to his canoe, and the proboscis as big as his wife's shovel. But he was favored with a still more extraordinary sight, in a gigantic ant, which passed him, as he was watching a beaver's lodge, dragging the·entire carcass of a hare.

At another time, for he was ever seeing or doing something wonderful, he got out of smoking weed, and in going into the woods in search of some, he discovered a bunch of the red willow, or maple bush, of such a luxuriant growth, that he was industriously occupied half a day in walking round it.[2]

NOTES

1. The muskellunge. [H. R. S.]
2. This melange of "tall tales" was reprinted without change in *M. H.,* pp. 85-87.

THE GRAVE LIGHT

OR

ADVENTURES OF A WARRIOR'S SOUL

FROM THE ODJIBWA

THERE WAS ONCE A BATTLE between the Indians, in which many were killed on both sides. Among the number was the leader of the Odjibwas, a very brave man, who had fought in many battles; but while he was shouting for victory, he received an arrow in his flesh, and fell as if dead. At last his companions *thought he was dead,* and treated him as if he were. They placed his body in a sitting posture, on the field of battle, his back being supported by a tree, and his face toward the enemies' country. They put on him his headdress of feathers, and leaned his bow against his shoulders, for it was before the white men had brought guns for the Indians. They then left him and returned to their homes.

The warrior, however, heard and saw all they did. Although his body was deprived of muscular motion, his soul was living within it. He heard them lament his death, and felt their touch as they set him up. "They will not be so cruel as to leave me here, he thought to himself. I am certainly not dead. I have the use of my senses." But his anguish was extreme, when he saw them, one after another depart, till he was left alone among the dead. He could not move a limb, nor a muscle, and felt as if he were buried in his own body. Horrid agonies came over him. He exerted himself, but found that he had no power over his muscles. At last he appeared to leap out of himself. He first stood up, and then followed his friends. He soon overtook them, but when he arrived at their camp no one noticed him. He spoke to them, but no one answered. He seemed to be *invisible* to them, and his voice appeared to have no *sound.* Unconscious, however, of his body's being left behind, he thought their conduct most strange. He determined to follow them, and exactly imitated all they did, walking when they walked, running when they ran, sleeping when they slept. But the most unbroken silence was maintained as to his presence.

When evening came he addressed the party. "Is it possible," said he, "that you do not see me, nor hear me, nor understand me? Will you permit me to starve when you have plenty? Is there no one who recollects me?" And with similar sentiments he continued to talk to them, and to upbraid them at every stage of their homeward journey, but his words seemed to pass like the sounds of the wind.

At length they reached the village, and the women and children, and old

232

men, came out, according to custom, to welcome the returning war party. They set up the shout of praise. "Kumaudjing! kumaudjing! kumaudjing! They have met, fought, and conquered," was heard at every side. Group after group repeated the cry.

> Kumaudjing! kumaudjing! kumaudjing!
> They have met, fought, and conquered
> The strong and the brave,
> See the eagle plumes nod,
> And the red trophies wave.
> Kumaudjing! kumaudjing!
> The war-banner waves,
> They have fought like our fathers,
> And scorn to be slaves,
> The sons of the noble,
> They scorn to be slaves.
> And he—where is he, who has led them to fight,
> Whose arrow was death,
> And whose war-club was might.
> Kumaudjing! kumaudjing!
> The hero is near,
> He is tying his enemies' scalp to his robe,
> And wiping the enemies' blood from his spear.
> He is near—he is near,
> And, hark, his Sa-sa-kwan
> Now bursts on the ear.

The truth, however, was soon revealed; although it caused a momentary check, it did not mar the *general* joy. The sight of scalps made every tongue vocal. A thousand inquiries were made, and he heard his own fate described, how he had fought bravely, been killed, and left among the dead.

"It is not true," replied the indignant chief, "that I was killed and left upon the field of battle. I am here. I live. I move. See me." Nobody answered. He then walked to his own lodge. He saw his wife tearing her hair, and lamenting his fate. He asked her to bind up his wounds. She made no reply. He placed his mouth close to her ear, and called for food. She did not notice it. He drew back his arm and struck her a blow. She felt nothing.

Thus foiled he determined to go back. He followed the track of the warriors. It was four days' journey. During three days he met with nothing extraordinary. On the fourth, toward evening, as he drew near the skirts of the battlefield, he saw a fire in the path. He stepped on one side, but the fire had also moved its position. He crossed to the other side, but the fire was still before him. Whichever way he took, the fire appeared to bar his approach. At this moment he espied the enemy of his fortunes in the moccasin, or flat-headed snake. "My son," said the reptile, "you have heretofore been considered a brave man—but beware of this fire. It is a strong spirit. You must appease it by the sacred gift." The warrior put his hand to his side, but he had left his sack behind him. "Demon," he exclaimed, addressing the flame, "why do you bar my approach? Know that I am a spirit. I have never been defeated by my enemies, and I will not be defeated by you."

So saying, he made a sudden effort and leaped through the flames. In this effort *he awoke from his trance.* He had lain eight days on the battle-field. He found himself sitting on the ground, with his back supported by a tree, and his bow leaning against his shoulder, as his friends had left him. He looked up and beheld a large Gha Niew, or war eagle, sitting in the tree, which he immediately recognized as his guardian spirit, or personal Manito. This bird had watched his body, and prevented the other birds of prey from devouring it.

He arose and stood for a few minutes, but found himself weak and emaciated. By the use of simples and such forest arts as our people are versed in, he succeeded in reaching his home. When he came near, he uttered the Sa-sa-kwan, or war cry, which threw the village into an uproar. But while they were debating the meaning of so unexpected a sound, the wounded chief was ushered into their midst. He related his adventures as before given. He concluded his narrative by telling them that it is pleasing to the spirits of the dead to have a fire lit upon their graves at night, after their burial. He gave as a reason, that it is four days' travel to the place appointed for the residence of the soul, and it requires a light every night at the place of its encampment. If the friends of the deceased neglect this rite, the spirit is compelled to build a fire for itself.[1]

> Light up the fire upon my grave
> $\qquad$ When I am dead.
> 'Twill softly shed its beaming rays,
> To guide the soul its darkling ways,
> And ever, as the day's full light
> Goes down, and leaves the world in night,
> These kindly gleams, with warmth possest,
> Shall show my spirit where to rest
> $\qquad$ When I am dead.
>
> Four days the funeral rite renew,
> $\qquad$ When I am dead.
> While onward bent, with typic woes,
> I seek the red man's last repose;
> Let no rude hand the flame destroy,
> Nor mar the scene with festive joy;
> While night by night, a ghostly guest,
> I journey to my final rest,
> $\qquad$ When I am dead.
>
> No moral light directs my way
> $\qquad$ When I am dead.
> A hunter's fate—a warrior's fame,

A shade, a phantom, or a name,
All life-long through my hands have sought,
Unblest, unlettered, and untaught:
Deny me not the boon I crave—
A symbol-light upon my grave,
            When I am dead.[2]

NOTES

1. This legend should be compared with "Gitchee Gauzinee."

2. Versions of this story may be found in *Travels* (1825), pp. 404-410; in Jones, II, 115-124; and in Jameson, III, 125-129. It was not printed in *M. H.* The terminal poem, however, was reprinted in "Wild Notes from the Pibbigwun," *M. H.*, p. 316.

PAUGUK

FROM THE MYTHOLOGY OF THE CHIPPEWAS

IN A PECULIAR CLASS OF LANGUAGES like the native American, in which symbols are so extensively used, it might be anticipated that Death should be thus denoted.

I asked SHAGUSH KODA WAIKWA,[1] from whom this allegory is derived, whether the Northern Indians discriminated between a corpse, a ghost, a spirit, an angel, and death, considered as a personification. The answer was affirmative, and I received the name for each.

Pauguk, according to this authority, is the personification of death. He is represented as existing without flesh or blood. He is a hunter, and besides his bow and arrows, is armed with a *puggamagon,* or war club. But he hunts only men, women, and children. He is an object of dread and horror. To see him is a sure indication of death. Some accounts represent his bones as covered by a thin transparent skin, and his eye sockets as filled with balls of fire.

Pauguk never speaks. Unlike the JEEBI or ghost, his limbs never assume the rotundity of life, neither is he to be confounded in form with the numerous class of minor Manitoes, or spirits. He does not possess the power of metamorphosis. Unvaried in repulsiveness, he is ever an object of fear; and often, according to Indian story, has the warrior, flushed with the ardor of battle, rushing forward to seize the prize of victory, clasped the cold and bony hand of PAUGUK.

"I shall never forget the fate of OWYNOKWA," continued the narrator. "She was a widow of my native village, who had been left with six sons. One after the other, as they became of suitable age, they had joined the war parties who went out against their enemies and fallen in battle. At last but one was left; he was her only stay and comfort, supplying her with food and protection in her old age. But he too, as he became old enough, spurning the dull life of a hunter, followed the war drum of his tribe, and went out against our enemies in the West. The absence of such a war party is a time of anxiety and suspense with the women of a village. To relieve this, and at the same moment to prepare them for more particular intelligence, the returning party gives the war-cry of triumph, and the death-wail indicating the number slain, as soon as they come within hearing. On the present occasion, Owynokwa rushed from her lodge, the moment she caught the first sound. She stood with her lips parted, in an attitude of intense and agonized suspense; and as soon as the death-wail broke upon her ear, despair appeared to rivet her to the spot. She heeded nothing; not a muscle moved; she neither inquired nor heard, who were the slain, but sank slowly

236

to the earth in the place where she stood. She was carried into her lodge, and the next morning showed signs of reanimation, but they were slight and brief—the rigidity of death soon seized upon her frame, and she followed her son to the land of spirits. Her son was indeed among the slain, but mortal tongue had not communicated the fact. It was generally supposed she had met the glare of Pauguk at the moment the death-wail or Chee kwau dum had broke on her ear.[2]

NOTES

1. Though unidentified, this personage was undoubtedly one of the many informants to whom Schoolcraft usually gave credit.

2. In *M. H.*, pp. 188-193, this bit of mythology is included in a general discussion of death and premonition of death. A poem, "To Pauguk," may be found in "Wild Notes from the Pibbigwun," *M. H.*, pp. 342-343.

THE VINE AND OAK

AN ALLEGORY IN THE MANNER OF THE ALGICS

A VINE WAS GROWING beside a thrifty oak, and had just reached that height at which it requires support. "Oak," said the ivy vine, "bend your trunk so that you may be a support to me." "My support," replied the oak, "is naturally yours, and you may rely on my strength to bear you up, but I am too large and too solid to bend. Put our arms around me, my pretty vine, and I will manfully support and cherish you, if you have an ambition to climb, even as high as the clouds. While I thus hold you up, you will ornament my rough trunk with your pretty green leaves and shining scarlet berries. They will be as frontlets to my head, and I shall stand in the forest like a glorious warrior, with all his plumes. We were made by the Master of Life to grow together, that by our union the weak should be made strong, and the strong render aid to the weak."

"But I wish to grow *independently*," said the vine, "why cannot you twine around me, and let me grow up straight, and not be a mere dependent upon *you*." "Nature," answered the oak, "did not *so* design it. It is impossible that you should grow to any height *alone*, and if you try it, the winds and rain, if not your own weight, will bring you to the ground. Neither is it proper for you to run your arms hither and yon, among the trees. The trees will begin to say—'It is not my vine—it is a stranger—get thee gone, I will not cherish thee.' By this time thou wilt be so entangled among the different branches, that thou canst not get back to the oak; and nobody will *then* admire thee, or pity thee."

"Ah me," said the vine, "let me escape from such a destiny:" and with this, she twined herself around the oak, and they both grew and flourished happily together.[1]

NOTE

1. Probably a Schoolcraft invention. It has the hallmark of sentimentalism, the popular stuff of the ladies' magazines of the period.

APPENDIX A

INDIAN TALES AND LEGENDS COLLECTED FROM OTHER WORKS OF SCHOOLCRAFT

PEZHIU AND WABOSE

OR

THE LYNX AND THE HARE

A CHIPPEWA FABLE

A LYNX ALMOST FAMISHED, met a hare one day in the woods, in the winter season, when food was very scarce. The hare, however, stood up on a rock, and was safe from its enemy.

"Wabose," said the lynx, in a very kind manner, "come here, my little white one,[1] I wish to talk to you."

"Oh no," replied the hare, "I am afraid of you, and my mother told me never to go and talk to strangers."

"You are very pretty," answered the lynx, "and a very obedient child to your parents, but you must know that I am a relative of yours. I wish to send some word to your lodge. Come down and see me."

The hare was pleased to be called pretty, and when she heard that it was a relative, she jumped down from the place where she stood, and was immediately torn in pieces by the lynx.[2]

NOTES

1. Such is the meaning of Wabose. [H. R. S.]
2. *M. H.*, p. 95. First printed in *Oneóta* (1844), p. 7; reprinted in *R. R. A.*, p. 81. Hereafter all *Oneóta* references will be assumed in references to *R. R. A.*

NEZHIK-E-WA-WA-SUN

OR

THE LONE LIGHTNING

ODJIBWA

A LITTLE ORPHAN BOY who had no one to care for him, was once living with his uncle, who treated him very badly, making him do hard things and giving him very little to eat; so that the boy pined away. He never grew much, and became, through hard usage, very thin and light. At last the uncle felt ashamed of this treatment, and determined to make amends for it, by fattening him up, but his real object was, to kill him by over-feeding. He told his wife to give the boy plenty of bear's meat, and let him have the fat, which is thought to be the best part. They were both very assiduous in cramming him, and one day came near choking him to death, by forcing the fat down his throat. The boy escaped and fled from the lodge. He knew not where to go, but wandered about. When night came on, he was afraid the wild beasts would eat him, so he climbed up into the forks of a high pine tree, and there he fell asleep in the branches, and had an aupoway, or ominous dream.

A person appeared to him from the upper sky, and said, "My poor little lad, I pity you, and the bad usage you have received from your uncle has led me to visit you: follow me, and step in my tracks." Immediately his sleep left him, and he rose up and followed his guide, mounting up higher and higher into the air, until he reached the upper sky. Here twelve arrows were put into his hands, and he was told that there were a great many manitoes in the northern sky, against whom he must go to war, and try to waylay and shoot them. Accordingly he went to that part of the sky, and, at long intervals, shot arrow after arrow, until he had expended eleven, in vain attempt to kill the manitoes. At the flight of each arrow, there was a long and solitary streak of lightning in the sky—then all was clear again, and not a cloud or spot could be seen. The twelfth arrow he held a long time in his hands, and looked around keenly on every side to spy the manitoes he was after. But these manitoes were very cunning, and could change their form in a moment. All they feared was the boy's arrows, for these were magic arrows, which had been given to him by a good spirit, and had power to kill them, if aimed aright. At length, the boy drew up his last arrow, settled in his aim, and let fly, as he thought, into the very heart of the chief of the manitoes; but before the arrow reached him, the manito

241

changed himself into a rock. Into this rock the head of the arrow sank deep and stuck fast.

"Now your gifts are all expended," cried the enraged manito, "and I will make an example of your audacity and pride of heart, for lifting your bow against me"—and so saying, he transformed the boy into the Nezhik-e-wä-wä-sun, or Lone Lightning, which may be observed in the northern sky, to this day.[1]

NOTE

1. *M. H.*, pp. 105-106. See *R. R. A.*, p. 168, for same story with slight variants in spelling.

THE AK UK O JEESH

OR

THE GROUNDHOG FAMILY

AN ODJIBWA FABLE

A FEMALE AKUKOJEESH, or groundhog, with a numerous family of young ones, was burrowing in her wauzh, or hole in the ground, one long winter, in the north, when the young ones became impatient for spring. Everyday the mother would go out and get roots and other things, which she brought in to them to eat; and she always told them to lie close and keep warm, and never to venture towards the mouth of the wauzh. But they became very impatient at last to see the light and the green woods. "Mother," said they, "is it not almost spring?" "No! no!" said she, in a cross humor, "keep still and wait patiently; it hails, it snows, it is cold—it is windy. Why should you wish to go out?" This she told them so often, and said it in such a bad temper, that they at last suspected some deception. One day she came in, after having been a long while absent, and fell asleep, with her mouth open. The little ones peeped in slyly, and saw on her teeth the remains of the nice white bulbous roots of the mo-na-wing, or adder's-tongue violet. They at once knew it was spring, and without disturbing the old one, who only wanted to keep them in till they were full grown, away they scampered, out of the hole, and dispersed themselves about the forest, and so the family were all scattered.[1]

NOTE

1. *M. H.*, pp. 107-108. First printed in *Oneóta*, p. 104, but not included in *R. R. A.* or later editions of *Oneóta* material.

SHINGEBISS

AN ALLEGORY OF SELF-RELIANCE

FROM THE ODJIBWA

THERE WAS ONCE A SHINGEBISS, the name of the fall duck living alone, in a solitary lodge, on the shores of the deep bay of a lake, in the coldest winter weather. The ice had formed on the water, and he had but four logs of wood to keep his fire. Each of these would, however, burn a month, and as there were but four cold winter months, they were sufficient to carry him through till spring.

Shingebiss was hardy and fearless, and cared for no one. He would go out during the coldest day, and seek for places where flags and rushes grew through the ice, and plucking them up with his bill, would dive through the openings, in quest of fish. In this way he found plenty of food, while others were starving, and he went home daily to his lodge, dragging strings of fish after him, on the ice.

Kabebonicca[1] observed him, and felt a little piqued at his perseverance and good luck in defiance of the severest blasts of wind he could send from the northwest. "Why! this is a wonderful man," said he; "he does not mind the cold, and appears as happy and contented as if it were the month of June. I will try whether he cannot be mastered." He poured forth tenfold colder blasts, and drifts of snow, so that it was next to impossible to live in the open air. Still, the fire of Shingebiss did not go out: he wore but a single strip of leather around his body, and he was seen, in the worst weather, searching the shores for rushes, and carrying home fish.

"I shall go and visit him," said Kabebonicca, one day, as he saw Shingebiss dragging along a quantity of fish. And, accordingly, that very night, he went to the door of his lodge. Meantime Shingebiss had cooked his fish, and finished his meal, and was lying, partly on his side, before the fire, singing his songs. After Kabebonicca had come to the door, and stood listening there, he sang as follows:

Ka	Neej	Ka	Neej
Be	In	Be	In
Bon	In	Bon	In
Oc	Ee.	Oc	Ee.
Ca	We-ya!	Ca	We-ya!

The number of words, in this song, are few and simple, but they are made up from compounds which carry the whole of their original meanings, and

244

are rather suggestive of the ideas floating in the mind than actual expressions of those ideas. Literally, he sings:

Spirit of the Northwest—you are but my fellow man.

By being broken into syllables, to correspond with a simple chant, and by the power of intonation and repetition, with a chorus, these words are expanded into melodious utterance, if we may be allowed the term, and may be thus rendered:—

Windy god, I know your plan,
You are but my fellow man;
Blow you may your coldest breeze,
Shingebiss you cannot freeze.
Sweep the strongest wind you can
Shingebiss is still your man;
Heigh! for life—and ho! for bliss,
Who so free as Shingebiss?

The hunter knew that Kabebonicca was at his door, for he felt his cold and strong breath; but he kept on singing his songs, and affected utter indifference. At length Kabebonicca entered, and took his seat on the opposite side of the lodge. But Shingebiss did not regard, or notice him. He got up, as if nobody were present, and taking his poker, pushed the log, which made his fire burn brighter, repeating, as he sat down again:

You are but my fellow man.

Very soon the tears began to flow down Kabebonicca's cheeks, which increased so fast, that, presently, he said to himself: "I cannot stand this— I must go out." He did so, and left Shingebiss to his songs; but resolved to freeze up all the flag orifices, and make the ice thick, so that he could not get any more fish. Still, Shingebiss, by dint of great diligence, found means to pull up new roots, and dive under for fish. At last, Kabebonicca was compelled to give up the contest. "He must be aided by some Monedo," said he. "I can neither freeze him nor starve him; he is a very singular being—I will let him alone."[2]

NOTES

1. A personification of the Northwest. [H. R. S.] The North. Cf. "Shawondasee," p. 222.
2. *M. H.*, pp. 113-115. Printed also in *R. R. A.*, pp. 85-86, and in *H. S. I.*, III, 324-326.

THE WHITE STONE CANOE

THERE WAS ONCE A VERY BEAUTIFUL YOUNG GIRL, who died suddenly on the day she was to have been married to a handsome young man. He was also brave, but his heart was not proof against this loss. From the hour she was buried, there was no more joy or peace for him. He went often to visit the spot where the women had buried her, and sat musing there, when, it was thought, by some of his friends, he would have done better to try to amuse himself in the chase, or by diverting his thoughts in the war-path. But war and hunting had both lost their charms for him. His heart was already dead within him. He pushed aside both his war-club and his bow and arrows.

He had heard the old people say that there was a path that led to the land of souls, and he determined to follow it. He accordingly set out, one morning, after having completed his preparations for the journey. At first he hardly knew which way to go. He was only guided by the tradition that he must go south. For a while he could see no change in the face of the country. Forests, and hills, and valleys, and streams had the same looks which they wore in his native place. There was snow on the ground, when he set out, and it was sometimes seen to be piled and matted on the thick trees and bushes. At length it began to diminish, and finally disappeared. The forest assumed a more cheerful appearance, and the leaves put forth their buds, and before he was aware of the completeness of the change, he found himself surrounded by spring. He had left behind him the land of snow and ice. The air became mild; the dark clouds of winter had rolled away from the sky; a pure field of blue was above him, and as he went he saw flowers beside his path, and heard the songs of birds. By these signs he knew that he was going the right way, for they agreed with the traditions of his tribe. At length he spied a path. It led him through a grove, then up a long and elevated ridge, on the very top of which he came to a lodge. At the door stood an old man, with white hair, whose eyes, though deeply sunk, had a fiery brilliancy. He had a long robe of skins thrown loosely around his shoulders, and a staff in his hands. It was Chebiabos.

The young Chippewa began to tell his story; but the venerable chief arrested him, before he had proceeded to speak ten words. "I have expected you," he replied, "and had just risen to bid you welcome to my abode. She whom you seek, passed here but a few days since, and being fatigued with her journey, rested herself here. Enter my lodge and be seated, and I will then satisfy your inquiries, and give you directions for your journey from this point." Having done this, they both issued forth to the lodge door. "You see yonder gulf," said he, "and the wide stretching blue plains beyond. It is the land of souls. You stand upon its borders, and

246

my lodge is the gate of entrance. But you cannot take your body along. Leave it here with your bow and arrows, your bundle, and your dog. You will find them safe on your return." So saying, he re-entered the lodge, and the freed traveler bounded forward, as if his feet had suddenly been endowed with the power of wings. But all things retained their natural colors and shapes. The woods and leaves, and streams and lakes, were only more bright and comely than he had ever witnessed. Animals bounded across his path, with a freedom and a confidence which seemed to tell him, there was no blood shed here. Birds of beautiful plumage inhabited the groves, and sported in the waters. There was but one thing, in which he saw a very unusual effect. He noticed that his passage was not stopped by trees or other objects. He appeared to walk directly through them. They were, in fact, but the souls or shadows of material trees. He became sensible that he was in a land of shadows. When he had traveled half a day's journey, through a country which was continually becoming more attractive, he came to the banks of a broad lake, in the center of which was a large and beautiful island. He found a canoe of shining white stone, tied to the shore. He was now sure that he had come the right path, for the aged man had told him of this. There were also shining paddles. He immediately entered the canoe, and took the paddles in his hands, when to his joy and surprise, on turning around, he beheld the object of his search in another canoe, exactly its counterpart in everything. She had exactly imitated his motions, and they were side by side. They at once pushed out from shore and began to cross the lake. Its waves seemed to be rising, and at a distance looked ready to swallow them up; but just as they entered the whitened edge of them they seemed to melt away, as if they were but the images of waves. But no sooner was one wreath of foam passed, than another, more threatening still, rose up. Thus they were in perpetual fear; and what added to it, was the *clearness of the water,* through which they could see heaps of beings who had perished before, and whose bones lay strewed on the bottom of the lake. The Master of Life had, however, decreed to let them pass, for the actions of neither of them had been bad. But they saw many others struggling and sinking in the waves. Old men and young men, males and females of all ages and ranks, were there; some passed, and some sank. It was only the little children whose canoes seemed to meet no waves. At length, every difficulty was gone, as in a moment, and they both leaped out on the happy island. They felt that the very air was food. It strengthened and nourished them. They wandered together over the blissful fields, where everything was formed to please the eye and the ear. There were no tempests —there was no ice, no chilly winds—no one shivered for the want of warm clothes: no one suffered for hunger—no one mourned the dead. They saw no graves. They heard of no wars. There was no hunting for animals; for the air itself was their food. Gladly would the young warrior have remained there forever, but he was obliged to go back for his body. He did not see the Master of Life, but he heard his voice in a soft breeze. "Go back," said this voice, "to the land from whence you came. Your time has not yet come. The duties for which I made you, and which you are to perform, are not yet finished. Return to your people and accomplish the duties of a good man. You will be the ruler of your tribe for many days. The rules you must observe will be told you by my messenger, who keeps the gate. When he surrenders back your body, he will tell you what to do. Listen to him, and you shall afterwards rejoin the spirit, which you must now leave behind. She is accepted, and will be ever here, as young and as happy as she was when I first called her from the land of snows." When this voice ceased, the narrator awoke. It was the fancy work of a dream, and he was still in the bitter land of snows, and hunger, and tears.[1]

NOTE

1. *M. H.*, pp. 223-227. Printed in *R. R. A.*, pp. 79-81, and as "The Island of the Blessed, or the Hunter's Dream," in *H. S. I.*, I, 321-323.

ONAIZO, THE SKY-WALKER

A LEGEND OF A VISIT TO THE SUN

AN OTTOWA MYTH

A LONG TIME AGO, there lived an aged Odjibwa and his wife, on the shores of Lake Huron. They had an only son, a very beautiful boy, whose name was O-no-wut-a-qut-o, or he that catches the clouds. The family were of the totem of the beaver. The parents were very proud of him, and thought to make him a celebrated man, but when he reached the proper age, he would not submit to the We-koon-de-win, or fast. When this time arrived, they gave him charcoal, instead of his breakfast, but he would not blacken his face. If they denied him food, he would seek for birds' eggs, along the shores, or pick up the heads of fish that had been cast away, and broil them. One day, they took away violently the food he had thus prepared, and cast him some coals in place of it. This act brought him to a decision. He took the coals and blackened his face, and went out of the lodge. He did not return, but slept without; and during the night, he had a dream. He dreamed that he saw a very beautiful female come down from the clouds and stand by his side. "O-no-wut-a-qut-o," said she, "I am come for you —step in my tracks." The young man did so, and presently felt himself ascending above the tops of the trees—he mounted up, step by step, into the air, and through the clouds. His guide, at length, passed through an orifice, and he, following her, found himself standing on a beautiful plain.

A path led to a splendid lodge. He followed her into it. It was large, and divided into two parts. On one end he saw bows and arrows, clubs and spears, and various warlike implements tipped with silver. On the other end were things exclusively belonging to females. This was the home of his fair guide, and he saw that she had, on the frame, a broad rich belt, of many colors, which she was weaving. She said to him: "My brother is coming and I must hide you." Putting him in one corner, she spread the belt over him. Presently the brother came in, very richly dressed, and shining as if he had points of silver all over him. He took down from the wall a splendid pipe, together with his sack of a-pa-ko-ze-gun, or smoking mixture. When he had finished regaling himself in this way, and laid his pipe aside, he said to his sister: "Nemissa" (which is, my elder sister), "when will you quit these practices? Do you forget that the Greatest of the Spirits had commanded that you should not take away the child from below? Perhaps you suppose that you have concealed O-no-wut-a-qut-o, but do I not know of his coming? If you would not offend me, send him back immediately." But this address did not alter her purpose. She would not send him back. Find-

249

ing that she was purposed in her mind, he then spoke to the young lad, and called him from his hiding-place. "Come out of your concealment," said he, "and walk about and amuse yourself. You will grow hungry if you remain there." He then presented him a bow and arrows, and a pipe of red stone, richly ornamented. This was taken as the word of consent to his marriage; so the two were considered husband and wife from that time.

O-no-wut-a-qut-o found everything exceedingly fair and beautiful around him, but he found no inhabitants except her brother. There were flowers on the plains. There were bright and sparkling streams. There were green valleys and pleasant trees. There were gay birds and beautiful animals, but they were not such as he had been accustomed to see. There was also day and night, as on the earth; but he observed that every morning the brother regularly left the lodge, and remained absent all day; and every evening the sister departed, though it was commonly but for a part of the night.

His curiosity was aroused to solve this mystery. He obtained the brother's consent to accompany him in one of his daily journeys. They traveled over a smooth plain, without boundaries, until O-no-wut-a-qut-o felt the gnaw-ings of appetite, and asked his companion if there were no game. "Patience! my brother," said he, "we shall soon reach the spot where I eat my din-ner, and you will then see how I am provided." After walking on a long time, they came to a place which was spread over with fine mats, where they sat down to refresh themselves. There was, at this place, a hole through the sky; and O-no-wut-a-qut-o looked down, at the bidding of his com-panion, upon the earth. He saw below the great lakes, and the villages of the Indians. In one place, he saw a war party stealing on the camp of their enemies. In another, he saw feasting and dancing. On a green plain, young men were engaged at ball. Along a stream, women were employed in gathering the a-put-wa for mats.

"Do you see," said the brother, "that group of children playing beside a lodge? Observe that beautiful and active boy," said he, at the same time darting something at him, from his hand. The child immediately fell, and was carried into the lodge.

They looked again, and saw the people gathering about the lodge. They heard the she-she-gwun of the meeta, and the song he sung, asking that the child's life be spared. To this request, the companion of O-no-wut-a-qut-o made answer: "Send me up the sacrifice of a white dog." Immediately a feast was ordered by the parents of the child, the white dog was killed, his carcass was roasted, and all the wise men and medicine men of the village assembled to witness the ceremony. "There are many below," continued the voice of the brother, "whom you call great in medical skill, but it is because their ears are open, and they listen to my voice, that they are able to succeed. When I have struck one with sickness, they direct the people to look to me; and when they send me the offering I ask, I remove my hand from off them, and they are well." After he had said this, they saw the sacrifice parceled out in dishes, for those who were at the feast. The master of the feast then said, "We send this to thee, great Manito," and immediately the roasted animal came up. Thus their dinner was supplied, and after they had eaten, they returned to the lodge by another way.

After this manner they lived for some time; but the place became wearisome at last. O-no-wut-a-qut-o thought of his friends, and wished to go back to them. He had not forgotten his native village and his father's lodge; and he asked leave of his wife to return. At length she consented. "Since you are better pleased," she replied, "with the cares and the ills, and the poverty of the world, than with the peaceful delights of the sky, and its boundless prairies, go! I give you permission, and since I have brought you hither, I will conduct you back; but, remember, you are still my husband. I hold a chain in my hand by which I can draw you back whenever I will. My power over you is not, in any manner, diminished. Beware, therefore, how you venture to take a wife among the people below. Should you ever do so, it is then that you shall feel the force of my displeasure."

As she said this, her eyes sparkled—she raised herself slightly on her toes, and stretched herself up, with a majestic air; and at that moment, O-no-wut-a-qut-o awoke from his dream. He found himself on the ground, near his father's lodge, at the very spot where he had laid himself down to fast. Instead of the bright beings of a higher world, he found himself surrounded by his parents and relatives. His mother told him he had been absent a year. The change was so great, that he remained for sometime moody and abstracted, but by degrees he recovered his spirits. He began to doubt the reality of all he had heard and seen above. At last, he forgot the admonitions of his spouse, and married a beautiful young woman of his own tribe. But within four days, she was a corpse. Even this fearful admonition was lost, and he repeated the offense by a second marriage. Soon afterwards, he went out of the lodge, one night, but never returned. It was believed that his Sunwife had recalled him to the region of the clouds, where, the tradition asserts, he still dwells, and walks on the daily rounds, which he once witnessed.[1]

NOTE

1. *M. H.*, pp. 228-232. In *R. R. A.*, pp. 82-84, this myth is entitled "The Worship of the Sun. An Ottowa Tradition."

BOSH-KWA-DOSH

OR

THE MASTODON

THERE WAS ONCE A MAN who found himself alone in the world. He knew not whence he came, nor who were his parents, and he wandered about from place to place, in search of something. At last he became wearied and fell asleep. He dreamed that he heard a voice saying, "Nosis," that is, my grandchild. When he awoke, he actually heard the word repeated, and looking around, he saw a tiny little animal hardly big enough to be seen on the plain. While doubting whether the voice could come from such a diminutive source, the little animal said to him, "My grandson, you will call me Bosh-kwa-dosh. Why are you so desolate? Listen to me, and you shall find friends and be happy. You must take me up and bind me to your body, and never put me aside, and success in life shall attend you." He obeyed the voice, sewing up the little animal in the folds of a string, or narrow belt, which he tied around his body, at his navel. He then set out in search of someone like himself, or other object. He walked a long time in the woods without seeing man or animal. He seemed all alone in the world. At length he came to a place where a stump was cut, and on going over a hill he descried a large town in a plain. A wide road led through the middle of it; but what seemed strange was, that on one side there were no inhabitants in the lodges, while the other side was thickly inhabited. He walked boldly into the town.

The inhabitants came out and said: "Why here is the being we have heard so much of—here is Anish-in-á-ba. See his eyes, and his teeth in a half circle—see the Wyaukenawbedaid! See his bowels, how they are formed;" —for it seems they could look through him. The king's son, the Mudjekewis, was particularly kind to him, and calling him brother-in-law, commanded that he should be taken to his father's lodge and received with attention. The king gave him one of his daughters. These people (who are supposed to be human, but whose rank in the scale of being is left equivocal) passed much of their time in play and sports and trials of various kinds. When sometime had passed, and he became refreshed and rested, he was invited to join in these sports. The first test which they put him to, was the trial of frost. At some distance was a large body of frozen water, and the trial consisted in lying down naked on the ice, and seeing who could endure the longest. He went out with two young men, who began, by pulling off their garments, and lying down on their faces. He did likewise, only keeping on the narrow magic belt with the tiny little animal sewed in it; for he felt

252

that in this alone was to be his reliance and preservation. His competitors laughed and tittered during the early part of the night, and amused themselves by thoughts of his fate. Once they called out to him, but he made no reply. He felt a manifest warmth given out by his belt. About midnight, finding they were still, he called out to them, in return, "What!" said he, "are you benumbed already? I am but just beginning to feel a little cold." All was silence. He, however, kept his position till early daybreak, when he got up and went to them. They were both quite dead, and frozen so hard, that the flesh had bursted out under their finger nails, and their teeth stood out. As he looked more closely, what was his surprise to find them both transformed into buffalo cows. He tied them together, and carried them towards the village. As he came in sight, those who had wished his death were disappointed, but the Mudjekewis, who was really his friend, rejoiced. "See!" said he, "but one person approaches—it is my brother-in-law." He then threw down the carcasses in triumph, but it was found that by their death he had restored two inhabitants to the before empty lodges, and he afterwards perceived that every one of these beings, whom he killed, had the like effect, so that the depopulated part of the village soon became filled with people.

The next test they put him to, was the trial of speed. He was challenged to the race ground, and began his career with one whom he thought to be a man; but everything was enchanted here, for he soon discovered that his competitor was a large black bear. The animal outran him, tore up the ground, and sported before him, and put out its large claws as if to frighten him. He thought of his little guardian spirit in the belt, and wishing to have the swiftness of the Kakake, i.e., sparrowhawk, he found himself rising from the ground, and with the speed of this bird he outwent his rival, and won the race, while the bear came up exhausted and lolling out his tongue. His friend the Mudjekewis stood ready, with his war-club, at the goal, and the moment the bear came up, dispatched him. He then turned to the assembly, who had wished his friend and brother's death, and after reproaching them, he lifted up his club and began to slay them on every side. They fell in heaps on all sides; but it was plain to be seen, the moment they fell, that they were not men, but animals—foxes, wolves, tigers, lynxes, and other kinds, lay thick around the Mudjekewis.

Still the villagers were not satisfied. They thought the trial of frost had not been fairly accomplished, and wished it repeated. He agreed to repeat it, but being fatigued with the race, he undid his guardian belt, and laying it under his head, fell asleep. When he awoke, he felt refreshed, and feeling strong in his own strength, he went forward to renew the trial on the ice, but quite forgot the belt, nor did it at all occur to him when he awoke, or when he lay down to repeat the trial. About midnight his limbs became stiff, the blood soon ceased to circulate, and he was found in the morning a stiff corpse. The victors took him up and carried him to the village, where the loudest tumult of victorious joy was made, and they cut his body into a thousand pieces, that each one might eat a piece.

The Mudjekewis bemoaned his fate, but his wife was inconsolable. She lay in a state of partial distraction, in the lodge. As she lay here, she thought she heard someone groaning. It was repeated through the night, and in the morning she carefully scanned the place, and running her fingers through the grass, she discovered the secret belt, on the spot where her husband had last reposed. "Aubishin!" cried the belt—that is, untie me, or unloose me. Looking carefully, she found the small seam which inclosed the tiny little animal. It cried out the more earnestly, "Aubishin!" and when she had carefully ripped the seams, she beheld, to her surprise, a minute, naked little beast, smaller than the smallest new-born mouse, without any vestige of hair, except at the tip of its tail; it could crawl a few inches, but reposed from fatigue. It then went forward again. At each movement it would *pupowee,* that is to say, shake itself like a dog, and at each shake it became larger. This it continued until it acquired the strength and size of a middle-sized dog, when it ran off.

The mysterious dog ran to the lodges, about the village, looking for the bones of his friend, which he carried to a secret place, and as fast as he found them arranged all in their natural order. At length he had formed all the skeleton complete, except the heel bone of one foot. It so happened that two sisters were out of camp, according to custom, at the time the body was cut up, and this heel was sent out to them. The dog hunted every lodge, and being satisfied that it was not to be found in the camp, he sought it outside of it, and found the lodge of the two sisters. The younger sister was pleased to see him, and admired and patted the pretty dog, but the elder sat mumbling the very heelbone he was seeking, and was surly and sour, and repelled the dog, although he looked most wistfully up in her face, while she sucked the bone from one side of her mouth to the other. At last she held it in such a manner that it made her cheek stick out, when the dog, by a quick spring, seized the cheek, and tore cheek and bone away and fled.

He now completed the skeleton, and placing himself before it, uttered a hollow, low, long-drawn-out howl, when the bones came compactly together. He then modulated his howl, when the bones knit together and became tense. The third howl brought sinews upon them, and the fourth, flesh. He then turned his head upwards, looking into the sky, and gave a howl, which caused every one in the village to startle, and the ground itself to tremble, at which the breath entered his body, and he first breathed and then arose. "Hy kow! I have overslept myself," he exclaimed; "I will be too late for the trial." "Trial!" said Bosh-kwa-dosh, "I told you never to let me be separate from your body, you have neglected this. You were defeated, and your frozen body cut into a thousand pieces, and scattered over the village; but my skill has restored you. Now I will declare myself to you, and show who and what I am!"

He then began to pupowee, or shake himself, and at every shake, he grew. His body became heavy and massy, his legs thick and long, with big clumsy ends, or feet. He still shook himself, and rose and swelled. A long snout grew from his head, and two great shining teeth out of his mouth. His skin remained as it was, naked, and only a tuft of hair grew on his tail. He rose up as high as the trees. He was enormous. "I should fill the earth," said he, "were I to exert my utmost power, and all there is on the earth would not satisfy me to eat. Neither could it fatten me or do me good. I should want more. The Great Spirit created me to show his power when there were nothing but animals on the earth. But were all animals as large as myself, there would not be grass enough for food. But the earth was made for man, and not for beasts. I give some of those great gifts which I possess. All the animals shall be your food, and you are no longer to flee before them, and be their sport and food." So saying, he walked off with heavy steps and with fierce looks, at which all the little animals trembled.[1]

NOTE

1. *M. H.*, pp. 233-238. In *R. R. A.*, pp. 106-109, the tale is called "Bosh-Kwa-Dosh, or The Quadruped with the Hair Blown off its Skin." In the latter case Schoolcraft added this note: "The preceding is a traditionary tale of Maidosegee, an aged and respected hunter, of Sault Ste Marie, who was the ruling chief of the band of Chippewas at those falls, and the progenitor of the present line of ruling chiefs. It is preserved through the Johnston family, where he was a frequent guest, prior to 1810, and was happy to while away many of his winter's evenings, in return for the ready hospitalities which were sure to await him at the house of the Indian's friend."

THE SUN-CATCHER

THE BOY WHO SET A SNARE FOR THE SUN

A MYTH OF THE ORIGIN OF THE DORMOUSE

FROM THE ODJIBWA

AT THE TIME WHEN THE ANIMALS REIGNED in the earth, they had killed all
but a girl, and her little brother, and these two were living in fear and
seclusion. The boy was a perfect pigmy, and never grew beyond the
stature of a small infant, but the girl increased with her years, so that the
labor of providing food and lodging devolved wholly on her. She went out
daily to get wood for their lodge-fire, and took her little brother along that
no accident might happen to him; for he was too little to leave alone. A big
bird might have flown away with him. She made him a bow and arrows, and
said to him one day, "I will leave you behind where I have been chopping
—you must hide yourself, and you will soon see the Gitshee-gitshee-gaun-
ia-see-ug, or snow birds, come and pick the worms out of the wood, where
I have been chopping" (for it was in the winter). "Shoot one of them and
bring it home." He obeyed her, and tried his best to kill one, but came home
unsuccessful. She told him he must not despair, but try again the next
day. She accordingly left him at the place she got wood, and returned. Towards nightfall, she heard his little footsteps on the snow, and he came in
exultingly, and threw down one of the birds which he had killed. "My
sister," said he, "I wish you to skin it and stretch the skin, and when I
have killed more, I will have a coat made out of them." "But what shall
we do with the body?" said she, for as yet men had not begun to eat animal
food, but lived on vegetables alone. "Cut it in two," he answered, "and
season our pottage with one half of it at a time." She did so. The boy, who
was of a very small stature, continued his efforts, and succeeded in killing
ten birds, out of the skins of which his sister made him a little coat.

"Sister," said he one day, "are we all alone in the world? Is there nobody
else living?" She told him that those they feared and who had destroyed
their relatives lived in a certain quarter, and that he must by no means go
in that direction. This only served to inflame his curiosity and raise his
ambition, and he soon after took his bow and arrows and went in that direction. After walking a long time and meeting nothing, he became tired,
and lay down on a knoll, where the sun had melted the snow. He fell fast
asleep; and while sleeping, the sun beat so hot upon him, that it singed and
drew up his bird-skin coat, so that when he awoke and stretched himself,
he felt bound in it, as it were. He looked down and saw the damage done

256

to his coat. He flew into a passion, and upbraided the sun, and vowed vengeance against it. "Do not think you are too high," said he, "I shall revenge myself."

On coming home, he related his disaster to his sister, and lamented bitterly the spoiling of his coat. He would not eat. He lay down as one that fasts, and did not stir, or move his position for ten days, though she tried all she could to arouse him. At the end of ten days, he turned over, and then lay ten days on the other side. When he got up, he told his sister to make him a snare, for he meant to catch the sun. She said she had nothing; but finally recollected a little piece of dried deer's sinew, that her father had left, which she soon made into a string suitable for a noose. But the moment she showed it to him, he told her it would not do, and bid her get something else. She said she had nothing—nothing at all. At last she thought of her hair, and pulling some of it out of her head, made a string. But he instantly said it would not answer, and bid her, pettishly, and with authority, make him a noose. She told him there was nothing to make it of, and went out of the lodge. She said to herself, when she had got without the lodge, and while she was all alone, "neow obewy indapin." From my body, some will I take. This she did, and twisting them into a tiny cord, she handed it to her brother. The moment he saw this curious braid, he was delighted. "This will do," he said, and immediately put it to his mouth and began pulling it through his lips; and as fast as he drew it changed it into a red metal cord, which he wound around his body and shoulders, till he had a large quantity. He then prepared himself, and set out a little after midnight, that he might catch the sun before it rose. He fixed his snare on a spot just where the sun would strike the land, as it rose above the earth's disk; and sure enough, he caught the sun, so that it was held fast in the cord, and did not rise.

The animals who ruled the earth were immediately put into a great commotion. They had no light. They called a council to debate upon the matter, and to appoint someone to go and cut the cord—for this was a very hazardous enterprise, as the rays of the sun would burn whoever came so near to them. At last the dormouse undertook it—for at this time the dormouse was the largest animal in the world. When it stood up it looked like a mountain. When it got to the place where the sun was snared, its back began to smoke and burn with the intensity of the heat, and the top of its carcass was reduced to enormous heaps of ashes. It succeeded, however, in cutting the cord with its teeth, and freeing the sun, but it was reduced to a very small size, and has remained so ever since. Men call it the Kug-e-been-gwa-kwa, the blind woman.[1]

NOTE

1. *M. H.,* pp. 239-242. In *R. R. A.* the story is called "The Boy Who Set a Snare for the Sun; or the Origin of the Kug-e-Beeng-Wa-Kwa, or Dormouse. From the Odjibwa—Algonquin," pp. 97-99. In *C. M.,* pp. 16-21, and *C-C,* pp. 1-6, it is called "The Boy Who Set a Snare for the Sun."

WA-WA-BE-ZO-WIN

THE SWING ON THE PICTURED ROCKS
OF LAKE SUPERIOR

A TRADITION OF THE ODJIBWAS

THERE WAS AN OLD HAG OF A WOMAN living with her daughter-in-law, and son, and a little orphan boy, whom she was bringing up. When her son came home from hunting, it was his custom to bring his wife the moose's lip, the kidney of the bear, or some other choice bits of different animals. These she would cook crisp, so as to make a sound with her teeth in eating them. This kind attention of the hunter to his wife at last excited the envy of the old woman. She wished to have the same luxuries, and in order to get them she finally resolved to make way with her son's wife. One day, she asked her to leave her infant son to the care of the orphan boy, and come out and swing with her. She took her to the shore of a lake, where there was a high range of rocks overhanging the water. Upon the top of this rock, she erected a swing. She then undressed, and fastened a piece of leather around her body, and commenced swinging, going over the precipice at every swing. She continued it but a short time, when she told her daughter [-in-law] to do the same. The daughter [-in-law] obeyed. She undressed, and tying the leather string as she was directed, began swinging. When the swing had got in full motion and well a-going, so that it went clear beyond the precipice at every sweep, the old woman slyly cut the cords and let her daughter [-in-law] drop into the lake. She then put on her daughter [-in-law]'s clothing, and thus disguised went home in the dusk of the evening and counterfeited her appearance and duties. She found the child crying, and gave it the breast, but it would not draw. The orphan boy asked her where its mother was. She answered, "She is still swinging." He said, "I shall go and look for her." "No!" said she, "you must not—what should you go for?" When the husband came in, in the evening, he gave the coveted morsel to his supposed wife. He missed his mother but said nothing. She eagerly ate the dainty, and tried to keep the child still. The husband looked rather astonished to see his wife studiously averting her face, and asked her why the child cried so. She said, she did not know—that it would not draw.

In the meantime, the orphan boy went to the lake shores, and found no one. He mentioned his suspicions, and while the old woman was out getting wood, he told [the son] all he had heard or seen. The man then

258

painted his face black, and placed his spear upside down in the earth, and requested the Great Spirit to send lightning, thunder, and rain, in the hope that the body of his wife might arise from the water. He then began to fast, and told the boy to take the child and play on the lake shore.

We must now go back to the swing. After the wife had plunged into the lake, she found herself taken hold of by a water-tiger, whose tail twisted itself round her body, and drew her to the bottom. There she found a fine lodge, and all things ready for her reception, and she became the wife of the water-tiger. Whilst the children were playing along the shore, and the boy was casting pebbles into the lake, he saw a gull coming from its center, and flying towards the shore, and when on shore, the bird immediately assumed the human shape. When he looked again, he recognized the lost mother. She had a leather belt around her loins, and another belt of white metal, which was, in reality, the tail of the water-tiger, her husband. She suckled the babe, and said to the boy—"Come here with him, whenever he cries, and I will nurse him."

The boy carried the child home, and told these things to the father. When the child again cried, the father went also with the boy to the lake shore, and hid himself in a clump of trees. Soon the appearance of a gull was seen, with a long, shining belt, or chain, and as soon as it came to the shore, it assumed the mother's shape, and she began to suckle the child. The husband had brought along his spear, and seeing the shining chain, he boldly struck it and broke the links apart. He then took his wife and child home, with the orphan boy. When they entered the lodge, the old woman looked up, but it was a look of despair: she instantly dropped her head. A rustling was heard in the lodge, and the next moment she leaped up and flew out of the lodge, and was never heard of more.[1]

NOTE

1. *M. H.*, pp. 243-245. "Wa-Wa-Be-Zo-Win, or The Swing on the Lake Shore," was published in *R. R. A.*, pp. 116-117.

MUKAKEE MINDEMOEA

OR

THE TOAD-WOMAN

AN ODJIBWA LEGEND

GREAT GOOD LUCK ONCE HAPPENED TO A YOUNG WOMAN who was living all alone in the woods, with nobody near her but her little dog, for, to her surprise, she found fresh meat every morning at her door. She felt very anxious to know who it was that supplied her, and watching one morning, very early, she saw a handsome young man deposit the meat. After his being seen by her, he became her husband, and she had a son by him. One day, not long after this, the man did not return at evening, as usual, from hunting. She waited till late at night, but all in vain. Next day she swung her baby to sleep in its tikenagun, or cradle, and then said to her dog: "Take care of your brother whilst I am gone, and when he cries, halloo for me." The cradle was made of the finest wampum, and all its bandages and decorations were of the same costly material. After a short time, the woman heard the cry of her faithful dog, and running home as fast as she could, she found her child gone and the dog too. But on looking around, she saw pieces of the wampum of her child's cradle bit off by the dog, who strove to retain the child and prevent his being carried off by an old woman called Mukakee Mindemoea, or the Toad-Woman. The mother followed at full speed, and occasionally came to the lodges inhabited by old women, who told her at what time the thief had passed; they also gave her shoes, that she might follow on. There were a number of these old women, who seemed as if they were all prophetesses. Each of them would say to her, that when she arrived in pursuit of her stolen child at the next lodge, she must set the toes of the moccasins they had loaned her pointing homewards, and they would return of themselves. She would get others from her entertainers further on, who would also give her directions how to proceed to recover her son. She thus followed in the pursuit, from valley to valley, and stream to stream, for months and years; when she came, at length, to the lodge of the last of the friendly old Nocoes, or grandmothers, as they were called, who gave her final instructions how to proceed. She told her she was near the place where her son was, and directed her to build a lodge of shingoob, or cedar boughs, near the old Toad-Woman's lodge, and to make a little bark dish and squeeze her milk into it. "Then," she said, "your first child (meaning the dog) will come and find you out." She did accordingly, and in a short time she heard her son, now grown, going out to hunt, with his dog, calling out to him, "Monedo Pewaubik (that is, Steel or Spirit Iron), Twee! Twee!" She then set ready the dish and filled it with her milk. The dog soon scented it and came into the lodge; she placed it before him. "See, my child," said she, addressing him, "the food you used to have from me, your mother." The dog went and told his young master that he had found his *real* mother; and informed him that the old woman, whom he *called* his mother, was not his mother, that she had stolen him when an infant in his cradle, and that he had himself followed her in hopes of getting him back. The young man and his dog then went on their hunting excursion, and brought back a great quantity of meat of all kinds. He said to his pretended mother, as he laid it down, "Send some to the stranger that has arrived lately." The old hag answered, "No! why should I send to her—the Sheegowish."[1] He insisted; and she at last consented to take something, throwing it in at the door, with the remark, "My son gives you, or feeds you this." But it was of such an offensive nature that she threw it immediately out after her.

After this the young man paid the stranger a visit, at her lodge of cedar boughs, and partook of her dish of milk. She then told him she was his real mother, and that he had been stolen away from her by the detestable Toad-Woman, who was a witch. He was not quite convinced. She said to him, "Feign yourself sick, when you go home, and when the Toad-Woman asks what ails you, say that you want to see your cradle; for your cradle was of wampum, and your faithful brother, the dog, bit a piece off to try and detain you, which I picked up, as I followed in your track. They were real wampum, white and blue, shining and beautiful." She then showed him the pieces. He went home and did as his real mother bid him. "Mother," said he, "why am I so different in my looks from the rest of your children?" "Oh," said she, "it was a very bright clear blue sky when you were born; that is the reason." When the Toad-Woman saw he was ill, she asked what she could do for him. He said nothing would do him good, but the sight of his cradle. She ran immediately and got a cedar cradle; but he said "That is not my cradle." She went and got one of her own children's cradles (for she had four), but he turned his head and said, "That is not mine." She then produced the real cradle, and he saw it was the same, in substance, with the pieces the other had shown him; and he was convinced, for he could even see the marks of the dog's teeth upon it.

He soon got well, and went out hunting, and killed a fat bear. He and his dog-brother then stripped a tall pine of all its branches, and stuck the carcass on the top, taking the usual sign of his having killed an animal— the tongue. He told the Toad-Woman where he had left it, saying, "It is very far, even to the end of the earth." She answered, "It is not so far but I can get it;" so off she set. As soon as she was gone, the young man and his dog killed the Toad-Woman's children, and staked them on each side of the door, with a piece of fat in their mouths, and then went to his real mother and hastened her departure with them. The Toad-Woman spent a long time in finding the bear, and had much ado in climbing the tree to get down the carcass. As she got near home, she saw the children looking out, apparently, with the fat in their mouths, and was angry at them, saying, "Why do you destroy the pomatum of your brother?" But her fury was great indeed, when she saw they were killed and impaled. She ran after the fugitives as fast as she could, and was near overtaking them, when the young man said, "We are pressed hard, but let this stay her progress," throwing his fire steel behind him, which caused the Toad-Woman to slip and fall repeatedly. But still she pursued and gained on them, when he threw behind him his flint, which again retarded her, for it made her slip and stumble, so that her knees were bleeding; but she continued to follow on, and gaining ground, when the young man said, "Let the Oshau shaw go min un (snake berry) spring up to detain her," and immediately these berries spread like scarlet all over the path for a long distance, which she could not avoid stooping down to pick and eat. Still she went on, and was again advancing on them, when the young man at last said to the dog, "Brother, chew her into mummy, for she plagues us." So the dog, turning round, seized and tore her to pieces, and they escaped.[2]

NOTES

1. *Sheegowiss,* a widow, and *mowigh,* something nasty. [H. R. S.]
2. *M. H.,* pp. 246-250. *R. R. A.,* pp. 101-103. "The Toad Woman" in *C. M.,* pp. 90-97, and in *C-C,* pp. 136-142.

WASBASHAS

OR

THE TRIBE THAT GREW OUT OF A SHELL

AN OSAGE LEGEND

THERE WAS A SNAIL living on the banks of the river Missouri, where he found plenty of food, and wanted nothing. But at length the waters began to rise and overflow its banks, and although the little animal clung to a log, the flood carried them both away; they floated along for many days. When the water fell, the poor snail was left in the mud and slime, on shore. The heat of the sun came out so strong, that he was soon fixed in the slime and could not stir. He could no longer get any nourishment. He became oppressed with heat and drought. He resigned· himself to his fate and prepared to die. But all at once, he felt a renewed vigor. His shell burst open, and he began to rise. His head gradually rose above the ground; he felt his lower extremities assuming the character of feet and legs. Arms extended from his sides. He felt their extremities divide into fingers. In fine he rose, under the influence of one day's sun, into a tall and noble man. For a while he remained in a dull and stupid state. He had but little activity, and no clear thoughts. These all came by degrees, and when his recollections returned, he resolved to travel back to his native land.

But he was naked and ignorant. The first want he felt was hunger. He saw beast and birds, as he walked along, but he knew not how to kill them. He wished himself again a snail, for he knew how, in *that* form, to get his food. At length he became so weak, by walking and fasting, that he laid himself down, on a grassy bank, to die. He had not laid long, when he heard a voice calling him by name. "Was-bas-has," exclaimed the voice. He looked up, and beheld the Great Spirit sitting on a white horse. His eyes glistened like stars. The hair of his head shone like the sun. He could not bear to look upon him. He trembled from head to foot. Again the voice spoke to him in a mild tone "Was-bas-has! Why do you look terrified?" "I tremble," he replied, "because I stand before Him who raised me from the ground. I am faint and hungry—I have eaten nothing since the floods left me upon the shore—a little shell."

The Great Spirit here lifted up his hands and displaying a bow and arrows, told him to look at him. At a distance sat a bird on a tree. He put an arrow to the string, and pulling it with force, brought down the beautiful object. At this moment a deer came in sight. He placed another arrow to the string, and pierced it through and through. "These," said he, "are

263

your food; and these are your arms," handing him the bow and arrows. He then instructed him how to remove the skin of the deer, and prepare it for a garment. "You are naked," said he, "and must be clothed; it is now warm, but the skies will change, and bring rains, and snow, and cold winds." Having said this, he also imparted the gift of fire, and instructed him how to roast the flesh. He then placed a collar of wampum around his neck. "This," said he, "is your authority over all beasts." Having done this, both horse and rider rose up, and vanished from his sight.

Was-bas-has refreshed himself, and now pursued his way to his native land. He had seated himself on the banks of the river, and was meditating on what had passed, when a large beaver rose up from the channel and addressed him. "Who art thou," said the beaver, "that comest here to disturb my ancient reign?" "I am a *man*," he replied, "I was once a *shell*, a creeping shell; but who art thou?" "I am king of the nation of beavers," he answered: "I lead my people up and down this stream; we are a busy people, and the river is my dominion." "I must divide it with you," retorted Was-bas-has. "The Great Spirit has placed me at the head of beasts and birds, fishes and fowl; and has provided me with the power of maintaining my rights." Here he held up the bow and arrows, and displayed the collar of shells around his neck. "Come, come," said the Beaver, modifying his tone, "I perceive we are brothers.—Walk with me to my lodge, and refresh yourself after your journey," and so saying he led the way. The Snail-Man willingly obeyed his invitation, and had no reason to repent of his confidence. They soon entered a fine large village, and his host led him to the chief's lodge. It was a well-built room, of a cone-shape, and the floor nicely covered with mats. As soon as they were seated, the Beaver directed his wife and daughter to prepare food for their guest. While this was getting ready, the Beaver chief thought he would improve his opportunity by making a fast friend of so superior a being; whom he saw, at the same time, to be but a novice. He informed him of the method they had of cutting down trees with their teeth, and of felling them across streams so as to dam up the water, and described the method of finishing their dams with leaves and clay. He also instructed him in the way of erecting lodges, and with other wise and seasonable conversation beguiled the time. His wife and daughter now entered, bringing in vessels of fresh peeled poplar, and willow, and sassafras, and alder bark, which is the most choice food known to them. Of this, Was-bas-has made a merit of tasting, while his entertainer devoured it with pleasure. He was pleased with the modest looks and deportment of the chief's daughter, and her cleanly and neat attire, and her assiduous attention to the commands of her father. This was ripened into esteem by the visit he made her. A mutual attachment ensued. A union was proposed to the father, who was rejoiced to find so advantageous a match for his daughter. A great feast was prepared, to which all the beavers, and other animals on good terms with them, were invited. The Snail-Man and the Beaver-Maid were thus united, and this union is the origin of the Osages. So it is said by the old people.[1]

NOTE

1. *R. R. A.*, pp. 95-97. Schoolcraft accumulated legends from the many informants who passed through the territory under his jurisdiction as Indian agent. Often Indians of one tribe learned the more "public" legends of another.

AMPATA SAPA

OR

THE FIRST-WIFE

A TRADITION OF THE DACOTAHS

AMPATA SAPA WAS THE WIFE of a brave young hunter and warrior, by whom she had two children. They lived together in great happiness, which was only varied by the changes of a forest life. Sometimes they lived on the prairies; sometimes they built their wigwam in the forest, near the banks of a stream, and they paddled their canoe up and down the rivers. In these trips they got fish, when they were tired of wild meats. In the summer season they kept on the open grounds; in the winter, they fixed their camp in a sheltered position in the woods. The very change of their camp was a source of pleasure, for they were always on the lookout for something new. They had plenty, and they wanted nothing.

In this manner the first years of their marriage passed away. But it so happened, that as years went by, the reputation of her husband in the tribe increased, and he soon came to be regarded as a Weetshahstshy Atapee, or chief. This opened a new field for his ambition and pride. The fame of a chief, it is well known, is often increased by the number of his wives. His lodge was now thronged with visitors. Some came to consult him; some to gain his favor. All this gave Ampata Sapa no uneasiness, for the Red People like to have visitors, and to show hospitality. The first thing that caused a jar in her mind, was the rumor that her husband was about to take a new wife. This was like a poison in her veins; for she had a big heart. She was much attached to her husband, and she could not bear the idea of sharing his affections with another. But she found that the idea had already got strong hold of her husband's mind, and her remonstrances did little good. He defended himself on the ground that it would give him greater influence in the tribe if he took the daughter of a noted chief. But before he had time to bring her to his lodge, Ampata Sapa had fled from it, taking her two children, and returned to her father's lodge. Her father lived at some distance, and here she remained a short time in quiet. The whole band soon moved up the Mississippi, to their hunting ground. She was glad to go with them, and would, indeed, have been glad to go anywhere, to get farther from the lodge of her faithless husband.

Here the winter wore away. When the Spring opened, they came back again to the banks of the river, and mended and fitted up the canoes, which they had left in the fall. In these they put their furs, and descended to the

266

Falls of St. Anthony. Ampata Sapa lingered behind a short time the morning of their embarkation, as they began to draw near the rapids which precede the great plunge. She then put her canoe in the water, and embarked with her children. As she approached the falls, the increasing velocity of the current rendered the paddles of but little use. She rested with hers suspended in her hands, while she arose, and uttered her lament:

"It was him only that I loved, with the love of my heart. It was for him that I prepared, with joy, the fresh killed meat, and swept with boughs my lodge-fire. It was for him I dressed the skin of the noble deer, and worked, with my hands, the moccasins that graced his feet.

"I waited while the sun ran his daily course, for his return from the chase, and I rejoiced in my heart when I heard his manly footsteps approach the lodge. He threw down the burden at the door—it was a haunch of the deer; —I flew to prepare the meat for his use.

"My heart was bound up in him, and he was all the world to me. But he has left me for another, and life is now a burden which I cannot bear. Even my children add to my griefs—they look so much like him. How can I support life, when all its moments are bitter! I have lifted up my voice to the Master of life. I have asked him to take back that life, which he gave, and which I no longer wish. I am on the current that hastens to fulfill my prayer. I see the white foam of the water. It is my shroud. I hear the deep murmur from below. It is my funeral song. Farewell."

It was too late to arrest her course. She had approached too near the abyss, before her purpose was discovered by her friends. They beheld her enter the foam—they saw the canoe for an instant, on the verge, and then disappear forever. Such was the end of Ampata Sapa; and they say her canoe can sometimes be seen, by moonlight, plunging over the falls.[1]

NOTE

1. *R. R. A.*, pp. 99-100. Although polygamy was common among the Indians, monogamy, especially among plains tribes, was not an unknown concept.

MASH-KWA-SHA-KWONG

OR

THE TRADITIONARY STORY OF THE RED-HEAD AND HIS TWO SONS

BY NABINOI, AN AGED ODJIBWA CHIEF

MASH-KWA-SHA-KWONG WAS A FIRST RATE HUNTER, and he loved the chase exceedingly, and pursued it with increasing vigilance. One day, on his return home, arriving at his lodge, he was informed by his two sons, who were but small then, that they were very lonesome, because their mother was in the habit of daily leaving them alone, and this occurred so soon as he started upon his daily chase. This circumstance was not unknown to Mash-kwa-sha-kwong, and he seemed fully aware of it; he took his boys in his arms and kissed them, and told them that their mother behaved improperly and was acting the part of a wicked and faithless woman. But Mash-kwa-sha-kwong behaved towards his wife as if ignorant of her vile course. One morning rising very early, he told his sons to take courage, and that they must not be lonesome; he also strictly enjoined them not to absent themselves nor quit their lodge; after this injunction was given to the boys, he made preparations, and starting much earlier than usual, he traveled but a short distance from his lodge, when he halted and secreted himself. After waiting a short time, he saw his wife coming out of their lodge, and immediately after a man made his appearance and meeting Mash-kwa-sha-kwong's wife, they greeted one another. His suspicions were now confirmed, and when he saw them in the act of carrying on an illegal intercourse, his anger arose. He went up to them and killed them with one blow; he then dragged them both to his lodge, and tying them together, he dug a hole beneath the fire-place in his lodge and buried them. He then told his sons that it was necessary that he should go away, as he would surely be killed if he remained, and their safety would depend upon their ability of keeping the matter a secret. He gave his eldest son a small bird, (Kichig-e-chig-aw-na-she) to roast for his small brother over the ashes and embers where their mother was buried. He also provided a small leather bag, and then told his sons the necessity of his immediate flight to heaven, or to the skies. And that it would be expedient for them to fly and journey southward, and thus prepared their minds for the separation about to take place. "By and by," said Mash-kwa-sha-kwong to his sons, "persons will come to you and inquire for me and for your mother. You will say to them that I am gone hunting, and your little brother in the meantime will continually point to the fireplace; this will lead the persons to whom I allude to make inquiries of the cause of this pointing, and you will tell them that you have a little bird roasting for your brother. This will cause them to desist from further inquiry at the time. As soon as they are gone, escape! While you are journeying agreeably to my instructions, I will look from on high upon you. I will lead and conduct you, and you shall hear my voice from day to day." Mash-kwa-sha-kwong at this time gave his sons an awl, a beaver's tooth, and a hone, also a dry coal, and directed them to place a small piece of the coal on the ground every evening, so soon as they should encamp, from which fire would be produced and given to them; he told his eldest son to place his brother in the leather bag, and in that manner carry him upon his back; he then bade them farewell.

The two boys being thus left alone in the lodge, and while in the act of roasting the little bird provided for them, a man came in, and then another, and another, until they numbered ten in all. The youngest boy would from time to time point at the fire, and the men inquired to know the reason. The eldest boy said that he was roasting a bird for his brother, and digging the ashes produced it. They inquired where their father and mother were. The boy answered them, saying that their father was absent hunting, and that their mother had gone to chop and collect wood. Upon this information the men rose and searched around the outskirts of the lodge, endeavoring to find traces of the man and his wife, but they were not successful, and returned to the lodge. Before this, however, and during the absence of the ten men, Mash-kwa-sha-kwong's eldest son placed his little brother in the leather bag (ouskemood), and ran away southward.

One of the ten men observed, that the smallest boy had repeatedly pointed to the fireplace, and that they might find out something by digging; they set to work, and found the woman and the man tied together. On this discovery their wrath was kindled; they brandished their weapons, denouncing imprecations upon Mash-kwa-sha-kwong, who was of course suspected of having committed the deed.   ,

The ten men again renewed their search in order to avenge themselves upon the perpetrator of this dark deed, but Mash-kwa-sha-kwong, in order to avoid instant death, had sought a large hollow tree, and entering at the bottom or root part, passed through and reached the top of it, from whence he took his flight upwards to the sky. His pursuers finally traced him, and followed him as far as the tree, and into the sky, with loud and unceasing imprecations of revenge and their determination to kill him. The spirit of the mother alone followed her children. About mid-day the boys heard, as they ran, a noise in the heavens like the rolling of distant thunder.[1] The boys continued their journey south when the noise ceased; towards night they encamped; they put a small piece of the coal on the ground, and a log of firewood was dropped down from the skies to them, from whence a good blazing fire was kindled. This was done daily, and when the fire was lit, a raccoon would fall from on high upon the fire, and in this manner the boys were fed, and this overruling care they experienced daily. In the evenings at their camping place, and sometimes during the day, the

Red Head's voice was heard speaking to his children, encouraging them to use their utmost exertions to fly from the pursuit of their mother. To aid them in escaping, they were told to throw away their awl, and immediately there grew a strong and almost impassable hedge of thorn bushes behind them, in their path, which the pursuing mother could scarcely penetrate, and thus impeding her progress, tearing away her whole body and leaving nothing but the head. So they escaped the first day.

The next day they resumed their march and could distinctly hear the noise of combat in the sky, as if it were a roaring thunder; they also heard the voice of their mother behind them, desiring her eldest son to stop and wait for her, saying that she wished to give the breast to his brother. Then again Mash-kwa-sha-kwong's voice, encouraged his sons to fly for their lives, saying that if their mother overtook them she would surely kill them.

In the evening of the second day the boys prepared to encamp, and the noise of combat on high ceased. On placing a small piece of the coal on the ground, a log and some firewood was let down as on the preceding night, and the fire was kindled, and then the raccoon placed on it for their food. This was fulfilling the promise made by their father, that they would be provided for during their flight. The beaver's tooth was here thrown away, and this is the cause why the northern country now abounds with beaver, and also the innumerable little lakes and marshes, and consequently the rugged and tedious traveling now experienced.

On the third day the boys resumed their flight, and threw away their hone, and it became a high, rocky, mountainous ridge, the same now seen on the north shore of these straits (St. Mary's), which was a great obstacle in the way of the woman of the Head, for this was now her name, because that part alone remained of her whole frame, and with it she was incessantly uttering determinations to kill her eldest son. The boys finally reached the fishing place known as the eddy of Wah-zah-zhawing, at the rapids of Bawating, situated on the north shore of the river. Here Mash-kwa-sha-kwong told his sons that he had himself been overtaken in his flight by his pursuers and killed, and he appeared to them in the shape of a red-headed woodpecker, or a *mama*. This is a bird that is seldom or never attacked by birds of prey, for no vestiges of his remains are ever seen or found by the Indian hunter. "Now my sons," said the red-headed woodpecker, "I have brought you to this river; you will now see your grandfather and he will convey you across to the opposite side." Then the boys looked to the southern shore of the river, and they saw, in the middle of the rapid, an Oshuggay [heron] standing on a rock. To the Oshuggay the boys spoke, and accosted him as their grandfather, requesting him to carry them across the river Bawating. The Oshuggay, stretching his long neck over the river to the place where the boys stood, told them to get upon his head and neck, and again stretching to the southern shore, he landed the boys in safety, upon a prairie: the Crane was seen walking in state, up and down the prairie.

The persevering mother soon arrived at Wah-zah-zhawing, and immediately requested the Oshuggay to cross her over, that she was in pursuit of her children, and that she wished to overtake them; but the Oshuggay seemed well aware of her character, and objected to conveying her across, giving her to understand that she was a lewd and bad woman. He continued giving her a long moral lecture upon the course she had pursued and the bad results to mankind in consequence, such as quarrels, murders, deaths, and hence widowhood.

The woman of the Head persisted in her request of being conveyed across. Objections and entreaties followed. She talked as if she were still a woman, whose favor was to be sought; and he, as if he were above such favors. After this dialogue the Oshuggay said that he would convey her across, on the condition that she would adhere strictly to his injunctions; he told her not to touch the bare part of his head, but to get upon the hollow or crooked part of his neck. To this she agreed, and got on. The Oshuggay then withdrew his long neck to about halfway across, when, feeling that she had forgotten her pledge, he dashed her head upon the rocks, and the small fish, that were so abundant instantly fed upon the brain and fragments of the skull and became large white fish. "A fish," said the Oshuggay, "that from this time forth shall be abundant, and remain in these rapids to feed the Indians and their issue, from generation to generation."[2]

After this transaction of the Oshuggay, landing the boys safely across, and dashing the woman's head upon the rocks, he spoke to the Crane and mutually consulting one another in relation to Mash-kwa-sha-kwong's sons they agreed to invite two women from the eastward, of the tribe of the Wassissig, and the two lads took them for wives. The Oshuggay plucked one of his largest wing feathers and gave it to the eldest boy, and the Crane likewise did the same, giving his feather to the youngest. They were told to consider the feathers as their sons after this. One feather appeared like an Oshuggay and the other like a young Crane. By and by they appeared like human beings to the lads. Thus the alliance was formed with the Wassissig, and the circumstance of the Oshuggay and Crane interesting themselves in behalf of the boys and the gift to them of their feathers and the result is the origin of the Indian *Totem*.

Here Mash-kwa-sha-kwong's sons were told that they would be comsidered as chieftains and that this office would be hereditary and continue in their generations. After this, they multiplied exceedingly and became strong and powerful. About this time the Obinangoes (or the Bears' Totem), came down from Shaugah-wah-mickong, near the extremity of Lake Superior. On their way eastward they were surprised on reaching Bawating to find such a numerous population of human beings; they were not aware of its being in existence. Fear came upon the Obinangoes, and they devised the plan of securing friendship with the Oshuggays and Cranes, by adopting and claiming a relationship with them, and calling them their grandsons. This claim was yielded, and they were permitted to remain at Bawating upon the score of relationship thus happily attained. The Obinangoes eventually emigrated eastward and settled upon the northern coast of Lakes Huron and Ontario.

Population increased so rapidly at Bawating, that it was necessary to form new villages, some settling on the Garden River, some upon the Pakaysaugauegan River, and others upon the island of St. Joseph's, and upon the Menashkong Bay and Mashkotay Saugie River.

About this time, a person in the shape of a human being came down from the sky; his clothing was exceedingly pure and white; he was seated as it were in a nest, with a very fine cord attached to it, by which this mysterious person was let down, and the cord or string reached heaven. He addressed the Indians in a very humane, mild, and compassionate tone, saying that they were very poor and needy, but telling them that they were perpetually *asleep,* and [that] this was caused by the Matche Monedo who was in the midst of them, and leading them to death and ruin.

This mysterious personage informed them also that above, where he came from, there was no night, that the inhabitants never slept, that it was perpetually day and they required no sleep; that Gézha Monedo was their light. He then invited four of the Indians to ascend up with him promising that they would be brought back in safety; that an opportunity would thereby present itself to view the beauty of the sky, or heavens. But the Indians doubted and feared lest the cord should break, because it appeared to them so small. They did not believe it possible it could bear their weight. With this objection they excused themselves. They were, however, again assured that this cord was sufficiently strong and that Gézha Monedo had the power to make it so. Yet the Indians doubted and feared, and did not accompany the messenger sent down to them. After this refusal the mysterious person produced a small bow and arrows with which he shot at the Indians in different parts of their bodies: the result was, the killing of multitudes of small white worms, which he showed to them, telling them that they were the Matche Monedo which caused them to sleep, and prevented their awakening from their death-like state.

This divine messenger then gave to the Indians laws and rules, whereby they should be guided: first, to love and fear Gézha Monedo; and next, that they must love one another, and be charitable and hospitable; and finally, that they must not covet their neighbors' property, but acquire it by labor and honest industry. He then instituted the grand medicine or metay-we-win dance: this ceremony was to be observed annually, and with due solemnity, and the Indians, said Nabinoi, experienced much good from it; but, unfortunately, the foolish young men were cheated by Matche Monedo, who caused them to adopt the Wabano dance and its ceremonies. This latter is decidedly an institution of the *sagemaus,* or evil spirits, and this was finally introduced into the metay-we-wining (i.e., medicine dance), and thereby corrupted it.

The old chief continued his moral strain thus: While the Indians were instructed by the heavenly messenger they were told that it would snow continually for the space of five years, winter and summer, and the end would then be nigh at hand; and again that it would rain incessantly as many winters and summers more, which would cause the waters to rise and overflow the earth, destroying trees and all manner of vegetation.

After this, ten winters and summers of drought would follow, drying up the land, and most of the lakes and rivers; not a cloud would be seen during this period. The earth would become so dry that it would then burn up with fire of itself, and it would also burn the waters to a certain depth, until it reached the first created earth and waters. Then the good Indians would rise from death to enjoy a new earth, filled with an abundance of all manner of living creatures. The only animal which would not be seen is the beaver. The bad Indians would not enjoy any portion of the new earth; they would be condemned and given to the evil spirits.

Four generations, he went on to say, have now passed away, since that brotherly love and charity, formerly known, existed among the Indians. There was in those ancient times an annual meeting among the Indians, resembling the French New Year's Day, which was generally observed on the new moon's first appearance, Gitchy Monedo gesus. The Indians of our village would visit those of another, and sometimes meet one another dancing; and on those occasions they would exchange bows and arrows, their rude axes, awls, and kettles, and their clothing. This was an annual festival, which was duly observed by them. In those days the Indians lived happily; but everything is now changed to the Indian mind, indicating the drawing near and approach of the end of time. The Indians who still adhere to the laws of the heavenly messenger experience happiness; and, on the contrary, concluded the old man, those who are wicked and adhere to the Wabano institution, generally meet with their reward; and it is singular to say that they generally come to their end by accidents, such as drowning, or miserable deaths.

He then reverted to the former part of his story. The Oshuggays and the Cranes quarreled, and this quarrel commenced on a trivial point. It appears that the Cranes took a pole, without leave, from the Oshuggays, and they broke the pole; this circumstance led to a separation. The Oshuggays emigrated south, and are now known as the Shawnees.[3]

NOTES

1. Note by Mr. George Johnston, from whom this tale was received.—Anything of the kind, or a similar noise heard, is attributed by the Indian, to this day, as an indication of the contention between Mash-kwa-sha-kwong and his pursuers, and hence a prelude to wars and contentions among the nations of the world. [H. R. S.]

2. The small white shells that the white fish live upon, and the white substance found in its gizzard are to this day considered by the Indians, the brain and skull of the woman of the Head. [H. R. S.]

3. *R. R. A.*, pp. 109-115. Compare with "Addik Kum Maig," where the Christian moralizing is omitted.

THE LITTLE SPIRIT, OR THE BOY-MAN

AN ODJIBWA FAIRY TALE

Written Out from the Verbal Narrative by the Late Mrs. H. R. Schoolcraft

THERE WAS ONCE A LITTLE BOY, remarkable for the smallness of his stature. He was living alone with his sister older than himself. They were orphans [and] they lived in a beautiful spot on the Lake shore. Many large rocks were scattered around their habitation. The boy never grew larger as he advanced in years. One day, in winter, he asked his sister to make him a ball to play with along shore on the clear ice. She made one for him, but cautioned him not to go too far. Off he went in high glee, throwing his ball before him, and running after it at full speed; and he went as fast as his ball. At last his ball flew to a great distance: he followed it as fast as he could. After he had run for sometime, he saw four dark substances on the ice straight before him. When he came up to the spot he was surprised to see four large, tall men lying on the ice, spearing fish. When he went up to them, the nearest looked up and in turn was surprised to see such a diminutive being, and turning to his brothers, he said, "Tia! look! see what a little fellow is here." After they had all looked a moment, they resumed their position, covered their heads, intent in searching for fish. The boy thought to himself, they imagine me too insignificant for common courtesy, because they are tall and large; I shall teach them, notwithstanding, that I am not to be treated so lightly. After they were covered up the boy saw they had each a large trout lying beside them. He slyly took the one nearest him, and placing his fingers in the gills, and tossing his ball before him, ran off at full speed. When the man to whom the fish belonged looked up, he saw the trout sliding away as if of itself, at a great rate—the boy being so small he was not distinguished from the fish. He addressed his brothers and said, "See how that tiny boy has stolen my fish; what a shame it is he should do so." The boy reached home, and told his sister to go out and get the fish he had brought home. She exclaimed, "where could you have got it? I hope you have not stolen it." "Oh no," he replied, "I found it on the ice." "How," persisted the sister, "could you have got it there?"— "No matter," said the boy, "go and cook it." He disdained to answer her again, but thought he would one day show her how to appreciate him. She went to the place he left it, and there indeed she found a monstrous trout. She did as she was bid, and cooked it for that day's consumption. Next morning he went off again as at first. When he came near the large men, who fished every day, he threw his ball with such force that it rolled into the ice-hole of the man of whom he had stolen the day before. As he happened to raise himself at

274

the time, the boy said, "Neejee, pray hand me my ball." "No indeed," answered the man, "I shall not," and thrust the ball under the ice. The boy took hold of his arm and broke it in two in a moment, and threw him to one side, and picked up his ball, which had bounded back from under the ice, and tossed it as usual before him. Outstripping it in speed, he got home and remained within till the next morning. The man whose arm he had broken hallooed out to his brothers, and told them his case, and deplored his fate. They hurried to their brother, and as loud as they could roar threatened vengeance on the morrow, knowing [from] the boy's speed that they could not overtake him, and he was near out of sight; yet he heard their threats and awaited their coming in perfect indifference. The four brothers the next morning prepared to take their revenge. Their old mother begged them not to go—"Better," said she, "that one only should suffer, than that all should perish; for he must be a monedo, or he could not perform such feats." But her sons would not listen; and taking their wounded brother along, started for the boy's lodge, having learned that he lived at the place of the rocks. The boy's sister thought she heard the noise of snowshoes on the crusted snow at a distance advancing. She saw the large, tall men coming straight to their lodge, or rather cave, for they lived in a large rock. She ran in with great fear, and told her brother the fact. He said, "Why do you mind them? give me something to eat." "How can you think of eating at such a time," she replied. "Do as I request you, and be quick." She then gave him his dish, which was a large *mis-qua-dace* shell, and he commenced eating. Just then the men came to the door, and were about lifting the curtain placed there, when the boy-man turned his dish upside down, and immediately the door was closed with a stone. The men tried hard with their clubs to crack it; at length they succeeded in making a slight opening. When one of them peeped in with one eye, the boy-man shot his arrow into his eye and brain, and he dropped down dead. The others, not knowing what had happened [to] their brother, did the same, and all fell in like manner; their curiosity was so great to see what the boy was about. So they all shared the same fate. After they were killed the boy-man told his sister to go out and see them. She opened the door, but feared they were not dead, and entered back again hastily, and told her fears to her brother. He went out and hacked them in small pieces, saying, "henceforth let no man be larger than you are now." So men became of the present size. When spring came on, the boy-man said to his sister, "Make me a new set of arrows and bow." She obeyed, as he never did anything himself of a nature that required manual labor, though he provided for their sustenance. After she made them, she again cautioned him not to shoot into the lake; but regardless of all admonition, he, on purpose, shot his arrow into the lake, and waded some distance till he got into deep water, and paddled about for his arrow, so as to attract the attention of his sister. She came in haste to the shore, calling him to return, but instead of minding her he called out, "Ma-mis-quon-je-gun-a, be-nau-wa-con-zhe-shin," that is, *"you, of the red fins come and swallow me."* Immediately that monstrous fish came and swallowed him; and seeing his sister standing on the shore in despair, he hallooed out to her, "Me-zush-ke-zin-ance." She wondered what he meant. But on reflection she thought it must be an old moccasin. She accordingly tied the old moccasin to a string, and fastened it to a tree. The fish said to the boy-man, under water, "What is that floating?" the boy-man said to the fish, "Go, take hold of it, swallow it as fast as you can." The fish darted towards the old shoe, and swallowed it. The boy-man laughed in himself, but said nothing, till the fish was fairly caught; he then took hold of the line and began to pull himself and fish to shore. The sister, who was watching, was surprised to see so large a fish; and hauling it ashore she took her knife and commenced cutting it open. When she heard her brother's voice inside of the fish, saying, "Make haste and release me from this nasty place," his sister was in such haste that she almost hit his head with her knife; but succeeded in making an opening large enough for her brother to get out. When he was fairly out, he told his sister to cut up the fish and dry it, as it would last a long time for their sustenance, and said to her, never, never more to doubt his ability in any way. So ends the story.[1]

NOTE

1. *R. R. A.*, pp. 127-130. It may also be found in *H. S. I.*, III, 318-320; in *C. M.*, pp. 172-189; and in *C-C*, pp. 285-294.

MOOWIS

OR

THE MAN MADE UP OF RAGS AND DIRT

A TRADITIONARY LEGEND OF THE ODJIBWAS

IN A LARGE VILLAGE, there lived a noted belle, or Ma mon dá go kwa, who was the admiration of all the young hunters and warriors. She was particularly admired by a young man, who from his good figure, and the care he took in his dress, was called the Beau-Man, or Ma mon dá gin in-e. The young man had a friend and companion, whom he made a confidant of his affairs. "Come," said he, one day in a sportive mood, "let us go a-courting to her who is so handsome, perhaps she may fancy one of us." But she would listen to neither of them, and when the handsome young man rallied from the coldness of her air, and made an effort to overcome her indifference, she put together her thumb and three fingers, and raising her hand gracefully towards him, deliberately opened them in his face. This gesticulatory mode of rejection is one of the highest contempt, and the young hunter retired confused and abashed. His sense of pride was deeply wounded, and he was the more piqued, that it had been done in the presence of others, and the affair was soon noised about the village, and became the talk of every lodge circle. Besides, he was a very sensitive man, and the thing so preyed upon him, that he became moody, and at last took to his bed. He was taciturn, often lying for days without uttering a word, with his eyes fixed on vacancy, and taking little or no food. From this state no efforts could rouse him; he felt abashed and dishonored, even in the presence of his own relatives, and no persuasions could induce him to rise. So that when the family prepared to take down the lodge to remove, he still kept his bed, and they were compelled to lift it over his head, and leave him upon his skin couch. It was a time of general removal and breaking up of the camp, for it was only a winter's hunting camp, and as the season of the hunt was now over, and spring began to appear, they all moved off, as by one impulse, to the place of their summer village, and in a short time, all were gone, and he was left alone. The last person to leave him was his boon companion, and cousin, who has been mentioned, as also one of the admirers of the forest belle. But even *his* voice was disregarded, and as soon as his steps died away on the creaking snow, the stillness and solitude of the wilderness reigned around.

As soon as all were gone, and he could no longer, by listening, hear the remotest sounds of the departing camp, the Beau-Man arose. It is to be

277

understood that this young man was aided by a powerful guardian spirit, or personal Moneto; and he resolved to make use of his utmost power to punish and humble the girl. For she was noted in the tribe for her coquetry, and had treated others, who were every way her equals, as she had done him. He resolved on a singular stratagem, by way of revenge. For this purpose, he walked over the deserted camp, and gathered up all the bits of soiled cloth, clippings of finery, and castoff clothing, and ornaments which had either been left or lost. These he carefully picked out of the snow, into which some of them had been trodden and partially buried, and conveyed them to one place. The motley heap of gaudy and soiled stuffs, he restored to their original beauty, and determined to make them into a coat and leggings, which he trimmed with beads, and finished and decorated after the best fashion of his tribe. He then made a pair of moccasins and garnished them with beads, a bow and arrows, and a frontlet and feathers for the head. Having done this, he searched about for cast-out bones of animals, pieces of skins, clippings of dried meat, and even dirt, and having cemented them together with snow, he filled the clothes with these things, and pressed the mass firmly in, and fashioned it externally in all respects, like a tall and well-framed man. He put a bow and arrows in his hands, and the frontlet on his head. And having finished it, he brought it to life, and the image stood forth, in the most favored lineaments of his fellows. Such was the origin of Moowis, or the Dirt and Rag Man.

"Follow me," said the Beau-Man, "and I will direct you, how you shall act." He was indeed, a very sightly person, and as they entered the new encampment, the many colors of his clothes, the profusion of ornaments which he had managed to give him, and his fine manly step, and animated countenance, drew all eyes. And he was received by all, both old and young, with marks of attention. The chief invited him to his lodge, and he was feasted on the moose's hump and the finest venison.

But no one was better pleased with the handsome stranger than Ma mon dá go kwa. She fell in love with him at the first sight, and he was an invited guest at the lodge of her mother, the very first evening of his arrival. The Beau-Man went with him, for it was under his patronage that he had been introduced, and, in truth, he had another motive for accompanying him, for he had not yet wholly subdued his feelings of admiration for the object, against whom he had, nevertheless, exerted all his necromantic power, and he held himself subject to any favorable turn, which he secretly hoped the visit might take, in relation to himself. But no such turn occurred. Moowis attracted the chief attention, and every eye and heart were alert to entertain him. In this effort on the part of his entertainers, they had well nigh revealed his true character, and dissolved him into his original elements of rags, and snow, and dirt; for he was assigned the most prominent place before the fire: this was a degree of heat which he could by no means endure. To ward it off he put a boy between himself and the fire. He shifted his position frequently, and evaded, by dexterous maneuvers, and timely remarks, the pressing invitation of his host to sit up, and enjoy it. He so managed these excuses, as not only to conceal his dread of immediate dissolution, but to secure the further approbation of the fair forest girl, who could not but admire one who had so brave a spirit of endurance against the paralyzing effects of cold.

The visit proved that the rejected lover had well calculated the effects of his plan. He withdrew from the lodge, and Moowis triumphed. Before he went, he saw him cross the lodge to the coveted *abinos*, or bridegroom's seat. Marriage in the forest race, is a simple ceremony, and where the impediments of custom are small, there is but little time demanded for their execution. The dart which Ma mon dá go kwa had so often delighted in sending to the hearts of her admirers, she was at length fated herself to receive. She had married an image. As the morning begun to break, the stranger arose and adjusted his warrior's plumes, and took his forest weapons to depart. "I must go," said he, "for I have an important business to do, and there are many hills and streams between me and the object of my journey." "I will go with you," she replied. "It is too far," he rejoined, "and you are ill able to encounter the perils of the way." "It is not so far, but that I can go," she responded, "and there are no dangers which I will not fully share for you."

Moowis returned to the lodge of his master, and detailed to him the events we have described. Pity, for a moment, seized the breast of the rejected youth. He regretted that she should thus have cast herself away upon an image and a shadow, when she might have been mistress of the best lodge in the land. "But it is her own folly," he said, "she has turned a deaf ear to the counsels of prudence, and she must submit to her fate."

The same morning the Image-man set forth, and his wife followed him, according to custom, at a distance. The way was rough and intricate, and she could not keep up with his rapid pace; but she struggled hard, and perseveringly to overtake him. Moowis had been long out of sight, when the sun arose, and commenced upon his snow-formed body the work of dissolution. He began to melt away, and fall to pieces. As she followed him, piece after piece of his clothing were found in the path. She first found his mittens, then his moccasins, then his leggings, then his coat, and other parts of his garments. As the heat unbound them, they had all returned also to their debased and filthy condition. The way led over rocks, through windfalls, across marshes. It whirled about to all points of the compass, and had no certain direction or object. Rags, bones, leather, beads, feathers, and soiled ribbons, were found, but she never caught the sight of Moowis. She spent the day in wandering; and when evening came, she was no nearer the object of her search than in the morning, but the snow having now melted, she had completely lost his track, and wandered about, uncertain which way to go, and in a state of perfect despair. Finding herself lost, she begun, with bitter cries, to bewail her fate.

"Moowis, Moowis," she cried. "Nin ge won e win ig, ne won e win ig"— that is—Moowis, Moowis, you have led me astray—you are leading me astray." And with this cry she continued to wander in the woods.

Sometimes the village girls repeat the above words, varying the expressions, till they constitute an irregular kind of song, which, according to the versions of a friendly hand, may be set down as follows:

Moowis! Moowis!
   Forest rover,—
Where art thou?
   Ah my bravest, gayest lover,
Guide me now.

Moowis! Moowis!
   Ah believe me,
List my moan,
   Do not—do not, brave heart, leave me
All alone.

Moowis! Moowis!
   Foot-prints vanished,
Whither wend I,
   Fated, lost, detested, banished,
Must I die.

Moowis! Moowis!
   Whither goest,
Eye-bright lover,
   Ah thou ravenous bird that knowest,
I see you hover.

Circling—circling,
   As I wander,
But to spy
   Where I fall, and then to batten,
On my breast.[1]

NOTE

1. It is a characteristic of some of the Indian legends, that they convey a *moral* which seems clearly enough to denote, that a part of these legends was invented to convey instruction to the young folks who listen to them. The known absence of all harsh methods among the Indians, in bringing up their children, favors this idea. This tale addresses itself plainly to girls; to whom it teaches the dangers of what we denominate coquetry. It would seem from this, that beauty, and its concomitant, a passion for dress, among the red daughters of Adam and Eve, has the same tendency to create pride, and nourish self-conceit, and self-esteem, and assume a *tyranny over the human heart,* which

writers tell us, these qualities have among their white-skinned, auburn-haired, and blue-eyed progeny the world over. The term Moowis is one of the most derogative and offensive possible. It is derived from the Odjibwa substantive, *mo*, filth, or excrement. [H. R. S.] *The Columbian Ladies' and Gentlemen's Magazine* (1844), I, 90-91. Reprinted in *R. R. A.*, pp. 164-167.

THE MAGICIAN OF LAKE HURON

AN OTTOWA TALE

Related by Nabunwa in the Indian Tongue, to Mr. George Johnston

AT THE TIME THAT THE OTTOWAS INHABITED the Manatoulin Islands, in Lake Huron, there was a famous magician living amongst them whose name was Masswäwëinini, or the Living Statue. It happened, by the fortune of war, that the Ottowa tribe were driven off that chain of islands by the Iroquois, and obliged to flee away to the country lying between Lake Superior and the Upper Mississippi, to the banks of a lake which is still called, by the French, and in memory of this migration, *Lac Courtoreille,* or the lake of the Cut-ears, a term which is their *nom de guerre* for this tribe. But the magician Masswäwëinini remained behind on the wide-stretching and picturesque Manatoulins, a group of islands which had been deemed, from the earliest times, a favorite residence of the manitoes or spirits. His object was to act as a sentinel to his countrymen, and keep a close watch on their enemies, the Iroquois, that he might give timely information of their movements. He had with him two boys; with their aid he paddled stealthily around the shores, kept himself secreted in nooks and bays, and hauled up his canoe every night, into thick woods, and carefully obliterated his tracks upon the sand.

One day he rose very early, and started on a hunting excursion, leaving the boys asleep, and limiting himself to the thick woods, lest he should be discovered. At length he came unexpectedly to the borders of an extensive open plain. After gazing around him, and seeing no one, he directed his steps across it, intending to strike the opposite side of it; while traveling, he discovered a man of small stature, who appeared suddenly on the plain before him, and advanced to meet him. He wore a red feather on his head, and coming up with a familiar air, accosted Masswäwëinini by name, and said gaily, "Where are you going?" He then took out his smoking apparatus, and invited him to smoke. "Pray," said he, while thus engaged, "wherein does your strength lie." "My strength," answered Masswäwëinini, "is similar to the human race, and common to the strength given to them, and no stronger." "We must wrestle," said the man of the red feather. "If you should make me fall, you will say to me, I have thrown you, *Wa ge me na.*"

As soon as they had finished smoking and put up their pipe, the wrestling began. For a long time the strife was doubtful. The strength of Masswäwëinini was every moment growing fainter. The man of the red feather, though small of stature, proved himself very active, but at length he was foiled

282

and thrown to the ground. Immediately his adversary cried out, "I have thrown you: *wa ge me na;*" and in an instant his antagonist had vanished. On looking to the spot where he had fallen, he discovered a crooked ear of *mondamin,* or Indian corn, lying on the ground, with the usual red hairy tassel at the top. While he was gazing at this strange sight, and wondering what it could mean, a voice addressed him from the ground. "Now," said the speaking ear, for the voice came from it, "divest me of my covering— leave nothing to hide my body from your eyes. You must then separate me into parts, pulling off my body from the spine upon which I grow. Throw me into different parts of the plain. Then break my spine and scatter it in small pieces near the edge of the woods, and return to visit the place, after *one moon.*"

Masswäwëinini obeyed these directions, and immediately set out on his return to the lodge. On the way he killed a deer, and on reaching his canoe, he found the boys still asleep. He awoke them and told them to cook his venison, but he carefully concealed from them his adventure. At the expiration of the moon he again, *alone,* visited his wrestling ground, and to his surprise, found the plain filled with the spikes and blades of new grown corn. In the place where he had thrown the pieces of cob, he found pumpkin vines growing in great luxuriance. He concealed this discovery also, carefully from the young lads, and after his return busied himself as usual, in watching the movements of his enemies along the coasts of the island. This he continued, till summer drew near its close. He then directed his canoe to the coast of that part of the island where he had wrestled with the Red Plume, drew up his canoe, bid the lads stay by it, and again visited his wrestling ground. He found the corn in full ear, and pumpkins of an immense size. He plucked ears of corn, and gathered some of the pumpkins, when a voice again addressed him from the cornfield. "Masswäwëinini, you have conquered me. Had you not done so, your existence would have been forfeited. Victory has crowned your strength, and from henceforth you shall never be in want of my body. It will be nourishment for the human race." Thus his ancestors received the gift of corn.

Masswäwëinini now returned to his canoe, and informed the young men of his discovery, and showed them specimens. They were astonished and delighted with the novelty.

There were, in those days, many wonderful things done on these islands. One night, while Masswäwëinini was lying down, he heard voices speaking, but he still kept his head covered, as if he had not heard them. One voice said, "This is Masswäwëinini, and we must get his heart." "In what way can we get it?" said another voice. "You must put your hand in his mouth," replied the first voice, "and draw it out that way." Masswäwëinini still kept quiet, and did not stir. He soon felt the hand of a person thrust in his mouth. When sufficiently far in, he bit off the fingers, and thus escaped the danger. The voices then retired, and he was no further molested. On examining the fingers in the morning, what was his surprise to find them long wampum beads, which are held in such high estimation by all the Indian tribes. He had slept, as was his custom, in the thick woods. On going out to the open shore, at a very early hour, he saw a canoe at a small distance, temporarily drawn up on the beach; on coming closer, he found a man in the bow and another in the stern, with their arms and hands extended in a fixed position. One of them had lost its fingers; it was evidently the man who had attempted to thrust his arm down his throat. They were two Pukwudjininees, or fairies. But on looking closer, they were found to be transformed into statues of stone. He took these stone images on shore, and set them up in the woods.

Their canoe was one of the most beautiful structures which it is possible to imagine, four fathoms in length, and filled with bags of treasures of every description and of the most exquisite workmanship. These bags were of different weight, according to their contents. He busied himself in quickly carrying them into the woods, together with the canoe, which he concealed in a cave. One of the fairy images then spoke to him and said: "In this manner, the Ottowa canoes will hereafter be loaded, when they pass along this coast, although your nation are driven away by their cruel enemies the Iroquois." The day now began to dawn fully, when he returned to his two young companions, who were still asleep. He awoke them, and exultingly bid them cook, for he had brought abundance of meat and fish, and other viands, the gifts of the fairies.

After this display of good fortune, he bethought him of his aged father and mother, who were in exile at the Ottowa lake. To wish, and to accomplish his wish, were but the work of an instant with Masswäwëinini.

One night as he lay awake, reflecting on their condition, far away from their native fields, and in exile, he resolved to visit them, and bring them back to behold and to participate in his abundance. To a common traveler, it would be a journey of twenty or thirty days, but Masswäwëinini was at their lodge before daylight. He found them asleep, and took them up softly in his arms and flew away with them through the air, and brought them to his camp on the Manatoulins, or Spirits' Islands. When they awoke, their astonishment was at its highest pitch; and was only equaled by their delight in finding themselves in their son's lodge, in their native country, and surrounded with abundance.

Masswäwëinini went and built them a lodge, near the corn and wrestling plain. He then plucked some ears of the corn, and taking some of the pumpkins, brought them to his father and mother. He then told them how he had obtained the precious gift, by wrestling with a spirit in red plumes, and that there was a great abundance of it in his fields. He also told them of the precious canoe of the fairies, loaded with sacks of the most costly and valuable articles. But one thing seemed necessary to complete the happiness of his father, which he observed by seeing him repeatedly at night looking into his smoking pouch. He comprehended his meaning in a moment. "It is tobacco, my father, that you want. You shall also have this comfort in two days." "But where," replied the old man, "can you get it—away from all supplies, and surrounded by your enemies?" "My enemies," he answered, "shall supply it—I will go over to the Nadowas of the Bear totem, living at Penetanguishine."

The old man endeavored to dissuade him from the journey, knowing their bloodthirsty character, but in vain. Masswäwëinini determined immediately to go. It was now winter weather, the lake was frozen over, but he set out on the ice, and although it is forty leagues, he reached Penetanguishine the same evening. The Nadowas discerned him coming—they were amazed at the swiftness of his motions, and thinking him somewhat supernatural, feared him, and invited him to rest in their lodges, but he thanked them, saying that he preferred making a fire near the shore. In the evening they visited him, and were anxious to know the object of his journey, at so inclement a season. He said it was merely to get some tobacco for his father. They immediately made a contribution of the article and gave it to him. During the night they however laid a plot to kill him. Some of the old men rushed into his lodge, their leader crying out to him, "You are a dead man." "No, I am not," said Masswäwëinini, "but you are," accompanying his words with a blow of his tomahawk, which laid the Nadowa dead at his feet. Another and another came, to supply the place of their fallen comrade, but he despatched them in like manner, as quickly as they came, until he had killed six. He then took all the tobacco from their smoking pouches. By this time, the day began to dawn, when he set out for his father's lodge, which he reached with incredible speed, and before twilight, spread out his trophies before the old man.

When spring returned, his cornfield grew up, without planting, or any care on his part, and thus the *maize* was introduced among his people and their descendants, who have ever been noted, and are at this day, for their fine crops of this grain, and their industry in its cultivation. It is from their custom of trading in this article, that this tribe are called Ottowas.[1]

NOTE

1. *R. R. A.,* pp. 175-178. Compare with "Mon-Daw-Min."

1. Excerpts from

GOVERNOR LEWIS CASS' *INQUIRIES RESPECTING THE HISTORY, TRADITIONS, LANGUAGES, MANNERS, CUSTOMS, RELIGION...,OF THE INDIANS LIVING WITHIN THE UNITED STATES (1823)*

(SHORTLY AFTER HIS RETURN from the expedition to Lake Superior and the upper Mississippi in 1820, Governor Lewis Cass had printed and circulated the queries listed below. Traders, military men, and Indian agents received copies and spent long hours drafting replies. To this printed circular must be credited much of the ferment of the thirties over Indian history, traditions, and antiquities. There is a reply from Doctor Alexander Wolcott in Schoolcraft's *Travels in the Central Portions of the Mississippi Valley*, pp. 380-386. It is known that celebrities like Col. William Dickson, James D. Doty, and William Morrison sent answers to General Cass. Schoolcraft wrote in 1825:

. . . the inquiries which he [Governor Cass] has since unremittingly directed to the history, languages, and moral and physical state of the Indian tribes living within the United States, have resulted in the collection of a mass of original information which constitutes in itself a MS. library. And the progress which has already been made in the digestion, examination, and comparison of these MSS. with authorities of every period, of every country, and of every degree of merit, justifies the public in anticipating from his pen an elementary work upon the aborigines, which every person who has directed his thoughts to the subject has admitted to be a desideratum in our vernacular literature. *Ibid.*, pp. 380-383.

On the other side of the ledger Cass had this to say to Schoolcraft:

My Indian materials are rapidly accumulating; but unfortunately, they are more valuable for quantity than quality. . . . There is a lamentable obtuseness of intellect manifested in both collector and contributor; and there is no systematic arrangement—no analytical process, and, in fact, no correctness of detail. I may safely say that what I received from you is more valuable than all my other stock. . . . The result of your inquiries into the Indian language is highly valuable and satisfactory. . . . I should be happy to have you prosecute your inquiries into the manners, customs, etc., of the Indians. You are favorably situated, and have withal such unconquerable perseverance, that I must tax you more than other persons. *Personal Memoirs,* letters from Cass to Schoolcraft in 1823 and 1824, pp. 184-186.

It is regrettable that Cass made no scientific use of the collection of Indian materials that his questionnaire brought him. Because everyone knew he had the data, he was frequently called the best informed man on the Indian in North America. Yet all posterity has to show for it is a few articles in the *North American Review.* His efforts were not wholly wasted, however, because the *Inquiries* stimulated private investigation and fired the public imagination on the subject.)

"The time for collecting materials to illustrate the past and present conditions of the Indians is rapidly passing away. The inquiries, which have heretofore been directed to this subject, have produced much authentic information; but it relates rather to the more prominent traits of Indian character, than to the constitution of their minds or their moral habits." Preface to the *Inquiries.*

INQUIRIES

Traditions

What is the original name of the tribe?

What is the present Indian name?

What is the meaning of the name in English?

To what other tribes are they related?

What is the degree of relationship?

What is the earliest incident they recollect in their history?

Whence did they come?

What migrations have they made, and when and why?

What memorable events in their history have been transmitted to them?

With whom have they been at war, and when?

How long did these wars continue? What were the incidents of them? Relate them as particularly as can now be done.

What belts have they, by which these wars, or any other events in their history are commemorated? Describe these belts.

How, and when, did these wars terminate?

When, and at what place, were they first acquainted with the whites?

What are the names, and the principal events in the lives of their great men, and when did they flourish?

What connection has this tribe with the council fire formerly held at Brownstown, at the mouth of the Detroit River?

Are there any mounds, or the remains of any other ancient work in the country occupied by this tribe? And if so, what are their traditions respecting these works and the people who erected them?

Astronomy, Mathematics, etc.

What is their opinion respecting the planetary system?

What do they think of the size, shape, etc., of the earth?

Do they divide the year into four seasons [and], if so, how are they denominated, in Indian and English?

What is their opinion respecting the sun, the moon and eclipses?

Do they name any of the stars, and have they any knowledge of the pole star?

To what number do they reckon in their language?

Do they know anything of addition, multiplication, subtraction or division?

Have they the four cardinal points, east, west, north and south?

Do they indulge in any prognostics respecting the weather?

What do they think of the meteors, called shooting stars?

Do they use any ceremonies on the appearance of the new moon [and], if so, what are they?

Can they calculate the time of the re-appearance of the new moon?

Have they any knowledge of the solstices or equinoxes?

Have they any idea of the situation [location] of Europe, or any of its states?

What do they think of the ocean?

Music and Poetry

What musical instruments do they use?

Are there wind instruments [and], if so, are they used exclusively, as is said, by the young men in love?

Has their music anything beyond simple cadences of thirds and fifths?

When it has these variations, does it always commence with the highest note?

Have they different music for different occasions, as for a medicine dance, a war dance, and for accompaniments to small games?

Can specimens of their music be noted down?

Give specimens of their songs.

Do they relate stories, or indulge in any work of imagination? Have they any poetry?

If so, is it poetry with measured verse, or without?

Have they any rhymes?

Give specimens of their poetry, of their measured verse, and of their rhymes.

Religion

What are their general opinions upon the subject of religion?

Do they believe in a future state of rewards and punishments?

Do they believe that good or bad conduct in this life will have any effect upon their future happiness or misery?

Do they believe in a Supreme Being [and], if so, by what name do they distinguish him?

Do they believe in subordinate deities, and by what names do they distinguish them?

How do they divide the powers and prerogatives of their different spirits, good and bad?

What is generally the state of their mythological opinions?

Do they believe in ghosts?

Do they believe in the moral superintendence of any invisible being over the affairs of the world?

Do they pray for favors or assistance?

When they deposit pieces of tobacco or any other article upon a stone or mountain, what is their idea?

Have they any ideas respecting a final judgment?

Do they associate with their opinions of a future state of existence, ideas of mental or corporeal pleasure?

State their general ideas respecting the situation of the soul from the time of death.

Have they any particular religious ceremonies or societies [and], if so, what are they?

Have they any priests [and], if so, how are they appointed, and what are their rights and duties?

What is their opinion respecting wizards or witches, or, in other words, the power of any man to suspend, alter or control the operations of nature?

Where is the local situation of the places to which they think the souls of good or bad men will go?

General Manners and Customs

Do they ever eat human flesh, and if so, upon what occasions and with what ceremonies?

What is their mode of salutation when they meet?

What do they say on these occasions?

Is shaking hands an Indian custom, and if not, what analogous custom have they?

Is any particular respect paid to age or rank?

Do they ever visit one another for the purpose of conversation?

Do they have regular parties, at which they entertain one another?

Are they in the practice of telling stories?

Mention any point of character, manners, government, or anything else, which is peculiar to them, or in which they differ from other tribes. (This is a subject, upon which I feel particular anxiety, and to which I request your particular attention.)

Do they use words equivalent to our habit of swearing?

By what do they regulate their course in an unknown country?
Do they exhibit strong feelings of love, friendship, or affection?
Is it common with them to endeavor to conceal such feelings?
Is it a matter of pride with them to suppress the expression of any strong
  feeling or excitement, either corporeal or mental?
When they return home, after being long absent, how do they conduct them-
  selves?
Are their powers of recollection strong?
Is there anything peculiar in their manner of encampment, or in their mode
  of building huts or temporary shelters?
Can an Indian, by examining an encampment which is abandoned, tell what
  tribe and nearly how many individuals occupied it; and if so, by what
  means?
What is their reason for sparing the lives of snakes?
What disposition is made of the property of a deceased person?
What is the general condition of the women among them?
Are they considered as menial servants by the men?

Games, Dances, and Amusements

How many different kinds of dances have they, such as the begging dance,
  the war dance, the buffalo dance, etc.?
Enumerate them and give the Indian names.
Describe the manner and ceremonies of each dance, and the occasion upon
  which it is used.
In what dances do the men and women intermingle, and from which is
  either sex excluded?
When both sexes join, do they dance together indiscriminately, or do the
  men occupy one side and the women the other?
Are some of these dances religious? If so, specify them particularly, to-
  gether with the opinions of the Indians respecting them.
Describe their games and amusements.
Describe the moccasin game.
What athletic games have they?
Are they fond of gambling?
What games of chance have they; either of cards or of any other kind?

Addenda

Have they any old hieroglyphical representations upon wood, designed
to aid the memory by the power of association, either in storytelling, or in
the singing of songs, or in the initiatory ceremonies of certain societies? If
any can be found describe them, and transmit a facsimile of each one. They
exist among some of the tribes, and are called music boards.

[Omitted from this list were 32 queries on Government; 41 on War, and Its Incidents; 11 on Peace; 17 on Death, and Its Incidents; 28 on Birth, and Its Incidents; 27 on Marriage, and Its Incidents; 9 on Social Relations; 15 on Medicine; 16 on Food, Mode of Living, Cooking; 10 on Peculiar Societies; 8 on International Relations; 8 on Hunting; 7 on Feasts and Fasts; 14 on Dress and Personal Appearance; 11 on Belts, Wampum, Hieroglyphics; and 8 on Statistical Information. The pamphlet also contained 36 pages of grammar review and word lists for the study of the Indian language, its grammar, orthography, vocabulary, and alphabet. Under the impact of such a sociological questionnaire, a device long believed to have been invented in the twentieth century, it is little wonder that agents complained and traders and missionaries grumbled: But the answers poured in, and the more interested began to study for themselves. The bibliography of contemporary works about Indians that follows reveals the degree to which the subject captured the interest of the English-speaking world.]

2. THE MYTH OF HIAWATHA

a. PREFACE

THERE IS BUT ONE CONSIDERATION of much moment necessary to be premised respecting these legends and myths. It is this: they are versions of oral relations from the lips of the Indians, and are transcripts of the thought and invention of the aboriginal mind. As such, they furnish illustrations of Indian character and opinions on subjects which the ever-cautious and suspicious minds of this people have, heretofore, concealed. They place the man altogether in a new phasis. They reflect him as he is. They show us what he believes, hopes, fears, wishes, expects, worships, lives for, dies for. They are always true to the Indian manners and customs, opinions and theories. They never rise above them; they never sink below them. Placing him in almost every possible position, as a hunter, a warrior, a magician, a pow-wow, a medicine man, a meda, a husband, a father, a friend, a foe, a stranger, a wild singer of songs to monedos or fetishes, a trembler in terror of demons and wood genii, and of ghosts, witches, and sorcerers— now in the enjoyment of plenty in feasts—now pale and weak with abstinence in fasts; now transforming beasts and birds, or plants and trees into men, or men into beasts by necromancy; it is impossible not to perceive what he perpetually thinks, believes, and feels. The very language of the man is employed, and his vocabulary is not enlarged by words and phrases foreign to it. Other sources of information depict his exterior habits and outer garb and deportment; but in these legends and myths we perceive the interior man, and are made cognizant of the secret workings of his mind, and heart, and soul.

To make these collections, of which the portions now submitted are but a part, the leisure hours of many seasons, passed in an official capacity in the solitude of the wilderness far away from society, have been employed, with the study of the languages, and with the very best interpreters. They have been carefully translated, written, and rewritten, to obtain their true spirit and meaning, expunging passages, where it was necessary to avoid tediousness of narration, triviality of circumstance, tautologies, gross incongruities, and vulgarities; but adding no incident and drawing no conclusion, which the verbal narration did not imperatively require or sanction. It was impossible to mistake the import of terms and phrases where the means of their analysis were ample. If the style is sometimes found to be bald, and of jejune simplicity, the original is characteristically so. Few adjectives are employed, because there are few in the original. The Indian effects his purposes, almost entirely, by changes of the verb and demonstrative pronoun or by adjective inflections of the substantive. Good and bad, high and low, black and white, are in all cases employed in a transitive sense, and with strict relation to the objects characterized. The Indian compound terms are so descriptive, so graphic, so local, so characterizing, yet so flexible and transpositive, that the legends derive no little of their characteristic features as well as melody of utterance from these traits. Sometimes these terms cannot be literally translated, and they cannot, in these cases, be left out without damaging the stories.

With regard to the thought-work of the legends, those who have deemed the Indians exclusively a cruel and bloodthirsty race, always seeking revenge, always invoking evil powers, will not be disappointed that giants, enchanters, demons, and dark supernatural agencies, should form so large a part of the *dramatis personae*. Surprise has been expressed, that the kindlier affections come in for notice at all, and particularly at the occurrence of such refined and terse allegories as the origin of Indian Corn, Winter and Spring, and the poetic conception of the Celestial Sisters, etc. I can only add, that my own surprise was as great when these traits were first revealed. And the trait may be quoted to show how deeply the tribes have wandered away from the type of the human race in which love and affection absorb the heart; and how little, indeed, we know of their mental character.

These legends have been out of print several years. They are now reproduced, with additional legendary lore of this description from the portfolios of the author, in a revised, and, it is believed, a more terse, condensed, and acceptable form, both in a literary and business garb.

HENRY R. SCHOOLCRAFT.

Washington, D. C., April 28, 1856.

b. INTRODUCTION

Hitherto, Indian opinion, on abstract subjects, has been a sealed book. It has been impossible to extract the truth from his evasive replies. If asked his opinion of religion in the abstract, he knows not the true meaning of the term. His ideas of the existence of a deity are vague, at best; and the lines of separation between it and necromancy, medical magic, and demonology are too faintly separated to allow him to speak with discrimination. The best reply, as to his religious views, his mythology, his cosmogony, and his general views as to the mode and manifestations of the government and providences of God, are to be found in his myths and legends. When he assembles his lodge-circle, to hear stories, in seasons of leisure and retirement in the depths of the forest, he recites precisely what he believes on these subjects. That restlessness, suspicion, and mistrust of motive, which has closed his mind to inquiry, is at rest here. If he mingles fiction with history, there is little of the latter, and it is very easy to see where history ends and fiction begins. While he amuses his hearers with tales of the adventures of giants and dwarfs, and the conflicts of Manito with Manito, fairies and enchanters, monsters and demons, he also throws in some few grains of instruction, in the form of allegory and fable, which enable us to perceive glimpses of the heart and its affections.

It is also by his myths that we are able to trace connections with the human family in other parts of the world. Yet, where the analogies are so general, there is a constant liability to mistakes. Of these foreign analogies of myth lore, the least tangible, it is believed, is that which has been suggested with the Scandinavian mythology. That mythology is of so marked and peculiar a character, that it has not been distinctly traced out of the great circle of tribes of the Indo-Germanic family. Odin, and his terrific pantheon of war-gods and social deities, could only exist in the dreary latitudes of storms and fire, which produce a Hecla and a Maelstrom. These latitudes have invariably produced nations, whose influence has been felt in an elevating power over the world; and whose tracks have everywhere been marked by the highest evidences of inductive intellect, centralizing energy, and practical wisdom and forecast. From such a source the Indian could have derived none of his vague symbolisms and mental idiosyncrasies, which have left him, as he is found today, without a government and without a God. Far more probable is it, in seeking for analogies to his mythology and cosmogony, to resort to the era of that primal reconstruction of the theory of a deity, when the human philosophy in the oriental world ascribed the godship of the universe to the subtile, ineffable, and indestructible essences of fire and light, as revealed in the sun. Such were the errors of the search for divine truth, power, and a controllable deity, which early developed themselves in the dogmas of the Assyrians, Egyptians, Persians, and wandering hordes of Northern Asia.

Authors inform us that the worship of the sun lies at the foundation of all the ancient mythologies, deeply enveloped as they are, when followed over Asia Minor and Europe, in symbolic and linguistical subtileties and refinements. The symbolical fires erected on temples and altars to Baal, Chemosh, and Moloch, burned brightly in the valley of the Euphrates, long before the pyramids of Egypt were erected, or its priestly-hoarded hieroglyphic wisdom resulted in a phonetic alphabet. In Persia, these altars were guarded and religiously fed by a consecrated body of magical priesthood, who recognized a deity in the essence of an eternal fire and a world-pervading light.

The same dogma, derived eastwardly and not westwardly through Europe, was fully installed at Atacama and Cuzco, in Peru, at Cholulu, on the magnificent and volcano-lighted peaks of Mexico; and along the fertile deltas of the Mississippi valley. Altar-beds for a sacred fire, lit to the Great Spirit, under the name and symbolic form of Ceezis, or the sun, where the frankincense of the nicotiana was offered, with hymns and genuflections, have been discovered, in many instances, under the earth-heaps and artificial mounds and places of sepulture of the ancient inhabitants. Intelligent Indians yet living, among the North American tribes, point out the symbol of the sun, in their ancient muzzinabikons, or rock-inscriptions, and also amid the idiographic tracery and bark-scrolls of the hieratic and magical medicine songs.

With a cosmogony which ascribes the creation of the Geezha Monedo, who is symbolized by the sun, the myth of Hiawatha is almost a necessary consequence in carrying out his mundane intentions to the tribes, who believed themselves to be peculiar objects of his love and benevolence. This myth is noticed by the earliest explorers of this continent, who have bestowed attention on the subject, under the various names of Inigorio, Yoskika, Taren-Yawagon, Atahentsic, Manabozho, and Micabo. A mythology appears indispensable to a rude and ignorant race like the Indians. Their vocabulary is nearly limited to objects which can be seen and handled. Abstractions are only reached by the introduction of some term which restores the idea. The Deity is a mystery, of whose power they must chiefly judge by the phenomena before them. Everything is mysterious which is not understood; and, unluckily, they understand little or nothing. If any phenomenon, or existence not before them, is to be described, the language must be symbolic. The result is, that the Indian languages are peculiarly the languages of symbols, metaphors, and figures. Without this feature, everything not in the departments of eating, drinking, and living, and the ordinary transactions of the chase and forest, would not be capable of description.

When the Great Sacred White Hare of Heaven, the Manabozho of the Algics, and Hiawatha of the Iroquois,[1] kills the Great Misshikinabik, or prince of serpents, it is understood that he destroys the great power of evil. It is a deity whom he destroys, a sort of Typhon or Ahriman in the system. It is immediately found, on going to his lodge, that it is a man, a hero, a chief, who is sick, and he must be cured by simples and magic songs like the rest of the Indians. He is surrounded with Indian doctors, who sing magic songs. He has all the powers of a deity, and, when he dies, the land is subjected to a flood; from which Hiawatha alone escapes. This play between the zoonic and mortal shapes of heroes must constantly be observed, in high as well as in ordinary characters. To have the name of an animal, or bird, or reptile, is to have his powers. When Pena runs, on a wager of life, with the Great Sorcerer, he changes himself sometimes into a partridge, and sometimes into a wolf, to outrun him.

The Indian's necessities of language at all times require personifications and linguistic creations. He cannot talk on abstract topics without them. Myths and spiritual agencies are constantly required. The ordinary domestic life of the Indian is described in plain words and phrases, but whatever is mysterious or abstract must be brought under mythological figures and influences. Birds and quadrupeds must be made to talk. Weeng is the spirit of somnolency in the lodge stories. He is provided with a class of little invisible emissaries, who ascend the forehead, armed with tiny war-clubs, with which they strike the temples, producing sleep. Pauguk is the personification of death. He is armed with a bow and arrows, to execute his mortal functions. Hosts of a small fairy-like creation, called Ininees, little men, or Pukwudj Ininees, vanishing little men, inhabit cliffs, and picturesque and romantic scenes. Another class of marine or water spirits, called Nebunabaigs, occupy the rivers and lakes. There is an articulate voice in all the varied sounds of the forest—the groaning of its branches, and the whispering of its leaves. Local Manitos, or fetishes, inhabit every grove; and hence he is never alone.

To facilitate allusion to the braggadocio, or the extravagant in observation, the *mythos* of Iagoo is added to his vocabulary. The North and the South, the East and the West, are prefigured as the brothers of Hiawatha, or the laughter-provoking Manabozho. It is impossible to peruse the Indian myths and legends without perceiving the governing motives of his reasons, hopes, wishes, and fears, the principles of his actions, and his general belief in life, death, and immortality. He is no longer an enigma. They completely unmask the man. They lay open his most secret theories of the phenomena of spirit life; of necromancy, witchcraft, and demonology; and, in a special manner, of the deep and widespread prevalence throughout the world of Indian opinion, of the theory and power of the local Manitos. It is here that the Indian prophet, powwow, or jossakeed, throws off his mask, and the Indian religionist discloses to us the secrets of his fasts and dreams. His mind completely unbends itself, and the man lives over, in imagination, both the sweet and the bitter scenes of a hunter's life. To him the clouds, which chase each other, in brilliant hues and constantly changing forms, in the heavens, constitute a species of wild pictography, which he can interpret. The phenomena of storms and meteorological changes connect themselves, in the superstitious mind, with some engrossing *mythos* or symbol. The eagle, the kite, and the hawk, who fly to great heights, are deemed to be conversant with the aerial powers, who are believed to have an influence over men, and hence the great regard which is paid to the flight of these birds in their war and hieratic songs.

Fictitious tales of imaginary Indian life, and poems on the aboriginal model, have been in vogue almost from the days of the discovery. But what has been fancied as life in the forest, has had no little resemblance to those Utopian schemes of government and happiness which rather denote the human mind run mad, than supply models to guide judgment or please philosophy. In general, these attempts have held up high principles of thought and action in a people, against truth, observation, and common sense. High heroic action, in the Indian, is the result of personal education in endurance, supported by pride of character; and if he can ever be said to rejoice in suffering, it is in the spirit of a taunt to his enemy. This error had been so long prevalent, that when, in 1839, the author submitted a veritable collection of legends and myths from the Indian wigwams, which reflected the Indian life as it is, it was difficult, and almost impossible, to excite interest in the theme, in the trade. He went to England and the continent, in hopes of better success. But, although philanthropists and men of letters and science appreciated the subject, as historical elements in the history of the human mind, the booksellers of London, Paris, Leipsic, and Frankfort-on-the-Main, to whose notice the subject was brought, exhibited very nearly the same nonchalant tone; and had it not been for the attractive poetic form in which one of our most popular and successful bards has clothed some of these wild myths, the period of their reproduction is likely to have been still further postponed.

In now submitting so large a body of matter, respecting the mental garniture of a people whose fate and fortunes have excited so much interest, the surprise is not that we know so little of their mental traits, but that, with so little research and inquiry, we should know anything at all. They have only been regarded as the geologist regards boulders, being not only out of place, but with not half the sure guides and principles of determining where they came from, and where the undisturbed original strata remain. The wonder is not that, as boulder-tribes, they have not adopted our industry and Christianity, and stoutly resisted civilization, in all its phases, but that, in spite of such vital truths, held up by all the Colonies and States, and by every family of them, they have not long since died out and become extinguished. No English colony could live three or four centuries, in any isolated part of the world, without the plow, the schoolbook, and the Bible; it would die out, of idleness and ignorance. If one century has kicked the Indian in America harder than another, it is because the kicks of labor, art, and knowledge are always the hardest, and in the precise proportion to the contiguity of the object.

By obtaining—what these legends give—a sight of the inner man, we are better able to set a just estimate on his character, and to tell what means of treatment are best suited for his reclamation. That forbearance, kindness, and teaching are best adapted to the object, there is no doubt. We are counseled to forgive an erring brother seventy and seven times. If, as some maintain, wrongfully, we believe, the Indian is not, in a genealogical sense, of the same stock, yet is he not, in a moral·sense a brother? If the knowledge of his storytelling faculty has had any tendency to correct the evils of false popular opinion respecting him, it has been to show that the man talks and laughs like the rest of the human family; that it is fear that makes him suspicious, and in ignorance superstitious; that he is himself the dupe of an artful forest priesthood; and that his cruelty and sanguinary fury are the effects of false notions of fame, honor, and glory. He is always, and at all times and places, under the strong influence of hopes and fears, true or false, by which he is carried forward in the changing scenes of war and peace. Kindness never fails to soften and meliorate his feelings, and harshness, injury, and contempt to harden and blunt them. Above all, it is shown that, in the recesses of the forest, he devotes a portion of his time to domestic and social enjoyment, in which the leading feature is the relation of traditionary legends and tales. Heroes and heroines, giants and dwarfs, spirits, Monetos or local gods, demons, and deities pass in review. It is chiefly by their misadventures and violations of the Indian theories, that the laugh is sought to be raised. The *dramatis personae* are true transcripts of Indian life; they never rise above it, or express a sentiment or opinion which is not true to Indian society; nor do they employ words which are not known to their vocabulary. It is in these legends that we obtain their true views of life and death, their religion, their theory of the state of the dead, their mythology, their cosmogony, their notions of astrology, and often of their biography and history—for the boundaries between history and fiction are vaguely defined. These stories are often told, in seasons of great severity in the depth of the winter, to an eagerly listening group, to while away the hour, and divert attention from the pressing claims of hunger. Under such circumstances to dole away time which has no value to him, and to cheat hunger and want, is esteemed a trait of philosophy. If there is a morsel to eat in the lodge, it is given to the children. The women imitate this stoicism and devotion of the men. Not a tone in the narration tells of dismay in their domestic circumstances, not an eye acknowledges the influence of grief. Tell me whether the dignity of this position is not worthy of remembrance. The man, it may be, shall pass away from the earth, but these tributes to the best feelings of the heart will remain, while these simple tales and legendary creations constitute a new point of character by which he should be judged. They are, at least, calculated to modify our views of the man, who is not always a savage, not always a fiend.

NOTE

1. The reader should observe that this is the *first* time that Schoolcraft makes this identification of Hiawatha and Manabozho—the year after the publication of Longfellow's poem. One can conclude that Schoolcraft was an opportunist.

3. SELECTIONS FROM SCHOOLCRAFT ILLUSTRATING HIS CONCEPTS OF PRESERVING INDIAN LEGENDS AND TRADITIONS

a. HISTORY AND TRADITIONS OF THE INDIANS

TO INVESTIGATE THE SUBJECT of the history and traditions of the Indians, would require more space, and better means of observation and comparison, than we can at present command. The collection of the traditions existing among the Indians is of itself a labor that demands years. The comparison of these traditions with the observations of the discoverers and early French, English, Spanish, and Scandinavian writers upon the aborigines, requires access to antique works, many of which are rarely to be found in America. ... The rejection of all that is vague, contradictory, or irrelevant, in these two great means of information, and the selection and composition of anything like a clear, methodical, and authentic history of our Indians, is a work that must demand time, and means and powers of discrimination, neither of which we possess. ... [*Travels in the Central Portions of the Mississippi Valley* (1825), pp. 379-380.]

b. METHOD OF RECORDING INDIAN TALES

These tales have been taken from the oral relation of the Chippewas at the Sault of St. Mary, the ancient seat of that nation. Written down at the moment, and consequently in haste, no opportunity for literary refinement was presented; and after the lapse of some time, we have not judged it expedient to make any material alterations in the language adopted, while our impressions were fresh. A literal adherence to the sense of the original, to the simplicity of the narration, and, in many instances, to the peculiar mode of expression of the Indians, is thus preserved, while the order of the incidents is throughout strictly the same. Our collections on this subject are extensive. We do not feel assured that the selections here given present a just specimen of their merits—particularly in relation to the poetical machinery or invention of the Indians. [*Travels in the Central Portions of the Mississippi Valley,* fn., p. 409. Schoolcraft was referring here to the four legends and to a collection of Indian Poetry which he had included in the *Travels.* All had been transcribed just before and after his marriage to Jane Johnston.]

301

c. GLEAN THE FRONTIERS

The accumulation of facts and materials on all, and each of the points which serve to illustrate their history and character, is an object of enlightened research. And it is a species of research which recommends itself particularly to our attention, situated as we are, in the vicinity of numerous, and some of them populous, tribes, who possess the living languages, and the traditions, customs and institutions of their ancestors. Other societies are favorably located to preserve the materials of our national history. It is our province to glean the frontiers.

As yet, no attempt at a general history of the North American Indian has been made. There are some accounts of particular tribes, several tracts on their languages, occasional papers, reports, and other materials, either in the evanescent form of pamphlets, or scattered through a variety of publications—all of which, it would be important to collect and preserve. By consulting the best informed chiefs, and some of our elder inhabitants, interesting facts might be gleaned from local tradition, and from unpublished letters and manuscripts. All that relates to languages is still within our grasp. Much of what is most desirable to be known has already perished with the prominent actors who have [dis]appeared from the scene. Much, however, still remains. To rescue, both what is written, and what is unwritten is an appropriate and laudable object of literary research.

["Some Remarks upon the Origin and Character of the North American Indians" (1832), *Historical and Scientific Sketches,* Detroit, (1834). pp. 57-58.]

d. TETRAMETER AND PARALLELISM IN INDIAN POETRY

The measure (tetrameter) is thought to be not ill adapted to the Indian mode of enunciation. Nothing is more characteristic of their harangues and public speeches, than the vehement, yet broken and continued strain of utterance, which would be subject to the charge of monotony, were it not varied by an extraordinary compass in the stress of voice, broken by the repetition of high and low accent, and often terminated with an exclamatory vigor, which is sometimes startling. It is not the less in accordance with these traits that nearly every initial syllable of the measure chosen is under accent. This at least may be affirmed, that it imparts a movement to the narrative, which, at the same time that it obviates languor, favors that repetitious rhythm, or pseudo-parallelism, which strongly marks their highly complex lexicography.

[*Alhalla, or The Lord of Talladega* (1843), pp. 2-3. Longfellow was quite aware of this poetic phenomenon of Indian linguistics as indicated in his letter to Ferdinand Freiligrath, January 11, 1856: "Your article . . . ("The Measure of Hiawatha," *London Athenaeum,* December 29, 1855, p. 1534) needs only one paragraph more to make it complete; and that is the statement that parallelism belongs to Indian poetry as well as to Finnish. . . . And this is my justification for adopting it in Hiawatha." Wilbur L. Schramm, in "*Hiawatha* and Its Predecessors," reviewed eleven narrative poems on Indian themes before *Hiawatha* and found the tetrameter line used in most of them. *Alhalla* was written entirely in trochaic tetrameter. While pursuing this vein it should be noted that another Schoolcraft poem, "The Birchen Canoe," appeared in *Knickerbocker Magazine*, X (1837), p. 295. Only three stanzas of this poem are concerned with the construction of the canoe, but the general concept is there.]

e. SCATTERED BONES OF ABORIGINAL HISTORY

But a people who live without letters, must expect their history to perish with them. Tradition soon degenerates into fable, and fable has filled the oldest histories of the world with childish incongruities, and recitals of gross immoralities. In this respect, the Indian race have evinced less imagination than the Greeks and Romans, who have filled the world with their lewd philosophy of genealogy, but their myths are quite as rational and often better founded than those of the latter. To restore their history from the rubbish of their traditions, is a hopeless task. We must rely on other data, the nature of which has been mentioned [geology, archeology, philology.] To seek among ruins, to decipher hieroglyphics, to unravel myths, to study ancient systems of worship and astronomy, and to investigate vocabularies and theories of language, are the chief methods before us; and these call for the perseverance of Sysiphus and the clear inductive powers of Bacon. Who shall touch the scattered bones of aboriginal history with the spear of truth, and cause the skeleton of their ancient society to arise and live? We may never see this; but we may hold out incentives to the future scholar to labor in this department.

["Incentives to the Study of Ancient American History," *New York Historical Society Proceedings*, Appended Address (1846), p. 33.]

f. HISTORICAL TRADITIONS OF THE CHIPPEWAS, ODJIBWAS, OR ODJIBWA-ALGONQUINS

Of all the existing branches of the Algonquin stock in America, this extensive and populous tribe appears to have the strongest claims to intellectual distinction, on the score of their traditions, so far, at least, as the present state of our inquiries extends. They possess, in their curious fictitious legends and lodge-tales, a varied and exhaustless fund of tradition, which is repeated from generation to generation. These legends hold, among the wild men of the north, the relative rank of story-books; and are intended both to amuse and instruct. This people possess also, the art of picture writing, in a degree which denotes that they have been either more careful, or more fortunate in the preservation of this very ancient art of the human race. Warriors, and the bravest of warriors, they are yet an intellectual people.

Their traditions and belief, on the origin of the globe, and the existence of a Supreme Being, are quite accordant with some things in our own history and theory. They believe that the Great Spirit created material matter, and that he made the earth and heavens by the power of his will. He afterwards made animals and men, out of the earth, and he filled space with subordinate spirits, having something of his own nature, to whom he gave a part of his own power. He made one great and master spirit of evil, to whom he also gave assimilated and subordinate evil spirits, to execute his will. Two antagonist powers, they believe, were thus placed in the world who are continually striving for the mastery, and who have power to affect the fortunes and lives of men. This constitutes the ground-work of their religion, sacrifices and worship.

They believe that animals were created before men, and that they originally had rule on the earth. By the power of necromancy, some of these animals were transformed to men, who, as soon as they assumed this new form, began to hunt the animals, and make war against them. It is expected that these animals will resume their human shapes [sic] in a future state, and hence their hunters feign some clumsy excuses for their present policy of killing them. They believe that all animals, and birds, and reptiles, and even insects, possess reasoning faculties, and have souls. It is in these opinions that we detect the ancient doctrine of trans-migration.

Their most intelligent priests tell us that their forefathers worshiped the sun; this luminary was regarded by them, as one of their medas told me, as the symbol of divine intelligence, and the figure of it is drawn in their system of picture writing to denote the Great Spirit. This symbol very often occurs in their pictures of the medicine dance, and the wabeno dance, and other sacred forms of their rude inscriptions.

They believe, at least to some extent, in a duality of souls, one of which is fleshly, or corporeal, [and] the other is incorporeal or mental. The fleshly soul goes immediately at death, to the land of spirits, or future bliss. The mental soul abides with the body, and hovers around the place of sepul-ture. A future state is regarded by them as a state of rewards, and not of punishments. They expect to inhabit a paradise, filled with pleasures for the eye, and the ear, and the taste. A strong and universal belief in divine mercies absorbs every other attribute of the Great Spirit, except his power and ubiquity; and they believe, so far as we can gather it, that this mercy will be shown to all. There is not, in general, a very discriminating sense of moral distinctions and responsibilities, and the faint out-shadowing, which we sometimes hear among them, of a deep and somber stream to be crossed by the adventurous soul, in its way to the land of bliss, does not exercise such a practical influence over their lives as to interfere with the belief of universal acceptance after death. So firm in this belief that their proper and most reverend term for the Great Spirit is Gézha Monedo, that is to say, Merciful Spirit. Gitchy Monedo, which is also employed, is often an equivocal phrase. The term Wäzheáud, or Maker, is used to designate the Creator, when speaking of his animated works. The compound phrase, Wäosemigóyan, or universal Father, is also heard.

The great spirit of evil, called Mudje Monedo, and Matche Monito, is regarded as a *created,* and not a pre-existing being. Subordinate spirits of evil are denoted by using the derogative form of the word, in *sh,* by which Moneto is rendered Monetosh. The exceeding flexibility of the language is well calculated to enable them to express distinction of this nature.

This tribe has a general tradition of a deluge, in which the earth was covered with water, reaching above the highest hills or mountains, but not above a tree which grew on the latter, by climbing which a man was saved. This man was the demi-god of their fictions, who is called Manabozho, by whose means the waters were stayed and the earth recreated. He employed for this purpose various animals who were sent to dive down for some of the primordial earth, of which a little was, at length, brought up by the beaver, and this formed the germ or nucleus of the new, or rather rescued planet. What particular allegories are hid under this story is not certain; but it is known that this and other tribes are much in the habit of employing allegories and symbols, under which, we may suspect, they have concealed parts of their historical traditions and beliefs. This deluge of the Algonquin tribes was produced, as their legends tell, by the agency of the chief of the evil spirits, symbolized by a great serpent who is placed, throughout the tale, in an antagonistical position to the demi-god, Manabozho. This Manabozho is the same, it is thought, as the Abou and the Michabou, or the Great Hare of older writers.

Of their actual origin and history, the Chippewas have no other certain tradition than that they came from Wabenong, that is to say, the land of the EAST. They have no authentic history, therefore, but such remembered events as must be placed subsequent to the era of discovery of the continent. Whether this tradition is to be interpreted as an ancient one, having reference to their arrival on the continent, or merely to the track of their migration, is a question to be considered. It is only certain that they came to their present position on the banks of Lake Superior from the direction of the Atlantic seaboard, and were, when discovered, in the attitude of an invading nation, passing westward and northward. Their distinctive name sheds no light on this question. They call themselves *Odjib-wäg,* which is the plural of Odjibwa—a term which appears to denote a peculiarity in their voice or manner of utterance. This word has been pronounced Chippewa by the Saxon race in America, and is thus recorded in our treaties and history. They are in language, manners and customs, and other characteristics, a well marked type of the leading Algonquin race, and indeed, the most populous, important, and widespread existing branch of that family now on the continent. The term Chippewa may be considered as inveterately fixed by popular usage, but in all disquisitions which have their philology or distinctive character in view, the true vernacular term of Odjibwa will be found to possess advantages to writers. The word Algonquin is still applied to a small local band, at the Lake of Two Mountains on the Utawas river, near Montreal, but this term, first bestowed by the French, has long been a generic phrase for the entire race, who are identified by the ties of a common original language in the United States and British America.

One of the most curious opinions of this people is their belief in the mysterious and sacred character of fire. They obtain sacred fire, for all national and ecclesiastical purposes, from the flint. Their national pipes are lighted with this fire. It is symbolical of purity. Their notions of the boundary between life and death, which is also symbolically the limit of the material verge between this and a future state, are revealed in connection with the exhibition of flames of fire. They also make sacrifices by fire of some part of the first fruits of the chase. These traits are to be viewed, perhaps, in relation to their ancient worship of the sun, above noticed, of which the traditions and beliefs are still generally preserved. The existence among them of the numerous classes of jossakeeds, or mutterers (the word is from the utterance of sounds low on the earth), is a trait that will remind the reader of a similar class of men, in early ages, in the eastern hemisphere. These persons constitute, indeed, the Magi of our western forests. In the exhibition of their art, and of the peculiar notions they promulgate on the subject of a sacred fire, and the doctrine of transmigration, they would seem to have their affiliation of descent rather with the disciples of Zoroaster and the fruitful Persian stock, than with the less mentally refined Mongolian hordes.

[*Red Race of America,* pp. 203-206. The twentieth century scholar must always remember, when reading the speculations of the nineteenth century writers, that they were the inheritors of the systems and rational schemes of the eighteenth century. It took many years of application of the scientific method to overthrow the method of armchair theorizing. Schoolcraft was a fireside theorist; so were Jefferson and Gallatin in their views about the Indians.]

g. DEDICATORY LETTER TO *THE MYTH OF HIAWATHA*

TO

PROF. HENRY WADSWORTH LONGFELLOW

Sir:

Permit me to dedicate to you this volume of Indian myths and legends, derived from the story-telling circle of the native wigwams. That they indicate the possession, by the Vesperic tribes, of mental resources of a very characteristic kind—furnishing, in fact, a new point from which to judge the race, and to excite intellectual sympathies, you have most felicitously shown in your poem of Hiawatha. Not only so, but you have demonstrated, by this pleasing series of pictures of Indian life, sentiment, and invention, that the theme of the native lore reveals one of the true sources of our literary independence. Greece and Rome, England and Italy, have so long furnished, if they have not exhausted, the field of poetic culture, that it is, at least, refreshing to find both in theme and metre, something new.

Very truly yours,

HENRY R. SCHOOLCRAFT

[*The Myth of Hiawatha* (1855), p. v.]

h. IGNORANCE OF INDIAN MATERIALS BY AMERICAN WRITERS

When the volume of *Algic Researches* was published, in 1839, the book-trade had hardly awakened to that wide and diffusive impulse which it has since received. No attention had been given to topics so obscure as inquiries into the character of the Indian mind—if, indeed, it was thought the Indian had any mind at all. It was still supposed that the Indian was at all times and in all places, "a stoic of the woods," always statuesque, always formal, always passionless, always on stilts, always speaking in metaphors, a cold embodiment of bravery, endurance, and savage heroism. Writers depicted him as a man who uttered nothing but high principles of natural right, who always harangued eloquently, and was ready, with unmoved philosophy on all occasions, to sing his death song at the stake to show the world how a warrior should die. [*The Myth of Hiawatha,* footnote, p. ix.]

4. EXCERPTS FROM SCHOOLCRAFT'S *PERSONAL MEMOIRS* DESCRIBING THE COLLECTION AND PREPARATION OF *ALGIC RESEARCHES*

[Taken from a no-longer-extant diary, the notes and observations set down in this memoir of thirty years among the Indian tribes form an invaluable source of information about both Schoolcraft and the Indians. Anyone reading a volume of Schoolcraft should have the *Personal Memoirs* beside him as a handbook. Comparison of letters quoted in the *Memoirs* with the originals, when available, indicates that Schoolcraft reproduced them exactly, thus increasing our credence in his account.]

July 28, 1822.

Mrs. Johnston [mother of Mrs. Schoolcraft] is a woman of excellent judgment and good sense; she is referred to on abstruse points of the Indian ceremonies and usages, so that I have in fact stumbled, as it were, on the only family in North West America who could, in Indian lore, have acted as my 'guide, philosopher, and friend.' pp. 107-108.

July 31, 1822.

Nothing has surprised me more in the conversation which I have had with persons acquainted with the Indian customs and character, than to find that the Chippewas amuse themselves with oral tales of a mythological or allegorical character. Some of these tales, which I have heard, are quite fanciful, and the wildest of them are very characteristic of their notions and customs. They often take the form of allegory, and in this shape appear designed to teach some truth or illustrate some maxim. The fact, indeed, of such a fund of fictitious legendary matter is quite a discovery, and speaks more for the intellect of the race than any trait I have heard. Who would have imagined that these wandering foresters should have possessed such a resource? What have all the voyagers and remarkers from the days of Cabot and Raleigh been about, not to have discovered this curious trait, which lifts up indeed a curtain, as it were, upon the Indian mind, and exhibits it in an entirely new character? p. 109.

September 27, 1822.

[After being solicited by a friend to pick the brains of the Johnstons for the "polite literature" of the Chippewas, Schoolcraft wrote:]

With a strong predisposition to these inquiries, with each additional excitement to the work, and with the very highest advantages of interpretation and no little fixity of application from boyhood, it must go hard with me this winter if I do not fish up something from the well of Indian researches and traditionary lore. p. 120.

May 30, 1824.
That the Indians should possess this mental trait of indulging in lodge stories impressed me as a novel characteristic which nothing I had ever heard of the race had prepared me for. I had always heard the Indian spoken of as [a] revengeful, bloodthirsty man, who was steeled to endurance and delighted in deeds of cruelty. To find him a man capable of feelings and affections, with a heart open to the wants and responsive to the ties of social life, was amazing. But the surprise reached its acme when I found him whiling away a part of the tedium of his long winter evenings in relating tales and legends for the amusement of the lodge circle. These fictions were sometimes employed, I observed, to convey instruction or impress examples of courage, daring, or right action. But they were, at all times, replete with the wild forest notions of spiritual agencies, necromancy, and demonology. They revealed abundantly the cause of his hopes and fears—his notions of a Deity, and his belief in a future state. pp. 196-197.

February 28, 1832.
The initial steps were taken for forming an association of persons interested in the cause of the reclamation of the Indians, to be known under the name of the Algic Society. Connected with this, one of its objects was to collect and disseminate practical information respecting their language, history, traditions, customs, and character; their numbers and conditions; the geographical features of the country they inhabit, and its natural history and productions. p. 403. [The society was also pledged to moral and spiritual regeneration of the Indians.]

May 25, 1835.
I have long deliberated what I should do with my materials, denoting a kind of oral literature among the Chippewas and other tribes in the shape of legends and wild tales of the imagination. The narratives themselves are often so incongruous, grotesque, and fragmentary as to require some hand better than mine to put them in shape. And yet, I feel that nearly all their value, as indices of Indian imagination, must depend on preserving their original form. . . . [Here he quotes a letter from Irving suggesting that he send materials—biographies, tales, and sketches—that Irving could exploit with his pen.]
I had never regarded these manuscripts, gleaned from the lodges with no little painstaking, as mere materials to be worked up by the literary loom, although the work should be done by one of the most popular and fascinating American pens. I feared that the roughness, which gave them their characteristic originality and Doric truthfulness, would be smoothed and polished off to assume the shape of a sort of Indo-American series of tales, a cross between the Anglo-Saxon and the Algonquin. pp. 514-515.

April 26, 1837.

I have filled the pauses of official duty, during the season, by preparing for the press the oral legends which have been gleaned from the Indians since my residence at Sault Ste. Marie, in the basin of Lake Superior, and at Michilimackinack, under the name of *Algic Researches*. p. 558.

January 26, 1838.

Completed the revision of a body of Indian oral legends, collected during many years with labor. These oral tales show up the Indian in a new light. Their chief value consists in their exhibition of aboriginal opinions. But, if published, incredulity will start up critics to call their authenticity in question. There are so many Indian tales, fancied, by writers, that it will hardly be admitted that there exist any *real* legends. If there be any literary labor which has cost me more than usual pains, it is this. I have weeded out many vulgarisms. I have endeavored to restore the simplicity of the original style. In this I have not always fully succeeded, and it has been sometimes necessary, to avoid incongruity, to break a legend in two, or cut it short off. p. 585. [On a visit to Gallatin in 1838, that old master warned him: "Take care that, in publishing your Indian legends, you do not subject yourself to the imputation made against Macpherson." *Personal Memoirs,* p. 596.]

May 20, 1839.

The Harpers, publishers of New York, send me copies of the first issue of my *Algic Researches,* in two vols., 12 mo. They intend to *publish* the work on the 1st proximo. p. 648.

[The book was favorably reviewed everywhere. Some of the most laudatory reviews appeared in the Albany *Argus* (June 13, 1839), the Detroit *Daily Advertiser* (June 17, 1839), and the Detroit *Free Press* (June 21, 1839). All the leading American periodicals noticed it in complimentary terms.]

5. A SELECT LIST OF EARLY NINE-TEENTH CENTURY BOOKS ABOUT THE LIFE, LEGENDS, AND ANTIQUITIES OF THE NORTH AMERICAN INDIANS

Atwater, Caleb, Description of Antiquities in the State of Ohio and Other Western States. *Trans. Amer. Antiq. Soc.* I (1820).

Bird, Robert M., Nick of the Woods. Philadelphia, 1837.

Black Hawk, Life of Black Hawk, Dictated by Himself. Boston, 1845.

Blake, Alexander V., Anecdotes of the American Indians. Hartford, 1850.

Bradford, Alexander W., American Antiquities. New York, 1841.

Buchanan, James, Sketches of the History, Manners, and Customs of the North American Indians. London, 1824.

Carver, Jonathan, Three Years' Travel through the Interior of North America. Philadelphia, 1796.

Catlin, George, Illustrations of the Manners and Customs and Conditions of the North American Indians. London, 1841.

Clark, J. V. H., Onondaga County, New York. Syracuse, 1849.

Colton, George H., Tecumseh. New York, 1836.

Cooper, James F., The Pioneers (1823), The Last of the Mohicans (1826), The Prairie (1827), The Pathfinder (1840), The Deerslayer (1841), Wyandotte (1843), The Oak Openings (1848).

Copway, George, The Traditional History of the Ojibway Nation, by Kah-ge-ga-gah-bowh [Copway]. Boston, 1850.

Cusik, David, Sketches of the Ancient History of the Six Nations. Lockport, N. Y., 1848.

Delafield, J[ohn], Inquiry into the Origin of the Antiquities of America. New York, 1839.

Drake, Benjamin, Life and Adventures of Black Hawk. Cincinnati, 1838.

Drake, Samuel G., Indian Biography. Boston, 1832.

Duponceau, Peter S., Memoir on the Indian Languages of North America. Paris, 1838.

Eastburn, James W., and Robert Sands, Yamoyden. New York, 1820.

Eastman, Mrs. Mary, Dahcotah. New York, 1849.

Flint, Timothy, Indian Wars of the West. Cincinnati, 1833.

Gallatin, Albert, A Synopsis of the Indian Tribes of North America. *Trans. Amer. Antiq. Soc.* II (1836).

Hall, James, Sketches of History, Life, and Manners of the West. Philadelphia, 1835.

Heckewelder, John, A Narrative of the Mission of the United Brethren among the Delaware and Mohigan Indians. Philadelphia, 1820.

311

Henry, Alexander, Travels and Adventures in Canada. New York, 1809.

Hildreth, Samuel P., Pioneer History of the Ohio Valley. New York, 1848.

Hoffmann, Charles F., A Winter in the West. New York, 1835; Wild Scenes in the Forest and Prairies. 2 vols. London, 1839.

Hosmer, Henry C., Yonnondio. New York, 1894.

Irving, John T., Indian Sketches. Philadelphia, 1835.

Irving, Washington, A Tour on the Prairies. Philadelphia, 1835; Astoria. Philadelphia, 1836; Adventures of Captain Bonneville. New York, 1847.

James, Edwin, Narrative of the Captivity of John Tanner. New York, 1830.

Jones, James A., Traditions of the North American Indians. London, 1830.

Lanman, Charles, Haw-Ho-Noo, or Records of a Tourist. Philadelphia, 1836.

Lanman, James H., History of Michigan. New York, 1839.

Long, Stephen H., Narrative of an Expedition to the Source of the St. Peter's River. Philadelphia, 1824.

Macomb, Alexander, Pontiac, or the Siege of Detroit. Boston, 1835.

McKenney, Thomas L., Sketches of a Tour to the Lakes. Baltimore, 1827.

McKenney, Thomas L., and James Hall, History of the Indian Tribes of North America. 3 vols. Philadelphia, 1837.

Matthews, Cornelius, Behemoth, a Legend of the Mound-Builders. New York, 1843.

Morgan, Lewis H., The League of the Iroquois. Rochester, N. Y., 1851.

Morse, Jedidiah, Report to the Secretary of War on Indian Affairs in 1820. New Haven, 1822.

Palmer, Joel, Journal of Travels over the Rocky Mountains to the Mouth of the Columbia River. Cincinnati, 1847.

Priest, Josiah, American Antiquities. Albany, 1838.

Rafinesque, Charles S., Ancient Monuments of North and South America. Philadelphia, 1838.

Schoolcraft, Henry R., Notes on the Iroquois. Albany, 1847; Alhalla, or the Lord of Talladega. New York, 1843.

Simms, William G., The Yemassee (1835), The Wigwam and the Cabin (1845).

Snelling, Mrs. Anna L., Kabaosa; or Warriors of the West. New York, 1842.

Snelling, William J., Tales of the Northwest. Boston, 1830.

Squier, Ephraim G., and Edwin H. Davis, Ancient Monuments of the Mississippi Valley. Washington, 1848.

Stone, John A., Metamora; or The Last of the Wampanoags. 1829.

Stone, William L., Life and Times of Red Jacket. New York, 1841.

Street, Alfred B., Frontenac. New York, 1849.

Whiting, Henry, Ontwa, The Son of the Forest. New York, 1823; Sannillac, A Poem [Notes by Schoolcraft]. Boston, 1831.

6. LONGFELLOW'S *HIAWATHA:* EXHIBITS IN THE CASE OF PUNDITS vs. LONGFELLOW

a. LONGFELLOW'S NOTES TO *HIAWATHA*

"THIS INDIAN EDDA—if I may so call it—is founded on a tradition, prevalent among North American Indians, of a personage of miraculous birth, who was sent among them to clear their rivers, forests, and fishing-grounds, and to teach them the arts of peace. He was known among different tribes by the several names of Michabou, Chiabo, Manabozo, Tarenya-wagon, and Hiawatha. Mr. Schoolcraft gives an account of him in his *Algic Researches,* vol. I, p. 154; and in his *History, Conditions and Prospects of the Indian Tribes of the United States,* Part III, p. 314, may be found the Iroquois form of the tradition, derived from the verbal narrations of an Onondaga chief.

"Into this old tradition I have woven other curious Indian legends, drawn chiefly from the various and valuable writings of Mr. Schoolcraft, to whom the literary world is greatly indebted for his indefatigable zeal in rescuing from oblivion so much of the legendary lore of the Indians.

"The scene of the poem is among the Ojibways on the southern shore of Lake Superior, in the region between the Pictured Rocks and the Grand Sable." pp. 351-352.

"The fanciful traditions of the Red Swan may be found in Schoolcraft's *Algic Researches,* vol. II, p. 9." [Followed by a long quotation from the story.] p. 357.

"The Indians hold the maize, or Indian corn in great veneration." [Followed by two quotations from Schoolcraft's *Oneóta.*] pp. 359-360.

[Longfellow attributes the song of Chibiabos, pp. 210-211, to Schoolcraft, p. 359, and quotes from *Oneóta* the explanations of both the corn-field thief, Wagemin, and the game of bowl, Pugasing, pp. 360-361. Had he wished he could have referred to Schoolcraft many more times. See the list of borrowings compiled by the Osborns in this appendix. The above notes were reprinted, by permission, from *The Poetical Works of Henry Wadsworth Longfellow,* Riverside Edition, Houghton Mifflin and Company (1886), vol. II.]

b. EXCERPTS FROM LONGFELLOW'S *JOURNAL* ON THE SUBJECT OF THE COMPOSITION, PUBLICATION AND RECEPTION OF *HIAWATHA*

[Longfellow had been interested in the Indians for many years prior to making up his mind to write an Indian epic. He had read widely in travel and exploration and had seen Schoolcraft's *Oneóta* when it first appeared. In 1849 Kah-ge-ga-gah-bowh, an Ojibwa chief, had lectured in Boston and had become a close acquaintance. From the chief Longfellow learned that the Indian had a mind and spirit worthy of the white man's respect.]

[June 22, 1854] I have at length hit upon a plan for a poem on the American Indians, which seems to me the right one, and the only. It is to weave together their beautiful traditions into a whole. I have hit upon a measure [trochaic dimeter],[1] too, which I think the right and only one for such a theme.

25th. I could not help this evening making a beginning of "Manabozho," or whatever the poem is to be called. His adventures will form the theme, at all events.

26th. Look over Schoolcraft's great book on the Indians; three huge quartos, ill-digested, and without any index. Write a few lines of the poem.

27th. Begin Manabozho's first adventure and lament for his brother.

28th. Work at "Manabozho;" or, as I think I shall call it, "Hiawatha"— that being another name for the same personage.

July 31st. Worked at Hiawatha—as I do more or less everyday. It is purely in the realm of fancy. After tea, read to the boys the Indian story of The Red Swan.

September 19th. Working away with Tanner, Heckewelder and sundry books about the Indians.

28th. Worked at the disentanglement of Indian legends.

October 19th. Hiawatha occupies and delights me. Have I no misgivings about it? Yes, sometimes. Then the theme seizes me and hurries me away, and they vanish.

November 13th. Read to . . . . some pages of Hiawatha. He fears the poem will want human interest. So does F[anny]. So does the author. I must put a live, beating heart into it.

December 8th. Cannot get back into the poetic mood. For a month I have written nothing. . . .

January 9, 1855. Began again upon Hiawatha, long neglected. . . .

February 19th. Worked at Hiawatha. I have now eighteen cantos, or chapters, finished.

March 18th. . . . I have been at work on the Song of Hiawatha pretty busily, and have it all finished except the last canto.

21st. Read Sumner some cantos of Hiawatha—the "Sailing" and the "Wooing." After he goes, finish the last canto, at noon.

June 4th. Proof-sheets of Hiawatha. I am growing idiotic about this song, and no longer know whether it is good or bad. Epimetheus!

August 20th. In great doubt about a canto of Hiawatha, whether to retain or suppress it. It is odd how confused one's mind becomes about such matters from long looking at the same object.

October 2nd. Go to town on business. The first edition of Hiawatha now in press—five thousand copies.

[The success of *Hiawatha* was phenomenal. Four of the five thousand copies were sold by the time it was published, November 10. Another edition of three thousand was immediately run off. An English edition appeared simultaneously; within a month 1800 of the five-shilling edition had been sold and 10,000 of a shilling edition.]

November 15th. Hiawatha makes some sensation. Sundry squibs and the like, imitations of the metre, as if it stirred the minds of the readers a little.

18th. Some of the newspapers are fierce and furious about Hiawatha, which reminds me of the days when Hyperion first appeared.

December 2nd. There is the greatest pother about Hiawatha. It is violently assailed, and warmly defended. Six English papers I have already received on my side, among them the Athenaeum and the Saturday Review, and as yet only one against me—the Illustrated News.

[Despite the attacks in English and American papers the book continued to sell. By mid-December the ninth, tenth, and eleventh thousand had been issued. In March of 1856 "Grace Darling" read the poem to packed houses in Philadelphia; Mrs. Barrow read "Hiawatha's Wooing" at the Boston Theatre; and a Mr. Gleason, a Boston woodcarver, began a carving of a figure-head of Minnehaha in a semi-public studio. French critics were reviewing the poem in 1857, one of them, Émile Montégut in the *Revue des Deux Mondes,* charging that the Mondamin legend had been taken from Robert Burns' "John Barleycorn." Edward Everett informed Longfellow in June 1857 that he had boarded a "noble first-class steamer," the *Hiawatha,* in St. Louis and had heard of another, the *Minnehaha.* Charles Sumner wrote him from Inverary Castle, Scotland, that William Stirling, a famous cattle breeder, had a fine bull and cow combination with the same names. In 1859 Longfellow heard the musical composition "Hiawatha" by Stoepel with explanatory readings by Matilda Heron, a tragedienne. *Sic transit gloria Hiawatha.*]

NOTE

1. So-called in Samuel Longfellow's footnote. Schoolcraft and modern commentators refer to it as "trochaic tetrameter."

c. LETTERS IN THE LONGFELLOW COLLECTIONS ABOUT *HIAWATHA*

[There is a mass of correspondence and critical evaluations, pro and con, to be examined by the student of *Hiawatha.* Much of this material is printed in Longfellow's *Journal* (edited by Samuel Longfellow); the remainder is scattered in magazines and collections. Only the more significant letters are reproduced here. The curious person may consult the *Journal* for letters about *Hiawatha* from Hawthorne, Taylor, Emerson, Parsons, and others.]

(1) Longfellow to Charles Sumner

December 3, 1855

This is truly one of the greatest literary outrages I ever heard of. [The tirade of T. C. Porter charging Longfellow with plagiarism from the *Kalevala,* a ridiculous charge never fully scotched to this day.] But I think it is done mainly to show the learning of the writer. He will stand finally in the position of a man who makes public assertions which he cannot substantiate. You see what the charge of imitation amounts to, by the extracts given. As to my having "taken many of the most striking incidents of the Finnish Epic and transferred them to the American Indians"—it is absurd. I can give chapter and verse for these legends. Their chief value is that they *are* Indian legends. I know the *Kalevala* very well; and that some of its legends *resemble* the Indian stories preserved by Schoolcraft is very true. But the idea of making me responsible for that is too ludicrous.

(2) Ferdinand Freiligrath to Longfellow

London, December 7, 1855

Are you not chuckling over the war which is waging in the [London] Athenaeum about the measure of Hiawatha? Of course William Howitt is right; and your trochaic meter is taken from the Finns, not from the Spaniards. The very moment I looked into the book I exclaimed,

Launawatar, Frau die alte,

and was laughing with you again over the pages of the *Finnische Runen,* as thirteen years ago on the Rhine. The characteristic feature, which shows that you have fetched the metre from the Finns, is the *parallelism* adopted so skillfully and so gracefully in Hiawatha. I wonder that just this decisive circumstance is overlooked by all the combatants. It settles the question at once. [Freiligrath, scholar-companion of Longfellow's *wanderjahre,* wrote a defense of Longfellow's Finnish metre for the English press. Longfellow, commenting on it privately in his journal, said, "But he does not seem aware that the parallelism, or repetition, is as much the characteristic of Indian as of Finnish song." January 11, 1856.]

(3) Henry Rowe Schoolcraft to Longfellow

Washington, December 19, 1855

Dear Sir,—I have received the copy of "Hiawatha" with which you have favored me, and have read the poem with equal avidity and high gratification. Its appearance from the American press constitutes, in my opinion, a period in our imaginative literature which cannot but be regarded as a progressive feature. From the days of "Atala" [Chateaubriand] and "Yamoyden" [James W. Eastburn and Robert C. Sands] to Mr. Street's poem of Iroquois life [*Frontenac*], of which I have only seen extracts, it has been an open question how far the Indian character and mythology is material for poetry. But notwithstanding much cleverness and some successful passages in each attempt, the general failure of popular attractiveness may be sufficient to convince us that there are some insuperable difficulties. One of the great faults of authors, it appears to me, has been treating the Indian as a stoic through every scene, thus disconnecting from the human sympathies. We may admire fortitude, wisdom, and eloquence, but we can only love, or be deeply interested in, the bosom that has kind affections, whether the expression be simple and rude, or highly refined.

The Indian must be treated as he is. He is a warrior in war, a savage in revenge, a stoic in endurance, a wolverine in suppleness and cunning. But he is also a father at the head of his lodge, a patriot in his love of his country, a devotee to noble sports in his adherence to the chase, a humanitarian in his kindness, and an object of noble grief at the grave of his friends or kindred. He is as simple as a child, yet with the dignity of a man in his wigwam. There has been no attempt, my dear sir, before "Hiawatha" to show this. To avoid the direct issue with Indian character, it has been aimed to excite interest by taking the hero or heroine from the half-breed class. The result has been that we have had a half-breed class of poetry. It is not to be asserted that success cannot be attained in this line, only it has not yet been demonstrated. It cannot be supposed that Roderick Dhu, a Highlander, could, in the hands of Sir Walter Scott, have been made more attractive by taking from him the strong marks of full-blooded clanship. If the Indian is ever to be made the material of popular poetry, it must be the full, free, wild Indian—the independent rover of the forests and prairies, who loves the chase, loves liberty, and hates labor and the white man, under the impression that the latter symbolizes the advent of his curse and downfall.

There are among the Indians persons who are called on at burials to recite the praises of the dead. These men generally cut the hieroglyphics on their wooden graveposts. Others are skilled in songs, which are often of a religious, mystic, or elegiac cast; or are noted as persons who recite legends and stories. I have frequently had these persons at my house during the long winter nights in the North, where the introduction of a good meal has put them in the best humor possible for whiling away the time in relating their lore. To assemble these on grand occasions, with their rude instruments of music, appears to me the most eligible mode of procuring a correct and pleasing delineation of the picturesque and social scenes and beliefs of aboriginal life. For Hiawatha to collect together this poetic force on the occasion of his wedding, was certainly a most felicitous and eligible method of celebrating his nuptials. To my taste, the thoughts of the poem are highly poetical, and the rhythm most harmonious; and I am free to say that by exhibiting these fresh tableaux of Indian life you have laid the reading world under great obligations.

Yours with regard,
Henry Rowe Schoolcraft.

[Compare with Schoolcraft's dedicatory letter, Appendix B, 3.]

d. PARALLEL PASSAGES IN SCHOOLCRAFT'S INDIAN LEGENDS
AND TRADITIONS AND LONGFELLOW'S *HIAWATHA*
(FROM THE OSBORN "INDEX" TO *"HIAWATHA"*
WITH ITS ORIGINAL INDIAN LEGENDS)

"Allegorical Traditions of the Origin of Men," *H.S.I.,* I, 317; 317-319.
    Hiawatha, VI [Chibiabos, the singer]; XV, [Death of Chibiabos],
    XXII, "Hiawatha's Departure."
"Chant to the Fire-Fly," *Oneóta,* p. 61.
    Hiawatha, III, [Song of Way-wah-taysee].
"Corn Planting and Its Incidents," *Oneóta,* pp. 82-83; 254-255.
    Hiawatha, XIII, [Minnehaha blesses the cornfield]; [The red and the
    crooked ears of corn].
"Gitchee-Gauzinee," *A.R.,* II, 128-131.
    Hiawatha, XIX [Burdens of the dead].
"Hiawatha, or the Origin of the Onondaga Council Fire," *H.S.I.,* III, 315-
    317.
    Hiawatha, I, [The gathering of the tribes].
"Iagoo," *A.R.,* II, 229-232.
    Hiawatha, XI, [Iagoo's tales at Hiawatha's wedding].
"Iamo, or The Undying Head," *A.R.,* I, 102-112.
    Hiawatha, II, [Mudjekeewiss kills Mishe-Mokwa].
"Indian Pictography," *H.S.I.,* I, 333-430.
    Hiawatha, XIV, "Picture-Writing."
"Indian Serenade," *Littell's Living Age,* XXV (April 1850), 45.
    Hiawatha, XI, [Song of Chibiabos at Hiawatha's wedding].
"Island of the Blessed" or "The White Stone Canoe," *H.S.I.,* I, 322.
    Hiawatha, XV, [Chibiabos' departure to the hereafter].
"Kabibonokka" (See "Shawondasee"), *H.S.I.,* III, 324-326.
    Hiawatha, II, [Kabibonokka and Shingebiss].
"Kezha Monedo," *Oneóta,* p. 144.
    Hiawatha, I, [The divine messenger working with the tribes].
"Kwasind," *A.R.,* II, 160-163; 163-164.
    Hiawatha, VI, [Kwasind, the strong man]; XVIII, [Death of Kwa-
    sind].
"La Poudre, or The Storm-Fool," *A.R.,* II, 123-125.
    Hiawatha, XVII, [Final paragraph].
"The Little Monedo," *Oneóta,* pp. 262-263.
    Hiawatha, VIII, "Hiawatha's Fishing."
"The Magic Canoe," *Oneóta,* p. 460 (and in several other stories).
    Hiawatha, VII, ["Paddles none had Hiawatha"].
"The Magician of Lake Huron," *Oneóta,* pp. 483-484.
    Hiawatha, V, [Hiawatha and Mondawmin].
"Manabozho," *A.R.,* I, 135-136; 136-138; 139-143; 144-146; 147-148;
    148-150; 151-154; 162-164; 171.
    Hiawatha, III, [Birth of Hiawatha]; [Hiawatha's life with Nokomis];
    IV, [Hiawatha's battle with his father]; [Hiawatha and the Arrow-

maker]; V, [Hiawatha's Fasting]; VIII, "Hiawatha's Fishing;" IX, "Hiawatha and the Pearl-Feather;" X, [Hiawatha and the Arrow-maker's Daughter]; XV, [Death of Chibiabos].

"Mash-kwa-sha-kwong," *Oneóta*, p. 144.
  Hiawatha, I, [The coming of a prophet].
"Megissogwon," *A.R.*, I, 143-154.
  Hiawatha, IX, "Hiawatha and the Pearl-Feather."
"Mon-daw-min, or The Origin of Indian Corn," *A.R.*, I, 122-128.
  Hiawatha, V, [Hiawatha and Mondawmin].
"Moose and Woodpecker," *A.R.*, II, 217.
  Hiawatha, XX, [The beginning of the famine winter].
"Mudjekeewiss," (See "Iamo," "Shawondasee").
"Nursery and Cradle Songs of the Forest," *Oneóta*, pp. 212-214.
  Hiawatha, III, [Little owl lullaby].
"Ojeeg Annung," *A.R.*, I, 62-63.
  Hiawatha, XVI, [Iagoo's story of the Summer-Maker].
"Ojibway Song," *Oneóta*, pp. 15-16.
  Hiawatha, XII, [Song of Chibiabos].
"Osseo," *A.R.*, II, 152-159.
  Hiawatha, XII, "The Son of the Evening Star."
"Pauguk," *A.R.*, II, 240-241.
  Hiawatha, XX, [Minnehaha sees Pauguk].
"Pau-Puk-Keewiss," *A.R.*, I, 200-220.
  Hiawatha, XVI, "Pau-Puk-Keewiss"; XVII, "The Hunting of Pau-Puk-Keewiss."
"Peboan and Seegwun," *A.R.*, I, 84-86.
  Hiawatha, XXI, [Allegory of Winter and Spring].
"Pugasaing," *Oneóta*, pp. 85-87.
  Hiawatha, XVI, [Pau-Puk-Keewiss teaches the game of bowl and counters].
"Puk-Wudj-Ininee," *A.R.*, II, 152-159; 163-164.
  Hiawatha, XII, "Son of the Evening Star"; XVIII, "The Death of Kwasind."
"The Red Swan," *A.R.*, II, 9-34.
  Hiawatha, IV, [Hiawatha's fleetness]; XII, [Introduction to Iagoo's tale].
"Shawondasee," *A.R.*, II, 214-215.
  Hiawatha, II, [Shawondasee and the dandelion].
"Shingebiss," *Oneóta*, pp. 11-12.
  Hiawatha, II, [Shingebiss' contest with Kabibonokka].
"Songs of the Wabeno," *H.S.I.*, I, 358-401.
  Hiawatha, XV, [The medicine men appease Hiawatha].
"The Two Jeebi," *A.R.*, II, 61-66.
  Hiawatha, XIX, "The Ghosts."
"Weeng," *A.R.*, II, 226-228.
  Hiawatha, XVIII, [Kwasind and the Puk-Wudjies].
"The White Stone Canoe," (See "Island of the Blessed").

BIBLIOGRAPHY

[A bibliography should be functional rather than a collection of *curiosa*. Only items that can contribute to knowledge and understanding of the subject are included here. For additional information see the Select List in Appendix B.]

Documents

American State Papers, Indian Affairs.
Michigan Pioneer and Historical Collections.
Wisconsin Historical Collections.

Periodicals

American Anthropologist.
American Monthly Magazine.
Columbian Ladies' and Gentlemen's Magazine.
Journal of American Folklore.
Knickerbocker Magazine.
North American Review.

Books and Articles

Bancroft, Hubert H., *Native Races of America.* 5 vols. San Francisco, 1886.

Beauchamp, William M., *Iroquois Folk Lore.* Syracuse, 1922; *The Iroquois Trail.* Fayetteville, N. Y., 1892.

Bingay, Malcolm B., "Good Morning," Detroit *Free Press,* Jan. 27, 1940, p. 23.

Brinton, Daniel G., *The Myths of the New World.* New York, 1868; *American Hero Myths.* Philadelphia, 1882.

Buley, R. Carlyle, *The Old Northwest: Pioneer Period 1815-1840.* Indianapolis, 1950.

Cass, Lewis, *Inquiries Respecting the History, Tradition, Language, Manners, Customs, Religion, etc. of the Indians living within the United States.* Detroit, 1823; "Remarks on the Condition, Character, and Languages of the North American Indian," *North Am. Rev.* (1826).

Choate, Florence, and Elizabeth Curtis, *The Indian Fairy Book.* New York, 1916.

Deming, Alden O., *Manabozho. The Indian Story of Hiawatha.* Philadelphia, 1938.

Densmore, Frances, Chippewa Customs. *Bur. Am. Ethnol. Bull.* No. 86. Washington, 1929.

Field, Thomas W., *An Essay towards an Indian Bibliography*. New York, 1873.

Fiske, C. L., "Mercerized Folklore in Hiawatha." *Poet Lore* (1920) 31: 538-575.

Gilman, G. R., *Life on the Lakes*. 2 vols. New York, 1836.

Hale, Horatio, "Huron Folk Lore," *Jour. Amer. Folklore* (1888) 1: 177-183.

Hallowell, A. Irving, "Concordance of Ojibwa Narratives in the Published Works of Henry R. Schoolcraft," *Jour. Amer. Folklore* (1946) 59: 136-153.

Hamilton, James C., "Famous Algonquins: Algic Legends," *Canadian Institute Semi-Centennial Volume*, pp. 285-312. Toronto, 1899.

Hatzan, A. Leon, *The True Story of Hiawatha*. Toronto, 1925.

Hewitt, J. N. B., Iroquoian Cosmology *Twenty-first Ann. Rep. Bur. Ethnol.* pp. 127-339. Washington, 1903. (Cont'd in *Forty-third Ann. Rep.* 1928); "Legend of the Founding of the Iroquois League," *Amer. Anthrop.* (1892) V, 131-148.

Hodge, Frederick W., Handbook of American Indians North of Mexico. *Bur. Am. Ethnol. Bull.* No. 30. Pts. 1 and 2. Washington, 1907, 1910.

Hoffman, Walter J., The Midewiwin of the .Ojibwa. *Seventh Ann. Rep. Bur. Ethnol.* pp. 143-300. Washington, 1891.

Jameson, Mrs. Anna, *Winter Studies and Summer Rambles*. 3 vols. London, 1838.

Jenks, Albert E., The Wild Rice Gatherers of the Upper Lakes. *Nineteenth Ann. Rep. Bur. Amer. Ethnol.* Pt. 2, pp. 1013-1137. Washington, 1900.

Jones, James A., *Tales of an Indian Camp*. 3 vols. London, 1829.

Jones, Peter, *History of the Ojebway Indians*. London, 1861.

Keiser, Albert, *The Indian in American Literature*, New York, 1933.

Kinietz, Vernon, "Schoolcraft's Manuscript Magazines," *Bibliog. Soc. of Amer. Papers,* (1941) 35: 151-154.

Longfellow, Henry W., *Poetical Works* (Riverside Ed.) Boston, 1886.

Longfellow, Samuel, *Life of Henry W. Longfellow*. 3 vols. Boston, 1891.

Matthews, Cornelius, *The Indian Fairy Book*. New York, 1869.

Michelson, Truman, Contributions to Fox Ethnology. *Bur. Amer. Ethnol. Bull.* No. 85. Washington, 1927.

Nichols, Francis S., Index to Schoolcraft's Historical and Statistical Information. *Bur. Amer. Ethnol. Bull.* No. 152. Washington, 1954.

Nyland, Waino, "*Kalevala* as a Reputed Source of Longfellow's *Song of Hiawatha*," *A.L.* (1950) 22: 1-20.

Osborn, Chase, and Stellanova Osborn, *Schoolcraft-Longfellow-Hiawatha*. Lancaster, Pennsylvania, 1943; *"Hiawatha" with Its Original Indian Legends*. Lancaster, Pennsylvania, 1944.

Powell, John W., Indian Linguistic Families of America North of Mexico. *Seventh Ann. Rep. Bur. Ethnol.* pp. 1-142. Washington, 1891.

Schoolcraft, Henry R., Algic Researches. New York, 1839; "Ante-Colum-

bian History of America." *American Biblical Repository* (1839)
2nd Ser. I, 430-449; Historical and Statistical Information re-
specting . . . the Indian Tribes of the United States. 6 vols.
Philadelphia, 1851-1857; "Incentives to the Study of the Ancient
Period of American History," *Proc. New York Hist. Soc.*
(1846), II, Appendix, (separate cover) 38 pp.; The Myth of
Hiawatha and Other Oral Legends. . . . Philadelphia, 1856;
"Mythology, Superstitions, and Language of the North American
Indians." *Literary and Theological Review* (1835) II, 96-121;
Narrative of an Expedition to Lake Itasca. New York, 1834;
Notes on the Iroquois. Albany, 1847; Personal Memoirs of a
Residence of Thirty Years with the Indian Tribes on the Ameri-
can Frontier. Philadelphia, 1851; The Red Race of America.
New York, 1847. [Comprising all eight issues of *Oneóta* pub-
lished in 1844-1845]; "Some Remarks upon the Origin and Char-
acter of the North American Indians," *Historical and Scientific
Sketches.* pp. 58-109. Detroit, 1834; Travels in the Central Por-
tions of the Mississippi Valley. New York, 1825.
Schramm, Wilbur L., "Hiawatha and Its Predecessors." *P.Q.* (1932), 11:
321-343.
Smith, Erminne A., Myths of the Iroquois. *Second Ann. Rep. Bur. Ethnol.*
pp. 47-116. Washington, 1883.
Swanton, John R., The Indian Tribes of North America. *Bur. Amer. Eth-
nol. Bull.* pp. 47-116. Washington, 1883.
Thompson, Stith, *Tales of the North American Indians.* Harvard U. Press,
1929; "The Indian Legend of Hiawatha," *Pub. Mod. Lang.
Assoc.* (1922) 37: 128-140.
Warren, William W., History of the Ojibways. *Coll. Minn. Hist. Soc.* vol. 5.
St. Paul, 1885.
Wissler, Clark, *The American Indian.* 3rd Ed. New York, 1938; *Indians of
the United States.* New York, 1940.
Woodford, Frank B., *Lewis Cass, the Last Jeffersonian.* Rutgers University
Press, 1950.